Reading Education Policy

A Collection
of Articles
From the
International
Reading
Association

Patrick Shannon
Jacqueline Edmondson
Pennsylvania State University
University Park, Pennsylvania, USA
Editors

INTERNATIONAL
Reading Association
800 BARKSDALE ROAD, PO BOX 8139
NEWARK, DE 19714-8139, USA
www.reading.org

Editorial Director   Matthew W. Baker
Managing Editor   Shannon T. Fortner
Permissions Editor   Janet S. Parrack
Acquisitions and Communications Coordinator   Corinne M. Mooney
Associate Editor   Charlene M. Nichols
Production Editor   Amy Messick
Books and Inventory Assistant   Rebecca A. Zell
Assistant Permissions Editor   Tyanna L. Collins
Production Department Manager   Iona Muscella
Supervisor, Electronic Publishing   Anette Schütz
Senior Electronic Publishing Specialist   R. Lynn Harrison
Electronic Publishing Specialist   Lisa M. Kochel
Proofreader   Elizabeth C. Hunt

Project Editor   Matthew W. Baker

Cover   Design, Linda Steere

Web addresses in this book were correct as of the publication date but may have become inactive or otherwise modified since that time. If you notice a deactivated or changed Web address, please e-mail books@reading.org with the words "Website Update" in the subject line. In your message, specify the Web link, the book title, and the page number on which the link appears.

Library of Congress Cataloging-in-Publication Data
Reading education policy : a collection of articles from the International Reading Association / Patrick Shannon, Jacqueline Edmondson, editors.
     p. cm.
  Includes bibliographical references.
  ISBN 0-87207-568-0
  1. Literacy–Government policy–United States. 2. Reading–United States. 3. Education–Standards–United States. I. Shannon, Patrick, 1951- II. Edmondson, Jacqueline, 1967- III. International Reading Association.
  LC151.R42 2005
  379.2'4'0973–dc22

2004026719

Contents

Introduction   1
Patrick Shannon

Reading Policies: Ideologies and Strategies for Political
Engagement   5
Jacqueline Edmondson

Section 1: Policy-Driven Work   23

Policy Studies   26
John T. Guthrie

The Current State of Quantitative Research   29
Michael L. Kamil

When Less May Be More: A 2-Year Longitudinal Evaluation
of a Volunteer Tutoring Program Requiring Minimal Training   41
Scott Baker, Russell Gersten, and Thomas Keating

The National Reading Panel Report   84
James W. Cunningham

Books Aloud: A Campaign to "Put Books
in Children's Hands"   104
Susan B. Neuman and Donna Celano

Looking Inside Classrooms: Reflecting on the "How" as Well
as the "What" in Effective Reading Instruction   117
Barbara M. Taylor, Debra S. Peterson, P. David Pearson, and Michael C. Rodriguez

Taking Seriously the Idea of Reform: One High School's Efforts
to Make Reading More Responsive to All Students   134
William G. Brozo and Charles H. Hargis

Behind Test Scores: What Struggling Readers *Really* Need   149
Sheila W. Valencia and Marsha Riddle Buly

Section 2: Policy Communications Concerns 167

Literacy Research in the Next Millennium: From Paradigms
to Pragmatism and Practicality   170
Deborah R. Dillon, David G. O'Brien, and Elizabeth E. Heilman

Can Teachers and Policy Makers Learn to Talk
to One Another?   201
Cathy A. Toll

Barriers to Literacy for Language-Minority Learners: An Argument
for Change in the Literacy Education Profession   214
Rachel A. Grant and Shelley D. Wong

What Can We Expect From a National Assessment
in Reading?   228
Robert E. Shafer

High-Stakes Testing in Reading: Today in Texas, Tomorrow?   237
James V. Hoffman, Lori Czop Assaf, and Scott G. Paris

The International Reading Association Responds to a Highly
Charged Policy Environment   256
Cathy Roller

The Voices of Researchers: Conflict and Consensus in Reading
Research and Policy   275
Claude Goldenberg

Educators Influencing Legislators: Commentary and the Kentucky
Case   278
Shirley C. Raines

Section 3: Critical Policy Action 281

Asking Different Questions: Critical Analyses and Reading
Research   284
Jacqueline Edmondson

The Use of Commercial Reading Materials in American Elementary
Schools   298
Patrick Shannon

Other Countries' Literacies: What U.S. Educators Can Learn From
Mexican Schools   325
Patrick H. Smith, Robert T. Jiménez, and Natalia Martínez-León

The Train Has Left: The No Child Left Behind Act Leaves Black
and Latino Literacy Learners Waiting at the Station   341
Dierdre Glenn Paul

Beyond Remediation: Ideological Literacies of Learning
in Developmental Classrooms   354
Eric J. Weiner

Hog Farms in Pennsylvania   382
Patrick Shannon

Literacy and the Other: A Sociological Approach to Literacy
Research and Policy in Multilingual Societies   387
Allan Luke

Conclusion: The Policy Culture of Reading Education
and Research: Places We Might Go   405
Jacqueline Edmondson

Introduction

Patrick Shannon

Every aspect of public schooling is subject to policy decisions. Something as apparently straightforward as gathering books for a classroom might involve policies at the school, district, state, and federal levels. For example, in most schools each book that enters a classroom must meet school and district censorship policy. Decisions on textbooks for each subject are made locally only if the state textbook policy allows. And if a school district is interested in federal funds from Title I or the Reading First Initiative, then all its reading materials must be considered sufficiently scientific in design and content to qualify for funding. For example, the U.S. federal government threatened to withhold school funding unless the New York City school district reconsidered its choice of phonics programs to qualify for the Reading First Initiative (Goodnough, 2003a, 2003b). Similar descriptions of policy influence on public schooling could be made for school subject matter, assessment, and even teaching methods within reading education. In a sense, public schools are made from policies.

Reading programs cannot avoid educational policy, and therefore this book is for reading educators, reading researchers, administrators, and anyone else interested in reading education in the United States. This collection of articles previously published in International Reading Association (IRA) journals opens spaces in reading education policy in which readers can insert themselves in order to develop ways of analyzing the policies decided for them and the ones they decide for themselves, and to extend their knowledge of the consequences of existing policies. We hope to encourage readers

- to analyze policy issues—such as scientifically based research, high-stakes testing, and cross-cultural understanding—and deepen the discussion about those issues;
- to engage in policymaking, interpretation, and realization with greater understanding; and
- to question reading policy, policymaking, and research on policy.

In addition to using the collection for personal use, we also expect teacher educators to use the material to help preservice teachers develop strategies for engaging policies that will affect their work.

The articles are as varied in form and substance as the IRA membership. The pieces do not represent a single position on any issue, nor are they limited to current policies at national and state levels. Although books that take a single position and those that consider contemporary policies are useful, they become dated too quickly in the particulars of an argument and lose much of their pedagogical power as a result. Rather, we have purposefully selected articles on a variety of policies across the 50 years of IRA's existence in order to help readers learn to analyze any reading policy or practice of policymaking at any level of schooling.

Note that we have not chosen to address strategies of reading policy reform in any explicit manner. Although we certainly have our opinions on current and potential policies, we do not see this book as a forum for advocacy of our positions. Rather we hope that we have created an open text in which readers can decide their own positions and choose their own course of action based on their new knowledge.

Reasonable people can examine the same policy and reach different conclusions about its worth. This is possible because people begin with different sets of assumptions about how education works and what is of most value. We designed this book with that possibility in mind. The articles are divided into three sections: Policy-Driven Work, Policy Communications Concerns, and Critical Policy Action. Understanding these categories should help you analyze, engage, and question policies and policymaking. Consider the Head Start program as an example.

One way of thinking about policy is driven by a process–product problem-solving metaphor. In this approach, efficiency and effectiveness are valued mostly highly, and it is assumed that the best policy is the one that yields the highest measure of change at the least cost. Policy-driven work set the basic design for the Head Start program during the early 1960s. In order to find the best method for preparing disadvantaged children for public schools, the U.S. federal government sponsored a grand competition among a wide variety of alternative models (Rivlin, 1971). The winner would be the model that delivered the highest scores on the academic measures that the federal Office of Management and Budget (OMB) valued. Analysis of the policy-driven work was (and is still) centered on whether or not particular models brought sufficient results to warrant their continuation. Engagement required the design of new, more effective and efficient models. The George W. Bush Administration has harnessed policy-driven work to reorganize the current Head Start program.

Other people see policy as more a process of communication in which groups bring various assumptions and values to the policy table in order to define and address a problem. People with this philosophy assume that clear communications of values, interests, and intentions are necessary for the best policy to be negotiated, articulated, and implemented. Without this process of interaction and negotiation, problems are likely to follow. Returning to the Head Start example, at its inception, various participants in the design of the program had different ideas about how to prepare disadvantaged children to begin school alongside their advantaged peers. The statisticians from the OMB brought policy-driven work assumptions, liberal politicians sought to level the differences in healthcare and nutrition, university experts recommended differing learning theories, and members of advocacy groups for the disadvantaged intended the programs to be community controlled. Lack of alignment among these groups' values led to an ill-defined program that later had difficulty defending itself against conservative criticism (McGill-Franzen, 1993). Analysis of the communication concerns leads to an initial clarification of values; engagement requires an open process of negotiation, compromise, and, perhaps, consensus; and questioning is always focused on the process because it determines the product and its consequences. Currently, advocates of policy communication concerns raise questions about the lack of debate among affected groups about the Bush Administration's design to improve Head Start.

Still other people are critical of both the policy-driven and policy communication understandings of policy. This critical action group interprets policymaking as a power game in which typically the policy-driven approach dominates communication among groups. Because the negotiations are skewed by power relationships, the consequences of policies are distributed along the lines of power. Critical policy action advocates suggest that the Head Start program was not negotiated primarily to help disadvantaged children to prepare for school; if it were, then it would not have been underfunded. Rather, winning the Cold War of world opinion was the objective. That is, members of the Lyndon Johnson Administration hoped that Head Start would demonstrate to the world that the United States was actively addressing its racist past. Critical analysis of policy, then, requires a historical treatment in which the assumptions, biases, and values expressed in policy are traced to larger social agendas. Critical engagement requires advocacy for the rights and involvement of the less powerful. And the critical question is always, Why this policy at this time and in this place? At present, critical policy action advocates identify the Bush Administration's efforts in Head Start as a project to repeal the last element of the Johnson Administration's War on Poverty.

Most often, we pay attention to policy only when it disrupts the normal patterns of our lives, changing our jobs, altering school curricula, or redistributing resources to and from different educational programs. This view gives reading education policy a negative connotation. Yet, we should realize that our "normal" patterns are also based on existing policy, which some one or some group negotiated and wrote. In order to uphold norms or to promote change of any sort in reading education, policies will direct our efforts. The more we know about them, the more we raise questions about them, and the more involved we become in their debate, the more powerful we can be in our efforts on behalf of public schools, reading education, and the communities that both serve.

REFERENCES

Goodnough, A. (2003a, January 24). Bush adviser casts doubt on the benefits of phonics program. *The New York Times*, p. B1.

Goodnough, A. (2003b, April 5). More intensive reading program is added for struggling pupils. *The New York Times*, p. D1.

McGill-Franzen, A. (1993). *Shaping the preschool agenda: Early literacy, public policy, and professional beliefs*. Albany: State University of New York Press.

Rivlin, A.M. (1971). *Systematic thinking for social action*. Washington, DC: Brookings Institution.

Reading Policies: Ideologies and Strategies for Political Engagement

Jacqueline Edmondson

I n 1989, as a brand new teacher, I received a small red, white, and blue pamphlet in my school mailbox. The pamphlet, tucked in with the announcements for "Back to School Night" and fire alarm testing schedules, included a list of President George H.W. Bush's new education initiative, America 2000. I remember reading the list of goals, which included statements about academic standards, graduation rates, achievement tests, and teacher education, then tossing the pamphlet in the nearby trash can. Nice ideas, I thought, but what does Bush know about teaching? And what do his policies have to do with me? I gathered my mail, grabbed a cup of coffee, and went down the hall to meet my kindergarten students, children who would be graduating from high school by the time America 2000 was to be realized.

As a young teacher, I wasn't sure that policy, particularly federal policy, had much to do with my work. Politics seemed to be for the rich and famous, and I was neither. I figured I would go to my classroom each day, close my door, and teach my students in the ways I knew they needed, a stance shared by many of my fellow teachers. Of course in my naivete, I didn't realize that closing my door was in fact a political act. My teaching always involved my own or someone else's vision for the way we should live together, and, whether I acknowledged it or not, someone's policies or values were always operating in and around the classrooms where I've taught. Whether the policies were about who parked in which space in the parking lot, whether school would be canceled because of falling snow, or how much I would pay to the local public library in fines when I returned my kindergarten students' favorite book late, someone's ideas about how we would carry on in this space called school prevailed.

This article is an effort to introduce teachers to the values and dominant ideologies that shape literacy policies in the United States and to offer educators information that will help them to become involved more strategically in political change. To do this, we will consider recent reading policies from the Bill Clinton administration (America Reads and the Reading

Reprinted from *The Reading Teacher*, 57, 418–428, February 2004.

Figure 1
Brief history of key literacy policies and ideological influences in the United States

1965:   Elementary and Secondary Education Act: Title I and Head Start programs (liberal policies)

1980s: Reports on reading and public education including *A Nation at Risk* (conservative report) and *Becoming a Nation of Readers* (liberal position on reading)

1989:   America 2000 (which later became Clinton's Educate America Act)

1996:   America Reads (neoliberal policy that emphasized a "reading success equation")

1997:   Reading Excellence Act (neoconservative response to America Reads)

1998:   *Preventing Reading Difficulties in Young Children* (liberal report). Congress commissioned the National Reading Panel (policy-driven research; see Shannon, 1991)

2001:   No Child Left Behind/Reading First Initiative (conservative policies)

Excellence Act) and the George W. Bush administration (Reading First), primarily because these policies are some of the most prescriptive about what should happen in schools (see Figure 1 for an outline of recent policies in reading). These policies also give an opportunity to consider the contemporary ideologies that influence today's reading policies. To begin, I offer a cursory definition of policy and ideology.

Policy and Ideology

Sociologist C. Wright Mills wrote that the powers of ordinary people are often "circumscribed by the everyday worlds in which they live, yet even in these rounds of jobs, family, and neighborhood, they often seem driven by forces they can neither understand nor govern" (1956, p. 3). This statement seems to ring particularly true where education policymaking is concerned. As educators, we all move in and around schools, but we rarely stop to question or understand why things are the way they are. Often the answer to this question relates to policies that structure our lives in particular ways. Policies are the articulation of someone's hope for the way something should be, and they are revealed through various texts, practices, and discourses that define and deliver these values (Schneider & Ingram, 1997). These articulations determine the ways in which we live together, but we are not always sure how they come to be or how we can become involved to change them. Policies always begin with their authors' images of an ideal society, and they are intended to be procedural and regulative statements to normatively realize that ideal. Ideals are based on values that always have social contexts and histories. Because of this, any discussion of policy must necessarily include considerations of values and ideologies, historical and social contexts, and power and prestige if it is to adequately capture the intricacies of the process. (See Figure 2 for an overview of theories of policymaking processes.)

Policy may come from a single point of view or from a negotiation that includes a series of compromises among different points of view. Allington (2002) noted that ideology, not research or any other factor, influenced the agendas and reports that resulted in U.S. federal literacy policies, especially in recent years. Aronowitz (1988) explained that ideologies (rather than ideology) are a type of discourse with special languages, rules, and values that establish parameters for our values and beliefs. However, he argued that ideologies are not completely determinate of people's understandings, and the effects of

Figure 2 Policymaking models	
Theory	Description
Group theory	This theory of policymaking argues that policy is a struggle among groups. Various groups in society (e.g., social, economic, ethnic) put pressure on government to produce policies favorable to them. This theory is associated with work by political scientists David Truman and Robert Dahl.
Elite theory	Policies are made by relatively small groups of influential leaders who share similar beliefs. Policy is determined by the preferences of a "power elite" (see C. Wright Mills, 1956; see also work by Ralph Miliband).
Corporatism	These theories explain policymaking as influenced by interest groups that become part of the decision-making and implementation system. In this way, groups help to manage society for the state or government. Philippe Schmitter is most associated with these theories.
Subgovernments	These theories endorse a view of policymaking whereby sections of government work with interest groups. The result, coalitions of Congress members, bureaucracy, and interest groups, develop policies around specialized areas of interest. Hugh Heclo writes about policymaking according to this theory.

From Theodoulou & Cahn (1995)

ideologies are never completely predictable. There are conflicts and contradictions within ideologies, and as they compete to define truth, they often match the social, political, or economic power of the groups who accept them.

As dominant groups attempt to define truth for others, they validate their own ideologies in sometimes subtle ways. Eagleton (1991) explained that ideologies are legitimized when dominant groups work to promote their own beliefs and values, often making these values appear to be natural and self-evident. He also noted that this process frequently includes the denigration of others' ideas, the exclusion of rival forms of thought, and efforts to obscure social reality (including masking social conflicts). In many ways, ideology assumes a sort of "phantom" presence in policymaking. In other words, we need to look closely at what is going on, particularly at the vision for reading education that is reflected in the statements and intent of policy authors, in order to fully understand the ideological influences. Awareness of these various strategies can help us to read policy more carefully. To help demonstrate the ideological influences in recent literacy policies in the explanation that follows, key values are in bold print (see Figure 3 for a summary).

Reading Policy in the United States

The Reading Excellence Act first was proposed in 1997 after President Clinton initiated his plans for the America Reads program. America Reads, introduced during Clinton's 1996 State of the Union Address, relied on volunteer reading tutors to help all children to read well and independently by the end of the third grade. It was a neoliberal policy and, for the first time, explicitly linked education to the economy by defining a "reading success equation" (see Edmondson & Shannon, 1998). While *A Nation At Risk* (National Commission on Excellence in Education, 1984) situated public education as necessary for the nation's security, America Reads named reading as the key to American success in a global economy. The intent was similar to other Clinton administration policies, including the School-to-Work Initiative and welfare reform (workfare), which required people to participate in education and job-training activities in order to receive assistance from the federal government. Neoliberalism is a dominant global political ideology that emphasizes capitalistic, or so-called "free market," principles in all areas of social, political, and business life. More specifically, America Reads reflected at least three core neoliberal values:

1. The primacy of fostering **economic growth**, in this case through education that would supposedly lead to eventual success in the job market;

Figure 3
Dominant political ideologies, values, and related literacy policies

Ideologies	Dominant values (based on Edmondson & Shannon, 1998; Shannon, 2000)	Policy examples
Conservatism	Most typically a reaction to a trend, policy, or phenomenon in society. Reflects a commitment to the protection of local values and beliefs and the right to accumulate property. In literacy education, this includes control of textbooks and a focus on hierarchical, systematic skill instruction as a "neutral" procedure.	• No Child Left Behind • Reading First initiative
Neoconservatism	Shares liberal values that no one should be restrained because of race, class, or position. Shares conservative beliefs that order, continuity, and community are important. Emphasizes character and moral education aligned with Euro-centric values and a belief that individuals are responsible for the world, so all should be equal.	• Reading Excellence Act
Neoliberalism	Liberal ideas ("free market" will solve social and public concerns) are combined with conservative solutions (such as local control). Belief in a reading success equation, where learning to read well will guarantee success in school and later in the job market.	• America Reads • School-to-Work
Liberalism	Emphasis on enlightenment ideals that knowledge will bring freedom. Science is the best knowledge maker. Literacy is a basic human right. We must search for the right method.	• Title I of 1965 Elementary and Secondary Education Act • *Becoming a Nation of Readers* • *Preventing Reading Difficulties in Young Children*

2. development of a **shared sense of community** that helps "them" to become more like "us"; and

3. development of **efficient** educational practices modeled after business principles, including standardization and increased accountability.

As the American Reads initiative was getting underway, Representative Bill Goodling (R-Pennsylvania), Chairman of the House Education and Workforce Committee, proposed the Reading Excellence Act in Congress. Many considered this proposal to be a Republican response to America Reads because it represented an ideological challenge to the neoliberal agenda evident in Clinton's program. The legislation espouses a commitment to teaching reading based on systematic, scientifically based materials with well-trained teachers. Specifically, in its final form, the Reading Excellence Act included four major goals:

1. Teach all children to read in their early childhood years, not later than the third grade. (In other words, **every child can learn.**)

2. Improve the reading skills of students and the instructional practices of teachers through the use of findings from reliable, replicable research in reading, including phonics. (Framed in neoconservative terms, this demonstrates the belief that **order** and **continuity** are important.)

3. Expand the number of high-quality family literacy programs. (This emphasizes the role of **community** and the need for communities to have particular, typically Judeo-Christian, **morals** in order to be successful.)

4. Reduce the number of children who are inappropriately referred to special education due to reading difficulties. (This reflects the neoconservative notion that every child can learn and reflects to some degree on conservative policies, particularly during the Ronald Reagan presidency, that attempted to **limit federal funding** for special education.)

This proposal in part reflected neoconservative values. Neoconservatism became a distinct political ideology in the 1960s when some liberals became disenfranchised with enlightenment ideals that **truth would "set people free."** In part, they opposed the tenets of President Lyndon Johnson's War on Poverty, and they were disenfranchised by what they considered to be a lack of **morals** in the "counterculture" and protest movements of the 1960s (Kristol, 1995). What resulted was a combination of liberal beliefs (specifically the notion that race, class, and position should not restrain individuals) and conservative concerns with **order**, **continuity**, and **community** (Gerson, 1996). In the Reading Excellence Act, these values become evident particularly in the emphasis on systematic instruction in reading education and teacher training in these methods (order, continuity, control), and in the push for a community that reflected particular moral values (Bennett, 1996) through family literacy programs. Underlying these emphases is a belief that individuals are ultimately responsible for their positions in society and that moral education will help to overcome poverty (see Shannon, 1998).

The Reading Excellence Act shows some of the messiness of policymaking. There were compromises between the neoconservative and conservative members of Congress and the neoliberal Clinton administration that converged to influence the final passage of the bill. Members of the U.S. Department of Education, including the national director for the America Reads program, worked with the Senate to change the legislation into a bipartisan bill that would be satisfactory to both parties. For example, while neoliberal members of the administration hoped for a bill that would emphasize volunteer tutoring and community building around literacy, the conservative and neoconservative members of Congress worked for more specificity about how reading should be taught. They emphasized reliable and replicable research, which they expected would give order to reading education. Conservatives in particular view order as a primary need for any society (Dunn & Woodard, 2003). In the end, tutorial assistance became a subgrant section of the legislation (Title III, Section 301), leaving liberal Democrats dissatisfied with the voucher-like nature attached to the tutoring component.

Once the Reading Excellence Act was enacted on October 21, 1998, it allocated approximately US$260–280 million to states between 1999 and 2001 for literacy needs in high-poverty schools (Roller & Long, 2001). In addition, many states adopted similar state-level policies that mirrored the language and intent of the federal policy. In Pennsylvania, for example, the Read to Succeed policy shared the same definitions of reading and research as the federal policy (see Edmondson, 2000).

Shortly after the Reading Excellence Act was enacted, the National Research Council (NRC) published the *Preventing Reading Difficulties in Young Children* report (Snow, Burns, & Griffin, 1998). This report, created by a panel of experts, recommended ways to promote quality reading instruction. Some of the expert suggestions included using reading to obtain meaning from print, having frequent and intensive opportunities to read, frequent exposure to regular spelling-sound relationships, learning about the nature of the alphabetic writing system, and understanding the structure of spoken words (p. 3). The report did not satisfy Congress for two reasons. First, the NRC did not specifically address how vital reading skills should be taught. During the first full National Reading Panel meeting on April 24, 1998, Duane Alexander, director of the National Institutes of Child Health and Human Development, explained these concerns to the panel:

> What the Congress has asked this panel to provide is that critical review and assessment of the literature as well as its readiness for implementation in the classroom in more detail probably in terms of the how's than maybe the National Research Council discussed.

Second, the NRC report was criticized for producing a "consensus document based on the best judgments of a diverse group of experts in reading research and reading instruction" (National Institute of Child Health and Human Development, 2000, p. 1).

In response, Congress proceeded to commission a National Reading Panel. The charge to this panel included (1) conducting a thorough study of the research and knowledge relevant to early reading development and instruction in early reading, (2) determining which research findings and what knowledge are available in the nation's classrooms, and (3) determining how to disseminate the research findings and knowledge to the nation's schools and classrooms. Although the panel could have considered this charge from Congress in any number of ways, it decided to investigate scientific studies of reading. Perhaps this was due to the political climate that emphasized reliable replicable research, or perhaps it had to do with the panel members' own ideologies (see Shannon, Edmondson, & O'Brien, 2002). Whatever the influence, the panel did not consider a significant number of studies in reading, nor did it consider various perspectives (e.g., historical, anthropological, sociological, moral). In spite of these limitations, The National Reading Panel's report *Teaching Children to Read: An Evidence-Based Assessment of the Scientific Research Literature on Reading and Its Implications for Reading Instruction* (National Institute of Child Health and Human Development, 2000) was the primary influence on the George W. Bush administration's Reading First Initiative, which highlighted the scientific research in areas of the National Reading Panel's subcommittee reports: phonemic awareness, phonics, vocabulary development, reading fluency, and reading comprehension.

The Reading First Initiative is directed toward individual schools that have a combination of low test scores and high poverty rates. Like most conservative policies, it is a **reaction** to something else (see Shannon, 2000). In this case, the Reading First Initiative was a reaction to supposed failures of the Reading Excellence Act, and an attempt to more closely monitor schools receiving federal grant money without following the scientifically based requirements of the 1998 bill (Manzo, 2002). Schools that are part of the Reading First program in Pennsylvania are expected to do the following:

1. Adopt scientifically based reading programs for K–3 students. This focus reflects a conservative faith in **prescription**, that reading education should be leveled hierarchically (Shannon, 2000). It also reflects a belief that skill instruction is neutral.

2. Train teachers in the implementation of these programs. Teachers are considered to be a problem for many legislators, and the increased surveillance of their work is a **reaction** to perceptions that they are not following the rules (Manzo, 2002).

3. Demonstrate adequate yearly progress in improving reading scores. For Pennsylvania, this means that schools cannot have more than 35% of their student scores at or below the basic level in math or more than 45% at or below that level in reading on the state exams. If each school in a district does not meet or make progress toward those selected targets, then the state places sanctions on the failing schools and district, which begins with school choice and over a four-year period will culminate in state takeover of the school. This effort to privatize public education (see Edmondson & Shannon, 2003) reflects a conservative belief that **property** and **freedom** are inseparable (Kirk, 1953). In other words, if the federal government's primary function is to protect the rights of private property (which includes more than material possessions), and if there is a belief that wide-ranging government planning should be distrusted (see Dunn & Woodard, 2003), then decisions about how and where money should be spent for education are best made in the private sector.

Of course, liberal responses to both the Reading Excellence Act and Reading First express dissatisfaction with limiting schools to particular forms of research and reading programs. Recently in New York, as one example, Month by Month phonics was selected amid controversy between National Institute of Child Health and Human Development Director of

Research on Learning and Behavior G. Reid Lyon, who argued that it wasn't scientifically proven to be effective, and the schools Chancellor Joel Klein, who determined that it was the best program for the New York public schools (Goodnough, 2003). Responses from educators and researchers debate the merits of particular programs and the quality of the science employed in determining a program's worth (see Yatvin, Weaver, & Garan, 2003). **Science** has been the most typical way for liberals to determine what is best (Shannon, 2000). This expectation is coupled with a belief that the best materials and teaching methods will work to **benefit all** students, regardless of race, class, or gender.

Across all these policies, teachers experienced different opportunities for their classrooms. With America Reads, they were given "extra hands" to help with reading instruction (and perhaps an insult in the premise that relatively untrained tutors could teach reading more effectively than they could). With the Reading Excellence Act, the *Preventing Reading Difficulties* report, and the National Reading Panel report, they were given specific criteria to determine what was best for their classroom reading instruction (i.e., reliable, replicable research). However, with the Reading First Initiative and the No Child Left Behind policy, the consequences became more severe as teachers were required to demonstrate adequate yearly progress in order for their schools to retain federal money that is crucial for many poor school budgets. The irony is that the current conservative Bush administration is not merely distributing patriotically colored brochures to inform teachers of policies, like the former Bush administration did. Instead, the consequences are more severe, and teachers are no longer tossing policy statements in the trash can. Test scores and adequate yearly progress now determine the extent of federal and state involvement in schools. To respond, teachers can engage current policies, become involved in changing policies, or go beyond the current policies. Each of these points is developed further in what follows, and summarized in Figure 4.

What To Do

Influencing policymaking processes is, of course, a complex matter (Luke, 2003). Legislation is never the sole product of one individual or group, and it rarely, if ever, reflects a straight "party line" (America Reads is one exception to this; see Edmondson, 2000). Instead, policies reflect negotiations and shared values and ideologies that can cross political groups. One recent example of this is Senator Ted Kennedy's involvement with the No Child Left Behind policy. Kennedy did not oppose the extensive testing involved with

Figure 4
Summary of policy activities in which teachers can engage

Activities	Description
Policy study	1. Functionalist study asks what the measurable effects of a policy are and focuses on works within a particular context. As teachers, we can learn from functionalist study, but we must not stop with these questions. 2. Critical policy study considers where a policy has come from; the social, historical, and political aspects of policy; the values and definitions of the author(s); the consequences; and who benefits and who is left out (see Edmondson, 2002). This study will help teachers to raise different questions about policy and its consequences.
Civic engagement	1. Teachers can be engaged as public intellectuals who help to inform the parents and taxpayers in their communities about particular policies and their effects. 2. Participation can take many forms, including writing in local newspapers, speaking in public town and school board meetings, and holding workshops for teachers and parents.
Different ideological positions	As educators, we can 1. Seek wide civic participation through our own civic engagement. 2. Engage differences as we seek consensus across values and respect different positions. 3. Formulate new identities, choices, and alternatives for literacy education. 4. Open new political spaces where we can discuss, debate, and influence political policy.

No Child Left Behind, perhaps in part because he shared with his brother Robert Kennedy a hope that tests would allow us to know who needs to be served through federal policies. Robert Kennedy endorsed the use of tests as part of the original Elementary and Secondary Education Act in 1965, largely because he thought these tests would show that poor and minority students needed the government to intervene to improve their education (see Shannon, 1998). On the surface, conservatives share this value for accountability, but for different purposes. Their aim is not necessarily to be sure that policies serve the neediest, but instead to show that policies work (or not) so that funding can be directed differently (see Shannon, 2000). Shared values can bring people and groups together around particulars to formulate policies based on common interests and concerns (see also Mouffe, 1995).

Teachers have known the complexity of policymaking for a long time, and reading teachers have often subverted and variously deflected, for better or worse, the policies that have come their way. Rather than reacting to or subverting policies, we can become more involved in influencing their content and purposes. It is toward this goal that we now turn our attention. (See Figure 4 for a summary.)

Engage in Policy Study

Teachers can and do engage in collaborative study. Some form study groups around books or other professional development activities, and some consider policy. Sometimes schools allow teachers time during their day to engage in these activities (see www.ncrel.org/sdrs/areas/issues/methods/technlgy/te10lk44.htm). At other times, teachers engage in after-school and Web-based study groups with other teachers (see www.teachers.net as one of many examples) or e-mail listservs (for example, The Reading Teacher listserv sponsored by the International Reading Association; see www.reading.org/virtual).

Generally speaking, policy study can take two forms (see Edmondson, 2002). Functionalist policy study engages questions of what works within a particular situation. This form of policy study is most typically ahistorical and risks being short sighted, and some have considered this form of policy analysis to be inappropriate for educational contexts because the assumptions are inimical to educational problems and issues (see Prunty, 1985). One example of a functionalist response to policy occurred in Minnesota in 1998 as teachers gathered at the state capitol to protest the new standards, called the Profile of Learning. The teachers voiced concern that the standards did not fit their current classroom practices, and in effect they felt that the new reform would not work within the current system. The teachers' resistance was primarily understood as complaints about the amount of work required, the difficulty of scoring the standards with the new rubrics, and a general lack of coherence with the already existing curriculum (see Edmondson, 2001). The result of the functionalist argument that these standards would not work did little to bring about substantive change to the standards and often cast teachers as lazy and unwilling to change.

Critical policy study aims to engage overtly political work that exposes sources of domination and oppression with the overall goal of searching for social justice and an improvement in the human condition. Those who employ critical policy study ask questions of policy that illuminate inequalities and injustices, particularly as these questions lead them to expose contradictions. Such study considers what policies offer as well as what they deny and in turn allows those who study policy to engage in an advocacy for change. Had the Minnesota teachers employed critical policy study as they planned their protest at the state capitol, they would have raised questions about the way in which the new standards were aligned with neoliberal human capital agendas, which effectively reduce literacy teaching and learning to a job skill. They would have exposed the limitations of this ideology in literacy education and schooling and asked important questions about the purposes of public education in a democratic society. Posing questions about the history, social contexts, and ideology of a particular reform raises different questions than functionalist policy questions can engage.

Join or Organize Citizens' Groups

Throughout the United States, there are various citizens' groups that have organized to educate the public about pressing issues and to subsequently effect changes in local communities. In "Prairie Town," Minnesota, for example, townspeople, educators, and high school students came together to decide how to best live together and survive in light of the neoliberal influences on their community. The ongoing farm crisis and government policies in agriculture and education threatened to erase them and the community's school from the map (see Edmondson, 2003, for more specifics on these policies and conditions).

During the first set of town meetings, those participating developed a vision statement to guide their work. The vision statement articulated goals in areas of economic opportunity, recreation/culture, community leadership, infrastructure/services, lifelong learning, and valuing diversity. The subtheme of the meetings, as articulated in a narrative written by the project coordinator, included

> connecting our community, first to itself, and then to the world. The designated projects all foster a connection of people to people, people to resources, and our community to the surrounding communities. Having successfully constructed a strong infrastructure of service, support, and accessibility the community is equipped to reach beyond its borders and impact a wider world. (Edmondson, 2003, p. 100)

This visioning process was followed by a series of meetings that brought people across four generations together to help the community move toward that vision. This vision was not just about nostalgia for the old days, but it included a vision for the future that linked the community to the world in ways community members defined. It involved generating shared languages and literacies as people worked to read their current circumstances in public forums that addressed pressing conditions (including employment rates, infrastructure needs, technological concerns, and more). This in turn involved employing a variety of literacies as people made decisions together that would eventually bring about changes to the community. Teachers continue to be instrumental in this process as they inform local community members about infrastructure needs, programmatic needs, and even trends among students. While this process is still ongoing, there have been positive changes, including consensus from a community vote for a new elementary school building, new recreational activities for young people in the town, and a renewed emphasis on local history and art (see Edmondson, 2003, for a more detailed account).

These meetings engaged different literacies than those endorsed by neoliberal perspectives, and they required teachers to have different understandings of literacy and language to negotiate and inform the public about the relationship between the school and the community. At the same time, these meetings did much to inform the local citizenry about education issues, which ultimately influenced their nominations and votes for school board members as well as their choices for local, state, and federal representatives. In this way, the teachers have worked as public intellectuals (Giroux, 1988) who understand the issues and challenges of education in their community and engage in educating the public about these issues.

Engage Alternative Positions

Political ideologies are socially constructed, and we do not have to subscribe to those that are dominant in today's society. Instead, we can work outside the existing ideologies to create new spaces and new possibilities. One example of this is fifth-grade teacher Bob Peterson's (2002) class and its study of which U.S. presidents owned slaves. This classroom inquiry began during a study of George Washington when Peterson noted that Washington owned 317 slaves. Students seemed interested in this and questioned how many other U.S. presidents owned slaves. Their questions led Peterson to develop an action research project that crossed subject areas (math, social studies, and language arts) and culminated in students writing a letter to Harcourt Publishers to ask about omissions of racism and slave ownership in their U.S. history textbooks.

Peterson's values reflect a radical democratic position, a political ideology that is committed to a view of democracy as "the development of individuals' identities that are committed to the values of freedom and equality (blended with the values of their other group memberships) and to active participation in civic life" (Shannon, 2000, p. 101). In particular, there are three values Shannon identified as central to radical democracy operating in Peterson's classroom: (1) a commitment to reflexive agency, (2) the will to act, and (3) respect for the position of adversaries. The commitment to reflexive agency is evident in the teacher's and students' commitment to evaluating their world, reflecting on these values, and acting thoughtfully on their new knowledge. Peterson and his class considered their own values (freedom for all people, truth in textbooks) and considered those in relation to others (such as the textbook publishers). They carefully investigated their own understandings of slavery in relation to those of others, and, from this investigation, they decided the most appropriate way to act. Their action in this case employed a sociological imagination that expected textbook contents to more accurately reflect people's lived experiences, and while they respected the opinion and perspective of the textbook publisher as they tried to understand the motives and beliefs that would result in the omission of racism from their text, they imagined that texts could be otherwise. The radical democratic values that are evident in this particular case did not stop with the letter writing or the end of the assignment. Instead, Peterson continued to reflect on the inquiry, to make the experience public through the *Rethinking Schools* publication, and to consider how it could be different.

Closing Thoughts

Public Agenda (2003) recently released a report entitled *Where We Are Now: 12 Things You Need to Know About Public Opinion and Public Schools*. Underwritten by Washington Mutual, the report is based on more than a dozen national surveys of parents, teachers, students, principals, superintendents, and school boards across the years 1998 to 2000. While there is not space in this article to adequately discuss questions around this document (for instance, why a financial institution would underwrite a project like this), it is interesting for our purposes to note that the authors of the report suggest that public opinion should not play a role in policy change, largely because

> People are not following some important debates in education very closely. They may have a vision of the kind of public schools they want, but few have struggled with the details of precisely how to get there. Parents

are understandably more focused on the needs of their own child than on those of children overall.... It is also worth remembering that some of the most significant developments in American history have not been led by public opinion. Americans now say that the civil rights movement benefited the country, but that was not always the case. (2003, pp. 6–7)

The report points to discrepancies in understandings and opinions of parents and educators. For example, the discussion of the findings opens with the following statement:

The specific provisions of the No Child Left Behind Act may be controversial among educators, but the public's support for the ideas behind the drive to raise standards is not in doubt. (p. 8)

If this concerns us, and if it is true that the public does not understand education policy issues in the same way that educators do, then we should be doing something to change these understandings. It seems to me that the three points raised above—engaging in policy study, working locally, and engaging alternative positions—should help to direct us.

As reading teachers, our critical policy study, our work to educate the public about literacy instruction in our classrooms, and our efforts to construct new and different understandings of literacy and ideology in our globalized society are more important than ever, particularly if we believe that public opinion does and should matter. Yet, this is not to suggest that we should always agree, or that we should expect to arrive at a consensus about each issue. With any truly democratic project, there is always dissent and compromise, and there is always change. However, we can work to change the meanings that are attached to our lives, and we can change the ways in which we come to understand and read the world as we work to write it anew.

Historian Robin D.G. Kelley (1997) has written that "decent countries are made, not born" (p. 101). Democratic projects are, as any policymaking should be, difficult work as we learn to respect and work with our differences, and to understand how these differences matter, not so we can put them aside, but rather so that we can begin to forge an understanding of our collective social needs. Literacy is central to every aspect of this work as we attempt to understand languages, meanings, and texts. Our engagement in critical policy study as it considers origins, contexts, and values of policies, as well as alternative positions, can lead us to historical, economic, cultural, and social understandings of the meanings and needs facing literacy education. Such study is a crucial first step in our work toward recognizing what is valuable about certain policies as we simultaneously strive to bring policy changes. The findings of our critical policy study should in turn allow us to respectfully and publicly raise our support or objection to particular policies or aspects of policies as we help to educate others about the cultural meanings and understandings that are reflected in these policies. Such work should strive to be publicly relevant as we hope to educate parents and others in our communities (geographic and professional) about the meanings we share, those we do not, and why. This in turn can open spaces for the discussion of different possibilities that should in turn influence our school boards, state and federal legislators, and the policies and meanings that affect our schools.

REFERENCES

Allington, R. (2002). *Big brother and the national reading curriculum*. Portsmouth, NH: Heinemann.

Aronowitz, S. (1988). *Science as power: Discourse and ideology in modern society*. Minneapolis: University of Minnesota Press.

Bennett, W. (1996). *Body count: Moral poverty and how to win America's war against crime and drugs*. New York: Simon & Schuster.

Dunn, C., & Woodard, J.D. (2003). *The conservative tradition in America*. Boulder, CO: Rowman & Littlefield.

Eagleton, T. (1991). *Ideology*. London: Verso.

Edmondson, J. (2000). *America Reads: A critical policy analysis*. Newark, DE: International Reading Association; Chicago: National Reading Conference.

Edmondson, J. (2001). Taking a broader look: Reading literacy education reform. *The Reading Teacher, 54*, 620–628.

Edmondson, J. (2002). Asking different questions: Critical analyses and reading research. *Reading Research Quarterly, 37*, 113–119.

Edmondson, J. (2003). *Prairie Town: Redefining rural life in an age of globalization*. Boulder, CO: Rowman & Littlefield.

Edmondson, J., & Shannon, P. (1998). Reading poverty and education: Questioning the reading success equation. *The Peabody Journal of Education, 73*, 104–126.

Edmondson, J., & Shannon, P. (2003). Reading First in rural Pennsylvania schools. *The Journal of Research in Rural Education, 18*, 31–34.

Gerson, M. (1996). *The neoconservative vision: From the Cold War to the culture wars*. Lanham, MD: Madison.

Giroux, H. (1988). *Schooling and the struggle for public life*. Minneapolis: University of Minnesota Press.

Goodnough, A. (2003, January 24). Bush adviser casts doubt on benefits of phonics program. *The New York Times*, p. 1B.

Kelley, R.D.G. (1997). *Yo mama's dysfunktional*. New York: Beacon.

Kirk, R. (1953). *The conservative mind: From Burke to Elliott*. Washington, DC: Regnery.

Kristol, I. (1995). *Neoconservativism: Selected essays 1949–1995*. New York: Free Press.

Luke, A. (2003). Literacy and the Other: A sociological approach to literacy research and policy in multilingual societies. *Reading Research Quarterly, 38*, 132–141.

Manzo, K. (2002, November 13). Department of Education to hike oversight of reading grants. Retrieved April 16, 2003, from www.edweek.org/ew/ewstory.cfm?slug=11read. h22&keywords=Manzo

Mills, C.W. (1956). *The power elite*. London: Oxford University Press.

Mouffe, C. (1995). Politics, democratic action, solidarity. *Inquiry, 38*, 99–108.

National Institute of Child Health and Human Development. (2000). *Report of the National Reading Panel: Teaching children to read: An evidence-based assessment of the scientific research literature on reading and its implications for reading instruction*. Washington, DC: U.S. Government Printing Office.

Peterson, B. (2002). Write the truth [Electronic version]. *Rethinking Schools, 16*(4). Retrieved September 1, 2003, from www.rethinkingschools.org

Prunty, J. (1985). Critical signposts for a critical educational policy analysis. *Australian Journal of Education, 29*, 133–140.

Public Agenda. (2003). *Where we are now: 12 things you need to know about public opinion and public schools*. Retrieved April 30, 2003, from www.publicagenda.org/aboutpa/pdf/ where_we_are_now_combined.pdf

Roller, C., & Long, R. (2001). Critical issues: Sounding like more than background noise to policy makers: Qualitative researchers in the policy arena. *Journal of Literacy Research, 33*, 707–725.

Schneider, A., & Ingram, H. (1997). *Policy design for democracy*. Lawrence: University of Kansas Press.

Shannon, P. (1991). Politics, policy, and reading research. In R. Barr, M.L. Kamil, P.B. Mosenthal, & P.D. Pearson (Eds.), *Handbook of reading research* (Vol. 2, pp. 147–167). White Plains, NY: Longman.

Shannon, P. (1998). *Reading poverty*. Portsmouth, NH: Heinemann.

Shannon, P. (2000). "What's my name?" A politics of literacy in the latter half of the 20th century in America. *Reading Research Quarterly, 35*, 90–107.

Shannon, P., Edmondson, J., & O'Brien, S. (2002). Expressions of power and ideology in the National Reading Panel. In D.L. Schallert, C.M. Fairbanks, J. Worthy, B. Maloch, & J.V. Hoffman (Eds.), *51st yearbook of the National Reading Conference* (pp. 383–395). Oak Creek, WI: National Reading Conference.

Snow, C., Burns, M., & Griffin, P. (1998). *Preventing reading difficulties in young children*. Washington, DC: National Academy Press.

Theodoulou, S., & Cahn, M. (1995). *Public policy: The essential readings*. Englewood Cliffs, NJ: Prentice Hall.

Yatvin, J., Weaver, C., & Garan, E. (2003). *The Reading First Initiative: Cautions and recommendations*. Retrieved April 16, 2003, from www.EdResearch.info/reading_first/ index.htm

SECTION 1

Policy-Driven Work

U.S. schools are responsible for teaching all citizens to read. Universal literacy across classes, races, genders, geographic regions, and capabilities poses daunting challenges for schools and teachers. Since the turn of the 20th century, educators, administrators, and reading experts have worked to develop the most efficient and effective system for teaching everyone to read. These efforts have been translated into policies that direct the actions of all school personnel, increasing the chances of success for all. With each new discovery about the reading process, instruction, and learning, new policies have followed in a steady progression toward the lofty goal.

Policy-driven work is based on functionalist social theory in which the human body is used as a metaphor for the working of complex social systems. Like the body, schools require the coordination of several systems to maintain a healthy status quo. If a problem arises in one part of a body, causing ill health, then other systems begin to troubleshoot the system of that part in order to regain a healthy norm. Policy-driven work is designed so that reading researchers and educators will gather and use data in order to address the problems in reading education, and then to inform the executive branch of schools so that healthy policy can be directed to all schools to maintain reading education generally.

Policy-driven work has four tenets:

1. Policy is the search for the one best method, which is effective and efficient for the largest possible context.
2. Policymaking is a rational process used to solve the problems within existing reading education systems.
3. Policy decisions are based on means–ends analysis.
4. Policy analyses should rely on empirical investigations and mathematical reasoning.

In his article in this section, Guthrie suggests that reading researchers and educators should use their expertise to conduct experiments and program evaluations in order to obtain empirically valid, straightforward solutions to the complex, practical problems facing reading programs (see also

Guthrie, 1987). Once completed, researchers and educators should share their results in clear language through popular media in order to inform the public about best practices in reading education. Within these public statements, researchers and educators should take responsibility to draw appropriate implications for instruction and policy. By engaging in such work, reading researchers and educators would raise their status among policymakers as the primary sources of the types of data necessary to develop informed policy.

Perhaps it is obvious that the U.S. federal government is interested in policy-driven work. Over the last 20 years the federal government has invested tens of millions of dollars to fund basic and applied reading research and programs to improve reading education in the United States. In his article, Kamil presents an apology for empirical theory as the driving force behind the content reform in reading education. He argues that new technology has provided new insights into the working of the mind during reading, and he finds it "difficult to imagine how policy might be set for the population of an entire country without collecting quantitative data." Note that Kamil assumes that research will develop generalizations, experimentation will decide the direction of action in reading education, and national policy in education is a foregone conclusion.

Baker, Gersten, and Keating offer a remarkably detailed evaluation study of a volunteer tutoring program in which a true experiment (allowing a random assignment of subjects) was possible. The authors take pains to elaborate why one method seemed superior to others despite its apparent weaknesses. In effect, they deliver the quantitative data that Kamil promotes as the driving force behind good policy decisions. Baker and his colleagues concur that their results should direct programs such as the America Reads Initiative.

Offering a cautionary tale to those who would place too much value on mathematics as a language that captures reality, Cunningham asks us to temper our enthusiasm for experimentation as the only means for gathering scientifically valid data on patterns in human behavior. While remaining within the parameters of functionalism, Cunningham deconstructs the 2000 National Reading Panel report as an example of overreach in its efforts to define science for reading education. He fears dire consequences for reading programs in schools because the U.S. federal government seems too aggressive in its use of the panel's report.

The next three articles provide examples of the scientific evidence that would be excluded if experimentation were to be the only method to drive policy. First, Neuman and Celano describe how their Books Aloud project changed the routines of preschoolers and their teachers, based on experimental and observational results. Second, Taylor, Peterson, Pearson, and Rodriguez explain how their observational results question a narrow definition of direct instruction. Third, Brozo and Hargis discuss how a program to encourage literacy instruction across the curriculum could bring similar results for other schools. Beyond the extension of data-gathering methods, these articles present policymaking as a rational process based on the best evidence.

Although the previous articles in this section demonstrate that there is disagreement among advocates of policy-driven work about the best way to gather and interpret data, Valencia and Buly seem to stretch this category beyond it limits. They do not, however, exceed its boundaries. While they provide a critique of No Child Left Behind assessment policies, demonstrating the naive assumptions about reading and testing, Valencia and Buly present a sophisticated version of functionalism in which the professional development for teachers can help them learn to prepare all students to pass state tests according to federal guidelines. Note that in the end, the authors discuss conditions that will allow teachers and schools to meet the demands of NCLB policy.

REFERENCE

Guthrie, J.T. (1987). Policy development in reading education. In D. Bloome (Ed.), *Literacy and schooling* (pp. 310-324). Norwood, NJ: Ablex.

Policy Studies

John T. Guthrie

F ervent attention to educational issues at the national level is welcome. The primary means of progress consists of the articulation of problems and debate about solutions. Recent suggestions for education, however, have come from government commissions, corporate barons, and political figures. The voices of educators and social scientists have been joined by others in the cacophony that surrounds education.

Renewed interest in education from legislative leaders and others is a first step toward the advancement of schooling. The primary agents of that advance, it should be noted, are educators themselves, including teachers and curriculum designers, superintendents and scholars. As Harold Howe pointed out in the November 1983 *Phi Delta Kappan*, "Now a new wave of reform appears to have been launched, and American educators must reflect on what they have learned in the past." We must assimilate the proposals from many quarters in terms of what we know from experiential and experimental sources to determine which of them merit adoption.

The challenge facing education is similar to the test that has been applied to many professions rooted in the social sciences. We must answer the call: "How do we stand as a body of citizens who share special skills, knowledge and insights, on those societal issues of transcendent national importance to which out competencies can make a useful contribution?" (William Bevan, *American Psychologist*, December 1982, p. 1303). As President of the American Psychological Association in 1983, Bevan set this as a standard for professional psychology. It is equally suited to education.

As educators, we are responsible for our own agenda of reform and improvement. We cannot afford, however, to ignore the lessons contained in the progress of other professions. Since 1969, the field of psychology has moved from isolationism to active participation in the public forum. This movement was spurred by the words of George Miller who said, in 1969, "I can imagine nothing we could do that would be more relevant to human welfare...than to discover how best to give psychology away."

Psychologists have found that they have reaped far more than they have sown by making charitable contributions of their knowledge through the court systems, national health care delivery systems, and agencies of human welfare such as the criminal justice department.

Reprinted from *Journal of Reading*, 27, 670-672, April 1984.

Progress by psychologists did not come haphazardly. As Bevan wrote its recent history, he compiled a list of needs for that profession. As he recounted, it is imperative to maintain a continuous overview of the state of knowledge and to chart the intellectual foundations of the field with increasing fullness. A second imperative, he claims, is to inform the lay public about the field and to engage interactively with previously unfamiliar groups such as legislators, executives, and journalists. Finally, he says the understandings of the field should be brought to impinge on matters of national urgency such as the economy, crime, and peace in a nuclear age.

In the educational enterprise, problems of policy are exceedingly complex. It will not aid us to yield to our tendency to shrink from these complications. Educators need effective statements of policy and an understanding of how to formulate them.

A policy is a desired or intended principle of operation. It is pragmatic because it relates means to goals in a consistent manner. A policy may capture past practice, but it is promissory in the sense that it obligates the policymaker to commitments under specified conditions. A policy is distinguished from a program, which is a more highly specified set of actions. A policy is not well construed as a procedure nor does it carry the theoretical connotation of an explanation. A policy is a goal, but is it more than that. It represents a rule of thought or action that commands the resources and the commitment of the policymaker.

One policy recommendation found in several national reports pertains to parent involvement with schooling. Reports submitted by the National Commission on Excellence in Education, the 20th Century Fund, and the Carnegie Foundation for the Advancement of Teaching all suggested that parents should be involved with schools at the local level. The suggestions, however, were vague and varied. They ranged from appeals to vote in school board elections to injunctions for parents to serve as model learners at home.

Specific parent involvement policies have been recommended by several social scientists. Herb Walberg and Tim Shanahan, in the *Educational Researcher*, September 1983, report that amount of homework was correlated with reading achievement in a study of 58,000 high school students. It is plausible that, within limits, the policy of increasing homework may accelerate reading growth.

Joyce Epstein of Johns Hopkins University analyzed home–school connections closely. Her recommendations are found in an article entitled "School Policy and Parent Involvement: Research Results" in *Educational Horizons*, Winter 1984. Epstein found that relatively few parents are typically involved in school activities. For example, about 70% of parents never helped a teacher in the classroom or on class trips.

Parents were found to be highly involved, however, in the sense that they assisted the children with homework, generated many home learning activities, and supported school routines. These activities were increased by teachers who gave specific suggestions to parents or who frequently communicated with parents by note, phone, memo, and conversations. Parents' belief, furthermore, that they should help the student at home was improved if the teacher assumed the initiating role of parent involvement. These studies show that the forward step from a policy to a program of parent involvement is informed by knowledge from research and that implementation of policies requires a certain measure of expertise and cannot be assumed to unfold automatically.

An agenda for policy studies in education for reading may be drawn in terms of three dimensions. First, what policies are supremely valuable in education for reading? We must articulate the possibilities and principles needed to sustain education for literacy. Although the policies of high priority will vary with changes in political, economic, and ideological trends, it is indispensable that we define the principles of importance to the present exigencies.

Second, it is rational to examine our knowledge base to guide us in adopting certain policies and rejecting others. Favorable policies should be elaborated and qualified based on the many modes of knowing available to educators.

Third, the findings from policy studies in which publicly sensitive and educationally important proposals are related to the scientific and experiential base must be communicated broadly. Audiences of other educators are insufficient.

The problems and predilections of legislators, politicians, journalists, and allied professionals are unavoidable. As their questions become ours, we may find that our answers become theirs.

The Current State of Quantitative Research

Michael L. Kamil

N ew technologies and methods have afforded new opportunities for re-searchers to address old questions with quantitative methods. However, to write about the issues surrounding new directions in quantitative research requires attention to some definitions. What is quantitative research? A commonly used opposition is quantitative versus qualitative research. In quantitative research, the emphasis is on counting and measuring. For example, a quantitative question might be "How many pages did a student read under a set of conditions?" Similarly, a qualitative question in a similar context might be "How did students interact while reading in a specific environment?" The important distinction here is whether the research is using measures that are quantifiable in numeric terms.

However, the terms *quantitative* and *qualitative* have become confused with other designations. One important set of distinctions that often over-laps with these is experimental and descriptive (or observational) research. Experimental research has as its goal the generation of theory by collecting data under a set of controlled, manipulated conditions. Observational re-search has as its goal the generation of theory by observation in naturalistic settings. What is important to understand is that neither of these definitions requires *quantitative* or *qualitative* measures as part of the design. Although many, if not most, experimental studies do collect quantitative data, this is not a necessary condition of an experiment. What is important for experi-mental research is that measurements or observations in experiments are taken or conducted under conditions in which many extraneous variables can be controlled. Moreover, experiments involve the manipulation of vari-ables under those controlled conditions. It is the design of the study that is most important in characterizing experimental work. That is, the logic is that any differences in measures of behavior under two conditions that vary in only a few dimensions are attributable to those variables, provided all of the "controls" have been effective. To the extent that a researcher can control the relevant variables and manipulate those of interest, the research can lead to causal formulations. All that is required is that there are controlled condi-tions under which data are collected.

Reprinted from *Reading Research Quarterly*, 39, 100–106, January/February/March 2004.

Other researchers do *not* control the environment in which they observe or measure. They observe and record as part of the environment or as a dispassionate observer, insofar that is possible. What is recorded can be counted or can be constructed into a narrative about the observations. As in experimental research, the important distinguishing characteristic is the methodology under which the observations are made. In this case, for at least one school of thought, the requirement is that the researcher *not* interfere with the context in which observations are being made. Of course, there are many variations on interference, with some researchers becoming fully immersed in the environment as participant observers.

To simplify this set of issues, I adopt the simple convention that quantitative research is determined by the treatment of the data collected. If it is numerical and involves counting and quantitative comparisons (e.g., Do students do more of this than that?), it is a quantitative study. Otherwise it qualifies as qualitative. But nothing is ever quite that simple. Many researchers adopt both quantitative and qualitative measures in experimental, descriptive, or ethnographic studies. I refer to this mixed methodology subsequently in this article.

What Are Some Current Directions to Experimental, Quantitative Research?

Two decades ago, experimental quantitative methodology dominated reading research. A decade ago, there were many who were suggesting the end of experimental quantitative research as a paradigm. Even a cursory examination of journals from 10 and 20 years ago shows a change in research orientations. *The Handbook of Reading Research* mirrors this trend. In Vol. 3, of 10 chapters on methodologies in reading research, at least 6 are nonexperimental.

Today, however, experimental quantitative research is alive and well in literacy research, policy, and practice, having staged something of a comeback after predictions of its demise. Most recently, the primary impetus for experimental quantitative research has come from the policy arena. Policymakers have become focused on experimental quantitative research to guide their formulation and implementation of instruction. One has only to examine the National Reading Panel report and legislation such as No Child Left Behind, Reading First, or earlier efforts like Reading Excellence or Goals 2000 to see the emphasis on quantitative work. While many in the reading research community have been vocal in their opposition to these efforts, it is important to look at why the use of experimental quantitative research is important.

Policymakers have different parameters within which to operate when compared with researchers. Policymakers have to be accountable to the public, which demands verifiable results. They have limited resources to bring to bear on the problems they are elected to solve. Researchers, on the other hand, are free to choose whatever problems that interest them. They are usually unaccountable for those choices unless they are unable to have the results published, at which point they become accountable in the tenure system.

Why is it that policymakers focus on experimental research? The answer is simple, at one level. The question that policymakers must ask is "Given a limited set of resources, which policies should be supported to maximize the educational effects?" Thus, the research question that is meaningful to policymakers is of the form "Does Method A produce better results than Method B?" (Method B could be a different educational intervention or it could be a control condition.) The answer to this question requires some sort of quantitative, comparative evidence, thus limiting the research paradigms that can be brought to bear on the issues in which policymakers are most interested. However, the extent to which policymakers ought to be legitimately involved in legislating methods (directly or indirectly) in a field of professional practice is an important one and one that requires public and professional debate.

For such decisions to be made on the basis of research, there has to be some way of determining what conclusions can be drawn about the results of that research. The sheer number of research studies requires a different sort of quantitative methodology in synthesizing the results of those studies. The current method of choice is meta-analysis. For an early discussion of these techniques, see Glass (1976). Meta-analysis is a quantitative method for summarizing the results of studies. The outcomes of meta-analyses are effect sizes, which are relative measures of how much improvement over a control group an intervention yields. Professional organizations have amended their publication policies to suggest the importance of reporting sufficient data to calculate effect sizes (e.g., American Psychological Association, 2001, pp. 25–26). These are important considerations when translating research into policy. The National Reading Panel report provides examples of several meta-analyses that allow policy to be set on the basis of extant research (National Institute of Child Health and Human Development, 2000).

Questions and Research

Almost every student in graduate school is taught that the *questions* should determine the methodology that one uses to investigate them. Somehow in the polarization attendant to what has been referred to as the "Reading Wars" the notion that different researchers were free to ask *different* questions and use different methodologies got lost. As a community, reading researchers became polarized, and different camps set off in different directions on a hunt for the "truth," somewhat akin to the philosopher Santayana's observation that a fanatic is someone who has lost his way and doubled his speed. Instead of understanding that asking different questions might require different methodologies, we began searching for singular solutions to complicated problems.

Recently there have been renewed calls for research methodologies to be guided by the questions being asked (Shavelson & Towne, 2002). One can hope that this call will be heeded by all educational researchers, including those in literacy. Peter Mosenthal and I (Mosenthal & Kamil, 1991) attempted to bring some sense to this situation by suggesting that progress in reading research is made by asking different questions (and thus using different methods) at different stages of knowledge about particular research areas. When knowledge is at a minimum, it is best to observe. Even one of the most quantitative of researchers, B.F. Skinner, suggested that a good *first* principle was to sit and watch (Skinner, 1956). At later stages, when more knowledge has accumulated to allow one to conceptualize matters, experimental work could be possible. Once results from experiments are obtained, it would be necessary to test out those results in new settings, perhaps more nearly authentic than the ones in which the earlier experimental results were obtained. This produces a spiral of research and accumulation of knowledge that utilize *both* of the methodologies, answering different questions at different stages. Lomax makes a similar point in a companion piece in this issue.

The important notion is that quantitative research can answer some questions and not others. There are times when it is crucial to use observational techniques, and there are other times when experimentation is important to determine or verify the locus of effects observed in more naturalistic settings.

Some Promising Areas of Experimental Quantitative Research

In the discussion that follows, four separate, but in some cases related, research areas in which experimental quantitative methods have been used are briefly described. They represent current directions for quantitative research.

Eye Movements and Reading Research

Since the beginning of the 20th century, researchers have been intrigued by the possibility that eye movements could reveal the cognitive processes involved in reading. Much work has been done in this area, although it has dropped out of the mainstream of reading research until recently. New work on multimedia displays has generated renewed interest in eye movements. The multimedia displays of interest are webpages and the ways in which readers find their way through the text and multimedia items on those pages. Several questions of interest seem to be the focus. For example, in one unpublished study (O'Toole, 2000) the question was whether readers spent more time reading the text or looking at the pictures displayed at websites. The researchers measured the duration and location of sequential eye fixations as the reader read the text.

The question itself requires a quantitative approach because the question it addresses requires a quantitative answer. Note that if the question had been asked somewhat differently (e.g., "How did readers enjoy the webpage?" or "What was the pattern of eye fixations during reading?") the answer would not necessarily be quantitative. The questions could have been addressed by gathering and analyzing qualitative data. Figure 1 shows an illustration of the type of data display that provides one answer to the quantitative question above. It provides a visualization of the quantitative data that underlie the answer.

This type of quantitative data has implications for the ways in which information is designed and presented in multimedia contexts. For example, it is important to understand whether or not most readers can find important information in the light of competing types of potentially distracting multimedia information. There are probably other ways in which to present data on these questions, but none so compelling as the visual display of the quantitative data in Figure 1.

Neuropsychology and Reading

Another type of research that depends on quantitative methods uses brain imaging to index reading behaviors. An excellent review of this work is available in Shaywitz et al. (2000). The illustration in Figure 2 shows the brain activation in dyslexic and nonimpaired readers during phonological processing. Figure 3 represents increases in activation during phonologic compared with orthographic coding in different brain regions for different readers. These two different displays represent different ways of illustrating the underlying quantitative measures. Figures 2 and 3 illustrate the amount of neural activation under various conditions.

This distinction implicit between Figure 2 and Figure 3 is important because it represents, in the first case, a type of descriptive methodology using quantitative data. In the second case, the underlying methodology is experimental. Yet, in both cases, the measures are quantitative.

Figure 1
Sample display of eye movements while reading a document with text and graphic materials

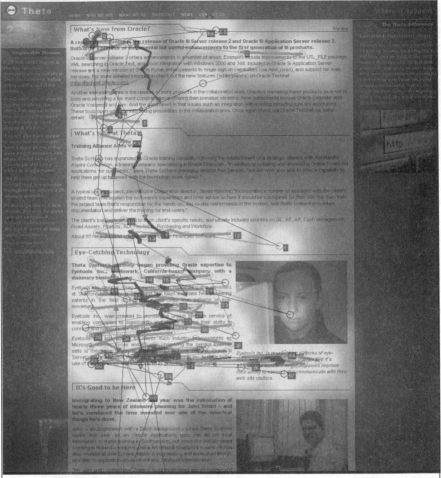

Reprinted with permission of Eyetools, Inc., San Francisco, CA.

What is important about neural imaging work is not that it reveals cognitive processes, but rather that it is yet another dependent measure reflecting the effectiveness of interventions. Brain imaging can be a more sensitive measure of the effects of instruction or it can assist in diagnosing specific and localized problems in reading. Moreover, the use of these quantitative data can help add to theory.

Figure 2
Composite activation maps in dyslexic and nonimpaired readers during phonological processing

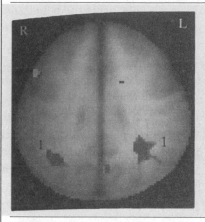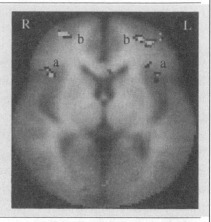

From "The Neurobiology of Reading and Reading Disability (Dyslexia)" by B. Shaywitz et al., 2000 (p. 243). In M.L. Kamil, P.B. Mosenthal, P.D. Pearson, & R. Barr (Eds.), *Handbook of Reading Research* (Vol. 3). Mahwah, NJ: Erlbaum. Copyright 2000 by Erlbaum. Reprinted with permission.

Figure 3
Relative increase in activation during phonologic compared to orthographic coding in different brain regions in nonimpaired and dyslexic readers

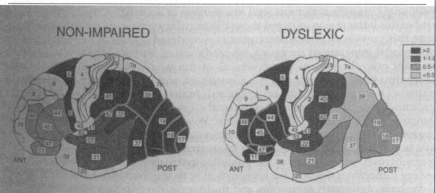

From "The Neurobiology of Reading and Reading Disability (Dyslexia)" by B. Shaywitz et al., 2000 (p. 243). In M.L. Kamil, P.B. Mosenthal, P.D. Pearson, & R. Barr (Eds.), *Handbook of Reading Research* (Vol. 3). Mahwah, NJ: Erlbaum. Copyright 2000 by Erlbaum. Reprinted with permission.

Readability of Texts

The study of readability of text has a long history. Much of the work is reviewed in Klare (1984). Because readability studies attempt to find quantitative correlates to text difficulty, this work clearly falls inside the boundaries of quantitative research. Two interesting developments in this area of research are worth noting. The first is the development of the Lexile framework for scaling texts (Wright & Stenner, 1999). This is a technique based on Rasch modeling concepts that assesses text materials in terms of sentence length and word frequency. The object is to find a metric for text difficulty that reduces sampling error insofar as possible. The way to accomplish this was to dramatically expand the corpus of words on which difficulty estimates are based. The models are based on a corpus of over 300 million words. Estimates from a corpus this size are possible *only* through the use of computer technology. For example, before the power afforded by today's computers, the Carroll, Davies, and Richman (1971) word list was compiled from more than 5 million words.

Whether or not this technique is useful has been the subject of a great deal of discussion. The National Center for Education Statistics (White & Clements, 2001) convened a panel that examined the efficacy of the Lexile framework. While they expressed some concerns about the framework, they did find value in its use. Of particular value in the framework is the ability to compare different texts, and even assessment instruments on the same scale, through the use of the Lexile values. What is important here is that the use of computer analyses of quantitative data provides new methods of examining old questions. In this case, the possibility of assigning text difficulty values to texts by computer analysis might make matching of students to materials much more efficient.

Large-Scale Policy Research

Finally, the use of quantitative methods is applicable to large-scale policy work. It is difficult to imagine how policy might be set for the population of an entire country without collecting quantitative data. In the United States, despite the shortcomings of large-scale assessments, the use of data from the National Assessment of Educational Progress or the National Assessment of Adult Literacy (NAAL) helps policymakers determine ways in which resources will be allocated.

Improvements in the types of data being collected and analyzed are being incorporated into new versions of these assessments. For example, the NAAL not only will assess the types of items from earlier administrations but also will incorporate measures of fluency that will be scored by computer. It will also incorporate a new supplemental assessment to the Adult Literacy Supplemental Assessment (ALSA) that assesses literacy in ways that differ from the previous versions of the NAAL. A unique feature of ALSA will be its use of highly familiar stimulus materials that can be manipulated (e.g., packaged food products) and contextualized (e.g., supported by visual information, logos, and sight words) (National Assessment of Adult Literacy, 2003).

The ALSA begins to combine standard test items with more authentic items, even though the end result is, ultimately, a quantitative score. These developments in the construction of large-scale, policy-driven assessments are promising directions for literacy research and increase the demand for appropriate quantitative analyses to analyze these new sources of data.

Technology and Quantitative Data Collection and Analysis

Many years ago, Bronfenbrenner (1977, 1979) proposed that one way to make research more ecologically valid was to use computers to collect a great deal of data about the conditions surrounding the research context. We have not made much progress in this regard because much quantitative research focuses on only a few variables. It remains an attractive concept, but one that awaits effective application.

In the meantime, computers are routinely used to collect and analyze data in ways that would have been unthinkable even a few years ago. The promising areas I have highlighted in previous sections here are examples of applications that would not have been possible without advances in computer technology. For example, the computer-based gathering of eye-movement data and the magnetic resonance imaging for brain functions are two divergent technologies that have made new advances in quantitative data collection possible.

Moreover, there are few researchers who do not make use of computerized data analysis to analyze the results of research. Even ethnographic data are often grouped and sorted with the use of computerized databases designed for that purpose.

As research becomes more complex, the research community will rely even more heavily on new technologies for collection and analysis of data. In turn, the possibilities for greater precision, additional information, and new ways of examining data will be forthcoming. While we have not yet fulfilled the promise of Bronfenbrenner's prediction, it seems as if we are on the verge of realizing much progress.

Preparation of Graduate Students and Researchers

Preparing graduate students as researchers is, perhaps, the most critical issue for the future of quantitative research because the graduate students of today will become the researchers of tomorrow. That issue is of great concern across the field of educational research (e.g., Good & Wandersee, 1991; Kamil, 1994; Pressley & Harris, 1994; Tuckman, 1990).

Perhaps the largest increment of time to prepare graduate students is necessary to provide intensive work in multiple methodologies. Duke and Mallette (2001) made this point. That is, students should be prepared to read across methodologies and to be able to conduct research that answers diverse questions. It would be unfortunate if students were to avoid asking quantitative questions, in which they are interested, because they feel unprepared to do that type of research. Of course the same would be true for observational questions.

To alleviate this shortcoming we will need to strengthen the methodology requirements, requiring that students become proficient in more than one methodology. This requirement will also increase demands on teaching as well because it is, perhaps, more important that students become good "consumers" of research *across* perspectives or paradigms.

A key role will be played by journal editors who must maintain high standards as prerequisites for publication. This will require the education of many reviewers. It will also require that editors select reviewers for particular methodological expertise, rather than hoping that one of the reviewers, who were selected because they were competent to judge the content, will be competent to judge the methodological rigor of a manuscript. By setting and maintaining these standards, the marketplace of research will eventually have to respond. Graduate programs that do not prepare their students for more rigorous research will change, albeit slowly. Students will slowly begin the process of selecting programs that prepare them better or they will demand changes in the programs they do attend. Literacy research will benefit from the better preparation of students.

Most of all, students will need to be prepared to use the mixed methods mentioned earlier in this article, using quantitative and qualitative analyses. Most questions do not easily fall into one of these categories. Some parts of many, if not most, research questions require quantitative data on which to base answers; others require qualitative data. Rather than design research around limited personal expertise, students should be prepared to do both types of research. Indeed, this preparation will require university faculties who have matching expertise in many areas, and it will require programs that insist students study more broadly in research methodologies. However, the field of literacy research will be richer for the change.

REFERENCES

American Psychological Association. (2001). *Publication manual of the American Psychological Association* (5th ed.). Washington, DC: Author.

Bronfenbrenner, U. (1977). Toward an experimental ecology of human development. *American Psychologist, 32*, 513-531.

Bronfenbrenner, U. (1979). *The ecology of human development*. Cambridge, MA: Harvard University Press.

Carroll, J.B., Davies, P., & Richman, B. (1971). *Word frequency book*. Boston: Houghton Mifflin.

Duke, N.K., & Mallette, M.H. (2001). Critical issues: Preparation for New Literacy researchers in multi-epistemological, multi-methodological times. *Journal of Literacy Research, 33*, 345-360.

Glass, G.V. (1976). Primary, secondary, and meta-analysis. *Educational Researcher, 5*(10), 3-8.

Good, R., & Wandersee, J. (1991). No royal road: More on improving the quality of published educational research. *Educational Researcher, 20*(8), 24-25.

Kamil, M.L. (1994). More on increasing the quality of educational intervention research: A response to Pressley and Harris. *Educational Psychology Review, 6*, 223-230.

Klare, G.R. (1984). Readability. In P.D. Pearson, R. Barr, M.L. Kamil, & P.B. Mosenthal (Eds.), *Handbook of reading research* (pp. 681-744). New York: Longman.

Lomax, R.G. (2004). New directions in research: Contemporary methods of quantitative data collection and analysis in literacy research: Whither the future of quantitative literacy research? *Reading Research Quarterly, 39*, 107-112.

Mosenthal, P.B., & Kamil, M.L. (1991). Research in reading and writing: A model of progress. In R. Barr, M.L. Kamil, P.B. Mosenthal, & P.D. Pearson (Eds.), *Handbook of reading research* (Vol. 2, pp. 1013-1046). White Plains, NY: Longman.

National Assessment of Adult Literacy. (2003). *National assessment of adult literacy design*. Retrieved June 11, 2003, from National Center for Education Statistics website: http://nces.ed.gov/naal/design/design.asp#instrument

National Institute of Child Health and Human Development. (2000). *Report of the National Reading Panel. Teaching children to read: An evidence-based assessment of the scientific research literature on reading and its implications for reading instruction: Reports of the subgroups* (NIH Publication No. 00-4769). Washington, DC: U.S. Government Printing Office.

O'Toole, K. (2000, May 8). Eye movement research points to importance of text over graphics on websites. *Stanford Online Report*. Retrieved May 20, 2003, from www.stanford.edu/dept/news/report/news/may10/eyetrack-55.html

Pressley, M., & Harris, K.R. (1994). Increasing the quality of educational intervention research. *Educational Psychology Review, 6*, 191-208.

Shavelson, R.J., & Towne, L. (Eds.). (2002). *Scientific research in education*. Washington, DC: National Academy of Sciences, National Research Council.

Shaywitz, B., Pugh, K.R., Jenner, A.R., Fulbright, R.K., Fletcher, J.M., Gore, J.C., et al. (2000). The neurobiology of reading and reading disability (Dyslexia). In M.L. Kamil, P.B. Mosenthal, P.D. Pearson, & R. Barr (Eds.), *Handbook of reading research* (Vol. 3, pp. 229-250). Mahwah, NJ: Erlbaum.

Skinner, B.F. (1956). A case history in the scientific method. *American Psychologist, 11*, 221-233.

Tuckman, B. (1990). A proposal for improving the quality of published educational research. *Educational Researcher, 19*(9), 22-25.

White, S., & Clements, J. (2001). *Assessing the Lexile Framework: Results of a panel meeting* (Working Paper No. 2001-08). Retrieved August 20, 2003, from National Center for Education Statistics website: http://nces.ed.gov/pubsearch/pubsinfo.asp?pubid=200108

Wright, B.D., & Stenner, A.J. (1999). One fish, two fish: Rasch measures reading best. *Popular Measurement, 2*(1), 34-38.

When Less May Be More: A 2-Year Longitudinal Evaluation of a Volunteer Tutoring Program Requiring Minimal Training

Scott Baker, Russell Gersten, and Thomas Keating

Start Making a Reader Today (SMART) is a volunteer tutoring program in Oregon to help kindergarten through second grade students learn to read (www.mytownnet.com/projects/OR/smart/smart.htm; Oregon Children's Foundation, 1992, 1998). It specifically focuses on those children who, according to their teachers, are having difficulty learning the basics. Conceived and developed in 1992 by former Oregon Governor Neil Goldschmidt, SMART has grown appreciably each year since its initial implementation in eight Oregon schools. Currently, 144 schools statewide have SMART programs operating in kindergarten, first grade, and second grade, and each year approximately 7,100 adult volunteers work one-on-one with 7,100 students (Janet Hurst, personal communication, January 1999).

SMART serves as a model for community members who wish to be more actively and positively involved with their local schools. In a series of town meetings throughout Oregon, Governor Goldschmidt consistently encountered a deep sense of disconnection between adults and the schools their children attended. What made SMART unique was that, from its inception, it attempted to reconnect communities and schools by asserting two basic premises. The first underlies virtually all tutoring programs (Juel, 1996; Shanahan, 1998; Wasik, 1998): Adults can make a vital difference in the lives of young students by spending time reading to them and teaching them to read. Even the best instructional environments for first graders in a public school setting, with one expert teacher responsible for teaching 20–30 students, cannot match the educational intensity of a one-to-one interaction. When an adult sits down with a child and shares in the pleasures of reading and then helps the child build literacy skills, progress accelerates.

SMART's second basic premise is that adults receive benefits as great as the students from the experience of meaningful involvement in the life of a young child (Oregon Children's Foundation, 1992, 1998). Not only would

Reprinted from *Reading Research Quarterly*, 35, 494–519, October/November/December 2000.

children with special needs become better readers, but adults, actively involved in the education of those children, would gain a better understanding of school life and, as they watched their students become better readers, would emerge from the experience with a sense of real accomplishment.

From the beginning, SMART was designed for rapid, wide-scale implementation. A major concern was that the program be low cost and feasible to implement and expand. Although SMART is in many ways similar to other tutoring programs such as those described by Shanahan (1998) and Wasik (1998), several important differences set it apart. Except for the use of Americorps volunteers as coordinators at some schools, SMART is entirely a private-sector enterprise. From the outset, the Oregon business community has played a large role in supporting the program by funding operating costs and paying for books, as well as by actively encouraging their employees to become reading volunteers and by facilitating their involvement as part of their paid employment. The individuals who conceived SMART believed that keeping government support to a minimum and relying primarily on support from local business and community organizations would increase its chances for survival.

SMART also differs from other programs in its approach to volunteer training and its minimal demands on teachers. Volunteer training is brief and focuses as much on the logistics of tutoring (e.g., where books are located, public school safety) as it does on reading instruction techniques. Tutors are provided with a broad framework to use during sessions, rather than specific techniques. SMART's approach to training contrasts sharply with the rather extensive training many educators suggest volunteers need to effectively tutor students in reading (e.g., Juel, 1994; Roller, 1998).

SMART's approach developed in part from the expectation that volunteer turnover from year to year was likely to be high and therefore intensive training would not be cost-effective. At approximately 50% per year, the turnover rate of SMART volunteers has proved to be an important training issue (Hurst, personal communication, January 12, 1999). There was also a sense that it would be far easier to recruit tutors to begin with if it were clear they were not expected to either know or acquire specialized instructional skills. Instead, the emphasis of recruiting was on asking volunteers, frequently under the auspices of their employers, to simply show up twice a week to read with students.

Similarly, to implement the program easily on a large scale, SMART was intentionally designed to place minimal demands on teachers whose students were being tutored and on coordinators supervising tutors and providing ongoing training. Parents and teachers were told that SMART's purpose was to supplement the daily reading instruction provided by the classroom teacher. There was no attempt to coordinate this supplemental program with the core reading program of each school or each classroom. This was due in part to the complex logistics that would have been necessary for such an arrangement, and in part because of the desire to keep implementation simple. Teachers were asked only to identify the students they felt needed extra support in reading.

What Is the Relative Impact of Different Approaches to Tutoring?

Given the high turnover rate typical of most volunteer programs and the extraordinary cost of training tutors, any program that is self-sufficient and serves a large number of students bears closer scrutiny. Compared with the volunteer reading programs evaluated in a recent review by Wasik (1998), SMART is low cost, serves a large number of students in predominantly low-income schools, and requires minimal training. Little systematically collected information is available, however, on the impact of volunteer reading programs on reading ability. The purpose of the current study was to evaluate the impact of the SMART tutoring program on the reading abilities of students deemed at risk for failure.

Only three previous studies of the impact of volunteer reading programs have been conducted that have used controlled experimental-comparison group designs (Wasik, 1998). These three programs—the Howard Street Tutoring Program (Morris, Shaw, & Perney, 1990), the Intergenerational Tutoring Program (American Academy of Arts and Sciences and Boston Partners in Education, 1999), and the School Volunteer Development Project (U.S. Department of Education, 1979, as cited in Wasik, 1998)—are drastically different than SMART in several ways. In these programs, training of tutors is much more intensive, lengthy, and highly structured. These programs also had an impact on a far smaller number of students, with less than 150 students being served at the time they were evaluated (American Academy of Arts and Sciences & Boston Partners in Education, 1999; Morris et al., 1990; U.S. Department of Education, 1981).

At the time we conducted our evaluation of SMART, over 7,000 students were being served. We believed it was crucial to understand the impact on reading achievement of programs like SMART, which provide minimal training and rely primarily on the judgment and instincts of literate adults to tutor struggling readers. We wished to examine whether these effects were comparable to the effects achieved by tutoring programs that are more intense and costly to implement. This information could be critical for policy makers and others who want to balance program effectiveness and breadth, trying to meaningfully serve as many students as possible who need assistance in the primary grades.

A secondary purpose of the study was to determine the impact of SMART on the referral and placement of students with reading problems in special education. A major goal of contemporary educational policy at both the federal and state or local levels (e.g., California Department of Education, 1998; Texas Reading Initiative, 1997) is to provide intensive beginning reading instruction—with any necessary support—in the primary grades to reduce unnecessary special education placement in later years. To our knowledge, this study is the only one conducted that has examined the impact of a volunteer reading program on special education referral and placement.

Before presenting the results of the evaluation, we briefly describe relevant research on tutoring, with particular attention to the three previous studies of volunteer tutoring programs that used controlled experimental designs. We then describe the SMART program, including the training of volunteers. Presentation of results and a discussion of implications follow.

Relevant Research on Tutoring

Considerable research indicates that one-to-one tutoring in which teachers and other paid professionals serve as tutors produces more substantial gains than any other dyad combination, including tutoring by peers, parents, or volunteers (Shanahan, 1998). Wasik and Slavin (1993) examined five of the most popular programs involving one-on-one tutoring by trained adults: Reading Recovery, Success for All, Prevention of Learning Disabilities, the Wallach Tutoring Program, and Programmed Tutorial Reading. They analyzed 16 studies of first-grade tutorials for children at risk of reading failure and found that the overall effect size was .51 standard deviation units, suggesting that the tutored children gained substantially more than untutored comparison students.

Most relevant to the SMART program and the current study is research on the effectiveness of tutoring by volunteers, which is typically conducted outside the normal classroom setting. Volunteer tutoring is increasingly popular because of the vast number of potential volunteers who could dramatically augment the amount of direct, one-to-one reading instruction students receive in the early grades. The popularity of volunteer tutoring has been enhanced considerably by the America Reads Challenge. While campaigning, President

Clinton (1996) promoted this challenge by calling for the mobilization of "a million volunteer reading tutors all across America...to help every eight-year-old learn to read" [because]..."we know that individualized tutoring works."

Wasik (1998) comprehensively summarized research on the impact of volunteer tutoring on early reading achievement. She identified 17 programs that met the following criteria: (a) adult volunteers were used as tutors, (b) the tutoring was in reading, and (c) the children being tutored were in kindergarten through Grade 3. Wasik concluded that empirical analysis of the impact of those programs is complicated since 5 of the 17 programs reviewed presented no evaluation data at all, and only 3 of them used designs of sufficient rigor to allow causal statements to be made about program effectiveness.

Although three programs had adequate outcome data in reading to determine their effects compared to a comparison group, they were quite different from SMART, most notably in the nature and extent of volunteer training and the number of children served. We review these three programs briefly and then provide a more lengthy description of SMART. We compare the effects all four of these programs had on reading outcomes later in the article.

Howard Street Tutoring Program (Morris et al., 1990). The Howard Street Tutoring Program provides one year of one-to-one tutoring for poor readers in Grades 2 and 3. The program began in 1979 and initially served approximately 20 students per year. It has remained a small-scale program. By 1990, at the time of the formal study, it served approximately 50 students per year. A paid reading specialist is essential to the program and trains non-paid volunteers in groups of two or three during approximately four 1-hour sessions. Volunteers then tutor children at the conclusion of the school day, following lessons individually planned for each child by the reading specialist. In addition to ongoing planning for each child, the reading specialists assist volunteers who need or want special training during the course of the year. Lessons focus on reading of connected text by students, developing alphabetic understanding, writing, and reading by tutors. The program resulted in statistically significant gains relative to the comparison group, on measures of word reading, accuracy of passage reading, and spelling.

Intergenerational Tutoring Program (American Academy of Arts and Sciences & Boston Partners in Education, 1999). The Intergenerational Tutoring Program represents a joint effort among Initiatives for Children of the American Academy of Arts and Sciences, Boston Partners in Education, and the Boston Public Schools to improve the reading skills of first graders who are identified by their teachers as having reading difficulties. At the time of the evaluation, 70 children in low-income Boston schools were being tutored. A certified teacher coordinates the program and does the training. Volunteer tutors receive four 3-hour training sessions prior to the start of tutoring, and ongoing support and training every 2 weeks once tutoring begins. Initial training addresses the basic format of the tutoring sessions, which are conducted three times per week for 45 minutes. Tutoring sessions address letter recognition, word study, phonemic awareness, printing and writing, and guided reading. Once tutoring begins, ongoing training for volunteers covers learning new reading activities and games, sharing tutoring experiences with one another, problem solving, and giving feedback to the Program Coordinator. Tutors keep daily written logs on each of the students they are tutoring. Preliminary analysis indicates the program has had impact on letter identification, but not on measures of word reading, phonemic awareness, or reading connected text.

School Volunteer Development Project (U.S. Department of Education, 1979, as cited in Wasik, 1998). This program was cited in the National Diffusion Network as an exemplary program, even though it was implemented in just two schools in Florida and was terminated during the 1980s. We were able to obtain only a brief description of this project and have relied to some extent on Wasik's (1998) review to help describe the program. The program was developed in Dade County, Florida, for children in Grades 2 through 6 who were functioning 1 or more years below grade level. Community volunteers tutored children for 30 minutes per day, 4 or 5 days per week. Tutors were trained prior to tutoring in a variety of skills. In addition, tutors worked with a reading specialist on the skills they were tutoring. Wasik reported that the program resulted in an overall effect size of .50 on a global measure of academic achievement, the Metropolitan Achievement Test (1984).

Although Wasik (1998) included 14 additional programs in her review of volunteer tutoring programs, none of the 14 had been evaluated by means of an acceptable research design. Salient differences between these 14 programs and Oregon's SMART program are that the training of coordinators and volunteers, and the content of tutoring sessions, are generally far less complex and structured in the SMART program.

The Start Making a Reader Today (SMART) Tutoring Program

Students are designated for participation in SMART by their teachers, who are asked to choose students who they believe are at risk for reading failure.

Students attend tutoring sessions for 30 minutes twice a week throughout the school year, and they may take home two books each month to keep for themselves for home reading. Popular books to read and take home in first grade include *The Very Hungry Caterpillar* (Carle, 1984), and *The Grouchy Ladybug* (Carle, 1996). Popular books in second grade include *A Pocket for Corduroy* (Freeman, 1980) and any number of books from the Arthur series (e.g., *Arthur Babysits* and *Arthur Accused*, Brown, 1997, 1998).

Volunteer tutors represent a diverse group, although considerable emphasis was placed on recruiting members of the business community. Two thirds of all SMART volunteers have been in the program less than 2 years. The greatest proportion of volunteers (33%) is in the 30–45-year-old age group, with the 45–65 age group the next largest (29%). One fifth are over 65.

Volunteers can be trained either in the fall before tutoring has begun or any time during the school year. An initial training session is held at the beginning of the year at a central location, such as the school district central office. The training lasts 1–2 hours, during which 30–40 minutes is devoted to actual reading strategies volunteers can use with students. The remaining time goes to orientation and discussion of logistical and administrative issues, school rules, and safety protocols. Training emphasizes the importance of reading to students and having students read. Volunteers are encouraged to try to increase students' interests in reading, to make the tutoring sessions fun, and to ask students questions about the material they read. After the initial 30-minute training session, volunteers are free to begin working with children on their own, and most receive no additional training.

SMART volunteers may also sign up to be tutors after the school year begins. In this case, training is conducted at the school in impromptu sessions organized by the coordinator. A common training activity is for the coordinator to model a few strategies during a reading session with a student before the volunteer takes over. Approximately half the volunteers are trained in this impromptu fashion.

The key resource for volunteers is the volunteer handbook (Oregon Children's Foundation, 1992, 1998). The handbook indicates that children will improve their reading if (a) they are provided with necessary background to appreciate the story being read, (b) they have opportunities to hear different types of books being read (i.e., some fiction, some science books, some biography, some poetry), (c) they learn something about letter-sound relationships to read unknown words, (d) they make predictions about the story, and (e) they derive meaning from illustrations.

To help children improve in these areas, four reading strategies a volunteer can use with the child are described: (1) the volunteer reads to the child, (2) the volunteer and child read together (e.g., at the same time), (3) the volunteer reads a section of text that the child then rereads, and (4) the volunteer asks the child questions during reading.

The handbook says that these strategies will work best if volunteers review books carefully before reading them with children by relating the content of a book to the child's experiences before reading it, skimming the book as a warm-up activity, and looking at and talking about the illustrations in the book as a way of engaging children in dialogue. A section of the handbook gives volunteers sample questions they can ask children before, during, and after reading, such as What are some words that might be in this story? (before); Is this what you expected to happen? (during); and Who was your favorite character? (after).

Each school has a half-time SMART coordinator who manages the program in that building. Most coordinators are Americorps volunteers or instructional assistants with no formal training in reading instruction or elementary education. Their coordinator training for SMART amounts to approximately 1 full day per year. The coordinator's main responsibilities are recruiting volunteers, setting up a place in the school for tutoring sessions, making sure there are a sufficient number of books, and working with teachers to identify tutoring times.

The present evaluation of SMART differs from evaluations of other volunteer tutoring programs in that students were in tutoring for 2 years at the time of the evaluation, compared to 1 year for the other programs. SMART also departs from two of the three other programs evaluated in that it provides tutoring to students in first grade. The Intergenerational Tutoring Program also tutored students in first grade, but the other two programs began tutoring students in second grade. The final difference is the number of students being served at the time of the evaluation. In SMART, the number of students tutored was far greater than in the other programs.

There are several important similarities in the evaluations of SMART and the other three volunteer tutoring programs that warrant their grouping as similar studies for comparative analysis. All of the evaluations examined effects on reading outcomes, and each expected its tutoring program to have a positive, measurable impact on reading achievement. All of the evaluations randomly assigned students to treatment and comparison groups. In all cases, the treatment was one-to-one tutoring and the comparison condition in all cases was no tutoring. It is important to note that in all of the programs, students in both treatment and comparison conditions continued to receive regular classroom reading instruction during the volunteer tutoring.

Method

Design

We used an experimental design with random assignment of eligible students within each classroom to either a SMART or comparison group. This type of design is considered optimal for field research (Cook & Campbell, 1979). Pairs of students in each classroom were matched on a salient pretest variable, Rapid Letter Naming (Kaminski & Good, 1996), and randomly assigned to treatment and comparison groups. Letter naming was used because it is one of the best predictors of subsequent reading achievement (Adams, 1990; Bond & Dykstra, 1967; Chall, 1967; Snow, Burns, & Griffin, 1998). For example, in Bond and Dykstra's classic first-grade study, letter naming at the beginning of first grade was the best predictor of end-of-year reading achievement. Summaries of the research on beginning reading by Chall (1967), Adams (1990), and Snow et al. (1998) have all concluded that letter naming is the single best predictor of beginning reading achievement.

Sample

Sampling procedures. In fall of the first evaluation year, all first-grade classrooms (24 total) in six schools across four school districts provided children for the study. These six schools were selected because they were all in the first year of implementing a SMART program, ensuring that none of the children nominated to participate had been in the SMART program in kindergarten. Typical of the procedure used to select students for SMART in classrooms across the state, approximately one quarter of the students in each classroom (four to six students) were selected by their teacher because they demonstrated reading difficulties. Teachers considered two criteria when nominating their students to participate in SMART: (a) the students' reading skills were among the lowest in their classrooms, and (b) in the teachers' opinions, it was likely the students had relatively few academic literacy experiences with adults or others in the home. The survey that teachers used to nominate students for the SMART program is included in Appendix A.

Teachers were asked to split their nominations approximately evenly between males and females. Teachers also nominated a group of four to six other students whom they believed had about average reading and language skills and who were likely to have had frequent academic literacy experiences in the home. Teachers were explicitly told to select average-ability readers, not high-ability readers (see Appendix A). This group served as a standard for assessing relative reading progress. After teachers' nominations, letters were sent to the parents of nominated children requesting permission for their child to participate in a study explained as an evaluation of a program designed to help students in the early grades become better readers. Parents of two students out of 129 nominated by teachers to participate in SMART declined permission.

When consent was obtained, all students were administered a battery of pretest measures (described in the Measures section). Rapid Letter Naming (Kaminski & Good, 1996; O'Connor, Notari-Syverson, & Vadasy, 1996) was used to evaluate students nominated by their teachers to participate in SMART and assign them to the SMART program or to the comparison group. In each classroom, the two students nominated for SMART who scored lowest on Rapid Letter Naming were paired. The same procedure was followed with the next two lowest scoring students until all students on the teacher nomination list were paired. Then, one member of each pair was randomly assigned to either the SMART group or the comparison group. In this way, random assignments were made at the classroom level, so there is no reason to expect that quality of classroom reading instruction differed for students in the experimental and comparison groups. The only difference was that students assigned to the SMART group received 1 hour of tutoring per week.

We were concerned about denying services to students who their teachers believed needed tutoring. But because all of the schools were in their first year of SMART implementation, there were not enough tutors available to serve all eligible students. Therefore, those students in the comparison group, who were eligible for tutoring but did not receive it, may not have received tutoring even if the study had not been conducted.

Sample attrition. The original sample—those students who were tested at the beginning of Grade 1—included 64 assigned to the SMART program and 63 assigned to the comparison group. Attrition rates over the 2 years were 33% in the SMART program and 35% in the comparison group. The final samples of students in the SMART and comparison groups were virtually identical on all of the measures administered at pretest.

Students in the comparison group were dropped from the study if they moved to a school outside of the two counties in which the study was being conducted. Students in the SMART group were dropped if they moved to a school outside one of the participating counties or if they moved to a school inside a participating county that did not have a SMART program.

Description of the sample. Students in the final sample were those students who participated in the full 2 years of the evaluation: 43 students in the SMART group and 41 students in the comparison group. All six participating schools were Title I schools located in two of the largest counties in the state. The schools represented a diverse range of communities, from low income/large city to working class/moderate size-city to rural. The communities were representative of the Title I school population of western Oregon. Student ethnicity was as follows: European American (47%) African American (30%), American Indian (10%), Asian American (6%), and Latino (6%). There were 44 female students in the sample and 40 males.

Average-achieving students. A third group of 36 average-ability students was also part of the evaluation. Data for these children were used to assess the progress SMART students made relative to a normative sample of students at the participating schools. Teachers were accurate in selecting average-achieving students as opposed to high-performing students. That is, the scores of these students on the reading measures reflect average as opposed to exceptional performance (see Table 1).

SMART Tutoring Procedures

Students in the SMART group received one-to-one tutoring for 6 months each year in first and second grade. Tutoring occurred in 30-minute sessions 2 days per week. Over the 2-year period, the number of one-to-one

Table 1
Pretest means, standard deviations, and percentiles
for SMART, comparison, and average-achieving groups

Measures	SMART (N = 43) M (SD)	Percentile	Comparison (N = 41) M (SD)	Percentile	ES(Δ)	Average achieving (N = 36) M (SD)	Percentile
Word Identification, WRMT-R (W score)	354.9 (12.6)	5th	357.5 (14.5)	6th	−.18	389.5 (30.0)	52nd
Letter Naming Fluency	27.7 (14.2)		25.2 (15.1)		.17	47.8 (15.1)	
Phonemic Segmentation	11.7 (7.5)		12.6 (8.8)		−.10	19.1 (7.4)	
Expressive One Word Picture Vocabulary Test-Revised(raw score)	43.3 (16.4)	19th	43.8 (18.3)	23rd	−.03	55.8 (11.4)	57th

sessions per student ranged from 49 to 98, with a mean of 73 (and a standard deviation of 10.9).

All students in the SMART and comparison groups (as well as the average-achieving group) received regular classroom reading instruction throughout the 2 years. We made no attempt to influence or interfere with school practices or decisions about how to teach reading to students, nor did we offer advice as to whether students in the study should receive any kind of specialized reading instruction or programs. Likewise, we made no attempt to influence student referral or placement decisions in special education.

Assessment Procedures

Students were tested three times in the study: at the beginning of Grade 1 (October, 1996), the end of Grade 1 (May, 1997), and the end of Grade 2 (May, 1998). The pretest battery took 20 to 30 minutes to administer; it was done in one session. First-grade posttesting took 40 to 60 minutes to complete and was done over the course of two sessions separated by no more than 2 days. Second-grade posttesting was completed in one session that took approximately 45 minutes.

As detailed below, all measures possess strong psychometric characteristics for the population of students in the evaluation and have been used in published research studies. Measures administered in the study, except for the commonly utilized measures—that is, the three subtests of the Woodcock Reading Mastery Test-Revised (1998) and the Expressive One Word Picture Vocabulary Test-Revised (1990)—are presented in Appendix B.

Certified teachers and graduate students in school psychology were trained by the first author to administer the battery of measures. Test administrators were kept blind as to which of the three groups students belonged. The reliable administration and scoring of each measure were established for each test administrator before any student in the study was tested. Each new examiner administered the test battery with the first author to their first student included in the study. Both adults scored student performance independently. Reliability was calculated by dividing the lowest raw score by the highest raw score. A checklist was used to ensure reliable administration procedures. When reliability was at least .95, the examiner tested students independently. In all cases, examiners tested students on their own after co-administering the battery with the first author with no more than 2 students. After that, two times per week, each examiner would determine reliability with another examiner using the same procedure. Reliability checks continued throughout the testing period and remained above .95 throughout.

Measures

Four types of measures were administered to students during the evaluation: (1) prereading measures, which included phonemic awareness and alphabetic understanding; (2) reading accuracy and fluency measures, which included word identification and reading fluency; (3) reading comprehension; and (4) vocabulary, which included a word comprehension measure and an expressive picture vocabulary measure. Table 2 summarizes the schedule for administration of measures at different phases of the study.

Because students' reading abilities change extensively during the course of first and second grade, only one measure (the Word Identification subtest of the Woodcock Reading Mastery Test-Revised) was administered at all three assessment periods. Measures were selected and administered at times when most students were considered to have sufficient skill to provide meaningful information. For example, the reading fluency measure was not administered until the end of first grade because, in the fall, most first graders—especially those considered at risk for reading difficulty—are not yet reading well enough to provide meaningful information in this area. Some early literacy measures were included in the first-grade battery to assess emerging phonemic awareness skills, but were dropped from the second-grade battery, because they no longer fit the children's level of reading development.

Table 2
Administration schedule of primary measures used in the evaluation

Measure	Fall first grade	Spring first grade	Spring second grade
Prereading			
Phonemic Segmentation	X	X	
Rapid Letter Naming	X	X	
Reading Accuracy and Fluency			
Word Identification: WRMT-R	X	X	X
Oral Reading Fluency First-Grade Passage		X	X
Oral Reading Fluency Second-Grade Passage			X
Reading Comprehension			
Passage Comprehension: WRMT-R		X	X
Vocabulary Knowledge			
Expressive One Word Picture Vocabulary Test-Revised	X	X	
Word Comprehension: WRMT-R			X

WRMT-R stands for the Woodcock Reading Mastery Test-Revised

Prereading Measures

In the fall and spring of first grade, children were administered two measures to assess the core underlying processes in learning to read: Phonemic Segmentation and Rapid Letter Naming (Adams, 1990; Kaminski & Good, 1996; O'Connor et al., 1996; Snow et al., 1998; Torgesen, Morgan, & Davis, 1992).

Phonemic Segmentation (O'Connor et al., 1996). On this measure of phonemic awareness, examiners orally presented 3-phoneme words to students one at a time. Students responded by saying the individual phonemes in each word. For example, the examiner would say "make." To answer correctly, children would say "/m/ /a/ /k/." As specified in the testing procedures, the task was modeled and practiced prior to administration. During administration, children received 1 point for each correct phoneme they produced (i.e., 0 to 3 points per word). The measure took 3–5 minutes to administer. Alternate-form reliability on a similar measure of phonemic segmentation (Kaminski & Good, 1996) was reported at .88, and predictive validity with reading measures that ranged from .73 to .91.

Rapid Letter Naming (Kaminski & Good, 1996). On this measure, students were presented with randomly ordered upper- and lowercase letters arranged in rows on a sheet of paper. They were asked to name as many letters as possible in 1 minute. The number of correctly named letters per minute was calculated. Reliability of the measure has been reported at .93 by Kaminski and Good (1996), who also reported 1-year predictive validity coefficients with reading criterion measures that ranged from .72 to .98.

Reading Accuracy and Fluency

We measured two aspects of reading accuracy and fluency: (1) reading isolated words correctly and (2) reading connected text fluently. The Word Identification subtest of the Woodcock Reading Mastery Test-Revised was used to assess accuracy of word reading. Oral Reading Fluency was used to assess ability to read words fluently (Shinn, 1998).

Word Identification Subtest of the Woodcock Reading Mastery Test-Revised (1998). The Word Identification subtest measures a student's ability to read words in isolation. The test begins with simple words and gradually becomes more difficult. The test takes from 2 to 15 minutes to administer, depending on a student's reading ability. This subtest was administered at all three testing times. Split-half reliability estimates are reported to be .98 for first graders. According to the examiner's manual, the correlation between the Word Identification subtest and the Woodcock-Johnson Total Reading score is .82 for first-grade students.

Oral Reading Fluency (Shinn, 1998). Oral Reading Fluency has been used in educational research and practice as a measure of reading proficiency for more than 15 years. Research has demonstrated consistently that the number of words students read correctly in 1 minute provides a reliable and valid measure of overall reading ability (Fuchs, Fuchs, & Maxwell, 1988; Potter & Wamre, 1990; Shinn, Good, Knutson, Tilly, & Collins, 1992). Standardized procedures were used for administration of this measure (Shinn, 1989). Each student read aloud a story written at either a first- or a second-grade level. The reading passages were taken from a basal reading series and were used by the first author on numerous occasions in schools as a method to assess the reading skills and progress of beginning readers. The number of words the student read correctly in 1 minute provided an index used in data analysis. The first-grade passage was administered during spring of first and second grade. The second-grade passage was administered only during the spring of second grade.

Estimates of the internal consistency, test-retest, and interscorer reliability for Oral Reading Fluency have ranged from .89 to .99. Correlations with other measures of reading, including measures of decoding and comprehension, have ranged from .73 to .91 (Shinn, Tindal, & Stein, 1988). Correlations between Oral Reading Fluency and standardized measures of reading comprehension are typically above .80 (Marston, 1989). Shinn et al. (1992) conducted a confirmatory factor analysis of Oral Reading Fluency and concluded that in the early grades the measure was as valid an indicator of reading comprehension as it was an indicator of decoding ability.

Reading Comprehension

The Passage Comprehension subtest of the Woodcock Reading Mastery Test-Revised was used to assess reading comprehension. This subtest provided an indication of the child's ability to comprehend short written text. The child read a portion of text silently and then supplied a missing word appropriate to the context of the passage. Administration time for this test ranged from 10 minutes to 25 minutes, depending on the ability of the student. Passage Comprehension was administered at the spring testing in first and second grade. According to the test manual, split-half reliability estimates for this measure were .94 for first graders. The correlation between Passage Comprehension and the Woodcock-Johnson Total Reading score was .63.

Vocabulary Knowledge

We measured two aspects of vocabulary knowledge. The Word Comprehension subtest of the Woodcock Reading Mastery Test-Revised was used to assess word comprehension. The Expressive One Word Picture Vocabulary Test-Revised (1990) was used to assess expressive vocabulary.

Word Comprehension: Antonyms, Synonyms, and Analogies Subtests of the Woodcock Reading Mastery Test-Revised. Word Comprehension assesses a student's reading vocabulary. On the Antonyms subtest, students read individual words out loud and state a word that means the opposite. On the Synonyms subtest, students read individual words and state another word with the same meaning. On the Analogies subtest, students read three words, two of which are related to each other, and are asked to supply a fourth word that completes the analogy. These subtests were administered at the end of second grade. Split-half reliability estimates for this subtest were .95 for first graders. The correlation of Word Comprehension with the Woodcock-Johnson Total Reading score for first graders was .82.

Expressive One Word Picture Vocabulary Test-Revised (EOWPVT-R). The Expressive One Word Picture Vocabulary Test-Revised (EOWPVT-R) is a measure of expressive language, an important component in reading comprehension. On this test, examiners asked children to name individual pictures (e.g., apple) or to tell what was happening in a picture (e.g., eating). Median split-half reliability coefficients for the EOWPVT-R are reported at .90. Criterion related validity coefficients with Peabody Picture Vocabulary Test-Revised, a measure of receptive language, was reported at .59. The measure was administered for two reasons: as a possible predictor of reading acquisition, and because it was hypothesized that the dialogic nature of SMART tutoring might result in improved vocabulary knowledge of students. The EOWPVT-R was administered in the fall and spring of Grade 1 only. Interim analyses (i.e., spring of Grade 1) revealed the SMART and comparison groups were virtually identical at both pretest and posttest. Consequently, the EOWPVT-R was not administered at the end of second grade.

Results

As seen in Table 2, data collection occurred in the fall of first grade, spring of first grade, and spring of second grade, with the measures varying somewhat at each point. Pretest data are presented first, confirming that the experimental and comparison samples are statistically equivalent. We then present an analysis of the impact of tutoring on reading achievement as measured through covariance procedures and growth curves, followed by comparison of rates of student placement in special education. Finally, we present a supplementary analysis of volunteers' perceptions of the impact of tutoring on their students and on their own view of schools.

Pretest Data

Table 1 presents means, standard deviations, and percentiles for the SMART, comparison, and average-ability groups, on the pretest battery: the Word Identification subtest of the Woodcock Reading Mastery Test-Revised, Rapid Letter Naming, Phonemic Segmentation, and the EOWPVT-R. Effect sizes are also presented using Glass's Δ (Cooper & Hedges, 1994), a commonly used measure of effect size. Glass's Δ was computed by subtracting the mean of the comparison group from the mean of the SMART group and dividing by the standard deviation of the comparison group (Cooper & Hedges, 1994).

There were no statistically significant differences between the SMART and comparison groups on any of the pretest measures: WRMT-R, t (82) = -.89, p = .37; Rapid Letter Naming, t (82) = .78, p = .44; Phonemic Segmentation, t (82) = -.53, p = .60; EOWPVT-R, t (82) = -.14, p = .89). Glass's Δ in Table 1 shows the high degree of comparability between the two groups at pretest. On all four measures, effect sizes are very small, and vary in a nonsystematic fashion. The mean effect size of -.05 is close to zero.

Differences in Achievement at End of First and Second Grades

Two reading measures were administered at the end of first and second grade, Oral Reading Fluency (First-Grade Passage) and the Passage Comprehension subtest of the Woodcock Reading Mastery Test-Revised. Analysis of covariance (ANCOVA) was used to analyze performance differences between SMART and comparison students at the end of second grade. The two covariates were pretest scores (beginning of first grade) on (a) Phonemic Segmentation and (b) the Word Identification subtest of the Woodcock Reading Mastery Test-Revised. Results indicated a statistically significant effect favoring SMART on the Oral Reading Fluency measure (First-Grade Passage); F (1, 80) = 7.61, p = .007. The effect on the Reading Comprehension subtest approached significance, F (1, 80) = 3.46, p = .067.

For the reading measures administered at the end of second grade only, ANCOVA results were statistically significant both for Oral Reading Fluency (Second-Grade Passage), F (1, 80) = 6.37; p = .014, and the Word Comprehension subtest of the Woodcock Reading Mastery Test-Revised, F (1, 80) = 5.20 ; p = .025.

Effect sizes for the different reading measures, using Glass's Δ were Word Identification, .44; Oral Reading Fluency (First-Grade Passage), .48; Oral Reading Fluency (Second-Grade Passage), .53; Word Comprehension, .43; and Passage Comprehension, .32. Except for Passage Comprehension, these effects are considered moderate in magnitude (Cohen, 1988). The effect on Passage Comprehension is considered small.

Supplemental analyses: Impact on predictive measures during Grade 1. Because SMART tutoring did not in any way stress phonemic awareness, we expected there to be no effect on that aspect of reading ability. As predicted, Phonemic Segmentation and Rapid Letter Naming were not affected by the SMART tutoring. ANCOVAs revealed no statistically significant differences on these measures at the end of the first grade. Effect sizes on Phonemic Segmentation and Rapid Letter Naming for SMART versus comparison groups were .07 and –.06, indicating virtually identical performance. In addition, an ANCOVA showed that there was no difference between SMART and comparison students on the measure of expressive language (EOWPVT-R) at the end of first grade. The effect size of .12 favoring SMART was small.

Analysis of Reading Growth Over Time (Word Identification Only)

Table 3 presents the results on measures of reading proficiency, at both the interim assessment (i.e., end of first grade), and for the final assessment (end of second grade).

The Word Identification subtest of the Woodcock Reading Mastery Test-Revised was administered at all three test phases (i.e., the beginning of first grade, the end of first grade, and the end of second grade). We used individual growth curve methodology (see Bryk & Raudenbush, 1992, or Stoolmiller, 1995, for more details and relevant example applications) to analyze change in student performance on this measure. This method allowed us to estimate (a) the mean rate of change and the extent to which individual children varied about the mean rate of change and (b) correlates of individual variability in change, which in this investigation focused on group status. Maximum likelihood estimation was used for nested chi-square tests

Table 3
Means, standard deviations, and percentiles for SMART and comparison groups at the end of first and second grades

Measures	SMART (N = 43) M (SD)	Percentile	Comparison (N = 41) M (SD)	Percentile	ES(Δ)	Average achieving (N = 36) M (SD)	Percentile
			Interim scores (end of first grade)				
Reading accuracy and fluency							
Word Identification, WRMT-R (W score)	409.2 (29.7)	33rd	398.9 (24.4)	21st	.42	438.6 (30.2)	69th
Oral Reading Fluency First-Grade Passage	27.8 (22.8)		18.7 (17.3)		.53	57.0 (34.2)	
Reading comprehension							
Passage Comprehension, WRMT-R (W score)	449.3 (24.4)	23rd	443.2 (14.2)	15th	.43	466.1 (16.0)	55th
			Posttest scores (end of second grade)				
Reading accuracy and fluency							
*Word Identification, WRMT-R (W score)	449.4 (30.2)	29th	437.9 (25.9)	21st	.44	470.4 (22.1)	47th
**Oral Reading Fluency First-Grade passage	71.3 (35.2)		55.9 (32.1)		.48	98.8 (35.1)	
*Oral Reading Fluency Second-Grade passage	61.5 (35.5)		45.9 (29.5)		.53	90.5 (38.3)	
Reading comprehension							
*Word Comprehension, WRMT-R (W score)	472.3 (17.3)	31st	465.4 (16.2)	19th	.43	487.8 (9.7)	69th
Passage Comprehension, WRMT-R (W score)	468.9 (16.0)	28th	464.7 (13.1)	22nd	.32	481.7 (10.9)	53rd

Means for the SMART and comparison groups are adjusted for pretest performance on the Phonemic Segmentation test and the Word Identification subtest of the WRMT-R using analysis of covariance. Significance tests are between the SMART and comparison groups. Percentiles and effect sizes are determined using the adjusted means. Means for the average-achieving group are unadjusted. *$p < .05$. **$p < .01$.

of variance components using the Mplus program (Muthen & Muthen, 1998). Restricted maximum likelihood estimation was used for estimation of group differences using the LME procedure in the S-plus 4 software package (Mathsoft, 1998).

We were interested in two questions regarding the growth parameters of students in these three groups. First, we predicted that students in SMART would have growth rates that would surpass the word reading growth of students in the matched comparison group. Second, we predicted that students in SMART would have growth rates that were similar to the growth rates of students in the average-achieving group.

To characterize the pattern of change over time, we first fit models to determine whether growth was linear or a curvilinear 2nd degree polynomial (i.e., a combination of linear and quadratic). We computed a nested chi-square statistic to assess the importance of the quadratic factor in understanding rate of growth in all 3 samples (SMART, the comparison group of at-risk readers, and the average-ability group). Within-subject error variance was fixed at about 2% of the total time 1 variance and $\chi^2 = 1953$, $df = 4$, was statistically significant. Inspection of the z test statistics associated with the individual quadratic growth factor parameters revealed that all 5 were highly statistically significant, the minimum z being –3.31. Thus, growth in word reading was best described by a curvilinear model (i.e., a combination of linear and quadratic trends), indicating that growth for all 3 samples was greatest in Grade 1 and tapered off in Grade 2.

To test for group differences in growth rates among the three groups, dummy coded group membership variables using two contrasts—SMART versus matched comparison and SMART versus average achieving—were added to the growth model. Differences were statistically significant among the instructional groups in terms of intercept and slope. The pooled within-group standard deviation of the linear growth rate factor was 1.63.

The SMART, matched comparison, and average-ability groups had estimated linear growth rates of 5.94, 5.20, and 5.20 words per month, respectively. The differences between SMART and the other groups were statistically significant in both cases ($z = -2.07$, one-tailed $p = .019$ for matched comparison; $z = -2.00$, one-tailed $p = .023$ for average ability). The effect sizes for the differences were .45 pooled standard deviation units for both comparisons.

Student Placement in Special Education

Relative rates of student referral and placement in special education were compared through chi-square analysis. Data were collected at the six evaluation schools in the fall of Grade 3 on special education referral and placement. We asked two questions of special education teachers at each school: (1) While the target students were attending that particular school, had they ever been referred for special education services? (2) While the target students were attending that particular school, had they ever been placed in special education?

At the beginning of third grade, 38 of the original 43 students in the SMART group (88%) were attending the same school they attended in Grades 1 and 2. Of the 41 students in the comparison group, 32 still attended the same school (78%). For these samples of students, we were able to trace special education referral and placement. By the beginning of third grade, 15 of the 38 students in the SMART group had been referred for special education (39%). Of these 15 students, 10 were actually placed in special education (26%). For the comparison group, 18 of the 32 were referred for special education placement (56%). Of these 18, 14 were placed in special education (44%).

Chi-square analysis showed that the difference in rate of special education placement by fall of grade 3, 39% for SMART versus 56% for the comparison group, approached statistical significance ($p = .12$). Power in this instance was limited by the relatively small sample size for chi-square analysis. We believe the lower special education placement rate for students in the SMART group is a potentially important finding. It is also worth noting that the special education placement rates are very high for both groups, providing additional evidence that SMART serves students who need as much support as possible learning to read.

Overall, the results of the evaluation suggest that in terms of reading achievement, students in SMART benefited a great deal from their participation in the tutoring program. Before discussing in detail the nature of those improvements and possible explanations, we examine the results of a survey of the program's volunteers.

Volunteers' Perceptions of the Impact of Tutoring

In 1993 and 1994, 3 years prior to beginning the longitudinal study of SMART reading outcomes, we asked all SMART volunteers in Oregon to complete a survey questionnaire in order to learn their impressions of the volunteer experience. A total of 903 volunteers submitted responses in 1993 and 986 in 1994. The responses were not significantly different statistically across the 2 years. About half of the SMART respondents rated their participation as an "excellent and valuable experience." Another 45% felt it was "a worthwhile experience." Ninety-five percent of volunteers felt the role of the SMART volunteer was a challenging experience.

Eighty-two percent felt their training was either excellent or good, while 17% felt the training did only a fair job of preparing them. About half of the volunteers indicated they "would like more guidance" in learning additional techniques and tools for improving children's reading and understanding. The need for more guidance, as opposed to extensive training, was frequently voiced. Volunteers desired information such as how to deal with students who have short attention spans, students who tell them "they did not want to read," or students who appeared unhappy or angry. Some requested more age-specific training, including information on what to expect at a given age or grade level. Several asked for ideas for alternative strategies or activities to increase motivation.

In open-ended responses, volunteers indicated that they would like more opportunities to meet with teachers, primarily to receive guidance on reading instruction, and to get a sense of how the teacher viewed the child's reading progress. The theme of emotional bonding consistently emerged from the open-ended responses. Many tutors described the intense nature of the one-on-one tutoring situation and the depth of feeling toward their students. For example, one volunteer noted that "so many of them are so angry and frustrated they can't listen or learn." Many volunteers indicated they would like to know more about their students' lives or more about the specific nature of their students' learning problems. Many volunteers complained about the fact that tutoring sessions had been canceled due to an array of school activities (such as assemblies or plays) and that tutors were rarely given advance notice. The quality and quantity of space provided were also a common concern.

Volunteers were very positive about the books that were available for students through SMART. About 80% indicated that they often or always found books appropriate for their students. Volunteers with Spanish-speaking students indicated a need for Spanish-language books and books appropriate for older children who were not yet fluent in English. Several suggested that books be organized according to reading or grade level. (This was later done.)

Volunteers disagreed somewhat about ways to improve SMART tutoring. Some indicated they wanted more games, puzzles, and other activities, while others believed these distracted from the reading tasks. Some volunteers indicated their roles should be simply to promote the joy of reading, while others felt it more important to teach reading skills.

Perhaps the most interesting survey finding was volunteers' responses to how the SMART experience changed their views of school. Many expressed an increased understanding of the challenging job teachers have and recognized the limited resources available to schools. One volunteer summarized the challenges by commenting how reading problems often are "coupled with emotional problems" in young learners. Most were impressed with the efforts schools directed towards these challenges.

One person summarized the intensity and importance of the tutoring experience this way: "As a parent with four kids, I have long viewed schools as the most critical battleground in our society. SMART rubs my face in it. SMART tutoring should be required of all adults, especially those voting against school funding."

Discussion

This study found that Oregon's SMART volunteer tutoring program improved the reading abilities of students deemed at risk for failure in reading. On most measures of reading, the performance of students in SMART was statistically higher than was the performance of students in a randomly assigned, matched comparison sample. Statistically significant differences were found on three aspects of reading: word reading, reading fluency, and word comprehension (i.e., reading vocabulary). The impact of the intervention on passage comprehension was not statistically significant, but the difference favored students in the SMART group and approached statistical significance ($p = .07$).

Effect sizes on all reading measures indicated the impact was at the level of educational importance. Effect sizes ranged from a low of .32 on reading comprehension to a high of .53 on the second-grade passage of Oral Reading Fluency. Taken together, the analysis indicated that SMART had a clear, positive impact on the reading achievement of students who received tutoring.

On the Word Identification measure (the subtest of the Woodcock Reading Mastery Test-Revised), the data were analyzed using growth curve analysis in order to determine the relative rates of growth for students in SMART, the comparison group, and average-achieving readers. The growth rate of students in the SMART group surpassed the growth of students in the comparison group, as well as the growth rate of students in the average-achieving group. The SMART group's greater growth compared with the average-achieving group is particularly important given what we know about the ever-expanding gap between good and poor readers over time unless intensive early intervention takes place (Foorman, Francis, Fletcher, Schatschneider, & Mehta, 1998; Stanovich, 1986).

Despite the greater growth rate of students in SMART versus the other two groups, at the end of second grade their level of performance was still much lower than the performance of students in the average-achieving group. At the end of second grade, the mean score for students in SMART corresponded to about the 30th percentile across the three subtests of the WRMT-R, compared to a mean score falling between the 47th and 69th percentiles for students in the average-achieving group. Thus many students in SMART remained at risk of reading-related difficulties in their subsequent school careers. At the end of second grade, students in the comparison group, with a mean score corresponding to about the 20th percentile across the three WRMT-R subtests, were at even greater risk for reading-related difficulties.

The data indicate that reading-related difficulties began to surface for some students in the study by third grade. For example, 44% of students in the comparison group had been placed in special education by the fall of third grade, compared to 26% for students in SMART. This difference is not statistically significant but suggests a possible trend that should be further investigated. It does show clearly, however, that students in SMART and students in the comparison group remain at considerable risk of reading-related difficulties. Current research is aimed at determining which children in SMART made the greatest reading growth, and a means for determining which students require a more intensive intervention than SMART beginning in first grade to avoid serious reading difficulties (Baker, Stoolmiller, & Gersten, 2000).

Strength of Effects of SMART Versus Other Volunteer Reading Programs

It is important to place the findings of this study in the context of other research on tutoring. Recent reviews by Wasik (1998) and Shanahan (1998) clearly indicated that there is a dearth of well-controlled research investigating the effects of volunteer tutoring programs on student reading. Because of this, Wasik and Shanahan indicated that all they actually could present were hypotheses about best practice. Neither the degree of impact that volunteer reading programs have on the reading achievement of students in the primary grades nor the degree to which the training of volunteers influences level of impact are clear from previous research.

A closer examination of SMART compared to the three other volunteer reading programs that used a similar experimental design in their evaluations provides some preliminary answers. When possible in these analyses, we rely on effect size comparisons on comparable measures of reading achievement.

The Howard Street Tutoring Program. The effect size on measures of word recognition for SMART and the Howard Street Tutoring Program was nearly identical, .44 and .42 respectively. Reading researchers have long considered word recognition to be the linchpin for successful reading (Adams, 1990; Foorman et al., 1998; Stanovich, 1986).

The School Volunteer Development Project. The overall effect size of the School Volunteer Development Project was .50 on a measure of overall achievement, the Metropolitan Achievement Test (Wasik, 1998). In SMART, the mean effect size across all reading measures was .44. The difference, though quite small, suggests a slightly stronger effect for the School Volunteer Program. It is not clear how many hours students were tutored in the School Volunteer Development Project, but sessions were 30 minutes long and were conducted four to five times per week. Thus, the total time in tutoring sessions over one year was likely to have been roughly the same as the SMART condition.

The Intergenerational Tutoring Program. Preliminary analysis of the Intergenerational Tutoring Program became available last year (American Academy of Arts and Sciences & Boston Partners in Education, 1999). The preliminary analysis is based on 140 students, assigned randomly to either the experimental tutoring group or the no-treatment comparison group. Across a number of outcome reading measures, the report indicates there was a statistically significant difference between the groups only on a measure of letter identification. On measures of word reading, phonemic awareness, and reading of text, there were no statistically significant differences between the groups. Further analysis needs to be conducted to determine impact, but it appears the effect of SMART is greater than the effect achieved in this program. Because the preliminary report on the effect of the Intergenerational Tutoring Program does not present data on the comparison group, calculating an effect size was not possible.

Implications

At the beginning of the study, we asked many of our colleagues with expertise in early reading instruction to make predictions about the outcome SMART would have on reading achievement. Like us, they were unsure what to predict. Some expressed concern that a program as loosely structured as SMART might not be able to affect the reading achievement of students who were clearly among the teachers' greatest concerns. After all, they reasoned, volunteers received only minimal training, and the wide latitude they were given in organizing the tutoring sessions could result in a pattern of tutoring decision making not particularly helpful to students struggling to learn to read. There was also concern that SMART in no way specifically supported the development of phonemic awareness skills.

However, other colleagues raised the possibility that the very looseness and flexibility of the program could be a strength. Without feeling burdened by extensive procedural expectations and routines, and without the need to attend more than one formal training session a year, the adult volunteers (many of whom were very successful in their respective occupations and active members of their communities) would rely on their own resources and insights to figure out how to best tutor children. Regardless of the specific positions we and our colleagues took in predicting reading outcomes, we agreed there would be positive benefits of regular one-to-one interactions between children and adults beyond the scope of reading achievement. We also agreed that such benefits could not be achieved easily in typical general education classrooms.

Comparison to Other Experimentally Evaluated Programs

What explains the impact of SMART; given similar effects compared to programs that provide more extensive training to their volunteers? Part of the explanation may be that, compared to the other three programs that were evaluated with the use of an experimental design, SMART provided tutoring to students over 2 years rather than 1. Although SMART lasted for 2 years, SMART students participated at a less intensive level during that time, with the result that they actually received either a comparable or lesser amount of time with an adult tutor as compared to the other programs.

For instance, students in SMART were tutored for 2 years and students in Howard Street were tutored for 1 year. In SMART, students received an average of 73 sessions over 2 years, in two 30-minute sessions per week. Howard Street sessions were 1 hour long, and 50 sessions were provided during the course of the year. Thus the total average time in tutoring sessions for each child was 36.5 hours for SMART (spread over 2 years) and 50 hours for Howard Street over 1 year.

SMART differed from the other volunteer programs in providing tutoring to students during both first and second grade. The Howard Street Tutoring Program and the School Volunteer Tutoring Project began tutoring students in second grade. The Intergenerational Tutoring Program provided tutoring to students in first grade only, and to date the reading outcomes have been mixed. Rapid growth in reading occurs in both Grades 1 and 2, and most reading experts agree these are excellent grades for adult tutoring (Juel, 1994).

The well-known Book Buddies intervention (Invernizzi, Juel, & Rosemary, 1996) found good effects at the end of first grade, after just 1 year of tutoring. Juel (1994) suggested, however, that the long-term benefits of Book Buddies would likely be much stronger if tutoring was provided to students while they are in first and second grade. She stated that

> successful intervention in first [grade] may be enough to ensure word recognition skill, or at least to have this skill under way so that a follow-up in the second grade could cement it. Without such a follow-up, those children who do not read during the summer are in danger of losing some of their skill in word recognition. (p. 59)

Researchers have long been aware of the problem of summer loss in reading achievement for many low-income students or students with reading difficulties (Natriello, McDill, & Pallas, 1990). Growth curve analysis in this study indicated that for all three groups (i.e., SMART, comparison, and average ability), greatest growth occurred in Grade 1 and tapered off slightly in Grade 2. We believe there are at least two reasonable explanations for this pattern.

For purposes of the growth curve analysis, we attempted to correct for the approximately 3 months of summer between the end of Grade 1 and the beginning of Grade 2—a period of time during which we did not expect students to make growth in reading. The three data points in the growth curve analysis represented the beginning of Grade 1, the end of Grade 1, and the end of Grade 2. We estimated 7 months between fall and spring testing in first grade and 9 months between end-of-first and end-of-second grade testing. The 9 months may have undercorrected for the loss in reading proficiency over the summer. This could have resulted in the slight curvilinear trend noted for all three samples. A second reasonable explanation is that it is quite possible that growth for all three samples was lower in second grade than first grade on norm-referenced tests.

The Ability to Serve a Large Number of Students

The flexible nature of SMART has played an important role in its rapid expansion. The founders of the program would like to implement SMART in as many low-income schools in the state as possible. Currently, SMART is in 16% of the elementary schools in the state, the great majority of which are located in low-income neighborhoods.

SMART is unique among volunteer reading programs in that it has used solid evaluation methods to demonstrate a positive impact on reading, and has achieved a widespread impact in terms of the number of students and geographic areas served. For students who have serious reading problems, tutoring by an adult in just two 30-minute sessions per week—1 hour total per week—might seem insufficient to yield measurable reading benefits. However, from the student's own perspective, 1 hour per week may be quite sufficient. To sit down with an adult for that amount of time each week and focus solely on books and reading may well have a profound effect on a struggling student, especially a student who may receive little literacy-related support at home.

Training of Volunteers

We believe one of the major attractions of the SMART program to volunteers (and to classroom teachers) is its simplicity. Volunteer tutors need not obtain knowledge of each classroom's reading program nor must teachers spend time explaining the reading program to tutors. SMART operates essentially independently of a given teacher's approach to reading instruction. On one hand, it is impressive that program impact is statistically significant even in the absence of substantive training and expectations of tutors. At the same time, it is unclear just exactly what the sessions consisted of. Clearly, a formal observational study of the range of methods SMART volunteers actually use during a tutoring session would be a logical next step in this line of research. When left largely to their own devices, what do adults do with struggling readers when the goal is reading improvement? It may be that a positive experience with a caring adult better characterizes the adult-student relationship than the use of specific reading instruction techniques. Perhaps the nature of the relationship leads tutored students to invest more effort in their interactions with the classroom teacher and thus benefit more from instruction.

In designing the present study, we did conduct informal observations in two schools to get a sense of the nature of the tutoring sessions and whether tutors seemed to be following the very general guidelines the program provided (Deathridge, 1993). Across a number of tutoring sessions in two schools, it was clear that volunteers took their roles as reading tutors seriously. They used an array of activities and approaches during the sessions, and in general, they had students practice reading independently, especially students in the second grade. Most volunteers demonstrated useful strategies for helping their students figure out what to do when they encountered difficult text. It also seemed clear that students felt supported during the tutoring sessions and looked forward to the time they would spend with their tutors. However, these qualitative observations of approximately 8 tutors are not sufficient to link tutoring methods to reading outcomes, or to generalize to the range of SMART volunteers tutoring children.

SMART is clearly less structured than most other volunteer reading programs. In terms of volunteer training, SMART provides less initial and ongoing training than other programs. Shanahan (1998) recently concluded that although most of the research on tutoring describes programs with intensive tutor training, extensive training may not always be necessary. Our results tend to support his hypothesis.

Most educators believe that careful training of tutors is an important component of volunteer tutoring programs. Roller (1998), for example, who directed a volunteer tutoring program at the University of Iowa for America Reads, said that

> Reading tutors need to know a great deal.... They need to know what tutoring looks like, they need to know how skilled reading operates, and they need to know how reading and writing develop.... Reading tutors need to know the letter-sound relations that characterize the English writing system and the high-frequency words that make up much of the English text. (p. 50)

Actually, few direct studies have been conducted that investigate the impact on reading achievement of different types of volunteer training (Shanahan, 1998). Shanahan found only one study that evaluated the impact of tutor training on the learning gains of the students tutored. Most relevant to the training of volunteer tutors was a study conducted by Leach and Siddall (1990), in which greater progress in reading accuracy and comprehension occurred for a group of young children when parent tutors were provided with 1-1/2 hours of training. Note that this amount of training is also quite minimal.

The findings from our study suggest that accelerated reading outcomes can be achieved by volunteers with minimal formal training, using their own judgment and instincts on how to support literacy development. Although desirable, intensive tutor training may not always be available or feasible, and considering the high turnover of adult volunteers that invariably occurs, intensive initial training may not be a good use of fiscal resources. The fact that minimally trained adult tutors can enhance meaningful growth in reading has important implications in designing programs such as those related to the America Reads initiative.

Author Note

This research was supported in part by a grant from the Oregon Children's Foundation and the U. S. Bank. The funds were used to support an independent evaluation of the SMART program by Eugene Research

Institute, which is the primary affiliation of the three authors. We conducted this evaluation free from any outside interference from the Oregon Children's Foundation (the parent organization of SMART), and have no vested interest in the outcome. Decisions about the evaluation—which measures to use, the number of students to sample, how to code and analyze the data—were made exclusively by the Eugene Research Institute.

REFERENCES

Adams, M.J. (1990). *Beginning to read: Thinking and learning about print*. Cambridge, MA: The MIT Press.

American Academy of Arts and Sciences & Boston Partners in Education. (1999). *The Intergenerational Tutoring Grogram*. Boston: Author.

Baker, S., Stoolmiller, M., & Gersten, R. (2000). *Predictors of students' ability to benefit from adult tutoring in first and second grade*. Manuscript in preparation.

Bond, G.L., & Dykstra, R. (1967). The cooperative research program in first-grade reading instruction. *Reading Research Quarterly, 2*, 5–142.

Brown, M.C. (1997). *Arthur babysits*. New York: Little, Brown.

Brown, M.C. (1998). *Arthur accused*. New York: Little, Brown.

Bryk, A.S., & Raudenbush, S.W. (1992). *Hierarchical linear models: Applications and data analysis methods*. Newbury Park, CA: Sage.

California Department of Education. (1998). *Reading/language arts framework for California public schools: Kindergarten through grade twelve*. Sacramento, CA: Author.

Carle, E. (1984). *The very hungry caterpillar*. New York: Putnam.

Carle, E. (1996). *The grouchy ladybug*. New York: HarperCollins.

Chall, J.S. (1967). *Learning to read: The great debate*. New York: McGraw-Hill.

Clinton, W.J. (1996, August 30). *Campaign train tour speech*. Chicago, IL.

Cohen, J. (1988). *Statistical power analysis for the behavioral sciences* (Rev. ed.). New York: Academic Press.

Cook, T.D., & Campbell, D.T. (1979). *Quasi-experimentation: Design and analysis issues for field settings*. Chicago: Rand-McNally.

Cooper, H., & Hedges, L.V. (Eds.). (1994). *The handbook of research synthesis*. New York: Russell Sage Foundation.

Deathridge, M. (1993). *Observations of SMART tutoring* (Tech. Rep. No. 93-01). Eugene, OR: Eugene Research Institute.

Freeman, D. (1980). *A pocket for Corduroy*. London: Puffin.

Foorman, B.R., Francis, D.J., Fletcher, J.M., Schatschneider, C., & Mehta, P. (1998). The role of instruction in learning to read: Preventing reading failure in at-risk children. *Journal of Educational Psychology, 90*(1), 37–55.

Fuchs, L.S., Fuchs, D., & Maxwell, L. (1988). The validity of informal reading comprehension measures. *Remedial and Special Education, 9*, 20–28.

Invernizzi, M., Juel, C., & Rosemary, C.A. (1996). A community volunteer tutorial that works. *The Reading Teacher, 50*, 304–311.

Juel, C. (1994). At-risk university students tutoring at-risk elementary school children. In E.H. Hiebert & B.M. Taylor (Eds.), *Getting reading right from the start* (pp. 39–61). Boston: Allyn & Bacon.

Juel, C. (1996). What makes literacy tutoring effective? *Reading Research Quarterly, 31*, 268–289.

Kaminski, R.A., & Good, R.H. (1996). Toward a technology for assessing basic early literacy skills. *School Psychology Review, 25*, 215-227.

Leach, D.J., & Sidall, S.W. (1990). Parental involvement in the teaching of reading: A comparison of hearing reading, paired reading, pause, prompt, praise, and direct instruction methods. *British Journal of Educational Psychology, 60*, 349-355.

Marston, D. (1989). Curriculum-based measurement: What is it and why do it? In M.R. Shinn (Ed.), *Curriculum-based measurement: Assessing special children* (pp. 18-78). New York: Guilford.

Mathsoft. (1998). *Splus 4 guide to statistics.* Seattle, WA: Author.

Morris, D., Shaw, B., & Perney, J. (1990). Helping low readers in grades 2 and 3: An after-school volunteer tutoring program. *The Elementary School Journal, 91*, 133-150.

Muthen, L.K., & Muthen, B.O. (1998). *Mplus user's guide.* Los Angeles, CA: Muthen & Muthen.

Natriello, G., McDill, E.L., & Pallas, A.M. (1990). *Schooling disadvantaged children.* New York: Teachers College Press.

O'Connor, R.E., Notari-Syverson, A., & Vadasy, P.F. (1996). Ladders to literacy: The effects of teacher-led phonological activities for kindergarten children with and without learning disabilities. *Exceptional Children, 63*, 117-130.

Oregon Children's Foundation. (1992). *SMART volunteer handbook.* Portland, OR: Author.

Oregon Children's Foundation. (1998). *SMART volunteer handbook.* Portland, OR: Author.

Potter, M.L., & Wamre, H.M. (1990). Curriculum-based measurement and developmental reading models: Opportunities for cross-validation. *Exceptional Children, 57*, 16-25.

Roller, C.M. (1998). *So...what's a tutor to do?* Newark, DE: International Reading Association.

Shanahan, T. (1998). On the effectiveness and limitations of tutoring in reading. In P.D. Pearson & A. Iran-Nejad (Eds.), *Review of research in education* (pp. 217-234). Washington, DC: American Educational Research Association.

Shinn, M.R. (1989). *Curriculum-based measurement: Assessing special children.* New York: The Guilford Press.

Shinn, M.R. (Ed.). (1998). *Advanced applications of curriculum-based measurement.* New York: Guilford.

Shinn, M.R., Good, R.H., Knutson, N., Tilly, W.D., & Collins, V. (1992). Curriculum-based measurement of oral reading fluency: A confirmatory analysis of its relation to reading. *School Psychology Review, 21*, 459-479.

Shinn, M., Tindal, G.A., & Stein, S. (1988). Curriculum-based measurement and the identification of mildly handicapped students: A research review. *Professional School Psychology, 3*(1), 69-85.

Snow, C.E., Burns, M.S., & Griffin, P. (Eds.). (1998). *Preventing reading difficulties in young children.* Washington, DC: National Academy Press.

Stanovich, K.E. (1986). Cognitive processes and the reading problems of learning-disabled children: Evaluating the assumption of specificity. In J.K. Torgesen & B.Y.L. Wong (Eds.), *Psychological and educational perspectives on LD* (pp. 87-131). Orlando, FL: Academic Press.

Stoolmiller, M. (1995). Using latent growth curve models to study developmental processes. In J.M. Gottman & G. Sackett (Eds.), *The analysis of change* (pp. 105-138). Hillsdale, NJ: Erlbaum.

Texas Reading Initiative. (1997). *Beginning reading instruction: Components and features of a research-based reading program.* Austin, TX: Author.

Torgesen, J.K., Morgan, S.T., & Davis, C. (1992). Effects of two types of phonological awareness training on word learning in kindergarten children. *Journal of Educational Psychology, 84,* 364–370.

U.S. Department of Education. (1979). *School volunteer development project.* Proposal submitted to the Program Effectiveness Panel of the National Diffusion Network. Washington, DC: Author.

U.S. Department of Education, National Diffusion Network Division. (1981). *Educational programs that work* (8th ed.). San Francisco: Far West Laboratory for Educational Research and Development.

Wasik, B.A. (1998). Volunteer tutoring programs in reading: A review. *Reading Research Quarterly, 33,* 266–292.

Wasik, B.A., & Slavin, R.E. (1993). Preventing early reading failure with one-to-one tutoring: A review of five programs. *Reading Research Quarterly, 28,* 178–200.

Appendix A

Student nomination forms

Teacher: _____ Grade & room: _____

Please consider these criteria for your students when making your selections for SMART:

> Lowest 25% of the class in reading skills
> Limited books in the home
> In need of one-on-one relationship with a caring adult
> Students not being served in other programs

Prioritize your list of students according to who could benefit the most from SMART. List up to 10 students in the space below, and give a brief explanation for your selection (e.g., improve reading skills, needs books, needs one-on-one time, etc.). Note any times that are particularly good or bad for your students to attend SMART.

SMART will try to serve as many students on your list as possible.

Student (grade)	Reason for selection	List the best times for your class to attend (half-hour slots)
1.		1.
2.		
3.		2.
4.		
5.		3.
6.		
7.		**Times not available**
8.		
9.		
10.		

(continued)

Appendix A

Student nomination forms (continued)

Teacher: _____ Grade & room: _____

Please select 4-6 additional students in your class who you believe are average readers. These students should not be the best readers in your class, but they should be solid readers who you believe will continue to make good progress in learning to read. For example, if you were to have low, middle, and high reading groups, these would be solid readers in the middle reading group.

Student (grade)
1.
2.
3.
4.
5.
6.

Appendix B

Measures

What the examiner says is in **bold/italics.**

Rapid Letter Naming

I am going to show you some letters and I want you to tell me the names of the letters as quickly as you can. Start here (point to the first letter) *and go across the page* (point across the first row). *Try to name each letter. If you don't know a letter, I'll tell it to you. Are you ready? Begin.*

- The child is given 1 point for each **letter or letter-sound** she or he states correctly.

- Mark a slash through each letter (or sound) said incorrectly. Put a bracket after the last letter the child says after 60 seconds.

- If the child takes more than 3 seconds to say a letter, tell the student the letter, and point to the next letter so the student continues.

Examiner copy:

D	N	b	H	f	i	m	O	A	R
s	E	W	y	L	T	c	X	g	K
B	F	o	j	a	S	p	r	U	e
M	z	K	C	t	q	n	J	P	x
u	G	Q	I	w	Z	I	v	Y	d
V	h								

Total correct _____ Seconds _____ (if less than 60)

Rapid Letter Naming
Student copy

D	N	b	H	f	i	m	O	A	R
s	E	W	y	L	T	c	X	g	K
B	F	o	j	a	S	p	r	U	e
M	z	K	C	t	q	n	J	P	x
u	G	Q	I	w	Z	I	v	Y	d
V	h								

(continued)

Appendix B

Measures (continued)

Segment words into three phonemes

This time I will say a word, and you will tell me the sounds in the word.
My turn. I can say the sounds in Mike. M—i—ke (pause 1 second between each sound). *Your turn. Say the sounds in Mike.*

- If the child is correct, go to item #1 (soap).
- If child gets the first sound right say: **Yes the first sound in Mike is /M/.**
  I'll say all the sounds in Mike. M—i—ke. Say all the sounds in Mike.
- If the child is incorrect say: *I'll say the sounds in Mike. M—i—ke. Say the*
  sounds in Mike.
- For children who get the first sound correct or no sounds correct on the
  first practice item, administer the next two practice items: shop *Sh—o—p;*
  cat *c—a—t*
- Begin timing the student with the first test item.
- For the test items, write the parts the child says, or a + if all 3 parts are cor-
  rect.
- If the child gets an item incorrect, tell the student the correct answer,
  but do not have the student repeat the correct answer.
- Score 1 point for each correct sound.
- Circle the number indicating how far the child got in one minute, but
  give all items!!!

1. soap _____	6. big _____
2. mom _____	7. fall _____
3. food _____	8. dad _____
4. gum _____	9. mud _____
5. ten _____	10. dog _____

Total segments correct (out of 30)   Words segmented correctly (out of 10)

(continued)

Appendix B

Measures (continued)

Reading Fluency Test

Place the unnumbered copy in front of the student. Place the numbered copy in front of you—but shielded so the student cannot see what you record. Say these specific directions to the student for each passage:

> *When I say "begin," start reading aloud at the top of this page. Read across the page (demonstrate by pointing). Try to read each word. If you come to a word you don't know, I'll tell it to you. Be sure to do your best reading. Are there any questions?"*

Say "Begin" and start your stopwatch when the student says the first word. If the student fails to say the first word of the passage after *three seconds,* tell the student the word and mark it as incorrect, then start your stopwatch. Follow along on your copy. Put a (/) through words read incorrectly. If a student stops or struggles with a word for *three seconds,* tell the student the word and mark it as incorrect. At the end of *one minute,* place a bracket ( ]) after the last word and say, ***"Stop."***

Scoring reading passages

Scoring the reading assessment is done by determining the number of words read correctly (WRC).

What is a "Word?"

Ex. 1.	cat	**TW** = 1
	read as:	
	"cat"	**WRC** = 1
Ex. 2.	I sat.	**TW** = 2
	read as:	
	"I sat."	**WRC** = 2

(continued)

Appendix B

Measures (continued)

What is a "Correctly Read Word?"

Rule 1. *Correctly read words are pronounced correctly.* A word must be pronounced correctly given the context of the sentence.

Ex. 1. The word "r-e-a-d" must be pronounced "reed" when presented in the **context** of:

He will *read* the book. **WRC** = 5

> **not as:**

"He will *red* the book." **WRC** = 4

Ex. 2. The word "l-e-a-d" must be **pronounced** "led" when presented in the **context** of:

She picked up a *lead* pipe. **WRC** = 6

> **not as:**

"She picked up a *leed* pipe." **WRC** = 5

Rule 2. *Self-corrected words are counted as correct.* Words misread initially but corrected within 3 seconds are counted as correctly read. Write the abbreviation "SC" over the corrected word.

Ex. 1. The river was *cold.* **WRC** = 4

> **read as:**

"The river was *could* . . . (2 sec) . . . *cold.*" **WRC** = 4

Ex. 2. Matt cleaned the house *for* Mom. **WRC** = 6

> **read as:**

"Matt cleaned the house *of...* (*1* sec).
cleaned the house *for* Mom." **WRC** = 6

(continued)

Appendix B

Measures (continued)

Rule 3. *Repeated words are counted as correct.* Words said over again correctly are ignored.

Ex. 1.   Ted *ran* swiftly.   **WRC** = 3

           read as:

           "Ted ran . . . *Ted ran* swiftly."   **WRC** = 3

Ex. 2.   Sally saw *a* cat.   **WRC** = 4

           read as:

           "Sally saw a . . . *a* cat."   **WRC** = 4

Rule 4. *Dialect or articulation.* Variations in pronunciation that are explainable by local language norms or individual speech difficulties are not errors.

Ex. 1.   They *washed* the car.   **WRC** = 4

           read as:

           "They *warshed* the car."   **WRC** = 4

Ex. 2.   Let's go to the *park*.   **WRC** = 5

           read as:

           "Let's go to the *pawk*."   **WRC** = 5

Rule 5. *Inserted words are ignored.* When a student adds extra words, they are not counted as correct words or as reading errors.

Ex. 1.   Sue was happy.   **WRC** = 3

           read as:

           "Sue was *very* happy."   **WRC** = 3

Ex. 2.   Kelly played the flute.   **WRC** = 4

           read as:

           "Kelly played *a* the flute."   **WRC** = 4

(continued)

Appendix B

Measures (continued)

What is an "Incorrectly Read Word?"

Rule 6. *Mispronounced or substituted words* are counted as incorrect.

Ex. 1.	The *dog* ate a bone.	**WRC** = 5
	read as:	
	"The *dig* ate a bone."	**WRC** = 4
Ex. 2.	Lynne has many *hats.*	**WRC** = 4
	read as:	
	"Lynne has many *hat.*"	**WRC** = 3
Ex. 3.	He *wanted* a new car.	**WRC** = 5
	read as:	
	"She *wants* a new car."	**WRC** = 3

Rule 7. *Omitted words* are counted as errors.

Ex. 1.	Mario climbed the *oak* tree.	**WRC** = 5
	read as:	
	"Mario climbed the tree."	**WRC** = 4
Ex. 2.	The king fought *with an alligator* in the moat.	**WRC** = 9
	read as:	
	"The king fought in the moat."	**WRC** = 6
Ex. 3.	Sewing is my favorite hobby. *I enjoy sewing dresses and suits.* What is your favorite hobby?	**WRC** = 16
	read as:	
	"Sewing is my favorite hobby. What is your favorite hobby?"	**WRC** = 10

(continued)

Appendix B

Measures (continued)

Rule 8. *Hesitations.* When a student hesitates or fails to correctly pronounce a word within *3 seconds,* the student is told the word and an error is scored.

Ex. 1.	Mark saw an elephant.	**WRC** = 4
	read as:	
	"Mark saw an . . . (3 sec)"	**WRC** = 3
	read as:	
	"Mark saw an elll-eee . . . (3 sec)"	**WRC** = 3

Rule 9. *Reversals.* When a student transposes two or more words, those words not read in the correct order are errors.

Ex. 1.	Charlie *ran quickly.*	**WRC** = 3
	read as:	
	"Charlie *quickly ran.*"	**WRC** = 1
Ex. 2.	Shelly bought a *beautiful sweater.*	**WRC** = 5
	read as:	
	"Shelly bought a *sweater beautiful.*"	**WRC** = 3

Rule 10. *Numbers written as numerals* are counted as words and must be read correctly within the context of the passage.

Ex. 1.	*May 5, 1989.*	**WRC** = 3
	should be read as:	
	"May *fifth, nineteen eighty-nine.*"	**WRC** = 3
	not as:	
	"May *five, one nine eight nine.*"	**WRC** = 1
Ex. 2.	He was in grade 3.	**WRC** = 5
	should be read as:	
	"He was in grade *three.*"	**WRC** = 5
	not as:	
	"He was in grade *third.*"	**WRC** = 4

(continued)

Appendix B

Measures (continued)

Rule 11. *Hyphenated words.* Each morpheme separated by a hyphen(s) is counted as an individual word if it can stand alone.

Ex.	Fifty-seven	**WRC** = 2
	Daughter-in-law	**WRC** = 3

Rule 12. *Hyphenated words.* If one or more of the morphemes separated by a hyphen(s) cannot stand alone, the entire sequence is counted as one word.

Ex.	re-evaluate	**WRC** = 1
	Bar-be-que	**WRC** = 1

Rule 13. *Abbreviations* are counted as words, and must be read correctly within the context of the sentence.

Ex. 1. Dr. Adams received a promotion. **WRC** = 5

> **should be read as:**

"Doctor Adams received a promotion." **WRC** = 5

> not as:

"D-R Adams received a promotion." **WRC** = 4

Ex. 2. Jan lives on Fifth *Ave.* **WRC** = 5

> **should be read as:**

"Jan lives on Fifth *avenue*" **WRC** = 5

> not as:

"Jan lives on Fifth *a-v-e*" **WRC** = 4

Ex. 3. Jan lives on Fifth *Ave.* **WRC** = 5

> **also should be read as:**

"Jan lives on Fifth *ave*" **WRC** = 4

(continued)

Appendix B

Measures (continued)

Ex. 4. John watched *T.V.*   WRC = 3

      can be read as:

      "John watched *tee-vee*"   WRC = 3

      or as:

      "John watched *television.*"   WRC = 3

Ex. 5. John watched *television.*   WRC = 3

      should be read as:

      "John watched *television.*"   WRC = 3

      not as:

      "John watched *tee-vee.*"   WRC = 2

Efficient scoring procedures:

1. If students appear to understand the instructions following the administration of the first passage, the examiner need only point to the first word at the top of subsequent passages saying **"Begin."** It is not necessary to reread the instructions each time.

2. Don't begin timing until the student says the first word. If necessary, supply the first word, put a slash through it, and begin timing.

3. If you completely lose track of where a student is reading, discontinue the reading and begin another passage.

4. If a student skips an entire row, put a line through it and continue the passage.

5. Score reading probes immediately after administration.

The National Reading Panel Report

James W. Cunningham

At the behest of the United States Congress in 1997, the Director of the National Institute of Child Health and Human Development (NICHD) and the U.S. Secretary of Education selected 14 persons to serve as a National Reading Panel (NRP). Most Panel members were reading researchers in various fields. All but two members held a doctorate. The Panel was charged to review and assess the research on teaching reading, with implications for both classroom practice and further research.

The report of the National Reading Panel was issued in two volumes. The first volume (00-4769) is a succinct summary of how the Panel came to be, the topics it chose to investigate, its procedures and methods, and its findings. The second volume (00-4754) contains the same introductory and methodological information, but presents at great length the work of each of the topical subgroups within the Panel. It is the second volume that one must read to fully understand the findings and recommendations for classroom practice and future research.

In this review, I refer to both volumes collectively as the NRP Report. Citations of the first volume contain only page numbers (e.g., p. 4); citations of the second volume contain a section number followed by page numbers because the second volume's pagination starts with 1 in each section (e.g., p. 3-13 means section 3, page 13 of the second volume). Some statements appear verbatim in both volumes.

The NRP's Philosophy of Science

The NRP Report should be seen as a manifesto for a particular philosophy of science as much as a summary of particular research findings. Marks of the manifesto are not subtle and, indeed, begin on the cover. The subtitle of both volumes of the report asserts that the Panel has provided us with "an evidence-based assessment of the *scientific* research literature" (covers, emphasis added). The Methodological Overview of the first volume begins with the sentence, "In what may be its most important action, the Panel then developed and adopted a set of *rigorous* research methodological standards" (p. 5, emphasis added). In their Reflections, the Panel claims that its goal

Reprinted from *Reading Research Quarterly*, 36, 326–335, July/August/September 2001.

had been to contribute "to a better *scientific* understanding of reading development and reading instruction" (p. 21, emphasis added). Upon looking back at its completed work, it assures us that "the evidence ultimately evaluated by the Panel met well-established *objective scientific* standards" (p. 21, emphasis added).

The Report makes it clear that the methodological standards adopted by the Panel did not arise from the research literature on reading, but rather were imposed upon it. Panel members tell us that they developed their criteria "*a priori*" (p. 27; p. 1-5) and that "Unfortunately, only a small fraction of the total reading research literature met the Panel's standards for use in the topic analyses" (p. 27; p. 1-5).

What are we to make of a report that so boldly lays claim to what science, rigor, and objectivity are in reading research, and first denigrates, then ignores, the preponderance of research literature in our field? Even though the NRP's philosophy of science is implied, its consequences are not discussed, so making it explicit and discussing it here is important. The Panel members' position about what kind of research is scientific fits within a historical philosophical context. To the extent that their views on science may affect how funding agencies, reviewers for journals and conference programs, and researchers conduct themselves, they have implications for the nature of future research in reading. If used to inform policy, their views on science will affect classroom reading experiences every day.

Demarcation

The Panel members' repeated and unapologetic appropriation of the term *scientific* to describe the results of their work places how they characterize their work in the subdomain of philosophy of science concerned with the demarcation problem. Positivism (Comte, 1830/1988) was an attempt to define *science* as knowledge with no vestige of theology or abstraction. Science was to be differentiated, or demarcated, from nonscience by being limited to beliefs that are so empirically supported they are certain or positive.

In the century after Comte's first work, scientific practice demonstrated that science couldn't be limited to what is known with certainty. Therefore, logical positivism (e.g., Carnap, 1934) took as its main task the establishment of criteria for what would constitute rational scientific inquiry, without regard for how scientists actually conduct their research (Garrison, 1996). In other words, the logical positivists sought a solution to the demarcation problem by defining and delimiting scientific logic.

When the approach to demarcation of the logical positivists was also found by scientists to be an inadequate guide, Karl Popper (1959) attempted to differentiate science from pseudoscience in yet another way. He argued that science progresses by submitting its hypotheses and theories to tests with the potential to falsify them, while the hypotheses and theories of pseudoscience cannot be falsified. Unfortunately, the falsification criterion of demarcation had trouble explaining why scientific theories are seldom discarded when one or a few investigations produce anomalous outcomes for them.

How successful have the various attempts been to demarcate science from nonscience or pseudoscience? Not very. In fact, the consensus view in philosophy of science is that all such efforts have failed completely (Gjertsen, 1989; Laudan, 1981). The issue is not that there is no difference between science and other thoughtful or creative endeavors, but rather that no one has yet devised a set of criteria that reliably distinguishes scientific from nonscientific practices. Contrary to the position of logical positivists, scientists and philosophers of science have been unable to reach consensus on what constitutes scientific logic or the scientific method (Laudan, 1983). It seems that science is recognized more by its discoveries than by whether its methods correspond to any formal standards. Generally, it appears that scientists are those who contribute new knowledge to the sciences, even when they employ unusual or unorthodox methods to do so. In fact, the breadth of what is usually considered scientific across the natural sciences, and their relatives in engineering and the professions, makes it probable that any attempt to narrowly define science is doomed to the failure of rejection by practicing scientists themselves (Laudan, 1983).

It is true that there are a few philosophers of science who still maintain that science can and should be demarcated from nonscience. Even these few (e.g., Fuller, 1985; Gieryn, 1983), however, generally advocate using a kind of jury system. They argue that in such a system the practicing researchers in a field have the right to label those among their peers *scientists* as part of a social phenomenon, without using any objective criteria of methodological form that demarcates their work from nonscience.

At times, the demarcation of science from nonscience has even been a political strategy. The philosopher and historian of science Imre Lakatos (1978) has pointed out that the Catholic Church in the 1600s engaged in demarcation to label findings of heliocentricity in astronomy as pseudoscience and then forced Galileo to recant. He also recalled that the Soviet Union in the mid-1900s used demarcation to label Mendelian genetics as pseudoscience and then tortured and executed its practitioners.

The National Reading Panel chose to engage itself in the messy and so far unsuccessful effort to solve the demarcation problem. The members boldly assert that they have differentiated the small amount of scientific, objective, and rigorous reading research from the great quantity of reading research that fails to merit one or more of these lofty labels. It has been more than 30 years since such a claim would not have appeared naive to anyone familiar with philosophy of science.

Moreover, the Panel's criteria can be applied to its own work, raising several difficult questions. Did the Panel conform to its own standards? By its demarcation criteria, is its own work scientific? Did the members of the Panel operate in a scientific, objective, and rigorous manner when they chose their procedures for conducting their review of reading research? Unfortunately, the answer seems obvious. Where are the scientific, objective, and rigorous studies that compare different ways of selecting and reviewing literature to improve practice? Is there experimental or quasi-experimental evidence demonstrating the superiority of the Panel's approach to determining which studies are a better guide to practice? No, members chose their demarcation criteria on logical rather than empirical grounds. Alas, the NRP's demarcation criteria do not pass its own standard: The Panel members' determination of what reading research is scientific is not scientific, as they themselves define it.

Verificationism

Ignoring how practicing scientists conduct their research, positivists of various stripes (old, logical, and neo) have privileged one or another brand of verificationism. For example, verifiability-in-principle was the criterion that the logical positivists employed to demarcate science from nonscience (Ayer, 1946; Carnap, 1934). To them, the meaning of any statement was the method of its verification. That is, any statement, however tentative, that could not be empirically verified was neither right nor wrong, but meaningless. Had scientists listened to the logical positivists—fortunately, most did not—they would have stopped searching for the truth of any hypothesis they did not then know how to verify. While the criterion of verifiability-in-principle was eventually abandoned by almost everyone, a broader and more nuanced neoverificationism still has a few adherents among philosophers today, principally Michael Dummett (1976, 1991).

Verificationism is always concerned with the meaning of statements rather than the nature of reality. It interposes a theory of knowledge and a theory of language between scientists and the objects of their investigation. Positivists want their a priori views of science and of scientific logic and language to dictate what can be known.

The National Reading Panel clearly holds a verificationist philosophy of science. It states that "To sustain a claim of effectiveness [for any instructional practice], the Panel felt it necessary that there be experimental or quasi-experimental studies of sufficient size or number, and scope...and that these studies be of moderate to high quality" (p. 1-7). Notice that the emphasis is not on effectiveness, but rather on *claims* of effectiveness. The true nature of reading or reading instruction is less important to the Panel than the need to "sustain [read "verify"] a claim" (p. 1-7) about it.

The Panel's positivism is strongly held. Because statements about reading development and instruction apparently have scientific meaning only to the extent that they are empirically and experimentally verifiable, even a review of the experimental research is "subjective" (p. 5) unless the findings of those experiments can be combined in "a formal statistical meta-analysis" (p. 5). In other words, the Panel holds both a verificationism about reading research and a metaverificationism about reviewing reading research.

The Panel's verifiable-by-experiment criterion is applied quite consistently throughout its examination of reading research. The language of the Report betrays no tentativeness about the Panel's criterion. When the Panel appears tentative, a careful reading reveals that this tentativeness is certainly not about the criterion:

> It should be made clear that these findings do not negate the positive influence that independent reading *may* have on reading fluency.... Rather, there are simply no sufficient data from well-designed studies capable of testing questions of causation to substantiate causal claims. (p. 13)

In other words, when its criterion for verification (data it considers sufficient from studies it considers well designed) is lacking, no claim can be verified.

A Critique of the NRP's Philosophy of Science

Most researchers, at least in the natural sciences, are scientific realists rather than positivists (Marsonet, 1995; Weinberg, 1992). Scientific realists are empiricists who build theoretical models, attempt to represent ever deeper layers of previously hidden reality, and seek full and satisfying explanations in order to achieve a clear and comprehensive understanding of cause-and-effect relationships (Cunningham & Fitzgerald, 1996). Scientific realists conduct experiments when experiments are called for, but they never confuse their methods with the reality their methods are used to discover.

Like all positivism, the Panel's work reveals a desire for certainty and a willingness to engage in reductionism to achieve it. All positivists have been antirealists (Cunningham & Fitzgerald, 1996), apparently because they are uncomfortable with the wide and never-closing gap between our knowledge and our questions (Searle, 1995). Their strategy has been to increase their comfort by reducing the questions one is permitted to ask, and reducing the ways one is permitted to answer them.

Practicing scientists of reading should be embarrassed by the simplistic, old-fashioned, and generally discredited verificationism of the National Reading Panel. In its assertions about the relationship between causal claims and the need for experimental evidence, the Panel has unwittingly allied itself with the research arm of the U.S. tobacco industry, the Tobacco Institute, which has long argued that the Surgeon General or anyone else has no right to claim that smoking causes cancer because the relationship is merely correlational (Giere, 1997).

The efforts of the NRP to formally demarcate science in reading from pseudoscience may actually be dangerous. While the members of the Panel I know personally are unquestionably well intentioned, one can be forgiven for being less certain about the Congress that requested the Report. I fear the philosophy of science that begins and permeates the NRP Report may have a chilling effect on the funding, publication, and influence of all reading research that fails to follow the positivist methodological standards it prescribes for our field.

The NRP's Doctrine of Research Design

The NRP Report should also be seen as a declaration of a particular doctrine of research design. By largely limiting itself to the examination of experimental and quasi-experimental studies of reading, the NRP echoes the raging battle between experimentalists and correlationists in the social sciences of the 1950s and early 1960s. Its repeated view is that "correlations tell us nothing about the direction or sequence of a relationship" (p. 3-10). In fact, the Methodological Overview of the NRP Report reads almost as if there had been an open copy of Campbell and Stanley's (1963) work in front of each of the Panel members as they developed their methodological standards.

In 1956, Lee Cronbach (1957) addressed an audience at the meeting of the American Psychological Association (APA). Unlike the NRP, Cronbach was willing in the title of his talk ("The Two Disciplines of Scientific Psychology") to refer to some of both experimental and correlational research as scientific. In his presentation, Cronbach famously called for a crossbreeding of experimental psychological research methods with those correlational methods used to investigate individual differences in psychology. This new genre of research came to be known as the study or science of Aptitude by Treatment Interactions (ATIs).

Eighteen years later, Cronbach returned to APA (1975) to discuss the state of the then-thriving subdiscipline of ATI research. Surely his comments were not what his audience had expected. After praising what ATI research, especially in instruction, had contributed, he stated that such research was no longer sufficient because "Interactions are not confined to the first order; the dimensions of the situation and of the person enter into complex interactions" (Cronbach, 1975, p. 116). Stepping back to evaluate the previous 30 years of research in psychology, Cronbach said that, "Taking stock today, I think most of us judge theoretical progress to have been disappointing" (p. 116). In this evaluation of research, including ATI studies, he especially noted the limitations of the "two-group experiment" (p. 116).

With courageous candor, Cronbach related how he and his coauthor, Richard Snow, had "been thwarted by the inconsistent findings from roughly similar inquiries" (Cronbach, 1975, p. 119) in their attempts to generalize from results of ATI studies on instruction. From this experience, he came to realize that untested interactions, especially of a higher order, can always be envisioned for any study. Then, in comments anyone today should find eerily prophetic, Cronbach questioned the eagerness of some social scientists of the time "to establish rigorous generalizations about social policy by conducting experiments in the field" (p. 122).

Cronbach (1975) did not conclude his remarks by opposing scientific psychology or calling for an end to experimentation. On the contrary, he expected both to continue and prosper. What he did call for was the end to simplistic and reductionist reporting of scientific research. If he were to make the same talk today, surely he would castigate the reporting of nothing but effect sizes with the same fervor he expressed then against the reporting of "nothing save F ratios" (p. 124). What he endorsed instead was "the scientific observation of human behavior" (p. 124) with an emphasis on descriptions. In opposition to purely numerical products of research, he cited Meehl (1957) to agree with him that "we [social scientists] have to use our heads" (p. 126).

Whether either of them were present to hear, or later read, Cronbach's (1975) remarks, Jay Samuels and David Pearson worked to establish a similar spirit of broadened and balanced inquiry in our field during their editorship of Reading Research Quarterly from 1979-1985. Early on, they expressed an appreciation for the strengths and limitations of both experiments and naturalistic observation and called for the recognition of "the symbiotic relationship between paradigms" (Pearson & Samuels, 1980, p. 430). Later in his tenure as coeditor, Samuels (1984) echoed Cronbach's concern with complex interactions that make it impossible to expect experimental science to find simple, all-embracing laws that generalize. He then discussed the implications for reading instruction of overlooking such interactions:

> Many of our educational pundits appear to believe there are universal approaches to instruction and development of curricular materials which will work for all children under all conditions. They seem to ignore differences in intelligence and home background conditions. Depending on these variables as well as the degree of motivation and prior knowledge brought to the task of learning to read, it is highly likely that some approaches to instruction should be better for some children and different approaches should work better for other children. (Samuels, 1984, p. 391)

In light of this historical background, the experimentalism of the NRP reminds me of Rip Van Winkle. It is almost as if the Panel fell mysteriously asleep 20 years ago and awoke just in time to do what the Congress and the NICHD convened them to do.

Equating Reading Education With Interventions

The NRP maintains that "The evidence-based methodological standards adopted by the Panel are essentially those normally used in research studies of the efficacy of interventions in psychological and medical research" and states its belief "that the efficacy of materials and methodologies used in the teaching of reading and in the prevention or treatment of reading disabilities should be tested no less rigorously" (p. 27; p. 1-5).

This argument is based on a metaphor of reading instruction being like the curing of psychological and physical diseases. The Panel's unquestioned assumption of this metaphor has the regrettable effect of reducing schooling in general, and reading education in particular, to a series of low- or noninteracting interventions. What if healthy human development is a better metaphor for schooling and the teaching of reading, pre-K through Grade 5 and beyond, than is the metaphor of treatments for specific mental or medical ailments? This metaphor would not negate the need for intervention research when particular treatments for specific reading disabilities or particular short-term learning outcomes are tested, but it would certainly broaden the research base for "the teaching of reading and in prevention...of reading disabilities" (p. 27; p. 1-5) beyond that considered scientific, objective, and rigorous by the Panel.

The NRP's findings relative to the value of systematic phonics instruction and attempts to increase independent reading illustrate the limitations of experimentalism as a doctrine of research design and treating ailments as a metaphor for reading education. To see the inadequacy, consider two possible claims one could make about reading instruction:

1. Systematic phonics instruction in first grade is a cause of better reading ability by fifth grade and beyond.

2. Increased independent reading in the elementary grades is a cause of better reading ability by fifth grade and beyond.

It is difficult to see anything unreasonable about either of these claims or anything unscientific about wanting to evaluate them.

Because of its doctrinaire experimentalism, however, the Panel chose to evaluate all allegations about the effectiveness of systematic phonics instruction and attempts to increase independent reading in ways that cannot serve to shed much light on important claims like the two stated above. First, the Panel limited the duration of the effect of instruction to the length of time between the official onset of the intervention and the final data collection in each particular study. Such studies of the effects of smoking would be far less threatening to the tobacco companies than the devastating studies of longer term effects have been. Indeed, it may be the long-term and complex nature of reading development, and indeed of all schooling, that makes the NRP's experimentalism most questionable.

Second, the Panel members forced themselves to attempt to select one or a few dependent variables that would permit them to conduct a meta-analysis or, at least, a "subjective qualitative analysis" (p. 5). So they tried to measure the short-term value of systematic phonics instruction using a reading comprehension dependent measure. Equally oddly, they tried to evaluate the short-term value of increased independent reading using a fluency dependent measure. Surely, these are examples of trying to pound square pegs into round holes because someone decided a priori that it would be easier to compare only round holes with one another.

What research designs would be more appropriate if healthy development were a better metaphor for learning to read than treating a range and sequence of diseases? They would be designs that test aspects of sophisticated theories of reading development. Wouldn't it have made much more sense for the Panel to attempt to test one or more theories of reading development that endeavor to come to grips with the long-term and interactive nature of schooling? Why not, for example, identify a theory or model of reading or of reading development that includes a complex causal network? I have argued, for example, that decoding by phonics has only small direct causal value for silent reading comprehension, but that it has important indirect causal value (Cunningham, 1993). That is, decoding by phonics contributes directly to the acquisition of automatic word recognition, which, in turn, has direct causal value for silent reading comprehension. This aspect of my model has much research to support it (e.g., Share, 1995), but it is difficult to imagine an experiment or quasi-experiment that would last long enough to conclusively test this indirect yet still causal relationship. Even if such an experimental study has been or could be done, it is a real stretch of the imagination to expect enough of them to make a meta-analysis possible. Yet do we want to ignore, or leave untested, theories that posit long-term, indirect causal relationships between decoding by phonics and ultimate reading comprehension ability, or between world knowledge, wide independent reading, and ultimate attitudes toward reading, self, and school?

When the Panel equated reading education with a series of interventions, it made a fatal error our field cannot afford to accept. It seems especially ironic that it made this error in the name of an organization given to the study of health and human development.

A Critique of the NRP's Doctrine of Research Design

I contend that education, including the teaching of reading, is more like fostering healthy human development, building a successful business, maintaining an effective military, and providing good parenting than it is like administering medical or psychological interventions. American business and the American military are each the envy of the world, yet imagine how little of their cumulative wisdom and common practice is supported by the kind of research the NRP would insist upon for investigating claims about reading instruction. For instance, what would happen if parents began to feel doubts about any practice that does not have enough experimental support to conduct a meta-analysis?

Get intelligent people together as a committee and sometimes they collectively act with less common sense than any individual among them has. The experimentalism held so unwaveringly by the NRP violates all common wisdom. Such a doctrine will not do in reading education and must not go unchallenged.

The NRP's Findings and Determinations

The members of the Panel divided themselves into five subgroups, with several members serving on more than one. These subgroups each examined the experimental and quasi-experimental research on the five main topics they had chosen: alphabetics, fluency, comprehension, teacher education and reading instruction, and computer technology and reading instruction. In this section, I will briefly review the findings and determinations of the five subgroups. Before doing so, however, it is important to consider whether such a review is even necessary after critiquing the Panel's philosophy of science and doctrine of research design that guided all five subgroups in their work.

If the Panel's philosophy of science and doctrine of research design are seriously flawed, as I have argued, does that mean its findings are inevitably also flawed? Positivists and other antirealists would think so, because they hold that reality is always determined by the methods and language employed to examine and interpret it. Scientific realists do not concur. We agree that a misunderstanding of science or a limited approach to research design will inevitably lead to some mistaken or limited findings, but not all findings will necessarily be mistaken or limited. In the case of the NRP Report, it may be that some or even all the findings of the Panel happen to be what would have been found had members approached their job differently. Therefore, I conclude that the findings of the Panel still need to be evaluated on their likelihood to conform to reality given a broader view of epistemology, a more versatile set of research tools, and a different metaphor of reading education.

Other questions also require an analysis of the Panel's results and interpretations. What is the relationship between the Panel's approach and its findings? How consistently did Panel members apply their own standards when they conducted their selection, analysis, and interpretation of literature on reading instruction and development? These questions can be answered only by a review of the actual findings and determinations of the subgroups.

Alphabetics

The word *alphabetics* is utilized by the Panel to group and label research on the topics of phonemic awareness (PA) and phonics instruction. The two topics are dealt with separately, with little explicit discussion of the relationship between them.

Phonemic awareness. The PA training that the Panel finds most effective is 5 to 18 hours of explicit and systematic, small-group instruction with one or two tasks of manipulating phonemes with letters, given to preschool and kindergarten children. Because the recommended instruction is "with letters" (p. 8; p. 2-4), the Panel's finding is tantamount to endorsing systematic phonics instruction in preschool and kindergarten (Yopp & Yopp, 2000). How should we, as a field, react to such a recommendation?

It does seem to me that, at the present time, the burden of proof (Giere, 1997) is on those who would have us do nothing instructional to foster the development of children's phonemic awareness. I believe we now have enough evidence that phonemic awareness is a necessary component of learning to identify words and that it is lacking in enough learners so we, as a field, must not leave its acquisition to chance. Had the Panel stopped there, I would endorse the finding wholeheartedly.

I also contend, however, that the burden of proof at this time is on those who would standardize PA training when so many questions about it remain unanswered. The chief question is the one that the Panel largely ignored throughout its entire work, even including its calls for future research: What are the long-term effects on silent reading comprehension ability, the reading habit, and attitudes toward reading, self, and school of its recommended changes in early reading instruction? Specific to PA training, would the future results in fifth grade and beyond justify the revolution in preschool and kindergarten education that implementing the Panel's PA findings would entail? When the first finding of the report is based primarily on short-term dependent measures of words in isolation that are not scientifically linked in a causal chain to appropriate long-term measures, the onus is on the Panel.

Another important question regarding PA training is one that the Panel also generally ignored throughout its work: What quality of instruction did the control group receive? Because of the Panel's verificationist philosophy of science, members were likely to be satisfied when they found enough well-designed experimental and quasi-experimental studies to generate a meta-analysis. They sometimes sugarcoat their findings and determinations with cautions, but by their own standards these cautions are not scientific. Their often mechanistic approach to selection, analysis, and interpretation of studies did not readily allow them to consult their professional judgment of what children actually need and when they need it, so their findings usually contain the implicit assumption that more and earlier are better. When such thinking rules, it can be all right if the control groups in many of the experiments received no instruction at all, mere placebos, or alternative treatments not developed by career reading educators committed to teaching phonemic awareness in a developmentally appropriate manner that recognizes the complex demands of the reading curriculum to come.

I contend that the burden of proof is with the Panel to show that research-based practices such as shared reading of books that play with sounds, writing with invented spelling, and teaching onsets using a variety of activities (key actions, students' names, and key foods or beverages) do not help most children develop the necessary phonemic awareness they need. Until this happens, the Panel's rush to standardization of how and when to best develop the essentials of phonemic awareness should be ignored or opposed.

Phonics instruction. The Alphabetics subgroup of the Panel makes three major distinctions among phonics instructional programs. First, it distinguishes explicit and systematic programs from programs providing nonsystematic phonics or no phonics at all. Second, it classifies explicit and systematic phonics programs into three categories: (1) synthetic, (2) larger unit, and (3) miscellaneous. Third, it looks at whether phonics is more effective when taught one-on-one, in small groups, or to the whole class. The principal findings of the meta-analyses are that explicit and systematic phonics is superior to nonsystematic or no phonics, but that there is no significant difference in effectiveness among the three kinds of systematic phonics instruction. The subgroup also found no significant difference in effectiveness among tutoring, small-group, or whole-class phonics instruction.

The Panel's findings, based on a meta-analysis of 66 comparisons from 38 experimental and quasi-experimental studies published since 1970, are consistent with the much broader body of literature on beginning reading instruction and the reading process. Surely, by now, the preponderance of logic and evidence is against those who contend that it is all right to provide young school children with reading instruction containing little or no phonics, with any phonics included being taught unsystematically. The NRP Report does nothing to change this.

What the Panel's findings may do, however, is move the burden of proof within the competition among advocates of different kinds of systematic phonics instruction. Historically, systematic phonics instruction has meant *synthetic* phonics instruction to many advocates. Recently, systematic phonics instruction in some states has come to mean *synthetic phonics instruction with at least 75 or 80% decodable text*. The onus has long been on those of us who believe that newer methods of systematic phonics instruction can be equally if not more effective than traditional synthetic programs over the long run. The NRP Report on phonics instruction may shift the burden of proof from advocates of these newer phonics methods to those who would impose synthetic phonics with high levels of decodable text on whole districts and states of children, because the advocates of such an imposition have always claimed that the research finds synthetic phonics to be superior to all other kinds. Will the NRP Report contribute to a shift of the burden of proof to those political activists who insist that synthetic phonics is best? Forgive me for not being overly optimistic, because the lack of scientific research supporting the link between retention in grade or grammar instruction hasn't kept these from being widely imposed on many public school children in the U.S. during the recent reforms.

The Panel's findings on phonics are also susceptible to the objection I raised earlier, that the studies to date really do not tell us that it matters—by fifth grade and beyond on the most important variables—how students were taught phonics in kindergarten and first grade. As an advocate of a type of systematic phonics instruction, I find this embarrassing for our field. Still, it was the responsibility of the Panel, and is the responsibility of us who read their report, to work to change that situation. Would that the Panel had taken the opportunity to instruct NICHD, Congress, and the nation on their responsibility to fund the kind of research that can eventually help us determine the long-term, multivariate, cause-and-effect chains that comprise healthy reading development. Sadly, the methods advocated by the Panel will almost certainly have the opposite effect-the funding and publication of more short-term, univariate, and single-cause studies.

Critique of the findings on alphabetics. I sense a hidden tension in this section of the Report between implicit or even subconscious views of the relationship linking phonemic awareness and phonics instruction. One view holds that phonemic awareness is prerequisite to learning phonics well; the other view holds that phonemic awareness is best taught when combined with systematic phonics instruction. The members of the subgroup resolve this tension by trying to have it both ways. They implicitly take the first or prerequisite view when they encourage the explicit and systematic teaching of phonemic awareness in preschool and kindergarten. They implicitly take the second or combined view when they advocate that phonemic awareness instruction be done with letters. A more straightforward approach would have been for them to acknowledge that two views exist and take one side or the other or admit that taking a side is currently premature.

Fluency

The Panel's discussion of reading fluency reveals another intriguing mix of opposing views underlying a report that feigns unanimity. One view is manifest in a summary of the theoretical relationship between automaticity and fluency that brings to bear eye movement research and a logical analysis of the reading task to include the roles of punctuation clues, grouping words into syntactic units, assigning emphasis to certain words, and pause behavior. Those in the subgroup who hold this view seem to see fluency as a construct and process underlying both oral and silent reading.

The other view is present in the identification of fluency with oral reading in both definition—"speed and accuracy of oral reading" (p. 3-28)—and measurement. "All [fluency] assessment procedures require oral reading of text" (p. 3-9). Those in the subgroup who hold this view seem to see fluency as a behavior and product of fluency instruction.

Because members of the Fluency subgroup were unaware of this tension in their midst or were unable to resolve it, they include independent silent reading as a treatment whose effectiveness should be measured with an oral reading dependent measure. No wonder they couldn't find a single study that evaluated interventions to encourage more independent silent reading with an oral reading fluency test. At that point, they should have realized that perhaps they had put the research on independent silent reading in the wrong subgroup.

Guided oral reading. The Fluency subgroup finds that guided oral reading, especially repeated reading, leads to improved oral reading fluency. With welcome candor, members admit they could locate no multiyear studies on this issue. Still, because professional wisdom and the literature the Panel ignored also support the claim that guided oral reading and repeated reading increase fluency, this finding of the Panel seems likely to hold up over time in the real world.

Independent silent reading. Beyond the questionable decision assigning this topic to the Fluency subgroup, the Panel's analysis of the research on independent silent reading manifests an appalling misunderstanding of even the narrow kind of research being endorsed by the NRP.

Although members claim that their methods are those used to study "the efficacy of interventions in psychological and medical research" (p. 27; p. 1-5), they misrepresent much psychological and medical research. No intervention to treat clinical depression is tested on patients who aren't depressed. No drug to treat kidney infections is tested on patients who don't have kidney disease. Moreover, treatments in psychological or medical research are ordinarily not administered even to patients having the targeted problems if they also have other problems that could prevent the intervention from working. For example, a treatment for heart disease probably won't be tested on patients who have heart disease combined with a serious lung ailment.

Yet, throughout its work, the NRP routinely selected and analyzed studies that tested the efficacy of a treatment in reading without ensuring that the participants needed what the treatment was designed to teach or that their other abilities made them likely candidates to benefit from the treatment. If the Panel was going to go the experimental and quasi-experimental route, it should have established criteria excluding any intervention study that did not screen participants to select those for whom the treatment would be appropriate and likely to work if effective.

Specific to this finding, if reading research should really be like psychological and medical intervention research, interventions designed to encourage students to increase their independent silent reading should only be tested using participants who have the ability and opportunity outside of school to read independently but who do not regularly do so.

Comprehension

This section of the NRP Report demonstrates the need and value of going beyond a critique of the methods the Panel adopted to look at the findings themselves. Members of the Comprehension subgroup found few studies that met the NRP criteria and did not perform any meta-analyses, but they chose to summarize the research they examined and make instructional recommendations anyway.

Vocabulary instruction. Because the 50 studies that were selected tested 21 different methods of teaching vocabulary, the Comprehension subgroup felt it should not perform a meta-analysis. Apparently, there was no consensus among members on a few distinctive features that some—but not all—methods shared. As a result, their instructional recommendations for vocabulary tend to be more balanced and less standardized than those of other subgroups.

Text comprehension instruction. Again, the subgroup found too few studies that met NRP criteria and too many different instructional methods to conduct a meta-analysis. Still, the subgroup found that seven of 16 types of text comprehension instruction have some support of effectiveness. Taking a balanced and practical, rather than verificationist tack, members recommend a combination of these and other types.

A critique of the findings on comprehension. This section of the Report is more like past major reviews of research on teaching reading comprehension (e.g., Pearson & Fielding, 1991; Tierney & Cunningham, 1984) than it is like other sections of the report. To me, at least, this section is more interesting and potentially valuable than the others, precisely because the Comprehension subgroup chose not to adhere too closely to the Panel's a priori methodological standards.

There is a definite downside, however, to the Panel's willingness to make instructional recommendations for comprehension based on looser criteria than it was willing to follow in the alphabetics and fluency sections. For example, members are willing to endorse text comprehension instruction but not interventions to increase independent silent reading, even though neither type of instruction met their original specifications for classroom implementation. Doesn't this reveal a bias toward explicit instruction rather than just a scientific finding of its superiority? Doesn't this suggest that the Panel thinks word identification and oral reading are more important and, therefore, more deserving of scientific, objective, and rigorous research standards than comprehension and independent silent reading?

Teacher Education and Reading Instruction

The Panel located 32 studies of the effects of teacher preservice or inservice education that met the general methodological standards, but again these studies represented too large a range of treatments to combine into a meta-analysis. The subgroup then added the additional criterion that "both teacher and student outcomes must be reported" (p. 17). The 11 studies with preservice teachers as participants all failed to meet this additional standard. Only about half of the 21 studies with inservice teachers met it. As a set, these studies of teacher inservice education indicated that professional development does increase student achievement, at least in the short-to-medium term.

In this section of the Report, the Panel's standard that preservice and inservice education be ultimately evaluated based on student outcomes is unfortunate. It certainly fits with the current political climate but ignores much that we know about professionalism. The members of no other profession are held accountable for client outcomes. No doctor, dentist, lawyer, or clinical psychologist is liable to be sued successfully or even professionally censured based on outcomes. (There is malpractice, but no such thing as a maloutcome suit.) Rather, these other professionals are held accountable for conforming to established best practices in their respective fields (Cunningham, 1999).

The purpose of research on teacher education is—or should be—to test theoretical models of how teachers gain and maintain professional competence and what conditions permit them to display that competence. To make every study on teacher education another experiment on teaching phonemic awareness, phonics, fluency, and so on is to place a burden on it that it cannot and should not bear. The research on teacher education should tell us how to promote professional practice.

Computer Technology and Reading Instruction

Again, the Panel located relatively few studies that met the NRP criteria and not enough of any kind to conduct a meta-analysis. Because all the studies reported positive results, the subgroup concluded that, "It is clear that some students can benefit from the use of computer technology in reading instruction" (p. 6-2). The subgroup also expressed some cautions. Let us hope the readers of the report do not conclude that anything taught on a computer will work.

A Critique of the NRP's Findings and Determinations

Most readers of the NRP Report will probably find themselves agreeing with at least one of the findings. Perhaps a majority of readers will agree with a majority of the findings. However, the test of quality for scientific research is whether knowledgeable and fair-minded skeptics find it persuasive. All research is persuasive to those who already agree with it. No research is persuasive to the person with a closed mind on the subject. The best science has the power to change the thinking of those who previously disagreed with its conclusions but who are fair-minded enough to admit they were wrong once the case has been made. Who is a fair-minded skeptic? Anyone who can point to several important issues in the past on which she or he has changed her or his mind because of research results.

The test of the scientific quality of the NRP's findings will be whether very many knowledgeable people who previously thought differently change their minds to agree with the Panel that preschool and kindergarten children should receive explicit and systematic phonemic awareness instruction with letters, or that efforts to increase independent silent reading are probably not effective in helping children acquire automaticity in reading.

How likely is that to happen? I predict that the knowledgeable and fair-minded skeptics who change their minds based on the NRP's findings will be few and far between. Too much professional and historical knowledge about teaching reading is ignored, too little common sense is brought to bear, and too little reading research is considered worthy of consultation.

The Context of the NRP Report

What if there had been no National Reading Panel, but the identical manifesto for a positivist philosophy of science in reading, the identical doctrine of experimentalism in reading research design, and the identical findings had been published in a series of articles in various major journals? I, for one, would have had the same substantive comments to make, but I would be much less fearful than I am now about what could come of it all. The U.S. Congress, the NICHD (an influential agency of the federal government), and the Secretary of Education convened the Panel and shaped its goals and operation. Does this mean the National Reading Panel was a bold attempt by powerful political forces to gain control of reading research? That will depend on whether persuasion or enforcement was the goal, and only time will tell.

REFERENCES

Ayer, A.J. (1946). *Language, truth and logic* (2nd ed.). London: V. Gollancz.

Campbell, D.T., & Stanley, J.C. (1963). *Experimental and quasi-experimental designs for research.* Chicago: Rand McNally.

Carnap, R. (1934). *The unity of science* (M. Black, Trans.). London: Kegan Paul, Trench, Trubner & Co.

Comte, A. (1988). *Introduction to positive philosophy* (P. Descours, H.G. Jones, & F. Ferré, Trans., F. Ferré, Ed.). Indianapolis, IN: Hackett. (Original work published 1830)

Cronbach, L.J. (1957). The two disciplines of scientific psychology. *American Psychologist, 12,* 671-684.

Cronbach, L.J. (1975). Beyond the two disciplines of scientific psychology. *American Psychologist, 30,* 116-127.

Cunningham, J.W. (1993). Whole-to-part reading diagnosis. *Reading and Writing Quarterly, 9,* 31-49.

Cunningham, J.W. (1999). How we can achieve best practices in literacy instruction. In L.B. Gambrell, L.M. Morrow, S.B. Neuman, & M. Pressley (Eds.), *Best practices in literacy instruction* (pp. 34-45). New York: Guilford.

Cunningham, J.W., & Fitzgerald, J. (1996). Epistemology and reading. *Reading Research Quarterly, 31,* 36-60.

Dummett, M. (1976). What is a theory of meaning? (II). In G. Evans & J. McDowell (Eds.), *Truth and meaning: Essays in semantics* (pp. 67-137). New York: Oxford University Press.

Dummett, M. (1991). *The logical basis of metaphysics.* Cambridge, MA: Harvard University Press.

Fuller, S. (1985). The demarcation of science: A problem whose demise has been greatly exaggerated. *Pacific Philosophical Quarterly, 66,* 329-341.

Garrison, J.W. (1996). Science, philosophy of. In J.J. Chambliss (Ed.), *Philosophy of education: An encyclopedia* (pp. 590-592). New York: Garland.

Giere, R.N. (1997). *Understanding scientific reasoning* (4th ed.). Orlando, FL: Harcourt Brace College.

Gieryn, T.F. (1983). Boundary work and the demarcation of science from non-science: Strains and interests in professional ideologies of scientists. *American Sociological Review, 48,* 781–795.

Gjertsen, D. (1989). *Science and philosophy: Past and present.* New York: Penguin.

Lakatos, I. (1978). *The methodology of scientific research programmes* (Philosophical Papers, Vol. 1, J. Worrall & G. Currie, Eds.). New York: Cambridge University Press.

Laudan, L. (1981). A problem-solving approach to scientific progress. In I. Hacking (Ed.), *Scientific revolutions* (pp. 144–155). New York: Oxford University Press.

Laudan, L. (1983). The demise of the demarcation problem. In R.S. Cohen & L. Laudan (Eds.), *Physics, philosophy and psychoanalysis: Essays in honor of Adolf Grunbaum* (pp. 111–127). Boston: D. Reidel.

Marsonet, M. (1995). *Science, reality, and language.* Albany: State University of New York Press.

Meehl, P.E. (1957). When shall we use our heads instead of the formula? *Journal of Counseling Psychology, 4,* 268–273.

National Institute of Child Health and Human Development. (2000). *Report of the National Reading Panel. Teaching children to read: An evidence-based assessment of the scientific research literature on reading and its implications for reading instruction* (NIH Publication No. 00-4769). Washington, DC: U.S. Government Printing Office.

National Institute of Child Health and Human Development. (2000). *Report of the National Reading Panel. Teaching children to read: An evidence-based assessment of the scientific research literature on reading and its implications for reading instruction: Reports of the subgroups* (NIH Publication No. 00-4754). Washington, DC: U.S. Government Printing Office.

Pearson, P.D., & Fielding, L. (1991). Comprehension instruction. In R. Barr, M.L. Kamil, P.B. Mosenthal, & P.D. Pearson (Eds.), *Handbook of reading research* (Vol. 2, pp. 815–860). White Plains, NY: Longman.

Pearson, P.D., & Samuels, S.J. (1980). Editorial. *Reading Research Quarterly, 15,* 429–430.

Popper, K.R. (1959). *The logic of scientific discovery.* London: Hutchinson.

Samuels, S.J. (1984). Editorial. *Reading Research Quarterly, 19,* 390–392.

Searle, J.R. (1995). *The construction of social reality.* New York: Free Press.

Share, D.L. (1995). Phonological recoding and self-teaching: Sine qua non of reading acquisition. *Cognition, 55,* 151–218.

Tierney, R.J., & Cunningham, J.W. (1984). Research on teaching reading comprehension. In P.D. Pearson, R. Barr, M.L. Kamil, & P.B. Mosenthal (Eds.), *Handbook of reading research* (pp. 609–655). New York: Longman.

Weinberg, S. (1992). *Dreams of a final theory.* New York: Pantheon.

Yopp, H.K., & Yopp, R.H. (2000). Supporting phonemic awareness development in the classroom. *The Reading Teacher, 54,* 130–143.

Books Aloud: A Campaign to "Put Books in Children's Hands"

Susan B. Neuman and Donna Celano

There's not much to read on the street in Philadelphia, Pennsylvania, where Deon (all children's names are pseudonyms) travels every day to his child-care center. In the windows of row houses, "For Sale" signs have long since given way to plywood. Illegible signs and graffiti tags mark much of the former candy-making factory and warehouse. A rusting teacher's desk barely visible through a blown-out window is the only vestige of what was once a neighborhood school.

But inside the child-care center, 3-year-old Deon looks at his favorite book, *Where the Wild Things Are* (Sendak, 1967) along with a gaggle of similarly aged children who implore him read it again. He flips the pages, jabbing his little finger hard at Sendak's witty monsters and carrying out a running commentary with his friends on the actions of the wild things "dancin' in the trees," and the sea monster "breathin' fire."

It looks so simple and natural. And yet there is nothing simple about what Deon is doing. Or where he is doing it. Or when. On this bleak street, at this struggling child-care center, at this age, it is something of a near-miracle that Deon has a book in his hands. With less than US$1 per week per child for supplies in government-subsidized child care, books are in short supply (Pennsylvania Department of Education, personal communication, June 8, 1998). That Deon is able to choose from so many selections is the result of a bold campaign to "put books in children's hands." The program, called Books Aloud (Neuman, 1999), a joint effort among philanthropists, educators, and librarians, has introduced Deon and others like him to the power and pleasure of reading.

Books Aloud came about as the result of a long plane ride during which two executives from a local foundation were deep in conversation. One was concerned about the state of child care and the lack of quality in early childhood curriculum. The other was equally concerned about libraries and their outreach to community organizations. What began as a casual conversation later became a US$2.5 million 2-year effort to improve language and literacy development for over 18,000 children in low-income areas. This article gives

Reprinted from *The Reading Teacher, 54,* 550–557, March 2001.

an overview of the project, detailing its progress, processes, and impact on children's literacy development.

Background

Books Aloud was designed as a loosely structured collaboration between the Office of Public Service Support of the Free Library of Philadelphia and seven county and city library systems in the Delaware Valley region of Pennsylvania. Its purpose was to enhance the language and literacy opportunities for children, from infants through age 5. But its target focus was perhaps its most innovative feature: Books Aloud was designed to enrich the lives of economically disadvantaged children in child-care centers and support the child-care providers who shepherd those toddlers and preschoolers through long days that stretch from before dawn to past supper time. In doing so, the Books Aloud program departed from the usual theme of getting parents to read to their children, to one of helping child-care workers read and read often to children. "We knew that these children often spend more waking hours at child-care centers than they do at home," reported Dick Cox, the now-retired vice president of the local foundation who conceived and helped launch Books Aloud. "And we hoped that if we could get teachers motivated to use printed material, then perhaps children would get excited about books and would take them home to parents."

The effort to put books in children's hands resulted in a dazzling display of ways in which libraries can support literacy. With funds from the foundation and special library discounts of 40%, the project provided more than 89,000 brand-new storybooks to 17,675 toddlers and preschoolers in child-care centers and family child-care homes, along with bookcases and storage and display racks to create library corners in classrooms. In a single month, 325 child-care centers and 250 family child-care homes—at a ratio of five books per child—were flooded with sturdy board books, beautiful picture books, and books that rhymed and counted and told wonderful stories. All of them came with special permabound covers, Books Aloud bookplates, and a promise from the program to help repair the books after they'd been played with and ripped and loved to the point of falling apart. "It felt like Christmas morning," remembers Ann Boyle, the director of Deon's facility. "We had always tried to buy books a few at a time, and even then, it would kill the budget just for glue and scissors and construction paper. Now we got boxes and boxes of them, so many that we were able to have multiple libraries for children to use in one classroom."

But the books came with something else that distinguished this program from other "book floods" in the past: 10 hours of training for child-care providers. The purpose of the training program was to emphasize the importance of the early years in establishing a foundation for literacy, to create environments that engage children in print activities, to foster effective read-aloud techniques, and to make books and story reading a constant presence in their everyday activities-not just a "fill-in" activity wedged between arts and crafts and nap time (Neuman, 1997).

To effectively train child-care workers, Books Aloud dispatched a small army of 22 "preschool specialists"—good-will ambassadors, many of whom were retired teachers—to help child-care providers set up library corners and display the new books in ways that would entice children to use them, play with them, and read them. At the beginning of the experiment, just 20% of the classrooms had some kind of a book nook, although 30% had TVs. By the end of the program, virtually all of the 325 centers and 250 child-care homes had a special book corner, with child-size display bookcases provided by Books Aloud.

In 2 years of intensive biweekly visits to centers, trainers like Jean Byrne encountered child-care providers who hustled the new books out of children's reach, in the belief that they were too precious to let children play with. Some simply did not see the point of exposing babies to books when they obviously couldn't read. Trainers heard some providers protest that they didn't read well aloud—a face-saving device, followed by a later admission that they couldn't really read well themselves. They found that some providers were so focused on teaching preschoolers the alphabet that they had no time—and no patience—for indulgences like storybooks.

These preschool specialist trainers realized that though they lacked formal training, child-care workers were hardly empty vessels waiting to be filled by expert knowledge from outside resource specialists. What they were teaching was based on their instincts, values, beliefs, and sense of what was right for young children. Trainers had to respect those values, and try not to change but to stretch their beliefs, selling what they knew about early literacy practices as something teachers might find of value, and then encouraging them to "take it out for a trial spin."

And sell they did. In visits to child-care centers, preschool specialists kept the message focused: "Put books in children's hands, whether it is potty time, free-play time, or nap time. Read them stories and let them play with and touch the books and see the pictures and print. Children will learn that words tell stories. They will begin to recognize letters and sounds, and without seeming to try, they will build a foundation for literacy."

Progress and Processes of Books Aloud

Several months before the project was to begin, I was invited to conduct a large-scale evaluation of Books Aloud. The funders had seen too many good-hearted service projects go by the wayside, and wanted a rigorous analysis of whether or not the project was successful. With colleague Donna Celano and 10 research assistants over the course of 2 years, we examined how books and staff training became integrated into the lives of children and their child-care providers in low income child-care centers. We designed an experimental study with more than 500 3- and 4-year-old children in centers across the region, and a series of naturalistic studies. Spending literally hundreds of hours in centers, we watched how teachers in the child-care community reacted to the critical message of Books Aloud, and to the importance of early literacy development. The story of Holy Day Child Care Center is one among many.

Holy Day Child Care Center

Holy Day Child Care Center (pseudonym) is housed in Sunday school classrooms of a former Baptist church, in a neighborhood that was once a bustling working-class community, but is now unquestionably poor. Although she has worked in child care for over 20 years and has an associate's degree in early childhood education, the director is new to the center. The center is run on a bare-bones budget since many of the families it serves are on public assistance. Basic supplies are difficult to come by, and books nonexistent.

Child care for the center's staff is largely about nurturance and social development. "We do what we can to make sure the children are well cared for and try to get them ready for kindergarten," said the director. Readiness training emphasizes self-help skills such as eating, dressing, and toilet training, along with some skills associated with academic readiness. There is no established curriculum. Teachers create lessons using flashcards, coloring books, and worksheets copied from old workbooks.

Ms. Helen is one of eight teachers at the school. With little formal training, she is highly experienced, having worked in child care for years. Visitors to her room find a warm and caring environment. As the 3- to 4-year-old children arrive each morning, they are greeted with smiles and informal conversation; parents are welcomed and eagerly exchange information on children's personal hygiene and social behaviors. Her interactions with parents and children make it clear that Ms. Helen enjoys her work.

Lessons begin first thing in the morning, focusing on rudimentary skills like days of the week and letter and number recognition. Ms. Helen arranges the children's seats carefully in rows. She holds up a flashcard, points to the number or letter, and asks the children to repeat it. Children are encouraged to name words that begin with different letters of the alphabet. On some occasions, after the lesson is over, Ms. Helen may try to read a storybook. However, she finds that children invariably turn disruptive, popping up out of their seats, shouting out something about the story, or asking questions. Further, the toddler teacher across the way usually insists on turning up the volume on the TV just as Ms. Helen is about to read. Resignedly, she has decided that children may not be ready to sit through a story.

Part of the problem, she recognizes, may be the physical design of her classroom. "There are so many distractions here," she explained. "No wonder they can't pay attention." On a good day the room is merely noisy, with the sound of toddlers playing and running around, but on other days, the noise level is deafening. There are sounds of children yelling, crying, roughhousing, and watching videos or daytime TV. Consequently, although the books they anticipate from the Books Aloud project are much needed, the staff is not exactly sure where to put them and what to do with them.

They decide to create a library for the entire center. On a follow-up visit, we find the new books up on the former altar of the church with beaming lights fixed on them as if they were beautiful trophies. The staff is eager for training, wanting to use the new resources to children's advantages. After many informal visits and conversations, Jean Byrne, the preschool specialist assigned to the center, has gained their confidence.

Jean wants to help teachers understand the importance of books in children's development and learning. Her training focuses on selecting age-appropriate books, storybook read-aloud techniques, story stretchers to promote vocabulary, and ways to enhance the physical environment to provide better access to books. Each visit includes new ideas and demonstrations, simple handouts that highlight key information, and many suggestions for good reading. For example, in one of her first visits, she encourages teachers to focus on children's age and developmental level when selecting books to read (see Figure 1). At the next visit, she emphasizes book-reading techniques and how different types of books may be used for different purposes. A book about feelings might lead to questions such as "How do you think this character feels?" or "How would you feel if this happened to you?"

Subsequent sessions focus on language and conversation as a way of stretching children's learning from the story. Jean describes how children

Figure 1
Ages and stages

Age	Characteristics	Types of materials
0-1	Becoming aware of environment and familiar people	Large, brightly colored pictures; simple rhymes (e.g., *The Real Mother Goose*, Iona Opie, 1996, Candlewick)
1-2	May begin to use words, and connect them to objects and people	Books with familiar objects; heavy cardboard or washable cloth books (e.g., *Pat the Bunny*, Dorothy Kunhardt, 1990, Golden Books)
2	Oral language increases	Predictable books, cumulative stories (e.g., *The House That Jack Built*, Pam Adams, 1995, Childs Play)
2-2-1/2	Oral language continues to increase; the child may verbalize a lot; may repeat phrases from books	Nonsense verse; funny books; pretends to read (*Henny Penny*, Paul Galdone, 1984, Houghton Mifflin)
2-1/2-3	Begins to talk in phrases and even sentences; may make up stories; may "read" to others; some memorization may also be evident	Simple informational books; alphabet or concept; simple narratives (e.g., *If You Give a Mouse a Cookie*, Laura J. Numeroff, 1985, HarperCollins)
3-1/2-4	Imaginative language becomes more developed; may ask for explanations; wants to be independent; may show definite reading preferences	Longer stories with more plot development; enjoys folk tales, fairy tales; explanations of how things work (e.g., *Mike Mulligan and His Steam Shovel*, Virginia Lee Burton, 1977, Houghton Mifflin)
4-5	Begins to recognize words in books/signs; can usually recite the alphabet; interested in retelling stories.	Enjoys a wide variety of books; may like wordless books that tell a story (e.g., *Frog, Where Are You?* Mercer Meyer, 1980, Dial)

need to ask questions to try to understand and resolve issues triggered by the text. "Children need to think about 'where the story is going,' and link what they already know to what they are learning and what they want to know more about." She shows them some simple ways of helping children reconstruct the story using paper-bag puppets, and gives them a simple ready-made flannel board and felt to make new characters. Throughout the sessions, Jean demonstrates the power of rereading books by showing teachers how children ask better questions, use new vocabulary from the book, and gain mastery of a wide variety of topics. "See what they've learned?" she says. She suggests changes in room arrangements so that children can read independently, and gives a few hints on keeping books healthy for little hands to enjoy (see Figure 2).

While the children are napping and the lights are turned out in the large room, Jean and the teachers hold their sessions. As they whisper softly and become more comfortable with one another, teachers raise issues about reading and ask questions. Ms. Fern asks, "How do I keep children's attention?" Jean shows them props and suggests Ms. Fern read the same story several times, each time with a different goal. "On the first day, you can just look at the pictures and talk about them. On the next, you can read it and point to the pictures. And on the third day, you can encourage the children to read along with you during predictable parts."

Jean talks about how to prepare for the storytime with age-appropriate books, "You may start with an attention book, one that requires the children

---

Figure 2
Suggestions for caring for books

A well-used book is a well-loved book

A few hints on keeping your "well-loved" book healthy for many little hands to enjoy:

- Invisible tape for ripped pages or flaps
  Use a good quality tape. Invisible (not glossy) will last longer.

- Gummy eraser
  Removes crayon marks from glossy pages. Use to erase pencil too.

- Book tape
  Heavy-duty tape to repair broken spines. Use one piece down outside of spine and on inside front and back seams and center seam. But don't use to repair ripped pages. It's too heavy.

- Glue
  Useful for repairing paper torn off cardboard jackets or board books (nontoxic only). Also put on broken spines before tape for extra hold.

- Disinfectant
  Dab diluted solution on paper towel to wipe covers clean. Also use spray bottles with water (10 parts) to ammonia or alcohol (1 part) to wipe covers and board books when they get that well-loved look.

Well-loved books, well cared for, will make many, many, friends.

---

to focus, and then a rhyming book to encourage lots of interaction." She discusses the room arrangement and the ways in which children can be better grouped to react to the book. She also raises the sensitive issue of collaboration among staff. "You need to be respectful of others' story times. When one is reading, the others need to be mindful and not turn on the TV or do loud activities. Don't let disruptions ruin the story."

In subsequent weeks, Jean emphasizes the importance of having children handle books on their own. She suggests that they move the bookcases down from the altar, using them as semifixed structures to more clearly define classroom spaces. Along with these suggestions, she conducts regular demonstration lessons in each class, showing teachers how to use the flannel board and how to raise questions that might generate discussion among young children. In one visit, the teacher tells us, "That Jean, she's helped move those bookcases down. Before, I would forget that the books were up there. The children would say, 'But we forgot to go to the library today.' And I would feel terrible. But now they are right here in the classroom and they can go get them themselves."

We began to notice not-so-subtle changes in classroom activities. One day, for example, we entered a freezing classroom. Children were sitting in this dark, windowless room, wrapped in sweaters and coats, the single fixture high up in the 14-foot ceiling adding little light to the room. Despite these discomforts, eight young children sat happily on the floor surrounding Ms. Helen, who quietly read *Letters From Felix* (Langen, 1994, Abbeville). The children listened intently. "Can you smell the cookies being baked?" Ms. Helen asked as she sniffed the air. The children followed her lead. "Let's smell them together," and each child touched the page with the cookies. After the reading, Ms. Helen told the children to get a book from the nearby open-faced bookcase, which now had about 20 high-quality hardcover children's books. They gathered around the bookcase, asking questions and telling their own stories to go along with the words.

By the end of the year, there are significant changes. Replacing the morning recitation of the alphabet is a regularly scheduled story hour for the children. After group readings children handle books, reenact stories, and engage in conversations. The toddler teacher, Ms. Robin, has selected age-appropriate books for her 2-year-olds and reads to them in small groups. The TV is off. The teachers are even making some beginning attempts at theme-based instruction, linking books with other subjects and field trips outside of the center. They have also created a small lending library for parents to take home books to read to their children. In short, book use and storytime now seem to be a significant part of the day.

Certainly the environment is not ideal, nor is the curriculum particularly developmentally appropriate. But teachers' beliefs and practices have clearly evolved from often relentless drill and worksheet practice to book-related activities. Jean's clear, focused, concrete, and realistic suggestions for ways in which to use books successfully addressed teachers' beliefs about their appropriateness and their cognitive value in daily activities. Her demonstrations provided concrete evidence that not only do children need to feel nurtured, but also they need and are motivated to learn, given the setting, time, and opportunity.

Even with a large quantity of new books, Jean reminded teachers that children will eventually tire of hearing the same familiar stories. Children want to be continually challenged with an ever-changing selection of books. As a parting gesture, Jean accompanied teachers and children on a field trip to the local library to help children register for their first library cards.

Impact of Books Aloud

The story of Holy Day Child Care Center is one that we would come to see more often than not. Among the more than 18,000 young children affected by Books Aloud in its first year, about 1 in 5 initially had library cards. Today, about 3 in 5 do. Small wins—not dramatic shifts in educational philosophy or curriculum change. But small wins can be bundled together to lead to big consequences, as in the case of Books Aloud.

Full documentation of the results of Books Aloud is available from other sources (Neuman, 1997, 1999), yet the description of the project would not be complete without briefly summarizing the findings. Comparing the abilities of children not involved in the project but in comparable low-income centers, we found striking differences in early literacy scores for children from Books Aloud child-care centers (see Neuman, 1997, for complete description of research design). Exposed to more storybooks in Books Aloud centers, children were better able to tell and recount stories, recognize letters, understand the conventions of print (that text and not artwork tells the story, for example, and that print moves from left to right), and grasp early writing skills than their counterparts not in the program. What was particularly interesting is that toddlers benefited just as much as preschool children. As a conceptually rich activity, book reading stimulated literacy growth and continuous development, suggesting its flexibility as well as its challenging cognitive benefits. For very young children, age-appropriate book reading involved labeling and feedback activities around board books and concept books; for other children, more continuous dialogue and interactions with predictable books and beginning narratives enhanced language and other critical skills.

Observations of classrooms, however, perhaps convey the effect of Books Aloud best. In Deon's classroom, book reading has become more than a segment in a day crowded with physical activity. It has become a point of departure for questions and conversation—something that many of these children get little of with parents who struggle to make ends meet. It has become a key to unlock the unending mysteries of how books work. In the act of turning pages gently and slowing down to gaze at pictures, highly active children like Deon have learned, literally, what it feels like to learn. Reports his teacher, "You really can't teach a child to have enthusiasm or motivation to learn, but if I give them a love of reading, their natural desire to keep at it will take them far—farther than anything else I can do for them. It gives them a fighting chance."

Put Books in Children's Hands

Books Aloud has now run its course; trainers have moved on to other teaching or library positions. Their efforts, however, are still producing results. Centers have maintained their book areas. Some are especially attractive and child centered, with spaces for book reading, play, and books in interest centers. Others have put in chairs or comfortable rugs so that children can sit and read nearby. Still others may have only a bookcase. Yet once again we find small wins. In one class, for example, we locate a bookcase, but are dismayed to see no books on it. Looking more closely, we find four very young children with books all around them, reading, pretending to read, giggling, and playing together. Even in the most sparsely lit, poorly configured spaces, books are in children's hands.

Following many of these children to kindergarten, we have asked teachers, "Do Books Aloud children seem interested in books, ask questions, and contribute to book discussions? Are children developing the skills that are critical for success in reading?" There seems to be a powerful consensus: Books Aloud children are better prepared to learn in kindergarten.

Teachers share many examples. One young girl is already familiar with the stories the teacher is reading to the class, answering questions sometimes before they are asked. Another seems to be reading, and her "book behavior is more advanced than that of the rest of the class." Another child regales the other children with his rendition of "The Gingerbread Man," reciting, "Run run as fast as you can, you can't stop me, I'm the gingerbread man." Some of the children who already know the predictable phrases chime them aloud along with him.

Children's literacy skills, measured against their counterparts who did not have the benefits of Books Aloud, also provide a telling picture. Even 6 months later, there were dramatic differences in phonological awareness, letter knowledge, narrative abilities, and writing (Neuman, 1999). It is not surprising that the shared book experience is considered the single most important activity in early literacy development: Children's growth in reading and writing serves to confirm and extend its power.

Results of Books Aloud corroborates the International Reading Association/National Association for the Education of Young Children declaration in their position statement on "Learning to Read and Write: Developmentally Appropriate Practices for Young Children" (International Reading Association/National Association for the Education of Young Children, 1998) that language and literacy teaching begins well before kindergarten. Whatever their economic status, young children thrive in print-rich environments with supportive caregivers to engage them in thinking and talking about storybooks. Through these interactions, children acquire new vocabulary and some level of print awareness, as well as play with and analyze the sounds of language long before formal reading instruction begins in elementary school. Books make a critical difference in this process, providing children as young as infants, toddlers, and preschoolers with models of good language teaching that prepare them for the task of learning to read. Consequently, for those in the early childhood community who still cling to the view that children are not intellectually ready to be exposed to reading or writing, we would urge them to heed the position statement's warning that, "failing to give children literacy experiences until they are school age can severely limit the reading and writing levels they ultimately attain" (International Reading Association/National Association for the Education of Young Children, 1998, p. 10).

Further substantiation for the importance of early language and literacy experiences comes from the National Research Council's report *Preventing Reading Difficulties* (Snow, Burns, & Griffin, 1998). The authors suggest that opportunities to engage with print may act as a primary prevention of reading difficulties. Stanovich and West (1989), focusing on the role of print exposure, found it to be a potent predictor of vocabulary growth, knowledge acquisition, and a variety of verbal skills. Print exposes children to words outside of their current vocabulary far more effectively than conversational talk or other media like watching television (Cunningham & Stanovich, 1998). Anderson and Nagy (1992), for example, estimated that children learn an average of 4,000 to 12,000 new words each year as a result of book reading. It is for this reason that the International Reading Association (2000) has recommended that at the very minimum, school library media centers have 20 books per child, and classroom libraries 7 books per child, with 2 additional new books per child to be purchased each year.

But it is not just exposure to books that makes a difference. Children need skillfully mediated assistance in book reading by their caregivers that can help to explain the workings of literacy. As a large number of scholars have reported (Dickinson & Smith, 1994; Whitehurst et al., 1994), it is the intensity of engagement—the quality of talk and conversational interactions between adult and child—that nurtures and helps them to construct vital literacy-related concepts. These conversations allow them to stretch their understanding of phenomena and use their increasingly rich vocabulary in other contexts. Playing with words, letters, and sounds in contexts that are meaningful to them, children begin to attend to the features of print and the alphabetic nature of reading.

Therefore, given the enormous disparities among different income groups, how can we ensure that all children have an equal opportunity to succeed in reading? As we confirmed in this research: Increase the volume, quality, and intensity of young children's stimulating experiences with good books at an early age. Provide opportunities for young children to hear, see, and participate in a wide range of activities with their caregivers who may help them to uncover the mysteries of written language. As Books Aloud has advocated, find every way to "put books in children's hands."

REFERENCES

Anderson, R.C., & Nagy, W.E. (1992). The vocabulary conundrum. *American Educator*, 14-18, 44-46.

Cunningham, A.E., & Stanovich, K. (1998). What reading does for the mind. *American Educator, 22*, 8-15.

Dickinson, D., & Smith, M. (1994). Long-term effects of preschool teachers' book readings on low-income children's vocabulary and story comprehension. *Reading Research Quarterly, 29*, 104-122.

International Reading Association. (2000). *Providing books and other print materials for classroom and school libraries: A position statement*. Newark, DE: Author.

International Reading Association/National Association for the Education of Young Children. (1998). Learning to read and write: Developmentally appropriate practices for young children. *The Reading Teacher, 52*, 193-216.

Neuman, S.B. (1997). *Getting books in children's hands: The book flood of '96*. Final report to the William Penn Foundation. Philadelphia, PA: Temple University.

Neuman, S.B. (1999). Books make a difference: A study of access to literacy. *Reading Research Quarterly, 34*, 286-311.

Snow, C., Burns, M.S., & Griffin, P. (1998). *Preventing reading difficulties in young children.* Washington, DC: National Academy Press.

Stanovich, K.E., & West, R.F. (1989). Exposure to print and orthographic processing. *Reading Research Quarterly, 24,* 402–433.

Whitehurst, G.J., Epstein, J., Angell, A., Payne, A., Crone, D., & Fischel, J. (1994). Outcomes of an emergent literacy intervention in Head Start. *Journal of Educational Psychology, 86,* 542–555.

Looking Inside Classrooms: Reflecting on the "How" as Well as the "What" in Effective Reading Instruction

Barbara M. Taylor, Debra S. Peterson, P. David Pearson, and Michael C. Rodriguez

We know a great deal about effective elementary teachers of reading (Taylor, Pressley, & Pearson, 2000). From the research of the 1960s and 1970s (Brophy, 1973; Dunkin & Biddle, 1974; Flanders, 1970; Stallings & Kaskowitz, 1974) we learned that effective teachers maintained an academic focus, kept more pupils on task, and provided direct instruction. Effective direct instruction included making learning goals clear, asking students questions to monitor understanding of content or skills covered, and providing feedback to students about their academic progress.

Roehler and Duffy (1984) focused on the cognitive processes used by excellent teachers. More effective teachers use modeling and explanation to teach students strategies for decoding words and understanding texts. Knapp (1995) found that effective teachers stressed higher level thinking skills more than lower level skills. Taylor, Pearson, Clark, and Walpole (2000) found that, compared with their less accomplished peers, more accomplished primary-grade teachers provided more small-group than whole-group instruction, elicited high levels of pupil engagement, preferred coaching over telling in interacting with students, and engaged students in more higher level thinking related to reading.

The National Reading Panel Report (National Institute of Child Health and Human Development, 2000) concluded that instruction in systematic phonics, phonemic awareness, fluency, and comprehension strategies was important in a complete reading program. The panel's conclusions are consistent with the findings of Pressley et al. (2001) regarding the balance that outstanding primary-grade teachers achieve in their classroom reading programs; Pressley et al. found that outstanding teachers taught skills, actively engaged students in a great deal of actual reading and writing, and fostered self-regulation in students' use of strategies.

Reprinted from *The Reading Teacher*, 56, 270–279, November 2002.

In short, we have learned different, but complementary, lessons about the teaching practices of outstanding elementary literacy teachers from research on effective teaching. In this article, we discuss a subset of findings from year 1 of a larger national study on school reform in reading (Taylor, Pearson, Peterson, & Rodriguez, 2001) funded by the Center for the Improvement of Early Reading Achievement (CIERA). The purpose of the larger study was to evaluate the impact of all aspects of school reform on student performance. The purposes of the present, more focused analysis are to (a) describe the teacher practices we observed in the classrooms, particularly those that are derived from the research of the last four decades; (b) examine the relationship between teachers' practices and students' growth in reading achievement; and (c) provide vignettes that vividly describe what those practices look like in action.

Participants and Assessments

Eight high-poverty schools (with 70–95% of the students qualifying for subsidized lunch) were included in the study. Across the schools, 2–68% of the students were nonnative speakers of English, and 67–91% were members of minority groups. The schools represented demographic and geographic diversity—the rural southeast, a large midwestern city, and a large southwestern city. Five of the schools implemented our CIERA School Change Framework (www.schoolchange.ciera.org), and three were comparison schools. In all schools, two teachers per grade (kindergarten through sixth) were randomly invited to participate in the classroom observations. Within these classrooms, teachers were asked to divide their classes into thirds (high, average, and low) in terms of reading performance, and two children from each third, six per classroom, were randomly selected to be assessed.

The children were given a number of literacy assessments in the fall and spring (depending on grade level and ability level), including the Gates-MacGinitie Reading Tests, 4th ed. (2000; grades 1–6) and assessments of letter names and sounds (Pikulski, 1996; K–1), phonemic awareness (Taylor, 1991; K–1), word dictation (Pikulski, 1996; K–1), concepts of print (Pikulski, 1996; K–1), and fluency (Deno, 1985; 1–6) on passages from the Basic Reading Inventory, 7th ed. (1997).

Documenting Classroom Practices

On three scheduled occasions (fall, winter, and spring) each participating teacher was observed for an hour during reading instruction to document classroom practices in the teaching of reading. The observers were graduate students in literacy or retired elementary teachers, all of whom were trained to use the CIERA Classroom Observation Scheme (Taylor & Pearson, 2000, 2001). The structure of our observation scheme was influenced by the work of Scanlon and Gelzheiser (1992). Each observer was required to meet a criterion (80% agreement with a "standard" coding at each of the seven categories of the coding scheme) in order to have his or her observations included in the study.

The observation system combined qualitative notetaking with a quantitative coding process. The observer took field notes for a five-minute segment, recording a narrative account of what was happening in the classroom, including, where possible and appropriate, what the teacher and children were saying. At the end of the five-minute notetaking segment, the observer first recorded the proportion of children in the classroom who appeared to be on task, that is, doing what they were supposed to be doing. The observer next coded the three or four most salient literacy events (category 4 codes) that occurred during that five-minute episode. Then for each category 4 event, the observer also coded who was providing the instruction (category 1), the grouping pattern in use for that event (category 2), the major literacy activity (category 3), the materials being used (category 5), the teacher interaction styles observed (category 6), and the expected responses of the students (category 7). An example of a five-minute observational segment is provided in the Figure. (See Table 1 for a list of the codes for all the categories.)

Coding the Observations

On the basis of research on effective teachers of reading, certain aspects of the data from classroom observations were analyzed to investigate the relationship between various classroom instructional practices and students' growth in reading. Except as noted, for a given teacher each of these variables was constructed by summing the number of five-minute segments in which the target practice was observed divided by the total number of observed segments. The numbers resulting from these calculations might be thought of as rates of inclusion of these practices into the teachers' instructional repertoires. The research-based classroom practices analyzed included the following:

> Whole group—the percentage of five-minute segments in which whole-group activities were coded.
>
> Small group—the percentage of five-minute segments in which small-group activities were coded.

Table 1
Codes for classroom observations

Category 1 Who	Code	4 Specific focus (cont.)	Code
Classroom teacher	c	p4 = multisyllabic	p4
Reading specialist	r	Word recognition strategies	wr
Special education	se	Phonemic awareness	pa
Other specialist	sp	Letter identification	li
Student teacher	st	Spelling	s
Aide	a	Other	o
Volunteer	v	Not applicable	9
No one	n		
Other	o	5 Material	Code
Not applicable	9	Textbook, narrative	tn
		Textbook, informational	ti
2 Grouping	Code	Narrative trade book	n
Whole class	w	Informational trade book	i
Small group	s	Student writing	w
Pairs	p	Board/chart	b
Individual	i	Worksheet	s
Other	o	Oral presentation	o
Not applicable	9	Pictures	p
		Video/film	v
3 General focus	Code	Computer	c
Reading	r	Other/not applicable	o/9
Composition/writing	w		
Spelling	s	6 Teacher interaction	Code
Handwriting	h	Tell/give info	t
Language	l	Modeling	m
Other	o	Recitation	r
Not applicable	9	Discussion	d
		Coaching/scaffolding	c
4 Specific focus	Code	Listening/watching	l
Reading connected text	r	Reading aloud	ra
Listening to text	l	Check work	cw
Vocabulary	v	Assessment	a
Meaning of text, lower		Other	o
m1 for talk	m1	Not applicable	9
m2 for writing	m2		
Meaning of text, higher		7 Expected pupil response	
m3 for talk	m3	Reading	r
m4 for writing	m4	Reading turn taking	r-tt
Comprehension skill	c	Orally responding	or
Comprehension strategy	cs	Oral turn taking	or-tt
Writing	w	Listening	l
Exchanging ideas/oral production	e/o	Writing	w
Word Identification	wi	Manipulating	m
Sight words	sw	Other/not applicable	o/9
Phonics p1 = letter sound	p1	Number of students on task/	
p2 = letter by letter	p2	number of students	
p3 = onset/rime	p3		

Word skills—a sum of the number of five-minute segments in which the level 4 activities dealing with word skills were observed, divided by the number of segments in which the level 3 code was designated as reading. An aggregate variable was formed by summing the data from the following practices: (a) word identification work, (b) sight word drill, (c) phonics work, (d) phonemic awareness work, and (e) letter identification work.

Comprehension skills or strategies—the percentage of five-minute segments in which comprehension skills and strategies were coded divided by the number of category 3 reading segments coded.

Low-level questioning or writing about text—the percentage of five-minute segments in which the category 4 activities dealing with lower level talking or writing about text were observed, divided by the number of category 3 reading segments coded.

Higher level questioning or writing about text—the percentage of five-minute segments in which the category 4 activities dealing with higher level talking or writing about text were observed, divided by the number of category 3 reading segments coded. Because word skill work, comprehension skill and strategy work, or questioning or writing about text were almost always coded when the general focus of the lesson was reading, a decision was made to consider the incidence of these three different types of reading activities out of the number of five-minute segments where reading was coded.

Teacher telling—the percentage of five-minute segments in which the teacher was coded as telling children information.

Teacher using recitation—the percentage of five-minute segments in which the teacher was coded as engaging children in recitation.

Teacher coaching—the percentage of five-minute segments in which the teacher was coded as coaching children for independence. Because only telling, recitation, and coaching were coded with regularity, analyses were limited to these three codes from category 6.

Students actively responding—an aggregate variable: the percentage of responses in which children were coded as engaged in reading, writing, or manipulating out of the total number of student responses coded.

Students passively responding—an aggregate variable: the percent of responses in which children were coded as engaged in reading turn taking, oral turn taking, or listening to the teacher out of the total number of student responses coded.

Because all category 7 codes were frequently coded and because multiple category 7 codes were almost always coded during a five-minute segment, a decision was made to consider the incidence of active (reading, writing, manipulation) and passive (reading turn taking, oral turn taking, and listening) out of all category 7 codes recorded.

To ensure maximum consistency across a large number of observers, one member of the research team read through all of the observations to assess interrater reliability. All disagreements were checked by a second member of the research team, and this second team member agreed with the first member in 97% of the cases. All disagreements between the first and second research team member were resolved by a third research team member.

Descriptive Data From the Classroom Observations

The results from the classroom observations are useful data in their own right (see Table 2), quite independent of their relationship to student growth. In a

Table 2
Incidence of classroom factors by grade

	Kindergarten mean percentage of segments observed	Grade 1 mean percentage of segments observed	Grades 2–3 mean percentage of segments observed	Grades 4–6 mean percentage of segments observed
$n =$	16	14	31	33
Whole group*	.72 (.28)	.51 (.29)	.59 (.29)	.68 (.27)
Small group*	.25 (.28)	.34 (.24)	.36 (.29)	.22 (.25)
Word skills**	1.07 (.80)	1.00 (.79)	.26 (.38)	.10 (.24)
Comprehension skills**	.05 (.09)	.04 (.09)	.12 (17)	.24 (.26)
Meaning of text**	.40 (.33)	.37 (.15)	.57 (.34)	.57 (.34)
Lower level	.36 (.31)	.34 (.15)	.44 (.26)	.45 (.26)
Higher level	.05 (.08)	.03 (.06)	.13 (.18)	.21 (.29)
Telling*	.50 (.22)	.55 (.16)	.51 (.22)	.60 (.25)
Recitation*	.58 (.19)	.65 (.20)	.64 (.16)	.56 (.19)
Coaching*	.20 (.25)	.25 (.15)	.19 (.15)	.13 (.12)
Active responding***	.27 (.13)	.28 (.11)	.29 (.15)	.34 (.14)
Passive responding***	.44 (.12)	.49 (.14)	.57 (.16)	.66 (.14)

*   Percentage of segments coded out of all five-minute segments coded.
**   Percentage of segments coded out of all five-minute reading segments.
***   Percentage of responses coded out of total number of category 7 responses.

sense, they capture the nature of classroom instruction in schools like those in which we spent the year observing teachers and testing children. These data also provide us with an opportunity to compare what was going on in these "aspiring" schools with the practices we observed two years earlier in our study of low-income, high-performing schools (Taylor et al., 2000) as well as with other research on effective teaching of reading.

Grouping Practices

Across all grades, whole-group instruction was coded more often than small-group instruction. In contrast, a greater occurrence of small-group rather than whole-group instruction was found to be a characteristic of the most effective schools in our earlier study of primary-grade reading instruction in schools that were beating the odds (Taylor et al., 2000). These findings from the observations are not exclusive to schools serving high-poverty populations. Similar results have emerged from a case study we conducted in a school where only 30% of the students qualified for subsidized lunch.

Balance Between Word Work and Comprehension Work

Not surprisingly, word-level activities during reading were observed more in grades K–1 than 2–3 or 4–6, and comprehension work was seldom observed in the primary grades. These findings are similar to those in our previous study of primary-grade reading instruction in effective, low-income schools (Taylor et al., 2000), where we found that word-level activities were infrequently observed in grade 3 and that comprehension skill or strategy work was seldom observed in grades 1–3. The findings related to word skill activities also suggest that teachers are focusing on phonics instruction in kindergarten and first grade, a finding compatible with the recommendations of the National Reading Panel Report (National Institute of Child Health and Human Development, 2000), "that phonics instruction taught early proved much more effective than phonics instruction introduced after first grade" (p. 2-85).

Across all grades a relatively small amount of higher level questioning or writing related to stories read was observed. These findings are, unfortunately, all too consistent with the results of our earlier study (Taylor et al., 2000). It is important to note that effective teachers and teachers in more effective schools are more frequently observed asking higher level questions than less effective teachers and teachers in less effective schools (Knapp, 1995; Taylor, Pressley, & Pearson, 2000).

Teachers' Interaction Styles

Telling and recitation were major interaction styles of teachers in all grades; coaching was seldom observed. In our earlier study (Taylor, Pearson, et al., 2000), teacher interaction style varied by level of teacher accomplishment: The least accomplished teachers preferred telling while the most accomplished preferred coaching as their primary interaction style.

Students' Active Versus Passive Involvement

Across all grades, students in the present study were engaged in passive responding more often than in active responding. Passive responding included turn taking during oral reading (e.g., round robin), oral turn taking, or listening to the teacher. Active responding included reading, writing, and manipulating. In contrast, Pressley et al. (2001) found that exemplary first-grade teachers had their students actively engaged in actual reading and writing.

Students' Reading Growth and Teacher Practices

To take a closer look at the relationships between teacher practices during literacy instruction and students' reading and writing growth, we conducted Hierarchical Linear Modeling (HLM) analyses (Bryk & Raudenbush, 1992). The outcome measures for these analyses were reading fluency (as measured by the number of words read correctly on a grade-level passage in one minute) and comprehension (as measured by the comprehension subtest of the Gates-MacGinitie reading tests). Although we were interested in the possible effects of all 11 coded practices, only those practices that were found to be significantly related to students' reading growth are discussed here. The details of these analyses appear in the report of the larger study (Taylor et al., 2001).

Fluency

The HLM analysis for grade 1 revealed that the incidence of students coded as actively responding was positively related to spring fluency scores, after accounting for fall scores. For grades 2–3, the HLM analysis revealed that telling had a significant negative relationship with regard to spring fluency scores (after accounting for fall scores).

Reading Comprehension

Only the classroom-level HLM analysis for grades 4–6 showed significant differences related to reading comprehension. Time spent on higher-level questions had a significant positive relationship and telling had a significant negative relationship with regard to spring comprehension scores (after accounting for fall scores).

Emergent Literacy in Kindergarten

For kindergarten, there were fall scores only for the children identified by their teachers as low and average in literacy abilities. The HLM analysis revealed that time spent on word-level activities (positively related) and telling (negatively related) had significant relationships with regard to spring letter-name scores (after accounting for fall scores). The HLM analysis showed that telling was negatively related to spring phonemic awareness scores (after accounting for fall scores). For concepts of print, the HLM analysis revealed that small-group instruction had a significant positive relationship and telling had significant negative relationship with regard to spring scores (after accounting for fall scores). For word dictation, the HLM analysis revealed that telling was negatively related to spring scores (after accounting for fall letter-name scores).

Summary of Classroom Findings and Descriptions of More Helpful and Less Helpful Classroom Practices

The descriptive data of typical effective classrooms indicate that, in general, a shift in certain teaching practices, such as higher level questioning, style of interacting, and encouraging active pupil involvement, may be warranted. The HLM results from the current study further underscore this point. Based on the HLM analyses, reliance on telling as an interaction style was not found to be beneficial to students' reading growth. Several practices were found to be beneficial at particular grade levels: active responding (grade 1), small-group instruction (kindergarten), word skill work (kindergarten), and higher-level questions (grades 4–6).

To better explain the findings related to classroom factors, we provide descriptions of teachers who illustrate positive practices. We also provide examples from classrooms in which telling was a common strategy in order to better describe this less helpful practice. These examples were reconstructed from our field notes, and wherever possible, we used direct quotes from teachers and students. All names are pseudonyms.

Kindergarten

Ginger Smith embodied all of the characteristics of an effective kindergarten teacher. She taught reading in groups of six. She emphasized word work: The children made words with plastic letters, practiced sight words in drill and game activities, generated rhyming words, generated words starting with the same sound as a key word such as *sun*, and tried to write the sounds they heard as they wrote in their journals.

Instead of telling children information, Ginger involved her students at every turn. For example, as they listened to the sounds in *fan*, they slid their hand from their shoulder to their elbow, then to their wrist and chorally chimed, /fff-aaa-nnn/. For rhymes, the children came up with the words themselves.

Ginger:	What rhymes with boat?
Students:	*moat, coat, boat, float, troat, soat.*
Ginger:	That's great. You can make up words.

During making words activities, the children manipulated their own set of letters as Ginger coached:

Let's do *tub*. Listen to the middle sound. It's not *tab*, it's not *tob*. It's /ttt-uuu-bbb/. You need a letter for /uuu/.

While reading leveled books, students tracked with their fingers as they read independently from their own copies. If they got stuck on a word, Ginger coached by providing hints instead of telling them the word. They frequently read chorally instead of taking turns. While completing a journal entry about their favorite book, children wrote their own sentence(s) while Ginger gave feedback. In another instance, a child needed help with *like*. Ginger enunciated the sounds but allowed the child to generate the letters.

Grade 1

Aaron Brown balanced whole-group and small-group instruction in approximately equal proportions. Instead of relying on telling, Aaron used a recitation framework for discussions, provided coaching through scaffolding techniques, and emphasized students' active involvement in their own learning experiences. As children were rereading familiar stories independently in their small guided reading group, Aaron often listened to individual children. In these settings, as the opportunity arose, he would coach them on a word-recognition strategy as they struggled to decode a word. The following example describes his actions when a child was stuck on *door*.

Aaron:	Think of how it begins.
Child:	Door.
Aaron:	How did you know it was *door*?
Child:	The *d* and the *r*.
Aaron:	What would be a good strategy to use if you didn't know that word?
Several students:	Chunk it, think about what would make sense, skip it.

Later in the lesson as they were reading, they skipped a word, came back to it, and talked about how they had used this particular strategy to figure out the word.

Additional interactions revealed Aaron's commitment to students' active involvement in all of their literacy activities:

1. When a different group couldn't answer a question about how a character had changed, Aaron suggested that they search the book for a clue instead of telling them the answer.

2. As an introduction to a writing activity, Aaron asked students to think of something they enjoyed doing with a family member and share that with a partner.

3. When a student asked about the spelling of a word, instead of spelling it for him, Aaron encouraged the student to think of other ways to find the answer. This elicited a range of independent strategies such as sound it out, look on the word wall, or look in the spelling book. Aaron circulated, checked work, and coached children with spelling and with ideas as they were writing.

In contrast, a first-grade teacher who relied on telling revealed a different pattern of interaction. For example, she generated a morning message for the class rather than asking the students to coconstruct it. Instead of asking students how to spell the words in her sentence, she spelled "Today is a rainy day" and then asked the class to recite what she wrote. When she asked the question, "Why do clouds make rain?" she called on two children who couldn't answer and then answered the question herself instead of coaching children to generate an answer by rephrasing the question or providing further prompts.

In word-level work, she sounded out a word herself and then had the children repeat it, instead of coaching them to sound out the word. After asking the meaning of a word and receiving no immediate answer, she answered herself when she could have had students generate a definition after providing the word in the context of a sentence. As children were writing in their journal, she consistently told her students how to spell a word instead of determining which parts they could spell themselves.

Another telling-oriented first-grade teacher reminded children that they had learned that /ea/ could have the short sound as in *feather*, as opposed to asking them what sounds they had learned for /ea/. When discussing a story on machines, this teacher explained how a shovel worked instead of involving the students in constructing an explanation.

Grades 2–3

Terry Miller was a second-grade teacher who relied on coaching and active responding on the part of the children instead of telling as a teaching style. As children were working on animal reports, Terry circulated and coached:

> How would you spell *nuts*? Say the word slowly.
>
> You need to add some more ideas to this paragraph. Where can you look?
>
> How can a polar bear live in the snow? They have thick fur to keep them warm? Okay, add that idea here.

Virginia Gray, a third-grade teacher, also used very little telling in her teaching. She started her reading lessons with the whole group, listing the lesson objectives on the chalkboard and having children read them aloud. She led them through a quick picture walk, looking at the pictures and making predictions, which she wrote on the chalkboard. Then the children read the story silently, paying attention because they knew they were expected to participate in the small-group discussions that followed. They then formed groups of four in which one student was the leader and one was the recorder. Each group had a list of lower and higher level questions to answer on the story. During this time, Virginia circulated, took notes, and coached as children answered their questions. When the whole group got back together to share their answers, Virginia used coaching techniques to encourage children to elaborate on their ideas.

In contrast, a telling-oriented second-grade teacher missed many opportunities to involve the children. Here is her introduction to a new book:

> Teacher: The previous book we read by Ezra Jack Keats, *The Trip* (1978, William Morrow), was a story about a boy who was moving to a new house. Now we'll read a new one, *Peter's Chair* (1998, Puffin). Keats's books look similar. He is the author and the illustrator. I think the pictures look like wallpaper.

There could have been many ways for the teacher to bring the children into the conversation. As the teacher was reading aloud to the group, she did not stop to ask questions, only to interject a few ideas.

> Teacher: He was being sneaky. I couldn't see him hiding, could you?

After reading, the teacher explained the story to the group as opposed to asking them to explain it to her.

> Teacher: At the beginning he wanted to keep the chair for himself. That's being selfish.

Grades 4–6

John Merryweather was a sixth-grade teacher who engaged his students in frequent lower and higher level questioning on the stories they read, emphasized small groups for discussing novels, taught comprehension strategies, and did all of this with less telling and more coaching as an interaction style. When reading *The Best Christmas Pageant Ever* (Barbara Robinson, 1982, HarperCollins), John had his students write a prediction in their journal before continuing to read.

> John: What do you think Alice is up to? Write your idea in your response journal.

As the class continued to read, John called four of his struggling readers to a table at the back of the room so he could coach them in word recognition. When John returned to the larger group, he asked them to agree or disagree in their response journal with a quote from the book. As the children were writing, he coached an English as a second language child with his answer and then told him he was going to call on him to share that answer with the class. After a few individuals shared their journal responses with the class, the class went to work preparing small-group presentations on questions and vocabulary related to the book to share the next day with the whole class.

In contrast, an intermediate teacher who relied on telling taught reading lessons to the whole class with a great deal of teacher talk, as in the following exchange:

Teacher: What kind of bird is an eaglet?

Without stopping for an answer, he continued,

Teacher: If you put *et*, or *ette* at the end of a word it refers to something being small. So an eaglet is a small eagle.

As the teacher read a basal story to the class, he frequently stopped to tell students about information in the story. As he continued to read aloud to the students from their basal, he stopped to explain the story to the class as opposed to asking them to explain it to him.

Teacher: The point of the story is that the father had to accept the fact that he would never have a son and should be happy with his daughter.

The overwhelming sense one gets in examining our observational notes is that some teachers feel so compelled to make sure that key information is discussed that they bring it up themselves, thereby robbing students of opportunities to test their own knowledge and skill acquisition, and themselves of opportunities to evaluate students' growth toward independence. This distinction is rendered all the more important by the consistent relationship we found between an emphasis on telling and lower student achievement at most grade levels.

How Is as Important as What

We believe that the most interesting data from the larger study (Taylor et al., 2001) came from the observational data on classroom reading instruction. A consistent finding of the HLM analyses was that the more a teacher was coded as telling children information, the less the children grew in reading achievement. This finding is compatible with our earlier research which

---

Sample of observational notes

9:38 Small group continues. T is taking running record of child's reading. Others reading familiar books. Next, T coaches boy on sounding out *discovered*. Covers up word parts as he says remaining parts. T: Does that make sense? T: What is another way to say this part [cov with short o]? T passes out new book. T has students share what the word *creature* means. Ss: animals, monsters, dinosaurs, Dr. Frankenstein. 9:42

11/12 OT (On Task)	C/s/r	r/t/a/r	wr/t/c/or(indv)	v/t/r/or-tt
	Levels 123	4567	4567	4567

---

found that less-accomplished teachers engaged in much more telling than highly accomplished teachers (Taylor et al., 2000).

This does not mean that teachers should never tell students information; it would be impossible to teach without doing so. However, excessive amounts of "telling," especially in situations where coaching students to come up with their own responses is possible, may rob children of the opportunity to take responsibility for their own skills and strategies. Telling is indicative of a strong teacher-directed stance, as opposed to a student-support stance toward teaching (e.g., coaching, modeling, and other forms of scaffolding). Our hope is that by receiving feedback on the incidence of telling in one's literacy teaching, teachers may be able to shift somewhat on the continuum of teacher-to-student directedness if their data from the classroom observations suggest that this would be beneficial. This shift, in turn, will ideally lead to enhanced student performance. Over the subsequent years of the current project, as we provide teachers and schools with data on teaching practices tied to students' performance, we plan to investigate the degree to which teaching practices at the classroom and the school level shift toward those practices identified as more effective.

Similarly, students in grade 1 demonstrated more growth in reading fluency the more they were coded as actively, as opposed to passively, responding to reading activities. Instead of listening to the teacher or engaging in reading turn taking or oral turn-taking, these students were observed actually reading or writing more often than other students. Similar findings about the large amounts of time students were actually reading and writing were reported by Pressley et al. (2001) in their study of exemplary first-grade teachers.

We did find some evidence for the differential impact of curricular activities across grade levels. Higher-level questions emerged as a significant predictor of growth in grades 4-6, while word work emerged most clearly in kindergarten. In light of these findings and those of the National Reading

Panel Report (National Institute of Child Health and Human Development, 2000), a gradual shift in emphasis may be warranted. However, this does not mean that comprehension should be delayed until grade 4 or that word work should end in the primary grades, only that some shift in emphasis seems warranted. Clearly more research is needed to help teachers determine the optimum balance between word work and comprehension work for their particular students at any given grade level.

Classroom literacy instruction needs to reflect best practices as identified in the research. In addition to *what* teachers teach, the findings at the classroom level in the current study in corroboration with earlier research suggest that how teachers teach is also important to consider when seeking to make changes in reading instruction to improve students' reading achievement. The results of this study show that an overreliance on telling as an interaction mode, indicative of a strong teacher-directed stance, does not appear to be very effective for enhancing students' reading growth. Currently, the improvement of children's reading achievement is a major goal in the United States (Bush, 2001). Schools know that a wealth of information exists to help them move toward this goal, but putting all of the relevant pieces together remains a challenge. Ongoing professional development in which teachers work together within buildings to reflect on their practice is one important piece of the total package that is needed to ensure that "no child is left behind" (Bush, 2001).

To paraphrase, we appear headed on a march toward full literacy that includes all U.S. children in the parade. If we are serious about the metaphor of "leaving no child behind," our data would suggest that we, as professionals, must possess the conviction, the knowledge, and the teaching techniques necessary to ensure that every child in that march is equipped with a "full backpack" of skills, strategies, habits, and dispositions toward literacy.

REFERENCES

Brophy, J. (1973). Stability of teacher effectiveness. *American Educational Research Journal, 10*, 245–252.

Bryk, A.S., & Raudenbush, S.W. (1992). *Hierarchical linear models*. Newbury Park, CA: Sage.

Bush, G.W. (2001). *No child left behind*. Washington, DC: Office of the President.

Deno, S. (1985). Curriculum-based measurement: The emerging alternative. *Exceptional Children, 52*(2), 199–232.

Dunkin, M., & Biddle, B. (1974). *The study of teaching*. New York: Holt, Rinehart, & Winston.

Flanders, N. (1970). *Analyzing teacher behavior*. Reading, MA: Addison-Wesley.

Knapp, M.S. (1995). *Teaching for meaning in high-poverty classrooms*. New York: Teachers College Press.

National Institute of Child Health and Human Development. (2000). *Report of the National Reading Panel. Teaching children to read: An evidence-based assessment of the scientific re-*

search literature on reading and its implications for reading instruction (NIH Publication No. 00-4769). Washington, DC: U.S. Government Printing Office.

Pikulski, J. (1996). *The emergent literacy survey*. Boston: Houghton Mifflin.

Pressley, M., Wharton-McDonald, R., Allington, R., Block, C.C., Morrow, L., Tracey, D., et al. (2001). A study of effective first-grade literacy instruction. *Scientific Studies of Reading, 5,* 35-58.

Roehler, L.R., & Duffy, G.G. (1984). Direct explanation of comprehension processes. In G.G. Duffy, L.R. Roehler, & J. Mason (Eds.), *Comprehension instruction: Perspectives and suggestions* (pp. 265-280). New York: Longman.

Scanlon, D.M., & Gelzheiser, L.M. (1992). *Study center observation system*. Unpublished manuscript, University of Albany, State University of New York, Child Research and Study Center, Albany, NY.

Stallings, J., & Kaskowitz, D. (1974). *Follow through classroom observation evaluation 1972-73* (SRI Project URU-7370). Stanford, CA: Stanford Research Institute.

Taylor, B.M. (1991). *A test of phonemic awareness for classroom use*. Minneapolis: University of Minnesota.

Taylor, B.M., & Pearson, P.D. (2000). *The CIERA school change classroom observation scheme*. Minneapolis: University of Minnesota.

Taylor, B.M., & Pearson, P.D. (2001). The CIERA School Change Project: Translating research on effective reading instruction and school reform into practice in high-poverty elementary schools. In C.M. Roller (Ed.), *Learning to teach reading: Setting the research agenda* (pp. 180-189). Newark, DE: International Reading Association.

Taylor, B.M., Pearson, P.D., Clark, K., & Walpole, S. (2000). Effective schools and accomplished teachers: Lessons about primary grade reading instruction in low-income schools. *The Elementary School Journal, 101,* 121-166.

Taylor, B.M., Pearson, P.D., Peterson, D., & Rodriguez, M.C. (2001). *Year one of the CIERA school change project: Supporting schools as they implement home-grown reading reform.* Minneapolis: University of Minnesota.

Taylor, B.M., Pressley, M.P., & Pearson, P.D. (2000). *Research-supported characteristics of teachers and schools that promote reading achievement.* Washington, DC: National Education Association, Reading Matters Research Report.

Taking Seriously the Idea of Reform: One High School's Efforts to Make Reading More Responsive to All Students

William G. Brozo and Charles H. Hargis

A hard fact of U.S. high school life is that within any classroom the range of reading abilities can be enormous (Hargis, 1997; Stanovich, 1986). This range may be wider than ever today as general education classes give way to growing numbers of inclusion students (Pearman, Huang, & Mellblom, 1997). We became reacquainted with the reality of this situation at Mountain View High School (the school's name and all names of individuals in this article are pseudonyms) where, as literacy consultants, we were asked to interpret for faculty the results of standardized reading testing. A 10th-grade teacher, for instance, had a staggering 15-grade-level spread in one of his classes. Within that tremendous range, we found 9 out of 24 students had reading levels at the 8th grade or below; 7 were within the 9th- to 10th-grade interval; and 8 had scores from the 11th-grade to nearly the 19th-grade level. When these results were considered relative to the 10.2 readability estimate of the textbook (as part of our work, we ran five 100-word text samples from every core textbook in use at Mountain View through a word-processing program and calculated readability using the built-in Flesch-Kincaid formula) we realized that for over one third of his students, the text was too difficult to read. For another third, it might not be challenging enough to make the content interesting or engaging. The teacher could only shake his head in bewilderment and respond, "That's why so many of us teach to the middle."

This article is a description of our experiences at Mountain View High, where teachers and administrators used a reading grant to re-create the literate culture of the school. We detail how reading achievement testing was conducted and the results were translated into effective literacy reforms designed to go beyond teaching to the middle. Within a discussion of these initiatives we track the experiences of two students at either end of the reading ability continuum and the effects the initiatives had on them.

Reprinted from *Journal of Adolescent & Adult Literacy*, 47, 14–23, September 2003.

The Testing Initiative

Allington (2002) asserted that good teachers know their students well, know where to begin appropriate instruction, and know how to recognize growth. Identifying a starting point requires gathering relevant information about students' skills, abilities, and knowledge. Without this essential information, teachers cannot account for individual differences in their planning or track progress. Although we believe the best assessments of learning should occur within the context of daily instruction and situated literacy activities (Brozo & Simpson, 2003; Hargis, 1999), we also believe, as do others (Stiggins, 2002), that if assessment results can inform teachers and learners in ways that lead to improvement of the teaching and learning process, then a range of potentially viable assessment options are possible. One of those options—standardized reading achievement testing—provided Mountain View teachers with important data for moving forward with needed literacy reforms.

In September of 2000, we were contracted by Mountain View High School to provide consulting services in fulfillment of the Tennessee Goals 2000 grant awarded to the school. The overarching goal of the grant was to determine the reading abilities of all students and the effectiveness of initiatives to improve them. Because Mountain View hadn't been notified of the grant award until nearly six weeks into its modified school year, which began in late July, we were faced with the immediate onset of the grant's timetable. One of the first questions we posed to the administrative team was whether current reading achievement scores were available for all students. We were eager to avoid redundant testing, if possible. When we were told the only test data the district had were Iowa Silent Reading Test scores for current ninth graders given the previous spring, we began an immediate search for a pre- and postproject assessment instrument appropriate for the entire student body.

In collaboration with school staff, it was decided that reading achievement testing would occur first to determine the students' range of needs before relevant initiatives would be implemented. It was also decided that the instruments used for this purpose would be used to evaluate the overall effectiveness of the grant program at the end of the school year.

The tests we administered had to have recognized technical adequacy and be sufficiently sensitive to measure achievement levels at the extremes of the reading achievement continuum in each of the high school grades. The tests would also have to be easy to administer to large groups in order to minimize disruption to teachers' and students' daily routines. We decided on the Gates-MacGinitie Reading Tests (2000) and the Nelson-Denny Reading Test

(1993). The two tests have similar formats with vocabulary and passage comprehension subtests. The different tests of the Gates-MacGinitie range from 1st through 12th grade; the Nelson-Denny tests range from grade 11 to 18.9. According to Buros (2001), both are psychometrically mature, and the two in combination made it possible to find the most sensitive level of test difficulty for each student. This was especially important when using the instruments to measure end-of-year progress.

Because of the wide range of ability we expected the students to exhibit, we needed a means of estimating which students should get which test or test level. This was vital to our intent to match individual students with the most sensitive test for each. Because information on students' reading achievement was not available, we searched for a convenient and efficient screening mechanism that would yield a reading level estimate for each student.

We discovered in a meeting with the curriculum specialist that the school had a site license to administer the STAR (see Buros, 2001, for a review of its technical qualities), the computerized reading test that accompanies the Accelerated Reader program. The program was not uniformly used at Mountain View but was serving as a supplement for the English teacher who taught the ninth graders. The school had a sufficient number of computers to make it possible for the entire student body to route through the two computer labs and take the STAR in one day. Make-ups were scheduled for the following day. STAR software calculated a score and an instructional reading level for each student.

With these results in hand, we assigned the appropriate Gates or Nelson-Denny test to students. With the help of the curriculum specialist, we set a testing date for early November and administered the tests during one 90-minute instructional block. Only a couple of mix-ups occurred in an otherwise smooth morning of testing. The make-ups were scheduled within a couple of days, which ensured that all 346 students had been tested. When pretest scoring was completed, the data were assembled alphabetically by grade so teachers could be apprised of the reading skill level of each of their students.

Building a Shared Reform Agenda and Implementing Literacy Reforms

Upon completion of pretesting we began intense collaboration with Mountain View faculty and staff. Although by then it was the middle of November and the administration was eager to see the implementation of a new literacy program, we had no desire to impose a unilaterally designed plan on teachers. Instead, in order to ensure that as many as possible felt vested in the reform process, we requested and were given the opportunity to meet several times within a couple of weeks with all potential stakeholders.

These meetings were critical because overall pretest results revealed that nearly 35% of Mountain View students were reading one or more grade levels below grade placement—and, in many cases, far below the expected grade level. Another 18% were reading one or more grade levels beyond expectation. Many teachers were not aware of the reading ability levels of their students, and once presented with the pretest results they found themselves forced to adjust their evaluation of individual student performance in their classes. For example, Martin, an 11th-grade math teacher, had to rethink whether Tony, one of his students, was performing poorly out of "laziness" or because he was reading at the fifth-grade level. Conversely, Pam, who taught 11th-grade English, began wondering if Tamika, who fell just one year shy of reaching the maximum on the Nelson-Denny by achieving a grade equivalent of 17.9, was disengaged in her class out of boredom.

Taking frequent opportunities to converse with individual faculty members about their students' pretest performances also allowed us to gather feedback on ideas for infusing the curriculum with a variety of literacy experiences and strategies to meet students' varied needs. Meetings occurred before and after classes and during lunch and planning periods. We held focus sessions with the grant-writing team to become better acquainted with the original goals of the grant and discuss which ones could be feasibly met given students' reading achievement. We brainstormed separately with department chairs, English teachers, the curriculum director, and the administrative team on potential initiatives to meet students' wide range of abilities. We attended whole-school faculty meetings where reading test results were shared again, the relative merits of proposed initiatives were debated, an action plan was approved, and the logistics of implementing the plan were reviewed. We also participated in a Q&A session about the literacy reform plan with the school board and superintendent.

In the end, three initiatives were endorsed by the administration and a majority of the faculty: sustained silent reading, reading young adult novels in the content classroom, and making alternatives to the textbook available for struggling students and superior readers. The Mountain View administrative staff wanted to add one additional support option for students who had very low scores on the achievement test but were not receiving special education services. This evolved into a "Reading Buddy" program arranged during the second half of one class block for qualifying students. After launching these initiatives, we held frequent formal and informal sessions with individuals, small groups, and the whole staff to share concerns and successes. These frank and open conversations proved invaluable for nurturing commitment to the literacy reforms.

For the remainder of this article we follow Tony and Tamika, the two students mentioned earlier, through the literacy initiatives launched at Mountain View. By following these students from their pretest performance, through strategies implemented on their behalf, to posttest performance, we hope to personalize the reforms and demonstrate how schoolwide efforts and classroom instructional modifications led to improved and sustained growth for individual students.

Sustained Silent Reading

Once children have mastered basic reading skills, the surest road to a richer vocabulary and expanded literacy is wide and sustained reading (Allington, 2002; Anderson, Wilson, & Fielding, 1988; Cipielewski & Stanovich, 1992; Taylor, Frye, & Maruyama, 1990). Yet, many adolescents read less than their peers of 30 years ago (Carlson, 1999; Glenn, 1994; Libsch & Breslow, 1996) or, even more alarming, choose not to read at all (Beers, 1996; Schumm & Saumell, 1994). The less time young people spend with books and print, the less growth they exhibit on measures of vocabulary and reading achievement (Durrell, 1969; Gardiner, 2001; Glenn, 1994). This pattern seems to be particularly common among minority youth (Larson, Richards, Sims, & Dworkin, 2001), who score lower on achievement tests and are admitted to colleges in smaller numbers relative to other groups (Ogbu, 1994).

The Sustained Silent Reading (SSR) initiative at Mountain View, which students named "Get Ready to Read," was launched to ensure that all students—regardless of ability—developed the reading habit, and all teachers participated in modeling the pleasure of self-selected reading. Using grant funds, the librarian and English department head purchased scores of high-interest young adult novels and magazines covering a wide range of reading levels, which were compiled into class sets. Metal racks were placed in every teacher's classroom to hold the SSR material. Drop boxes were set up at several locations in the building, and students were encouraged to donate a favorite paperback to the cause. This netted many additional books for the classroom libraries. One day per week during homeroom, approximately 25 minutes were set aside for SSR; many teachers added days on their own as they discovered the advantages of having students involved in focused, constructive activity and the enjoyment of recreational reading during the school day.

Tony

Tony's homeroom was with Mr. Watson, the chemistry teacher. Mr. Watson, one of the assistant football coaches, had many of his players in homeroom, including Tony. Mr. Watson would spend the 25 minutes between A and B blocks planning strategy with other coaches, making telephone calls, and talking with players. After a couple of weeks of SSR, however, this routine was slowly replaced by reading. We emphasized to Mr. Watson that his leadership role offered him a special opportunity to model recreational reading habits for his ballplayers, many of whom were struggling readers. Initially, Tony's SSR material mimicked the selections of his coach, as he chose magazines such as *Sports Illustrated* and *Football Digest*. Tony eventually made his way through a couple of simple illustrated football biographies, one on Emmitt Smith (Stewart, 1996) and another about Brett Favre (Dougherty & Dougherty, 1999). By the end of the year, Tony became engrossed in an easier reading football novel, *The Heartbeat of Halftime* (Wunderli, 1996). Mr. Watson, knowing Tony's reading level, helped him select these books and encouraged Tony to give him feedback on how difficult they were. If Tony said a book was too "hard" Mr. Watson did his best to find an alternative from the SSR material on his bookrack or borrow books from other teachers.

Advocates of secondary school reform (Alvermann et al., 2002; Langer, 2000; Moore, Bean, Birdyshaw, & Rycik, 1999; Ruiz-de-Velasco, Fix, & Clewell, 2001) concur that students need multiple opportunities for engaged, sustained print encounters in the classroom every day. More to the point, the easier access is to interesting print materials, the more frequently adolescents read (McQuillan & Au, 2001). Lack of opportunities for regular, engaged reading may help account for why most students who are poor readers upon entry into high school remain so by the time of graduation (Cappella & Weinstein, 2001).

Tamika

From the outset, Tamika needed little encouragement to find reading material for SSR. Ms. Bly, her French and homeroom teacher, knew that with Tamika's exceptional reading abilities she was capable of handling any book on the adult market, so she brought to class several from her own collection. From January through May, Tamika went through *Drowning Ruth* (Schwarz, 2000), *She's Come Undone* (Lamb, 1997), *Vinegar Hill* (Ansay, 1994), and *Where the Heart Is* (Letts, 1998). Ms. Bly often chatted with Tamika during class breaks about the books they shared, and found her level of appreciation for the plots and characters remarkably sophisticated for a 16-year-old.

Reading Young Adult Novels in the Content Classroom

The practice of using novels anywhere other than the English classroom is rare at the high school level (Brozo & Simpson, 2003). We found that several Mountain View teachers were willing to try this approach once they knew that many of their students were unlikely to benefit from assigned textbook reading, because it was too difficult. We also overcame some initial reluctance by acquiring a large number of used class sets of books suitable for a variety of content area topics and themes and by conducting classroom demonstrations with novels.

Among the novels and information books that found their way into the subject area classrooms at Mountain View were the following: *Beggar's Ride* (Kress, 1996) in 10th-grade biology for the topic of genetics and genetic engineering; *Visions of Symmetry: Notebooks, Periodic Drawings, and Related Works of M.C. Escher* (Schattschneider, 1990) in a geometry class; and *King: Volume 1* (Anderson, 1993), a graphic novel about Martin Luther King used in ninth-grade English during the study of biography.

Tamika and Tony

Both Tamika and Tony were members of Mr. Turner's history class. We estimated his course textbook had a readability level of around 10.8, so it was ostensibly an appropriate book for the average 11th grader. However, Tamika's superior and Tony's limited reading abilities represented the range in his class. In a unit on World War II, we collaborated with Mr. Turner to develop curricular plans that included three different young adult novels related to the Holocaust: *Jacob's Rescue* (Drucker, 1994), *No Pretty Pictures* (Lobel, 1998), and *The Night Crossing* (Ackerman, 1995). In addition, several engaging, though easier to read, picture books were also made available to students [e.g., *Rose Blanche* (Innocenti, 1998); *The Holocaust, a History of Courage and Resistance* (Stadtler, 1996); *Tell Them We Remember: The Story of the Holocaust* (Bachrach, 1994)]. These materials were purchased with Goals 2000 grant monies. Mr. Turner introduced the novels with brief book talks, then allowed self-selection of favorites. With tactful prompting, he steered Tony in the direction of *Jacob's Rescue*, while inviting Tamika to read any of the books she would like. At least 15 minutes of class time were allotted for silent reading, after which students wrote answers to general questions meant to draw their attention to content in their books that coincided with or embellished upon ideas from the lectures. Each class session students discussed what was learned in the novels, comparing and contrasting that information with newly learned facts about the Holocaust and the Nazis.

Because *Jacob's Rescue* was written on a level of difficulty in line with Tony's reading ability, he was able to make steady progress over the three-week unit. He didn't complete the novel, but was enjoying it so much he finished it during "Get Ready to Read" time. Tamika, on the other hand, was able to complete all three novels within the three weeks. For extra credit, she created a multimedia report with character analyses, plot summaries, and major similarities and differences of the books. She also used special software to create graphic displays of the facts of the war and their effects on characters from the novels.

Alternative Texts in the Content Classroom

This initiative seemed necessary given the large number of Mountain View students who were reading two or more grade levels below their grade placement. As stated, for these students, engagement with the textbooks they encounter in their subject area classes is unrealistic if not impossible. This situation poses special challenges because most high school teachers do not have at their immediate disposal texts at a range of difficulty levels on the same topic. We discovered that the Internet offers access to vast amounts of public domain material on virtually any school-related topic. We gathered and reviewed course syllabi to guide our selection of readings. For example, for chemistry, we located and prepared easy readings on carbon bonding, the periodic table, and balancing equations. These texts were reformatted and given inviting covers to avoid stigmatizing struggling readers. When students were expected to consult their textbooks for information to solve problems or describe processes, the chemistry teacher, Mr. Watson, allowed his less skillful readers to use the alternative texts as their information source. See Sidebar for some helpful websites.

Tony

Modified texts became an important learning tool for Tony. According to his world geography teacher, Mr. Combs, Tony paid close attention during lecture but rarely was seen consulting the textbook to locate information or read assignments. Mr. Combs agreed to make available to Tony and his other struggling readers a variety of passages we had compiled from the Internet as well as the

URLs for content area topics and passages

Math
www2.hawaii.edu/suremath/home.html
www.tc.cornell.edu/Edu/MathSciGateway
http://forum.swarthmore.edu/dr.math/dr-math.html

Biology and Chemistry
www.ala.org/parentspage/greatsites/science.html
www.cellsalive.com
www.ornl.gov/hgmis/education/education.html
www.chem4kids.com

History
http://bensguide.gpo.gov
www.ala.org/parentspage/greatsites/people.html
http://grid.let.rug.nl/~welling/usa/revoultion.html

actual sites where easier readings on geopolitical topics could be found. One day, the class was studying the ethnic fighting in the former Yugoslavia. Sorting out the complexities of nationalism, culture, and historical boundaries in the region was particularly vexing for Tony. Mr. Combs gave the class a set of questions to answer using the textbook, other print sources and reference material, or the World Wide Web. Tony was provided with the URLs to two websites from which he was able to locate informative and simply composed passages about the topic. Reading them directly from the screen, Tony was able to complete most of the assignment.

Mr. Combs acknowledged that before modified text and URLs with easier readings were made available to Tony, he had completed very little reading and independent work. Now that these resources were available to Tony, he was able to remain a participating member of the geography class for the full 90-minute block.

Tamika

In her American government class, Ms. Hammond, the teacher, made available numerous readings taken off the World Wide Web on topics from federalism to details of the 14th Amendment to the U.S. Constitution. These texts were at a level of difficulty suitable for her best readers, several of whom, including Tamika, had achieved levels on the Nelson-Denny test well above the 10.7 readability level of her course textbook. To ensure involvement with these readings, Ms. Hammond had Tamika and her other high-ability students use them to gather additional information on textbook topics and report to the class about what was learned.

In one case, Tamika and a classmate read a number of Web-based articles on the topic of the Electoral College, which was the focus of much class conversation and analysis in the aftermath of the 2000 U.S. presidential election. The two students presented the views of current political scientists on the strengths and limitations of this unique electoral process in a point-counterpoint format.

Buddy Reading

The overarching goal of the literacy grant awarded to Mountain View was to improve the reading abilities of all the students and close the gap between the reading achievement level and the potential reading skill level for those students who had fallen significantly behind. The Mountain View administrative staff wanted a service created for struggling students who (a) had reading skill levels at or below the sixth grade and (b) did not qualify for or were not already receiving special education or special language support. Instead of relying exclusively on pull-out tutoring for these neediest students, we worked with the curriculum specialists at the elementary and the high school to implement a buddy reading program. The most potent benefit of such a program is that it imbues struggling readers with a sense of responsibility and purpose for improving their own abilities (Avery & Avery, 2001; Wilhelm, Dube, & Baker, 2001). Our approach matched a high schooler with a second or third grader.

Because the high school students' schedules were already set, those participating in the program had to take time out of one of their classes. The faculty who taught the students we identified for the program agreed to allow them to leave during the second half of an instructional block for three days per week. After a couple of orientation sessions, we settled into a routine that began by gathering at 10:30 a.m. and walking the short path around a duck pond to Mountain View Elementary, where our high schoolers paired up with their reading buddies in the library.

Tony

A total of 12 high school students, including Tony, participated in the program. Tony and his reading buddy, like the others, spent the 30 minutes involved in the following activities: (a) reading aloud from a favorite children's book, (b) filling out a log sheet upon a book's completion, (c) making an entry in a shared response journal, and (d) writing and making a book of their own. All participants were monitored to ensure they were reading material within or very close to their independent ranges and that they were making optimal use of their time together.

With our guidance, Tony prepared for the read-aloud by orally rehearsing the story at least two times, identifying vocabulary that might pose difficulty for his reading buddy, and preparing strategies to assist in decoding and contextual understanding.

One of the books Tony and his buddy, Mia, read together was *The Rainbow Fish* (Pfister, 1997). Tony helped her pronounce and work out the meanings of several words. When they concluded the story, Mia wanted to make her own cartoon book, so Tony helped her draw, color, and write captions.

The book they created was based on a fall outing to pick apples. The experience left a lasting impression on Mia. Mia brought in photographs her mother had taken of her in an apple tree, filling a bushel and eating apples. These and the text were placed on pages Tony cut in the shape of apples. At the end of the year, we held a reception to showcase the reading buddies' work. The principal, curriculum specialists, parents, and other teachers attended and offered their praise and congratulations.

During the four months of the program, Tony and Mia read several children's books, and although they were relatively simple, the additional reading practice seemed to improve Tony's fluency and confidence. For instance, as Tony learned of Mia's interest in soccer, he helped her find books on the topic in the elementary school library and read several others to her that we supplied for him.

Buddy reading helped Tony view himself as a reader in a new way. We observed how his former complacent attitude toward reading gave way to active participation, concern replaced antipathy, and engagement overcame disinterest. Not all students in the buddy reading program responded as enthusiastically, but each participant did spend more time in sustained print encounters that might not have occurred without the program.

Posttesting and a Postscript

In mid-May 2001, just a couple of weeks before the end of the school year, Mountain View students were administered the same tests they took in November in order to determine if reading achievement gains had been made. Overall, there was significant improvement. For example, nearly half the students increased their scores by two or more grade levels, while another third maintained their pretest scores with an average grade equivalent of 12.5. Tony's Gates-MacGinitie posttest reading level of 7.0 was nearly two grade levels higher than his pretest score of 5.2. Although Tamika's exceptionally high pretest score of 17.9 on the Nelson-Denny left little room for improvement, she did manage to raise it to 18.2.

Improved test performance may be a good indicator of reading growth, but perhaps more significant were reports from Tony's and Tamika's teachers that specific information on students' reading levels and strategies for accommodating them brought about improved classroom performance. Feedback from his teachers indicated that Tony was participating more actively in class, completing more assignments, and generally making a greater effort to read. His participation seemed to contribute to the modest though meaningful rise in his grade point average (GPA) from the equivalent of a low "D" the first six weeks to a solid "C" in the last grading period. By the end of the school year, Tamika's high academic potential was realized as she raised her GPA from a 3.0 to a 3.78 on a 4.0 scale.

Whether the gains observed are greater and the class performance better than might have occurred without the literacy initiatives undertaken at Mountain View, we cannot say. This project was not a controlled experiment, and previous reading achievement data were not available to compare with our findings. We believe, however, that it is unlikely any of the reforms would have been implemented but for two critical factors: building and maintaining a reform community, and making teachers and administrators aware of students' specific reading ability levels through reading achievement testing.

As professors and researchers in adolescent literacy, we realize that none of the initiatives established at Mountain View High School are especially novel. At the same time, we know that getting content area teachers to play an active role in integrating literacy throughout the curriculum is never easy (Barry, 1997; Bintz, 1997; O'Brien, Stewart, & Moje, 1995). Some recent findings have confirmed earlier explanations for the lack of penetration of literacy innovations into secondary school culture. For example, in one study (Zipperer, Worley, Sisson, & Said, 2002) over 40% of high school teachers said they did not feel competent addressing reading problems or planning instruction to foster reading development, while another 30% were unsure of their competencies. In another study (Sunderman, Amoa, & Meyers, 2001) of the constraints on implementation of California's reading initiative in middle and high schools, the authors concluded that "The organization of secondary schools and middle and high school teachers who are trained as subject matter specialists are challenges schools confront as they respond to the reading deficiencies of their students" (p. 675). In Lester's (2000) review of the literature, he found that many secondary-level teachers perceived literacy instruction in high school as low priority, unnecessary, the responsibility of an English or reading teacher, or a burdensome addition to an already full workload. Given this state of affairs it should not be surprising to learn that comprehensive and coherent reading programs in U.S. high schools are not common, and, in fact, the trend has been toward a reduction in secondary reading services (Barry, 1997). This explains why secondary school reformers continue to assert that much remains to be done to make reading more engaging and literacy instruction more responsive to adolescents' needs.

Making instruction more responsive to students' reading needs was achieved by many teachers at Mountain View, even though the initiatives they employed to do so might appear to be commonplace to many of us. In our year there, we witnessed several intelligent and concerned teachers and administrators taking seriously the idea that the grant they received could be used as a catalyst for change. Certainly, not all teachers bought into this idea. For instance, Pam, Tamika's English teacher, made no instructional modifications for students in spite of being apprised of their reading achievement levels. However, like all of her colleagues, Pam chose to participate once a week in SSR time. Many of the other teachers recognized the potential of enacting all of the reforms they had helped craft and remained committed to the idea that better readers make better students in every subject area (Campbell, Hombo, & Mazzeo, 2000).

REFERENCES

Ackerman, K. (1995). *The night crossing*. New York: Random House.

Allington, R.L. (2002). What I've learned about effective reading instruction. *Phi Delta Kappan, 85*, 740-747.

Alvermann, D., Boyd, F., Brozo, W., Hinchman, K., Moore, D., & Sturtevant, E. (2002). *Principled practices for a literate America: A framework for literacy and learning in the upper grades*. New York: Carnegie Corporation.

Anderson, H.C. (1993). *King: Volume 1*. Seattle, WA: Fantagraphics.

Anderson, R.C., Wilson, P., & Fielding, L. (1988). Growth in reading and how children spend their time outside of school. *Reading Research Quarterly, 23*, 285-303.

Ansay, A.M. (1994). *Vinegar hill*. New York: Viking Penguin.

Avery, C., & Avery, K.B. (2001). Kids teaching kids. *Journal of Adolescent & Adult Literacy, 44*, 434-435.

Bachrach, S. (1994). *Tell them we remember: The story of the Holocaust*. New York: Little, Brown.

Barry, A. (1997). High school reading programs revisited. *Journal of Adolescent & Adult Literacy, 40*, 524-531.

Beers, K. (1996). No time, no interest, no way: The three voices of aliteracy. *School Library Journal, 42*, 30-41.

Bintz, W. (1997). Exploring reading nightmares of middle and secondary school teachers. *Journal of Adolescent & Adult Literacy, 41*, 12-25.

Brozo, W.G., & Simpson, M. (2003). *Readers, teachers, learners: Expanding literacy across the content areas.* Upper Saddle River, NJ: Merrill/Prentice Hall.

Buros, O.K. (2001). *The mental measurements yearbook* (14th ed.). Highland Park, NJ: Gryphon.

Campbell, J., Hombo, C., & Mazzeo, J. (2000). *NAEP 1999 trends in academic progress.* Washington, DC: National Center for Education Statistics.

Cappella, E., & Weinstein, R. (2001). Turning around reading achievement: Predictors of high school students' academic resilience. *Journal of Educational Psychology, 91,* 758-771.

Carlson, D. (1999, October 4). Poll shows continuing strong American reading habits. *Gallup Poll News Service.* Retrieved August 2, 2002, from www.gallup.com/poll/releases/pr991004b.asp

Cipielewski, J., & Stanovich, K. (1992). Predicting growth in reading ability from children's exposure to print. *Journal of Experimental Child Psychology, 54,* 74-89.

Dougherty, D., & Dougherty, T. (1999). *Brett Favre.* Medina, MN: Abdo & Daughters.

Drucker, M. (1994). *Jacob's rescue: A Holocaust story.* New York: Yearling.

Durrell, D. (1969). Listening comprehension versus reading comprehension. *Journal of Reading, 12,* 455-460.

Gardiner, S. (2001). Ten minutes a day for silent reading. *Educational Leadership, 59,* 32-35.

Glenn, N. (1994). Television watching, newspaper reading, and cohort differences in verbal ability. *Sociology of Education, 67,* 216-230.

Hargis, C. (1997). *Teaching low achieving and disadvantaged students* (2nd ed.). Springfield, IL: Charles C. Thomas.

Hargis, C. (1999). *Teaching and testing in reading.* Springfield, IL: Charles C. Thomas.

Innocenti, R. (1998). *Rose Blanche.* Minneapolis, MN: Econo-Clad.

Kress, N. (1996). *Beggar's ride.* New York: Tor.

Lamb, W. (1997). *She's come undone.* New York: Gale Group/Scribners.

Langer, J. (2000). *Beating the odds: Teaching middle and high school students to read and write well* (2nd ed., revised). (CELA Research Report 12014). Albany, NY: National Research Center on English Learning and Achievement.

Larson, R., Richards, M., Sims, B., & Dworkin, J. (2001). How urban African American young adolescents spend their time: Time budgets for location, activities, and companionship. *American Journal of Community Psychology, 29,* 565-597.

Lester, J.H. (2000). Secondary instruction: Does literacy fit in? *The High School Journal, 83,* 10-16.

Letts, A. (1998). *Where the heart is.* New York: Warner.

Libsch, M., & Breslow, M. (1996). Trends in non-assigned reading by high school seniors. *NASSP Bulletin, 80,* 111-116.

Lobel, A. (1998). *No pretty pictures: A child of war.* New York: Greenwillow.

McQuillan, J., & Au, J. (2001). The effect of print access on reading frequency. *Reading Psychology, 22,* 225-248.

Moore, D., Bean, T., Birdyshaw, D., & Rycik, J. (1999). Adolescent literacy: A position statement. *Journal of Adolescent & Adult Literacy, 43,* 97-112.

O'Brien, D., Stewart, R., & Moje, E. (1995). Why content literacy is difficult to infuse into the secondary school: Complexities of curriculum, pedagogy, and school culture. *Reading Research Quarterly, 30,* 442-463.

Ogbu, J. (1994). Racial stratification and education in the United States: Why inequality persists. *Teachers College Record, 96,* 264-298.

Pearman, E., Huang, A., & Mellblom, C. (1997). The inclusion of all students: Concerns and incentives of educators. *Education and Training in Mental Retardation and Development, 32,* 11-19.

Pfister, M. (1997). *The rainbow fish.* Union City, CA: Pan Asian.

Ruiz-de-Velasco, J., Fix, M., & Clewell, B. (2001). *Overlooked and underserved—Immigrant students in U.S. secondary schools: Core findings and conclusions.* Retrieved April 5, 2002, from www.urban.org/pdfs/overlooked.pdf

Schattschneider, D. (1990). *Visions of symmetry: Notebooks, periodic drawings, and related works of M.C. Escher.* New York: W.H. Freeman.

Schumm, J., & Saumell, K. (1994). Aliteracy: We know it is a problem, but where does it start? *Journal of Reading, 37,* 24-27.

Schwarz, C. (2000). *Drowning Ruth.* New York: Gale Group/Scribners.

Stadtler, B. (1996). *The Holocaust: A history of courage and resistance.* Springfield, NJ: Behrman House.

Stanovich, K. (1986). Matthew effects in reading: Some consequences of individual differences in the acquisition of literacy. *Reading Research Quarterly, 21,* 360-407.

Stewart, M. (1996). *Emmitt Smith.* New York: Children's Press.

Stiggins, R. (2002). Assessment crisis: The absence of assessment for learning. *Phi Delta Kappan, 85,* 758-765.

Sunderman, G., Amoa, M., & Meyers, T. (2001). California's reading initiative: Constraints on implementation in middle and high schools. *Educational Policy, 15,* 674-698.

Taylor, B., Frye, B., & Maruyama, G. (1990). Time spent reading and reading growth. *American Educational Research Journal, 27,* 351-362.

Wilhelm, J., Dube, J., & Baker, T. (2001). *Strategic reading: Guiding students to lifelong literacy.* Portsmouth, NH: Heinemann.

Wunderli, S. (1996). *The heartbeat of halftime.* New York: Henry Holt.

Zipperer, F., Worley, M., Sisson, M., & Said, R. (2002). Literacy education and reading programs in the secondary school: Status, problems, and solutions. *NASSP Bulletin, 86,* 3-17.

Behind Test Scores: What Struggling Readers *Really* Need

Sheila W. Valencia and Marsha Riddle Buly

Every year thousands of U.S. students take standardized tests and state reading tests, and every year thousands fail them. With the implementation of the No Child Left Behind legislation (www.ed.gov/nclb/landing.jhtml), which mandates testing all children from grades 3 to 8 every year, these numbers will grow exponentially, and alarming numbers of schools and students will be targeted for "improvement." Whether you believe this increased focus on testing is good news or bad, if you are an educator, you are undoubtedly concerned about the children who struggle every day with reading and the implications of their test failure.

Although legislators, administrators, parents, and educators have been warned repeatedly not to rely on a single measure to make important instructional decisions (Elmore, 2002; Linn, n.d.; Shepard, 2000), scores from state tests still seem to drive the search for programs and approaches that will help students learn and meet state standards. The popular press, educational publications, teacher workshops, and state and school district policies are filled with attempts to find solutions for poor test performance. For example, some schools have eliminated sustained silent reading in favor of more time for explicit instruction (Edmondson & Shannon, 2002; Riddle Buly & Valencia, 2002), others are buying special programs or mandating specific interventions (Goodnough, 2001; Helfand, 2002), and some states and districts are requiring teachers to have particular instructional emphases (McNeil, 2000; Paterson, 2000; Riddle Buly & Valencia, 2002). Furthermore, it is common to find teachers spending enormous amounts of time preparing students for these high-stakes tests (Olson, 2001), even though a narrow focus on preparing students for specific tests does not translate into real learning (Klein, Hamilton, McCaffrey, & Stecher, 2000; Linn, 2000). But, if we are really going to help students, we need to understand the underlying reasons for their test failure. Simply knowing which children have failed state tests is a bit like knowing that you have a fever when you are feeling ill but having no idea of the cause or cure. A test score, like a fever, is a symptom that demands more specific analysis of the problem. In this case, what is

Reprinted from *The Reading Teacher*, 57, 520–531, March 2004.

required is a more in-depth analysis of the strengths and needs of students who fail to meet standards and instructional plans that will meet their needs.

In this article, we draw from the results of an empirical study of students who failed a typical fourth-grade state reading assessment (see Riddle Buly & Valencia, 2002, for a full description of the study). Specifically, we describe the patterns of performance that distinguish different groups of students who failed to meet standards. We also provide suggestions for what classroom teachers need to know and how they might help these children succeed.

Study Context

Our research was conducted in a typical northwestern U.S. school district of 18,000 students located adjacent to the largest urban district in the state. At the time of our study, 43% were students of color and 47% received free or reduced-price lunch. Over the past several years, approximately 50% of students had failed the state fourth-grade reading test that, like many other standards-based state assessments, consisted of several extended narrative and expository reading selections accompanied by a combination of multiple-choice and open-ended comprehension questions. For the purposes of this study, during September of fifth grade we randomly selected 108 students who had scored below standard on the state test given at the end of fourth grade. These 108 students constituted approximately 10% of failing students in the district. None of them was receiving supplemental special education or English as a Second Language (ESL) services. We wanted to understand the "garden variety" (Stanovich, 1988) test failure—those students typically found in the regular classroom who are experiencing reading difficulty but have not been identified as needing special services or intensive interventions. Classroom teachers, not reading specialists or special education teachers, are solely responsible for the reading instruction of these children and, ultimately, for their achievement.

Data Collection and Assessment Tools

Our approach was to conduct individual reading assessments, working one-on-one with the children for approximately two hours over several days to gather information about their reading abilities. We administered a series of assessments that targeted key components of reading ability identified by experts: word identification, meaning (comprehension and vocabulary), and fluency (rate and expression) (Lipson & Wixson, 2003; National Institute of Child Health and Human Development, 2000; Snow, Burns, & Griffin, 1998). Table 1 presents the measures we used and the areas in which each provided information.

To measure word identification, we used two tests from the 1989 Woodcock-Johnson Psycho-Educational Battery-Revised (WJ-R) that assessed students' reading of single and multisyllabic words, both real and pseudowords. We also scored oral reading errors students made on narrative and expository graded passages from the 1995 Qualitative Reading Inventory-II (QRI-II) and from the state test. We calculated total accuracy (percentage of words read correctly) and acceptability (counting only those errors that changed the meaning of the text). Students also responded orally to comprehension questions that accompanied the QRI-II passages, providing a measure of their comprehension that was not confounded by writing ability. To assess receptive vocabulary, we used the 1981 Peabody Picture Vocabulary Test-Revised (PPVT-R), which requires students to listen and point to a picture that corresponds to a word (scores of 85 or higher are judged to be average or above average). As with the comprehension

Table 1
Diagnostic assessments

Assessment	Word identification	Meaning	Fluency
Woodcock-Johnson–Revised			
Letter-word identification	X		
Word attack	X		
Qualitative Reading Inventory-II			
Reading accuracy	X		
Reading acceptability	X		
Rate			X
Expression			X
Comprehension		X	
Peabody Picture Vocabulary Test-Revised			
Vocabulary meaning		X	
State fourth-grade passages			
Reading accuracy	X		
Reading acceptability	X		
Rate			X
Expression			X

questions, the vocabulary measure does not confound understanding with students' ability to write responses. Finally, in the area of fluency, we assessed rate of reading and expression (Samuels, 2002). We timed the readings of all passages (i.e., QRI–II and state test selections) to get a reading rate and used a 4-point rubric developed for the Oral Reading Study of the fourth-grade National Assessment of Educational Progress (NAEP) (Pinnell et al., 1995) to assess phrasing and expression (1–2 is judged to be nonfluent; 3–4 is judged to be fluent).

Findings

Scores from all the assessments for each student fell into three statistically distinct and educationally familiar categories: word identification (word reading in isolation and context), meaning (comprehension and vocabulary), and fluency (rate and expression). When we examined the average scores for all 108 students in the sample, students appeared to be substantially below grade level in all three areas. However, when we analyzed the data using a cluster analysis (Aldenderfer & Blashfield, 1984), looking for groups of students who had similar patterns across all three factors, we found six distinct profiles of students who failed the test. Most striking is that the majority of students were not weak in all three areas; they were actually strong in some and weak in others. Table 2 indicates the percentage of students in each group and their relative strength (+) or weakness (−) in word identification, meaning, and fluency.

Table 2
Cluster analysis

Cluster	Sample percentage	English Language Learner percentage	Low socio-economic status percentage	Word identification	Meaning	Fluency
1-Automatic Word Callers	18	63	89	+ +	−	+ +
2-Struggling Word Callers	15	56	81	−	−	+ +
3-Word Stumblers	17	16	42	−	+	−
4-Slow Comprehenders	24	19	54	+	+ +	−
5-Slow Word Callers	17	56	67	+	−	−
6-Disabled Readers	9	20	80	− −	− −	− −

The Profiles

We illuminate each profile by describing a prototypical student from each cluster (see Figure) and specific suggested instructional targets for each (all names are pseudonyms). Although the instructional strategies we recommend have not been implemented with these particular children, we base our recommendations on our review of research-based practices (e.g., Allington, 2001; Allington & Johnston, 2001; Lipson & Wixson, 2003; National Institute of Child Health and Human Development, 2000), our interpretation of the profiles, and our experiences teaching struggling readers. We conclude with several general implications for school and classroom instruction.

Cluster 1: Automatic Word Callers

We call these students Automatic Word Callers because they can decode words quickly and accurately, but they fail to read for meaning. The majority of students in this cluster qualify for free or reduced-price lunch, and they are English-language learners who no longer receive special support. Tomas is a typical student in this cluster.

Tomas has excellent word identification skills. He scored at ninth-grade level when reading real words and pseudowords (i.e., phonetically regular nonsense words such as *fot*) on the WJ-R tests, and at the independent level for word identification on the QRI-II and state fourth-grade passages. However, when asked about what he read, Tomas had difficulty, placing his comprehension at the second-grade level. Although Tomas's first language is not English, his score of 108 on the PPVT-R suggests that his comprehension difficulties are more complex than individual word meanings. Tomas's "proficient" score on the state writing assessment also suggests that his difficulty is in understanding rather than in writing answers to comprehension questions. This student's rate of reading, which was quite high compared with rates of fourth-grade students on the Oral Reading Study of NAEP (Pinnell et al., 1995) and other research (Harris & Sipay, 1990), suggests that his decoding is automatic and unlikely to be contributing to his comprehension difficulty. His score in expression is also consistent with students who were rated as "fluent" according to the NAEP rubric, although this seems unusual for a student who is demonstrating difficulty with comprehension.

The evidence suggests that Tomas needs additional instruction in comprehension and most likely would benefit from explicit instruction, teacher modeling, and think-alouds of key reading strategies (e.g., summarizing,

Prototypical students from each cluster

Cluster 1-Automatic Word Callers (18%)

Word identification	Meaning	Fluency
+ +	−	+ +

Tomas

Word identification = ninth grade (WJ-R)
>fourth grade (QRI-II)
= 98% (state passages)
Comprehension = second/third grade
Vocabulary = 108
Expression = 3
Rate = 155 words per minute
Writing = proficient

Cluster 2-Struggling Word Callers (15%)

Word identification	Meaning	Fluency
−	−	+ +

Makara

Word identification = fourth grade (WJ-R)
<second grade (QRI-II)
= 75% (state passages)
Comprehension = <second grade
Vocabulary = 58
Expression = 2.5
Rate = 117 words per minute
Writing = below proficient

Cluster 3-Word Stumblers (17%)

Word identification	Meaning	Fluency
−	+	−

Sandy

Word identification = second grade (WJ-R)
= second-grade accuracy/third-grade
acceptability (QRI-II)
= 80% accuracy/99% acceptability
(state passages)
Comprehension = fourth grade
Vocabulary = 135
Expression = 1.5
Rate = 77 words per minute
Writing = proficient

Cluster 4-Slow Comprehenders (24%)

Word identification	Meaning	Fluency
+	+ +	−

Martin

Word identification = sixth grade (WJ-R)
>fourth grade (QRI-II)
= 100% (state passages)
Comprehension = >fourth grade
Vocabulary = 103
Expression = 2.5
Rate = 61 words per minute
Writing = proficient

Cluster 5-Slow Word Callers (17%)

Word identification	Meaning	Fluency
+	−	−

Andrew

Word identification = seventh grade (WJ-R)
>fourth grade (QRI-II)
= 98% (state passages)
Comprehension = second grade
Vocabulary = 74
Expression = 1.5
Rate = 62 words per minute
Writing = not proficient

Cluster 6-Disabled Readers (9%)

Word identification	Meaning	Fluency
− −	− −	− −

Jesse

Word identification = first grade (WJ-R)
<first grade (QRI-II)
<50% (state passages)
Comprehension = <first grade
Vocabulary = 105
Writing = not proficient

self-monitoring, creating visual representations, evaluating), using a variety of types of material at the fourth- or fifth-grade level (Block & Pressley, 2002; Duke & Pearson, 2002). His comprehension performance on the QRI-II suggests that his literal comprehension is quite strong but that he has difficulty with more inferential and critical aspects of understanding. Although Tomas has strong scores in the fluency category, both in expression and rate, he may be reading too fast to attend to meaning, especially deeper meaning of the ideas in the text. Tomas's teacher should help him understand that the purpose for reading is to understand and that rate varies depending on the type of text and the purpose for reading. Then, the teacher should suggest that he slow down to focus on meaning. Self-monitoring strategies would also help Tomas check for understanding and encourage him to think about the ideas while he is reading. These and other such strategies may help him learn to adjust his rate to meet the demands of the text.

Tomas would also likely benefit from additional support in acquiring academic language, which takes many years for English-language learners to develop (Cummins, 1991). Reading activities such as building background; developing understanding of new words, concepts, and figurative language in his "to-be-read" texts; and acquiring familiarity with genre structures found in longer, more complex texts like those found at fourth grade and above would provide important opportunities for his language and conceptual development (Antunez, 2002; Hiebert, Pearson, Taylor, Richardson, & Paris, 1998). Classroom read-alouds and discussions as well as lots of additional independent reading would also help Tomas in building language and attention to understanding.

Cluster 2: Struggling Word Callers

The students in this cluster not only struggle with meaning, like the Automatic Word Callers in Cluster 1, but they also struggle with word identification. Makara, a student from Cambodia, is one of these students. Like Tomas, Makara struggled with comprehension. But unlike Tomas, he had substantial difficulty applying word identification skills when reading connected text (QRI-II and state passages), even though his reading of isolated words on the WJ-R was at a fourth-grade level. Such word identification difficulties would likely contribute to comprehension problems. However, Makara's performance on the PPVT-R, which placed him below the 1st percentile compared with other students his age, and his poor performance on the state writing assessment suggest that language may contribute to his comprehension difficulties as well—not surprising for a student acquiring a second language. These language-related results need to be viewed with caution, however, because the version of the PPVT–R available for use in this study may underestimate the language abilities of students from culturally and linguistically diverse backgrounds, and written language takes longer than oral language to develop. Despite difficulty with meaning, Makara read quickly—117 words per minute. At first glance, this may seem unusual given his difficulty with both decoding and comprehension. Closer investigation of his performance, however, revealed that Makara read words quickly whether he was reading them correctly or incorrectly and didn't stop to monitor or self-correct. In addition, although Makara was fast, his expression and phrasing were uneven and consistent with comprehension difficulties.

Makara likely needs instruction and practice in oral and written language, as well as in constructing meaning in reading and writing, self-monitoring, and decoding while reading connected text. All this needs to be done in rich, meaningful contexts, taking into account his background knowledge and interests. Like Tomas, Makara would benefit from teacher or peer read-alouds, lots of experience with independent reading at his level, small-group instruction, and the kinds of activities aimed at building academic language that we described earlier, as well as a more foundational emphasis on word meanings. Makara also needs instruction in self-monitoring and fix-up strategies to improve his comprehension and awareness of reading for understanding. Decoding instruction is also important for him, although his teacher would need to gather more information using tools such as miscue analysis or tests of decoding to determine his specific decoding needs and how they interact with his knowledge of word meanings. Makara clearly cannot be instructed in fourth-grade material; most likely, his teacher would need to begin with second-grade material that is familiar and interesting to him and a good deal of interactive background building. At the same time, however, Makara needs exposure to the content and vocabulary of grade-level texts through activities such as teacher read-alouds, tapes, and partner reading so that his conceptual understanding continues to grow.

Cluster 3: Word Stumblers

Students in this cluster have substantial difficulty with word identification, but they still have surprisingly strong comprehension. How does that happen? Sandy, a native English speaker from a middle class home, is a good example of this type of student. Sandy stumbled on so many words initially that it seemed unlikely that she would comprehend what she had read, yet she did. Her word identification scores were at second-grade level, and she read the state fourth-grade passages at frustration level. However, a clue to her strong comprehension is evident from the difference between her immediate word recognition accuracy score and her acceptability score, which takes into account self-corrections or errors that do not change the meaning. In other words, Sandy was so focused on reading for meaning that she spontaneously self-corrected many of her decoding miscues or substituted words that preserved the meaning. She attempted to read every word in the reading selections, working until she could figure out some part of each word and then using context clues to help her get the entire word. She seemed to over-rely on context because her decoding skills were so weak (Stanovich, 1994). Remarkably, she was eventually able to read the words on the state fourth-grade reading passages at an independent level. But, as we might predict, Sandy's rate was very slow, and her initial attempts to read were choppy and lacked flow—she spent an enormous amount of time self-correcting and rereading. After she finally self-corrected or figured out unknown words, however, Sandy reread phrases with good expression and flow to fit with the meaning. Although Sandy's overall fluency score was low, her primary difficulty does not appear in the area of either rate or expression; rather, her low performance in fluency seems to be a result of her difficulty with decoding.

With such a strong quest for meaning, Sandy was able to comprehend fourth-grade material even when her decoding was at frustration level. No doubt her strong language and vocabulary abilities (i.e., 99th percentile) were assets. As we might predict, Sandy was more than proficient at expressing her ideas when writing about her experiences. She understands that reading and writing should make sense, and she has the self-monitoring strategies, perseverance, and language background to make that happen.

Sandy needs systematic instruction in word identification and opportunities to practice when reading connected text at her reading level. She is clearly beyond the early stages of reading and decoding, but her teacher will need to determine through a more in-depth analysis precisely which decoding skills should be the focus of her instruction. At the same time, Sandy needs supported experiences with texts that will continue to feed and challenge her drive for meaning. For students like Sandy, it is critical not to sacrifice intellectual engagement with text while they are receiving decoding instruction and practice in below-grade-level material. Furthermore, Sandy needs to develop automaticity with word identification, and to do that she would benefit from assisted reading (i.e., reading along with others, monitored reading with a tape, or partner reading) as well as unassisted reading practice (i.e., repeated reading, reading to younger students) with materials at her instructional level (Kuhn & Stahl, 2000).

Cluster 4: Slow Comprehenders

Almost one fourth of the students in this sample were Slow Comprehenders. Like other students in this cluster, Martin is a native English speaker and a relatively strong decoder, scoring above fourth-grade level on all measures of decoding. His comprehension was at the instructional level on the fourth-grade QRI-II selections, and his vocabulary and writing ability were average for his age. On the surface, this information is puzzling because Martin failed the fourth-grade state test.

Insight about Martin's reading performance comes from several sources. First, Martin was within two points of passing the state assessment, so he doesn't seem to have a serious reading problem. Second, although his reading rate is quite slow and this often interferes with comprehension (Adams, 1990), results of the QRI-II suggest that Martin's comprehension is quite strong, in spite of his slow rate. This is most likely because Martin has good word knowledge and understands that reading should make sense, and neither the QRI-II nor the state test has time limits. His strong score in expression confirms that Martin did, indeed, attend to meaning while reading. Third, a close examination of his reading behaviors while reading words from the WJ-R tests, QRI-II, and state reading selections revealed that he had some difficulty reading multisyllabic words; although, with time, he was able to read enough words to score at grade level or above. It appears that Martin has the decoding skills to attack multisyllabic words, but they are not yet automatic.

The outstanding characteristic of Martin's profile is his extremely slow rate combined with his relatively strong word identification abilities and comprehension. Our work with him suggests that, even if Martin were to get the additional two points needed to pass the state test, he would still have a significant problem with rate and some difficulty with automatic decoding of multisyllabic words, both of which could hamper his future reading success. Furthermore, with such a lack of automaticity and a slow rate, it is unlikely that Martin enjoys or spends much time reading. As a result, he is likely to fall further and further behind his peers (Stanovich, 1986), especially as he enters middle school where the amount of reading increases dramatically. Martin needs fluency-building activities such as guided repeated oral reading, partner reading, and Readers Theatre (Allington, 2001; Kuhn & Stahl, 2000; Lipson & Wixson, 2003). Given his word identification and comprehension abilities, he most likely could get that practice using fourth-grade material where he will also encounter multisyllabic words. It is important to find reading material that is interesting to Martin and that, initially, can be completed in a relatively short time. Martin needs to develop stamina as well as fluency, and to do that he will need to spend time reading short and extended texts. In addition, Martin might benefit from instruction and practice in strategies for identifying multisyllabic words so that he is more prepared to deal with them automatically while reading.

Cluster 5: Slow Word Callers

The students in this cluster are similar to Tomas, the Automatic Word Caller in Cluster 1. The difference is that Tomas is an automatic, fluent word caller, whereas the students in this cluster are slow. This group is a fairly even mix of English-language learners and native English speakers who have difficulty in comprehension and fluency. Andrew is an example of such a student. He has well-developed decoding skills, scoring at the seventh-grade level when reading words in isolation and at the independent level when reading connected text. Even with such strong decoding abilities, Andrew had difficulty with comprehension. We had to drop down to the second-grade QRI–II passage for Andrew to score at the instructional level for comprehension, and, even at that level, his retelling was minimal. Andrew's score on the PPVT–R, corresponding to first grade (the 4th percentile for his age), adds to the comprehension picture as well. It suggests that Andrew may be experiencing difficulty with both individual word meanings and text-based understanding when reading paragraphs and longer selections. Like Martin, Andrew's reading rate was substantially below rates expected for fourth-grade students (Harris & Sipay, 1990; Pinnell et al., 1995), averaging 62 words per minute when reading narrative and expository selections. In practical terms, this means he read just one word per second. As we might anticipate from his slow rate and his comprehension difficulty, Andrew did not read with expression or meaningful phrasing.

The relationship between meaning and fluency is unclear in Andrew's case. On the one hand, students who realize they don't understand would be wise to slow down and monitor meaning. On the other hand, Andrew's lack of automaticity and slow rate may interfere with comprehension. To disentangle these factors, his teacher would need to experiment with reading materials about which Andrew has a good deal of background knowledge to eliminate difficulty with individual word meanings and overall comprehension. If his reading rate and expression improve under such conditions, a primary focus for instruction would be meaning. That is, his slow rate of reading and lack of prosody would seem to be a response to lack of understanding rather than contributing to it. In contrast, if Andrew's rate and expression are still low when the material and vocabulary are familiar, instruction should focus on both fluency and meaning. In either case, Andrew would certainly benefit from attention to vocabulary building, both indirect building through extensive independent reading and teacher read-alouds as well as more explicit instruction in word learning strategies and new words he will encounter when reading specific texts (Nagy, 1988; Stahl & Kapinus, 2001).

It is interesting that 50% of the students in this cluster scored at Level 1 on the state test, the lowest level possible. State guidelines characterize these students as lacking prerequisite knowledge and skills that are fundamental for meeting the standard. Given such a definition, a logical assumption would be that these students lack basic, early reading skills such as decoding. However, as the evidence here suggests, we cannot assume that students who score at the lowest level on the test need decoding instruction. Andrew, like others in this cluster, needs instruction in meaning and fluency.

Cluster 6: Disabled Readers

We call this group Disabled Readers because they are experiencing severe difficulty in all three areas—word identification, meaning, and fluency. This is the smallest group (9%), yet, ironically, this is the profile that most likely comes to mind when we think of children who fail state reading tests. This group also includes one of the lowest numbers of second-language learners. The most telling characteristic of students in this cluster, like Jesse, is their very limited word identification abilities. Jesse had few decoding skills beyond initial consonants, basic consonant-vowel-consonant patterns (e.g., *hat*, *box*), and high-frequency sight words. However, his knowledge of word meanings was average, like most of the students in this cluster, which suggests that receptive language was not a major problem and that he does not likely have limited learning ability. With decoding ability at the first-grade level and below, it is not surprising that Jesse's comprehension and fluency were also low. He simply could not read enough words at the first-grade level to get any meaning.

As we might anticipate, the majority of students in this cluster were not proficient in writing and scored at the lowest level, Level 1, on the state fourth-grade reading test. It is important to remember, however, that children who were receiving special education intervention were not included in our sample. So, the children in this cluster, like Jesse, are receiving all of their instruction, or the majority of it (some may be getting supplemental help), from their regular classroom teachers.

Jesse clearly needs intensive, systematic word identification instruction targeted at beginning reading along with access to lots of reading material at first-grade level and below. This will be a challenge for Jesse's fifth-grade teacher. Pedagogically, Jesse needs explicit instruction in basic word identification. Yet few intermediate-grade teachers include this as a part of their instruction, and most do not have an adequate supply of easy materials for instruction or fluency building. In addition, the majority of texts in other subject areas such as social studies and science are written at levels that will be inaccessible to students like Jesse, so alternative materials and strategies will be needed. On the social-emotional front, it will be a challenge to keep Jesse engaged in learning and to provide opportunities for him to succeed in the classroom, even if he is referred for additional reading support. Without that engagement and desire to learn, it is unlikely he will be motivated to put forth the effort it will take for him to make progress. Jesse needs a great deal of support from his regular classroom teacher and from a reading specialist, working together to build a comprehensive instructional program in school and support at home that will help him develop the skill and will to progress.

Conclusions and Implications

Our brief descriptions of the six prototypical children and the instructional focus each one needs is a testimony to individual differences. As we have heard a thousand times before, and as our data support, one-size instruction will not fit all children. The evidence here clearly demonstrates that students fail state reading tests for a variety of reasons and that, if we are to help these students, we will need to provide appropriate instruction to meet their varying needs. For example, placing all struggling students in a phonics or word identification program would be inappropriate for nearly 58% of the students in this sample who had adequate or strong word identification skills. In a similar manner, an instructional approach that did not address fluency and building reading stamina for longer, more complex text or that did not provide sufficient reading material at a range of levels would miss almost 70% of the students who demonstrated difficulty with fluency. In addition to these important cautions about overgeneralizing students' needs, we believe there are several strategies aimed at assessment, classroom organization and materials, and school structures that could help teachers meet their students' needs.

First and most obvious, teachers need to go beneath the scores on state tests by conducting additional diagnostic assessments that will help them identify students' needs. The data here demonstrate quite clearly that, without more in-depth and individual student assessment, distinctive and instructionally important patterns of students' abilities are masked. We believe that informal reading inventories, oral reading records, and other individually tailored assessments provide useful information about all students. At the same time, we realize that many teachers do not have the time to do complete diagnostic evaluations, such as those we did, with every student. At a minimum, we suggest a kind of layered approach to assessment in which teachers first work diagnostically with students who have demonstrated difficulty on broad measures of reading. Then, they can work with other students as the need arises.

However, we caution that simply administering more and more assessments and recording the scores will miss the point. The value of in-depth classroom assessment comes from teachers having a deep understanding of reading processes and instruction, thinking diagnostically, and using the information on an ongoing basis to inform instruction (Black & Wiliam, 1998; Place, 2002; Shepard, 2000). Requiring teachers to administer grade-level classroom assessments to all their students regardless of individual student needs would not yield useful information or help teachers make effective instructional decisions. For example, administering a fourth-grade reading selection to Jesse, who is reading at first-grade level, would not provide useful information. However, using a fourth- or even fifth-grade selection for Tomas would. Similarly, assessing Jesse's word identification abilities should probably include assessments of basic sound/symbol correspondences or even phonemic awareness, but assessing decoding of multisyllabic words would be more appropriate for Martin. This kind of matching of assessment to students' needs is precisely what we hope would happen when teachers have the knowledge, the assessment tools, and the flexibility to assess and teach children according to their ongoing analysis. Both long-term professional development and time are critical if teachers are to implement the kind of sophisticated classroom assessment that struggling readers need.

Second, the evidence points to the need for multilevel, flexible, small-group instruction (Allington & Johnston, 2001; Cunningham & Allington, 1999; Opitz, 1998). Imagine, if you will, teaching just the six students we have described, who could easily be in the same class. These students not only need support in different aspects of reading, but they also need materials that differ in difficulty, topic, and familiarity. For example, Tomas, Makara, and Andrew all need instruction in comprehension. However, Tomas and Andrew likely can receive that instruction using grade-level material, but Makara would need to use easier material. Both Makara and Andrew need work in vocabulary, whereas Tomas is fairly strong in word meanings. As second-language learners, Tomas and Makara likely need more background building and exposure to topics, concepts, and academic vocabulary as well as the structure of English texts than Andrew, who is a native English speaker. Furthermore, the teacher likely needs to experiment with having Tomas and Makara slow down when they read to get them to attend to meaning, whereas Andrew needs to increase his fluency through practice in below-grade-level text.

So, although these three students might be able to participate in whole-class instruction in which the teacher models and explicitly teaches comprehension strategies, they clearly need guided practice to apply the strategies to different types and levels of material, and they each need attention to other aspects of reading as well. This means the teacher must have strong classroom management and organizational skills to provide small-group instruction. Furthermore, he or she must have access to a wide range of books and reading materials that are intellectually challenging yet accessible to students reading substantially below grade level. At the same time, these struggling readers need access to grade-level material through a variety of scaffolded experiences (i.e., partner reading, guided reading, read-alouds) so that they are exposed to grade-level ideas, text structures, and vocabulary (Cunningham & Allington, 1999). Some of these students and their teachers would benefit from collaboration with other professionals in their schools, such as speech and language and second-language specialists, who could suggest classroom-based strategies targeted to the students' specific needs.

The six clusters and the three strands within each one (word identification, meaning, fluency) clearly provide more in-depth analysis of students' reading abilities than general test scores. Nevertheless, we caution that there is still more to be learned about individual students in each cluster, beyond what we describe here, that would help teachers plan for instruction. Two examples make this point. The first example comes from Cluster 1, Automatic Word Callers. Tomas had substantial difficulty with comprehension, but his scores on the vocabulary measure suggested that word meanings were likely not a problem for him. However, other students in this cluster, such as Maria, *did* have difficulty with word meanings and would need not only comprehension instruction like Tomas but also many more language-building activities and exposure to oral and written English. The second example that highlights the importance of looking beyond the cluster profile is Andrew, our Slow Word Caller from Cluster 5. Although we know that in-depth assessment revealed that Andrew had difficulty with comprehension and fluency, we argue above that the teacher must do more work with Andrew to determine how much fluency is contributing to comprehension and how much it is a result of Andrew's effort to self-monitor. Our point here is that even the clusters do not tell the entire story.

Finally, from a school or district perspective, we are concerned about the disproportionate number of second-language students who failed the test. In our study, 11% of the students in the school district were identified as second-language learners and were receiving additional instructional support. However, in our sample of students who failed the test, 43% were second-language learners who were *not* receiving additional support. Tomas and Makara are typical of many English-language learners in our schools. Their reading abilities are sufficient, according to school guidelines, to allow them to exit supplemental ESL programs, yet they are failing state tests and struggling in the classroom. In this district, as in others across the state, students exit supplemental programs when they score at the 35th percentile or above on a norm-referenced reading test—hardly sufficient to thrive, or even survive, in a mainstream classroom without additional help. States, school districts, and schools need to rethink the support they offer English-language learners both in terms of providing more sustained instructional support over time and of scaffolding their integration into the regular classroom. In addition, there must be a concerted effort to foster academically and intellectually rigorous learning of subject matter for these students (e.g., science, social studies) while they are developing their English-language abilities. Without such a focus, either in their first language or in English, these students will be denied access to important school learning, will fall further behind in other school subjects, and become increasingly disengaged from school and learning (Echevarria, Vogt, & Short, 2000).

Our findings and recommendations may, on one level, seem obvious. Indeed, good teachers have always acknowledged differences among the students in their classes, and they have always tried to meet individual needs. But, in the current environment of high-stakes testing and accountability, it has become more of a challenge to keep an eye on individual children, and more difficult to stay focused on the complex nature of reading performance and reading instruction. This study serves as a reminder of these cornerstones of good teaching. We owe it to our students, their parents, and ourselves to provide struggling readers with the instruction they *really* need.

REFERENCES

Adams, M.J. (1990). *Beginning to read: Thinking and learning about print*. Cambridge, MA: MIT Press.

Aldenderfer, M., & Blashfield, R. (1984). *Cluster analysis*. Beverly Hills, CA: Sage.

Allington, R.L. (2001). *What really matters for struggling readers*. New York: Longman.

Allington, R.L., & Johnston, P.H. (2001). What do we know about effective fourth-grade teachers and their classrooms? In C.M. Roller (Ed.), *Learning to teach reading: Setting the research agenda* (pp. 150–165). Newark, DE: International Reading Association.

Antunez, B. (2002, Spring). Implementing reading first with English language learners. *Directions in Language and Education, 15*. Retrieved October 15, 2003, from www.ncela.gwu.edu/ncbepubs/directions

Black, P., & Wiliam, D. (1998). Assessment and classroom learning. *Assessment in Education, 5*(1), 7–74.

Block, C.C., & Pressley, M. (Eds.). (2002). *Comprehension instruction: Research-based best practices.* New York: Guilford.

Cummins, J. (1991). The development of bilingual proficiency from home to school: A longitudinal study of Portuguese-speaking children. *Journal of Education, 173,* 85–98.

Cunningham, P.M., & Allington, R.L. (1999). *Classrooms that work* (2nd ed.). New York: Longman.

Duke, N.K., & Pearson, P.D. (2002). Effective practices for developing reading comprehension. In A.E. Farstrup & S.J. Samuels (Eds.), *What research has to say about reading instruction* (3rd ed., pp. 9–129). Newark, DE: International Reading Association.

Echevarria, J., Vogt, M.E., & Short, D. (2000). *Making content comprehensible for English language learners: The SIOP model.* Boston: Allyn & Bacon.

Edmondson, J., & Shannon, P. (2002). The will of the people. *The Reading Teacher, 55,* 452–454.

Elmore, R.F. (2002, Spring) Unwarranted intrusion. *Education Next.* Retrieved March 21, 2003, from www.educationnext.org

Goodnough, A. (2001, May 23). Teaching by the book, no asides allowed. *The New York Times.* Retrieved March 21, 2003, from www.nytimes.com

Harris, A.J., & Sipay, E.R. (1990). *How to increase reading ability* (9th ed.). New York: Longman.

Helfand, D. (2002, July 21). Teens get a second chance at literacy. *Los Angeles Times.* Retrieved March 21, 2003, from www.latimes.com

Hiebert, E.H., Pearson, P.D., Taylor, B.M., Richardson, V., & Paris, S.G. (1998). *Every child a reader: Applying reading research to the classroom.* Ann Arbor, MI: Center for the Improvement of Early Reading Achievement, University of Michigan School of Education. Retrieved March 21, 2003, from www.ciera.org

Klein, S.P., Hamilton, L.S., McCaffrey, D.F., & Stecher, B.M. (2000). What do test scores in Texas tell us? *Education Policy Analysis Archives, 8*(49). Retrieved March 21, 2003, from http://epaa.asu.edu/epaa/v8n49

Kuhn, M.R., & Stahl, S.A. (2000). *Fluency: A review of developmental and remedial practices* (CIERA Rep. No. 2-008). Ann Arbor, MI: Center for the Improvement of Early Reading Achievement, University of Michigan School of Education. Retrieved March 21, 2003, from www.ciera.org

Linn, R.L. (2000). Assessments and accountability. *Educational Researcher, 29*(2), 4–16.

Linn, R.L. (n.d.). *Standards-based accountability: Ten suggestions.* CRESST Policy Brief. 1. Retrieved March 21, 2003, from www.cse.ucla.edu

Lipson, M.Y., & Wixson, K.K. (2003). *Assessment and instruction of reading and writing difficulty: An interactive approach* (3rd ed.). Boston: Allyn & Bacon.

McNeil, L.M. (2000). *Contradictions of school reform: Educational costs of standardized testing.* New York: Routledge.

Nagy, W.E. (1988). *Teaching vocabulary to improve reading comprehension*. Urbana, IL: ERIC Clearinghouse on Reading and Communication Skills and the National Council of Teachers of English.

National Institute of Child Health and Human Development. (2000). *Report of the National Reading Panel. Teaching children to read: An evidence-based assessment of the scientific research literature on reading and its implications for reading instruction* (NIH Publication No. 004 769). Washington, DC: U.S. Government Printing Office. Retrieved March 21, 2003, from www.nationalreadingpanel.org

Olson, L. (2001). Overboard on testing. *Education Week, 20*(17), 23–30.

Opitz, M.F. (1998). *Flexible grouping in reading*. New York: Scholastic.

Paterson, F.R.A. (2000). The politics of phonics. *Journal of Curriculum and Supervision, 15*, 179–211.

Pinnell, G.S., Pikulski, J.J., Wixson, K.K., Campbell, J.R., Gough, P.B., & Beatty, A.S. (1995). *Listening to children read aloud*. Washington, DC: U.S. Department of Education.

Place, N.A. (2002). Policy in action: The influence of mandated early reading assessment on teachers' thinking and practice. In D.L. Schallert, C.M. Fairbanks, J. Worthy, B. Maloch, & J.V. Hoffman (Eds.), *Fiftieth yearbook of the National Reading Conference* (pp. 45–58). Oak Creek, WI: National Reading Conference.

Riddle Buly, M., & Valencia, S.W. (2002). Below the bar: Profiles of students who fail state reading tests. *Educational Evaluation and Policy Analysis, 24*, 219–239.

Samuels, S.J. (2002). Reading fluency: Its development and assessment. In A.E. Farstrup & S.J. Samuels (Eds.), *What research has to say about reading instruction* (3rd ed., pp. 166–183). Newark, DE: International Reading Association.

Shepard, L.A. (2000). The role of assessment in a learning culture. *Educational Researcher, 29*, 4–14.

Snow, C.E., Burns, M.S., & Griffin, P. (Eds.). (1998). *Preventing reading difficulties in young children*. Washington, DC: National Academy Press.

Stahl, S.A., & Kapinus, B.A. (2001). *Word power: What every educator needs to know about vocabulary*. Washington, DC: National Education Association Professional Library.

Stanovich, K.E. (1986). Matthew effects in reading: Some consequences of individual differences in the acquisition of literacy. *Reading Research Quarterly, 21*, 360–407.

Stanovich, K.E. (1988). Explaining the difference between the dyslexic and garden-variety poor reader: The phonological-core variable-difference model. *Journal of Learning Disabilities, 21*, 590–612.

Stanovich, K.E. (1994). Romance and reality. *The Reading Teacher, 47*, 280–290.

Policy Communications Concerns

S ome people interested in education policy argue that policymaking is a social action in which rules are set to direct institutional behavior (Mitchell & Green, 1986). Even an autocrat delivering personal fiats for others to follow works within a context in which social theories influence his or her thinking, through a language that has been socially constructed, and from a vision of social remedy. All social actions are directed by intentions, interests, and values (Bernstein, 1978). Therefore, policymaking is a negotiation among groups, each attempting to realize its intentions through institutional rules. Sometimes the negotiations are formal among groups directly involved in the decision-making process. At other times, the negotiations are informal, in which outside groups seek to influence the direct participants before, during, and even after policy decisions are made. Political lobbyists might be the most visible example of this informal practice, but reading education has its textbook and basal lobbyists as well.

Although research and rationality might enter into policy negotiations, they do not drive the intentions of participants necessarily, and they certainly do not trump participants' interests. They are factors, but not *the* factors. Rather it is the means and methods of communication that determine the outcome of policymaking. Open and free communications in which groups clearly articulate their definitions of issues as well as their positions on those issues will enable them to determine common elements on which to base the best policy for a particular situation. Bad policy and problems within policymaking are caused by barriers to this open and free interchange among interested parties. Good policy results when groups can coordinate their intentions within a common set of rules and meanings.

Policy communications concerns have four tenets:

1. Policy is a consensus among the groups participating about the rules that will direct institutional behavior.

2. Policymaking is a political negotiation among those groups.

3. Policy decisions are based on groups' values, interests, and intentions.

4. Policy negotiations require open and free communications among groups leading to mutual understanding within a particular context.

In the first article in this section, Dillon, O'Brien, and Heilman push the goals of reading education to the center of policy consideration. They charge that empirical theory moves too quickly to technical issues of method and procedures without careful and repeated discussions of where those methods might lead. For them, goal setting in reading education requires all stakeholders to clarify and declare their intentions in an open forum, enabling participants to get a clearer picture of the desired endpoint, which will enable a pragmatic evaluation of any subsequent policy. Within these discussions universal best practices will not be the driving force. The authors explain,

> An individual researcher's beliefs and expertise no longer can be the sole rationale for the research questions selected and pursued. Instead, the complexity of problems and social situations that affect practice and concern local constituents must be key to the creation of school research agenda.

Toll contrasts teachers' and administrators' understanding of school change and wonders how they communicate with each other because of the differences. She explains that interests, intentions, and values are not personal decisions, but rather markers of group membership. In her study, she found that teachers are consumed by establishing classroom communities and meeting students' needs, while administrators value general methods that address and solve problems once and for all time. To avoid poor school policies for change, Toll seeks ways to engage teachers and administrators in conversations (to reach consensus, if possible, but more likely) to begin the difficult work toward collaboration through the invention of a common language about schooling among teachers and administrators.

Because the population in school is becoming more diverse, Grant and Wong suggest that policymaking should adjust accordingly. Not only should the topics of reading research be broadened to include topics of interest to teachers of nonnative students but the policymaking also should include representatives of these groups and teachers. To date, the authors' concerns have not figured prominently in reading education policy and policymaking.

Pragmatism requires that policy be judged by its likely consequences. Although 30 years apart, the articles by Shafer and by Hoffman, Assaf, and Paris describe the consequences of large-scale testing. Shafer discusses what became the National Assessment of Educational Progress and Hoffman et al. tell the tale of what happened in Texas when the state increased the stakes for student testing. Both articles note that the assessment policies were set without the input of all effected groups. Shafer comments that the goal of national reading testing for secondary school students was not defined carefully, and Hoffman et al. note that teachers and community members were not well represented when the assessment policy was passed at the state level. With full participation, some of the problems with large-scale testing could be avoided.

Roller explains her role as the new IRA Director of Research and Policy within the "volatile and explosive U.S. government policy environment confronting reading professionals." Although she admits a fondness for policy-driven work, she acknowledges that research does not necessarily point the field in one direction nor does it represent the interests of all parties. Rather, different groups use different research to defend their position. Accordingly, Roller suggests that the best role for IRA in policymaking is to ensure that all participants have the best information available and to sponsor forums in which that information can be thoroughly examined and discussed.

In brief rejoinders to Hoffman and Roller, Goldenberg and Raines discuss how free, open communication about reading education might take place. Goldenberg counsels reading researchers on how to communicate with researchers, teachers, legislators, and the public if they want to be taken seriously in reading education reform. Raines describes a specific example in which communication was successful. However, after two pages of optimism, she levels a threat about reading education: Unless the achievement gap between rich and poor is closed "the next round of legislation will not be kind to educators."

REFERENCES

Bernstein, R.J. (1978). *The restructuring of social and political theory.* Philadelphia: University of Pennsylvania Press.

Mitchell, B., & Green, J. (1986). Of searchers, solons, and soldiers: How do educational research, policy, and practice relate? In J.A. Niles & R.V. Lalik (Eds.), *Solving problems in literacy: Learners, teachers, and researchers* (35th yearbook of the National Reading Conference, pp. 395–405). Rochester, NY: National Reading Conference.

Literacy Research in the Next Millennium: From Paradigms to Pragmatism and Practicality

Deborah R. Dillon, David G. O'Brien, and Elizabeth E. Heilman

I t is a daunting (some would say foolhardy) task to attempt to predict what will happen to literacy research in the next decade, let alone in the next millennium. Artist Mary Engelbreit stated in a recent interview (1998), "So the millennium is just around the corner—get over it; get on with it." Engelbreit noted that we might place too much stock in calendar benchmarks, particularly those that end in zero. Her message is well taken. Nonetheless, the approaching triple-zero date provides an opportunity to pause, reflect, and review what we have learned about the conduct of our inquiry and to consider future directions for literacy research. We had four goals in writing this article: (1) to examine broadly how inquiry paradigms have been defined, (2) to critique how paradigms are used in inquiry in literacy and to question their usefulness, (3) to consider pragmatism as a perspective that may be more useful in helping us decide what we study and how we engage in inquiry, and (4) to discuss the future of literacy inquiry.

In literacy research, as in the broader arena of educational research, there are three classes of scholars. The first group tries to anticipate the newest research topic, methodology, and paradigm. These individuals look intently ahead with little attention to historical grounding for a simple reason: In higher education, where most of the research is supported and conducted, researchers are rewarded for carving out new directions, generating articles and grant proposals, and positioning themselves as leaders in the field. To invent new genres, coin new terms, set directions for others to follow, and create new paradigms is to cement one's reputation as a scholar. In contrast, less glamour is associated with grounding one's work solidly on others' research or refining and improving upon existing ideas.

The second group of researchers achieves credibility and enjoys career-long success by introducing a single groundbreaking idea, mapping out a portion of some new territory, or working consistently on a set of problems within a given paradigm over time. In examining types of black intellectuals, Cornel West (1993) described these scholars as the "bourgeois model"

Reprinted from *Reading Research Quarterly, 35*, 10-26, January/February/March 2000.

who are "prone to adopt uncritically prevailing paradigms predominant in the bourgeois academy" (p. 76).

The third group of scholars is motivated by a position or an issue and is philosophically and ethically driven to find an answer. These researchers focus on collaboratively identifying a problem with participants in a community and working together over time to generate theories and explanations that can be used in local settings.

Researchers in all three groups have generated valuable literacy research findings. Nevertheless, endless debates challenge the credibility of various paradigms (e.g., quantitative versus qualitative, cognitive vs. socially constructed) in which research questions have been grounded and critique the appropriateness of questions posed for inquiry as well as the impact of inquiry on practice.

Paradigms and Inquiry

In this article we posit that the political affiliation with paradigms and the continued preoccupation with debates have resulted in literacy research that has made less difference than it could in practice. We offer pragmatism, and the discourse from which it is constructed, as a promising stance for moving us beyond paradigm affiliations and debates. We conjecture that the field of literacy, like the broader field of education, has not embraced pragmatism because it has been misunderstood and ill defined. Researchers have characterized pragmatists as individuals who fail to take a firm stance one way or the other on a given issue. We will discuss this further in a later section of the article. An example from within literacy research and practice is the term *balanced* or *eclectic approach*, which has been associated with "a little of this and a little of that" (Graves, 1998, p. 16), or "two very distinct, parallel approaches coexisting in a single classroom in the name of 'playing it safe'" (Strickland, 1996, p. 32). However, as Graves (1998) stated: "The purpose of creating balanced programs is to provide students with the best possible experiences for becoming competent and eager readers [and quality instruction] goes beyond a simple concept of balance [to] balancing instruction across a number of dimensions" (p. 16).

Graves and Strickland, who take a pragmatic stance, both noted that there are dimensions that undergird balance, but that there "is not one specific Balanced Approach" (Strickland, 1996, p. 32). Both imply, however, that the selection and articulation of the dimensions are important for progress to occur and that our guiding principle should be the end in view—students' learning.

In the next section we define paradigms and critique their usefulness in literacy inquiry. The following questions organize the discussion: What are paradigms? What do paradigms mean to inquiry in literacy? Has the multiplicity of paradigms we draw from helped or hindered our inquiry? What paradigms could make a difference in our inquiry and why? Following this discussion we present pragmatism as an alternative to paradigmatic perspectives.

Paradigms: A Plethora of Perspectives

The term *paradigm* is used in so many ways that it is meaningless to talk about it without selecting a definition prior to discussing its usefulness. For example, Patton (1990), a research methodologist, defined a paradigm as a "worldview, a general perspective, a way of breaking down the complexity of the real world" (p. 37). The term has been used to refer to a philosophical position, a research tradition or theoretical framework, and a methodology perspective.

Scholars across the disciplines have looked to philosophers of science for help in defining the term *paradigm*. Like other researchers who have struggled with the term during the last 20 years, we perused Kuhn's (1970) postpositivist position on inquiry in science and scientific revolutions, realizing that Kuhn also proliferated multiple meanings for the term in his classic work. Drawing from Kuhn's work, we defined a paradigm to be a conceptual system, clearly separate from other conceptual systems, with a self-sustaining, internal logic, constituted as a set of epistemological rules directed at solving problems matched to the logic and rules.

Kuhnian perspectives often focus on paradigm shifts. Shifts involve a process in which researchers, in the act of doing normal science (the day-to-day pursuit of problems within a chosen paradigm), are confronted with problems they cannot solve or assimilate, and thus adopt new paradigms following a period of crisis. Kuhn has characterized these shifts as developmental processes. A new paradigm, perhaps more technical or esoteric than the last, is viewed as a sign of scholarly maturity and development in a field. Yet, a certain amount of snobbery accompanies membership in the community aligned with a new paradigm. As new paradigms are accepted, old paradigms are rejected by the dominant research faction (e.g., Mosenthal, 1985).

Polkinghorne (1983) characterized Kuhn's notion of paradigm shifts as an "irrational, discontinuous jump, not an evolutionary or developmental change" (p. 113). Polkinghorne believes that research, when practiced day to day *within* a paradigm, can lead to progress, albeit progress constrained by the constitutive rules and questions permitted within the paradigm. Hence, progress in research not only is made by shifting to *better,* more comprehensive paradigms, but also is made within the conduct of normal science

(Kuhn, 1970). That is, cumulative progress means continuing to do research within existing paradigms by choosing problems that are solvable, that the community agrees are worth solving, and that the community encourages its members to undertake. However, members of a paradigm may insulate themselves culturally and politically from other paradigmatic communities (Mosenthal, 1985), satisfied to make progress within a paradigm and to buttress it against other paradigms.

In its broadest sense a paradigm refers to a fully realized worldview that suggests not only a research methodology but also a value system or axiology, and ontological and epistemological premises. For example, paradigms as diverse as empiricism, behaviorism, progressivism, existentialism, capitalism, Marxism, feminism, romanticism, and postmodernism can be considered to be philosophical worldviews. Philosophical worldviews offer fully realized theoretical systems for understanding the world. Traditions, however, are distinct from philosophical worldviews. Traditions are disciplines from which we glean theories that guide our research methodologies (often referred to as theoretical frameworks). These traditions often reflect a worldview as well as a methodology, though the dominant worldviews and methodologies are subject to change as the research tradition or discipline changes. For example, anthropology is a discipline within which social and cultural theoretical frameworks are used to guide research; social psychology traditions are linked with symbolic interactionism; from psychology comes cognitive psychology and constructivism; and from theology, philosophy, and literary criticism comes hermeneutics. Both traditions and theoretical worldviews guide methodologies and yet commonly are referred to as paradigms; they are important philosophical choices in research.

For instance, researchers who want to study the social organizations in classrooms and how these affect learning and teaching could draw upon the discipline of anthropology, the theoretical perspectives of cultural and social theories, and the methodology of ethnography. The methodology chosen would dictate the types of data collected and how these data are analyzed. The assumptions undergirding the selected theoretical perspectives would affect the interpretation of the analysis, which also would be heavily influenced by a researcher's philosophical worldviews. Research typically involves many layers of paradigms including a philosophical worldview, a tradition or discipline, and a methodology. Further, each of these paradigms typically makes or implies ontological, epistemological, and axiological claims. The nature of these claims and the meaning of these terms, drawn from several sources (Hitchcock & Hughes, 1989; Lincoln & Guba, 1985; Scheurich & Young, 1997), are elaborated as follows:

- *Ontology:* the nature of reality (what is understood to be real). Ontological assumptions get at what people believe and understand to be the case—the nature of the social world or the subject matter that forms the focus of our research. Ontological beliefs give rise to beliefs about epistemology.

- *Epistemology:* ways of knowing reality (what is true). Epistemological assumptions are those that people hold about the basis of knowledge, the form it takes, and the way in which knowledge may be communicated to others. Scheurich and Young (1997) related that these assumptions arise out of the social history of specific groups and that our typical epistemologies are often biased (e.g., racially). Epistemological assumptions have methodological implications.

- *Axiology:* basic beliefs that form the foundation of conceptual or theoretical systems; the idea that the truth of propositions generated from inquiry depends on shared values between the researcher and participants. These beliefs include what is good or the disputational contours of right and wrong or morality and values (e.g., the need for shared information about knowledge generated during a study and protection for the participants from knowledge generated about them being used against them).

- *Methodology:* ways of undertaking research including frames of reference (e.g., theoretical frameworks), models, concepts (e.g., conceptual frameworks), methods, and ideas that shape the selection of a particular set of data-collection techniques and analysis strategies.

A more narrow interpretation of a paradigm may focus on one or more of the dimensions above. For example, literacy researchers may work primarily from a methodological paradigm and may not feel that a philosophical worldview, complete with ethical or ontological concerns, is necessary. Other researchers, such as postmodern and poststructuralist inquirers, eschew the very authority of scientism that supports assumptions, preferring to work unbound by these perceived constraints. Alternatively, one could argue that any research suggests ontological, epistemological, and axiological concerns, even if researchers do not explicitly acknowledge these assumptions.

Critical, then, to understanding the nature of paradigms is knowing the assumptions, values, shared beliefs, and practices held by communities of inquirers. Literacy researchers seldom address these ontological, epistemological, or axiological assumptions explicitly (if at all) in their writings or their research practices, although methodologies are addressed. Yet many researchers embrace the paradigmatic assumptions as crucial to an internally cohesive, quality research project. Others argue that specific philosophical paradigmatic allegiance, grounded in the assumptions, is neither critical nor even necessary; in fact, opponents argue that philosophical debates over such esoteric matters keep us from the real work we should be doing (e.g., Patton, 1990). The latter group of individuals is more interested in finding new ways to solve problems or in re-creating and subsequently shifting the field in the direction of new paradigms. When discussing methodological issues, Patton (1990) noted,

> [Paradigms are] deeply embedded in the socialization of adherents and practitioners: Paradigms tell them what is important, legitimate, and reasonable. Paradigms are also normative, telling the practitioner what to do without the necessity of long existential or epistemological consideration. But it is this aspect of paradigms that constitutes both their strength and weakness-their strength in that it makes action possible, their weakness in that the very reason for action is hidden in the unquestioned assumptions of the paradigm. (p. 37)

Patton is concerned that "too much research, evaluation, and policy analysis is based on habit rather than situational responsiveness and attention to methodological appropriateness" (p. 38). He reminds us that paradigmatic blinders constrain methodological flexibility and creativity: Instead of being concerned about shifting from one paradigm to another, we may adhere rigidly to the tenets of a paradigm, perhaps because of philosophical arguments about adherence to assumptions underlying our worldview, rather than adjust the paradigm to meet the challenges of new issues and problems we encounter in research.

We have cited Patton throughout our discussion of paradigms because he is a self-proclaimed pragmatist. His stance is that researchers do not need to shift to a new paradigm when the existing one is not broad enough for researchers' needs; nor do they need to stay trapped within the philosophical constraints of a particular worldview. Instead, researchers work to "increase the options available to evaluators, not to replace one limited paradigm with another limited, but different paradigm" (Patton, 1990, p. 38). He differs from Polkinghorne (1983), who suggested that one should work within an existing paradigm and adjust research questions within it. Rather, Patton suggested that researchers work within a paradigm but bring in new frameworks, methods, and tools—whatever is needed—to better address the research questions at hand. In the next section we discuss the use and usefulness of paradigmatic reasoning to literacy inquiry.

Paradigms in Literacy Inquiry: Have They Been Useful?

Recent research in literacy has been influenced by broad shifts in approaches to both natural and social science research. Earlier educational research can be characterized by the use of classical empirical scientific paradigms, which were grounded in a nearly utopian belief in the possibilities of science. Scientific methods were understood to be capable of capturing truth about reality and phenomena that were not available through ordinary discourse and observation. Research was driven by epistemological concerns. A scientific epistemology was thought to reveal ontological certainty upon which actions should be based. For example, the scientific positivist study of literacy was thought to reveal unequivocal universal truths about learners and learning that would allow for the unequivocally scientific application of teaching.

Researchers in both natural and social sciences, however, have become increasingly aware of the role of context, subjectivity, interpretation, and social values in all aspects of what was earlier understood to be an objective research process. What is observed and the meaning that is made of inquiry both are understood to be deeply influenced by the theoretical assumptions of researchers. This recognition has underscored the value of research approaches that shed light on the complexity of learners, researchers, and research settings. This includes paradigms such as sociolinguistics, various qualitative approaches, and phenomenological and hermeneutical interpretations as well as the critical and postmodern. These paradigms are increasingly being pursued not only because of their intrinsic capacity to help clarify complexity, or, in the case of critical theory, to champion the perceptions of the oppressed and underserved, but also because of their popularity in some settings.

A historical glance shows clearly that the field of literacy is not one that has evolved through the adoption, adaptation, and rejection of successive paradigms generated from within. Rather, paradigms in literacy research have been borrowed from various fields that have richly informed research topics and methods, albeit with arguments both supporting and criticizing the multiplicity of paradigms.

A Variety of Paradigms Can Enrich Literacy Inquiry

The diversity of fields and their accompanying paradigms that have informed literacy research can be viewed as enriching our perspectives and methods of inquiry (Beach, 1994; Beach, Green, Kamil, & Shanahan, 1992; Harris, 1969; Pearson & Stephens, 1994; Ruddell, 1998). Pearson and Stephens noted that about 30 years ago scholarship in the field of reading consisted primarily of the study of perceptual processes. They stated that the field was transformed suddenly in the mid- to late-1960s not because of paradigm shifts from within the community of reading researchers, but because scholars in other fields (e.g., linguistics, psycholinguistics, cognitive psychology, sociolinguistics) had become interested in reading. Each of these fields defined the reading process using descriptive and operational definitions, constitutive rules, and research methods that fit their individual paradigms. The field of reading (and indeed the broader field of literacy as we define it) is what Pearson and Stephens (1994) referred to as a transdisciplinary field that permits scholars to solve myriad problems using a variety of perspectives.

Pearson and Stephens's (1994) retrospect is validated by Harris (1969), who summarized the field of reading as he saw it at the time. In his chapter called "Reading" in the fourth edition of the *Encyclopedia of Educational Research,* he viewed reading research as a mirror image of research in the broader educational community, a field he characterized as being influenced by other disciplines. Harris traced reading research in this century from an early focus on perception (1910); to case studies (1920s); to evaluation and behaviorism (1930s); to reading comprehension defined by psychometrics and factor analysis (1940s); to experimental research with accompanying hypothesis testing and statistical tests (1950s, 1960s); to the most current work by scholars in other disciplines including psychology, linguistics, sociology, and medicine "who bring conceptual and experimental tools to bear on reading phenomena" (p. 1069). Harris took the perspective that researchers in the reading field should try to mirror the quality of the research being conducted in the multiplicity of fields informing the education field. He positioned the research methodology affecting reading research from outside the field proper as a standard to attain.

A Variety of Paradigms Can Hamper Literacy Inquiry

The notion of paradigm incommensurability (Donmoyer, 1996), if taken literally, means that fields such as literacy, informed by a range of disciplines, remain a set of subcommunities with incompatible assumptions and methodologies and little common language. The pragmatic stance, which we will discuss later, allows for compatibility. But we will explore the literal argument that the field has been hampered in its progress because of the multiplicity of voices emanating from incompatible paradigms (Clay, 1994; Mosenthal, 1985, 1999; Weintraub & Farr, 1976).

Mosenthal, who drew partly from Kuhn's (1970) work on paradigms, discussed the progress of educational research in general (1985) and reading research in particular (1987). He explored three different approaches to defining progress in research: (1) *literal approaches* in which researchers work diligently within a chosen paradigm to refine existing theories, find new features and examples compatible with the theory's higher order features (normal science), or discover anomalies leading to the creation of recombinant theories more inclusive than that developed within the paradigm supported by normal science (extraordinary science); (2) *interpretive approaches* in which researchers abandon the preoccupation with the fit between empirical definitions and reality in favor of the belief that reality is constructed; and, (3) *evaluative approaches* in which ideological implications of inquiry for society are central to the researcher's work. After careful discussion of these idealized ways of making progress, Mosenthal stressed that each group of researchers, or speech communities, embraces and advances their respective beliefs and abides by the rules that support definitions, cementing their solidarity with discursive practices that promote each definition as the normative one. Hence, progress, he contended, is defined not by a systematic testing and reconceptualizing of theoretical perspectives, but by political dominance and power of one speech community over others (Mosenthal, 1999). This is a less optimistic view of multiple paradigms and transdisciplinary research perspectives.

We can demonstrate further the negative side of positioning and repositioning of paradigms in literacy by drawing on multiple sources in which scholars synthesized research and discussed trends in the field. Almost 25 years ago, Weintraub and Farr (1976) noted that research in reading was being conducted using the classical empirical design because of what they referred to as "methodological incarceration." They contended that the model was used even though it was inappropriate for some of the research questions posed in the field. Weintraub and Farr also posited that reading researchers adhered to this paradigm to prove to allied professions, particularly psychology, that reading researchers could conduct quality research in that era of classical experimental studies. Although literacy research conducted within this paradigm has been valuable and moved the field forward, one could argue that the self-imposed methodological incarceration did limit methodological vision.

Paradigms That Could Have Made a Difference But Did Not

The field of literacy is one microcosm illustrating the systematic positioning and repositioning of paradigms and their inherent communities. For example, in the first three editions of *Theoretical Models and Processes of Reading* (Singer & Ruddell, 1970, 1976, 1985), each table of contents maps out the dominant research communities. Not surprisingly, the contents of these texts include mostly psychological studies of processes of reading wherein authors have attached operational definitions of various systems such as phonological systems, lexical systems, decoding, recoding, and visual perceptual span. The section on models in the second edition (1976) is divided into four types of models (types based on substantive theories in psychology), tested against theories using methodology grounded in positivist science. Editors Singer and Ruddell hoped that the volume would enhance further theorizing and research productivity, resulting in better reading instruction in the United States.

Embedded within the predominantly psychological perspectives in the 1976 volume is a piece written by Ray McDermott in a section called "Cultural Interaction." In his chapter, McDermott drew on anthropological theories and methods to look at the social reproduction of minority-community pariah status among poor children in school, and how this pariah/host (black children/white teacher) relationship plays out in the social organization of reading instruction. At the time most literacy researchers first acquired the second edition of *Theoretical Models*, they were interested in the dominant psychological paradigm. Few individuals seem to have noticed the unobtrusive McDermott piece, which fell clearly outside the dominant paradigm. In today's current context of interpretive research, significantly influenced by anthropological theories and methods, we can historically situate McDermott as a scholar who was ahead of his time.

In reviewing our own literacy research careers (Dillon & O'Brien), we wonder what would have happened if we had embraced McDermott's 1976 work instead of the dominant psychological paradigm. Might we have engaged in research at the beginning of our careers (in the early 1980s) that would be retroactively viewed as groundbreaking? However, like most of our colleagues, we overlooked McDermott because the dominant paradigm in the early 1980s was reading comprehension research, grounded in cognitive science using positivist and postpositivist methodologies. And even though we both studied qualitative research methodology and conducted such research starting in 1982, it was not readily embraced by our research community at conferences or by journal editors until years later. Hence, paradigms, although useful if considered in their broadest sense, have restricted the potential of research by limiting vision and polarizing competing research communities. Pragmatism, we contend, is a viable alternative.

Implications for the Future: Pragmatism and Practical Discourse

To meet the challenges that literacy researchers and practitioners will face in the new millennium, we look outside the field of literacy to a broader perspective in education—pragmatism (Dewey, 1916, 1919/1993a; Rorty, 1982, 1991). In the following section we define pragmatism and discuss why it is a useful alternative to paradigmatic reasoning.

What Is Pragmatism?

Pragmatism, a branch of philosophy, is 100 years old and is currently undergoing a revival (Dickstein, 1998) as a new way of approaching old problems in several diverse fields (e.g., law, social thought, literary theory). William James introduced pragmatism in his published lectures (1907/1991), but he built his arguments largely on the work of Charles S. Peirce. In its inception, pragmatism was considered highly controversial, but it interested many scholars because "like modernism, it reflects the break-up of cultural and religious authority, the turn away from any simple or stable truth [truth is provisional, grounded in history and experience or context, not fixed in the nature of things], the shift from totalizing systems and unified narratives to a more fragmented plurality of perspectives" (Dickstein, 1998, pp. 4-5).

In 1917 pragmatism was sharply criticized, and the downfall of this perspective was initiated:

> Dewey's pragmatic justification for America's entry into World War I, which shocked many of his followers, [and] showed up his concern with technique and efficiency at the expense of consistent values...it was a narrowly expedient philosophy of "adaptation" and "adjustment" bereft of ultimate goals. (Dickstein, 1998, p. 8)

Critics were dismayed that a pragmatic approach could be used to support such repugnant ends. Conservatives and Marxists as well as cultural critics rejected pragmatism. After World War II the rejection of pragmatism became even more pronounced because of new influences in thought including existentialism, psychoanalysis, European modernism, and a cultural conservatism linked with a fear of communism (cf. Morton White's 1949 text *Social Thought in America: The Revolt Against Formalism*).

The label *pragmatism,* like other vague terms, has been avoided by leading educational philosophers and researchers because it is overused and misconstrued, and a "terminological lightening rod" (Boisvert, 1998, p. 11). Even Dewey, who considered himself a pragmatist, left the term out of his texts, noting, "Perhaps the word lends itself to misconception…so much misunderstanding and relatively futile controversy have gathered about the word that it seemed advisable to avoid its use" (Dewey as cited in Boisvert, 1998, p. 11).

In this article we use pragmatism to support what Bernstein (1983) called "radical critiques of the intellectually imperialistic claims made in the name of method" (p. xi). In calling for pragmatism we are not advocating the approach of one or another theorist who is identifiable as a pragmatist; instead, we are advocating the spirit of the pragmatic tradition, which asserts that conducting inquiry to useful ends takes precedence over finding ways to defend one's epistemology. It is important to remember, as Dewey noted, that pragmatism does not mean "if it works then it's true" (Boisvert, 1998, p. 31), even though the term had been so cast. Paradigmatic critiques of research, when played out in the community, especially the popular media, show that researchers are often more concerned about their theoretical positions than about answering important questions. However, pragmatists are not simply persons who push philosophical arguments—particularly metaphysical ones—aside to get research done. Nor are they wishy-washy inquirers who do not know which epistemology to support or individuals who have neglected worldviews to which their work is linked. Rather, they have decided, after careful consideration of the effort and involvement, that the broader epistemological arguments, particularly those based in foundational epistemology, can never be solved because meaning is inseparable from human experience and needs and is contingent upon context. This perspective in some ways prefigures the postmodern worldview.

The value of inquiry using the "pragmatic method" (James, 1907/1991, p. 23) is in looking at the practical consequences of a notion (a method or perspective of inquiry) before deciding to employ it. James argued that when comparing alternative views of science, one must examine the differences these views would make in the world if each were true. If the world is unchanged across alternative views, then discussing them is insignificant. The pragmatic method is not a way to get certain results but, rather, an "attitude of orientation" that looks beyond principles (metaphysics) toward consequences and "facts" (p. 27). Within this stance, ideas, which are based in our experiences, are true only insofar as they help us relate to other facets of our experience and to achieve our goals. As Misak (1998) explained, "The pragmatist argues, were we to forever achieve all of our local aims in inquiry, were we to get a belief which would be as good as it could be, that would be a true belief" (p. 410). Paradigms, or theories developed within paradigms, each may contribute something useful, but ultimately the usefulness in summarizing or synthesizing existing ideas that lead to new ideas (rather than the theoretical purity) is what is important.

Similarly Dewey (1938/1981) noted that the value of scientific research must be considered in terms of the projected consequences of activities—the end in view. Dewey identified genuine problems that were part of actual social situations as those researchers should address. These problems (from practice), stated Dewey, should be identified and carefully defined before inquiry is undertaken. In fact, this latter point—the need to convert a problematic situation into a set of conditions forming a definite problem—was recognized by Dewey as a weakness of much inquiry (i.e., researchers selected a set of methods without a clear understanding of the problem). After the problem or subject matter (the phenomenon under study) was identified and the dimensions clearly defined, Dewey recommended that the issue be investigated from various perspectives, depending on the purpose or objective of the inquiry. Finally, as Dewey stated, "the ultimate end and test of all inquiry is the transformation of a problematic situation (which involves confusion and conflict) into a unified one" (p. 401).

The usefulness of pragmatic inquiry, however, as conceived by Dewey, also should be considered in terms of its capacity to contribute to a democratic life, broadly defined. Dewey observed that democracy "has not been adequately realized in any time" (Boisvert, 1998, p. 299), and the goal of democracy is the "creation of a freer and...more humane experience in which all contribute." (Dewey, 1939/1993c, p. 245). Similarly, Rorty (1982) stated,

> Our identification with our community—our society, our political tradition, our intellectual heritage—is heightened when we see this community as ours rather than nature's, shaped rather than found, one among many which men have made. In the end, the pragmatists tell us what matters is our loyalty to other human beings, clinging together against the dark, not our hope of getting things right. (p. 166)

Because the problems that pragmatists address are to contribute to a more democratic way of life characterized by the creation of a freer and more humane experience, the identification of problems for inquiry is particularly important. Democracy is not simply a set of political institutions. For Dewey, democracy is most centrally a way of life, and also a way of inquiry. Dewey wrote, "Apart from the social medium, the individual would never 'know himself'; he would never become acquainted with his needs and capacities" (1908/1982, p. 388) and "Apart from the ties that bind him to others, he is nothing" (1932/1987, p. 323). Dewey emphasized the inherently social nature of all problem posing, and he believed that people cannot understand themselves, or develop their practical reasoning, in isolation from others. This ontological assumption is consistent with Hegel and, more recently, Charles Taylor's (1994) argument that our very psychology is collectively, situationally constructed. According to this understanding, a crucial feature of human life is its fundamentally dialogical character. As Taylor explained,

> We become fully human agents, capable of understanding ourselves, and hence of defining our identity, through our acquisition of rich human languages of expression...we learn these modes of expression through exchanges with others...the genesis of the human mind is in this sense not monological, not something each person accomplishes on his or her own, but dialogical. (p. 32)

Therefore, problems need to be socially situated and identified to be legitimate foci of inquiry. Dewey believed that all inquiry is "natural, situational, grounded in problems, interrogations of theory and practice and evaluative." Further, "The integration of particular nonexpert experience, fostered by the establishment of interaction and discussion, enables the community to better use the insights" (Campbell, 1995, p. 199).

The inquiry process suggested by a pragmatic stance is quite different from traditional inquiry in which a researcher establishes a question or problem and proceeds without the integration of nonexpert opinion. In fact, for some researchers the integration of nonexpert opinion, which was key to Dewey, is understood as a sign of methodological weakness. The importance of dialogue and listening in inquiry requires new roles for researchers and also for the community of learners and practitioners, or what traditional research would call the subjects of research.

Another issue, which has been pointed out by critics of pragmatism, focuses on the practical challenge of using a method that requires the identification of problems. For example, Thompson (1997) noted, "The contextual, problem-centered character (of pragmatism) limits its ability to identify and analyze structural problems" (p. 426). For those living under hegemonic power structures, the deep structural problems of inequality may not be perceived as such, or for those who benefit from inequity, power structures would not necessarily be considered problematic. Bernstein (1991) described Rorty's pragmatism as failing to engage in radical democratic critique and becoming "an apologia for the status quo—the very type of liberalism that Dewey judged to be 'irrelevant and doomed'" (p. 233). Therefore, Thompson (1997) recommended political pragmatism, which recognizes "systemic conflict between social groups" and "understands experience under such conditions as itself political" (p. 428). We believe that a researcher's biggest challenge within this stance will be working with diverse groups of stakeholders to identify and define the dimensions of problems, resisting the temptation to become fixated on methods yet employing empirical, ethical tools and strategies that yield insightful albeit sometimes unsettling answers to real problems, and writing up the findings to illuminate both the processes and results of inquiry. The following section further explores the implications of these issues for literacy inquirers.

Using a Pragmatic Stance for Literacy Inquiry in the New Millennium

Scrutiny from within and outside the field of literacy has forced internal examination of our research and the ways that we engage in inquiry. As Chall (1998) noted in a recent article, the public "seems to place less confidence now than in the past in the power of research and analysis to find better solutions" (pp. 21–22). And although we have a proliferation of research that informs practice, "it has also contributed to the loss of faith in its use. Perhaps it is too vast and confusing and not sufficiently interpreted and synthesized" (pp. 21–22). Chall commented on the unorganized plethora of research findings that seem to have little impact on pedagogy or on solving current literacy problems, whereas Marty Ruddell (1998) emphasized that, in a time when our theoretical frameworks and methods are more diverse than at any time in our scholarly history in literacy, policymakers, politicians, and others who inform them have marginalized important forms of inquiry. This marginalization has occurred because research does not conform to the accepted, albeit narrow, politically correct paradigm. Moreover, Ruddell contended that the denial of a multiplicity of inquiry paradigms by politically visible national panels and policymakers is an attempt to force compliance to a "party line" (p. 8). The party line requires us to disavow our allegiance to paradigms outside of the canon of research rooted in developmental psychology and traditional scientism. Specifically, researchers who address questions generated in local settings and use interpretive methods to understand how particular teachers and students work together to support learning are positioned as being less scientific and, hence, less credible in terms of their processes and results.

Alternatively, literacy researchers who have conducted research projects that would be characterized by their peers as "scientific" (e.g., use large samples of children in multiple settings with experimental designs to measure growth or impact of programs or strategies) also feel marginalized in the literacy research community, hence the formation of a new organization, the Society for the Scientific Study of Reading (SSSR). Accepted by those in power in governmental agencies (e.g., national boards created to study why we have low reading scores in the United States), these researchers are often positioned even further away from their colleagues whose research is not deemed scientific enough.

Thus, political entities in government and elsewhere, the struggle for resources (grant monies) and jobs (tenure and promotion at universities), and a human need to feel that one has made a mark in the field all have contributed to a preoccupation with paradigm debates resulting in literacy research that has not made the difference it could in practice. Clearly, we need to regroup as a research community and consider the value of pooling our considerable intellectual resources. Difficult questions must be asked about why we engage in inquiry and who benefits from or is affected by the results of our efforts.

Dimensions of Literacy Inquiry for the Future

Although it is difficult to change particular large systems or structures (e.g., university systems, government agencies) and their value systems, we can begin to make changes as individuals and as a research community. We believe that a pragmatic perspective offers literacy researchers a way to approach inquiry that will enable us to agree to disagree, to get over it—ego involvement, and to get on with it—the important work of defining the literacy problems we need to solve, determining how best to solve these problems, and ensuring that the results inform practice (Mosenthal, 1999). In the next section we move in this direction by presenting dimensions of literacy inquiry that we believe must be defined, articulated, put into practice, and evaluated.

Dimension #1: Building Communities of Inquiry

Dewey reminded us that from a pragmatic perspective it is critical that we reconceptualize how inquiry is conducted, who we involve in the inquiry process, and the roles various participants assume within the process.

Community partnerships. A 1999 Kellogg Commission publication by the National Association of State Universities and Land-Grant Colleges (NASULGC) presents a key issue relating to the reconceptualization of how inquiry is conducted. The report challenges university personnel to work toward organizing staff and resources to better serve local and national needs in meaningful and coherent ways. The Kellogg Commission noted that university personnel must go beyond traditional notions of outreach and service to what is termed engagement. This concept disrupts traditional notions of a one-way distribution of services (e.g., the expert at the university reaches out to the community and transfers knowledge) to promote the creation of partnerships (e.g., among university staff, K–12 teachers and administrators, parents, students, and members of the community) in which all parties come together with resources and expertise. Mutual respect is crucial, and individuals glean valuable information for specified purposes through collaboration. Engagement among partners involves seven key elements:

1. *Responsiveness:* the need to listen to community members and ask appropriate questions to identify public problems;

2. *Respect for partners:* the need to jointly identify problems, solutions, and definitions of success;

3. *Academic neutrality:* the need for activities that involve contentious issues that have profound social, economic, and political consequences and a change in the role university faculty assume in these issues;

4. *Accessibility:* the need to ensure that community members are aware of and can access resources that may be useful to solving problems;

5. *Integration:* the need for faculty members to seek new ways to integrate their outreach/service missions with their teaching and scholarship while also committing to interdisciplinary work;

6. *Coordination:* the need for overall coordination of engagement efforts across the university and community and the assessment and communication of these efforts;

7. *Resources partnerships:* the need for adequate resources (time, effort, funding) to be committed to the tasks identified by all members of the partnership.

The idea of engagement is consonant with Dewey's pragmatic conception of social inquiry. Clearly, a commitment to engagement is necessary in forming partnerships. Strong leadership, coupled with support by administrators, promotion and tenure committees, and funding agencies, is also necessary. Communities must be open to diverse solutions to problems and varying roles of persons involved in partnerships. Challenges to this new concept of engagement and social inquiry revolve around logistical and accountability issues: How will communities of inquiry come together and function? Who will ultimately be responsible for the success or failure of partnerships? Will personnel be supported and rewarded for their efforts in both the short and long term? How do we know that people in communities of inquiry have the critical skills needed to deliberate problems? How will we mediate power and get along?

These challenges of pragmatism highlight what Bernstein (1983) understood to be a "paradox of praxis": "The type of solidarity, communicative interaction, dialogue, and judgment required for the concrete realization of praxis already presupposes incipient forms of community life that such praxis seeks to foster" (p. 175). Similarly, Dewey (1927/1993b) observed, "A class of experts is inevitably so removed from common interests as to become a class with private interests and private knowledge, which in social matters is not knowledge at all" (p. 187). It is difficult to conduct pragmatic inquiry that relies on communication and dialogue when teachers, community members, and researchers are not accustomed to working together; when literacy researchers are often separated by paradigmatic boundaries reinforced by power interests; and when researchers are similarly unaccustomed to communicative dialogue and interaction across disciplines both within education and across the academy.

Dewey (1916) envisioned communities of inquiry as communities that internally reflect "numerous and varied interests" and "full and free interplay with other forms of association" (p. 83). This conception is opposite our usual conception of independent research or academic communities in which interests and memberships are explicitly narrow. As Foucault (1975/1977, 1980) delineated, disciplinary practices with distinct types of knowledge and knowledge makers are disciplined and understood as systems of power and authority. The suggestion of a more inclusive notion of research participants and academic communities through pragmatism implicates deeply entrenched notions of power and authority.

Partners as advocates for learners. A desire to work collaboratively to identify and solve problems is key to the formation of partnerships between school-based personnel, literacy researchers, and community members. This stance requires a form of advocacy by members of the partnership, what Rorty (1982) called "loyalty to other human beings" (p. 162) in order to promote "the creation of a freer and more humane experience" (Dewey, 1939/1993c, p. 245). For instance, partners might take up the cause of students who have been tracked using limited assessment measures. To give an example of the dynamics of such advocacy, and to present a stark contrast to education, we turn to medical research. The following example shows how a pragmatic perspective, with participants in the role of advocate for themselves and others, influences research and practice.

The National Breast Cancer Coalition (NBCC), whose members have demanded a significant role in the scientific research designed to find a cure for their disease, advocate strongly for scientific research that asks the right questions, that is designed in credible ways, and that will yield answers that are appropriate and adequately translated for the public. An article in a recent newsletter ("Science and Research: Call to Action," 1999, January/February) of the NBCC links science and advocacy:

> Science is supposed to be pure, based on data, and objective observation. So how can advocacy give us anything but bad science? Scientists are individuals with their own perspectives and biases. Individuals, who design protocols, determine which questions to ask and decide how to frame issues. The perspective of trained breast cancer activists can enrich the scientific process and through collaboration we can end up with better science and more meaningful answers. (p. 10)

During the design of high-stakes clinical research comparing the use of the drugs tamoxifen and raloxifene for women at high risk of breast cancer, advocates questioned the need for requiring control groups and placebos as well as large numbers of women in the study. Researchers refused to approve a placebo component, claiming that it would be unethical. NBCC advocates questioned what was ethical in the long term. It is crucial to a pragmatic view of research to define what is ethical within the community in which the research is conducted. As a result of many conversations, NBCC advocates are creating partnerships with industry and government as they design new therapies. These partnerships ensure that the participants (and later recipients of the therapies) are able to play a role in the design, implementation, and dissemination of results from clinical trials; the advocates also serve on peer review teams for funding agencies. This advocacy has resulted in what is referred to as a new paradigm for breast cancer research, with collaborative efforts resulting in answers about whether new therapies are effective much sooner than in previous years.

This medical example is interesting in comparison to advocacy efforts of researchers and educators in K-12 education settings. It presents a marked contrast to educators' advocacy for themselves and their students. A challenging question for educators is why we see little need for advocacy with such a large number of stakeholders, including researchers, teachers, parents, students, and citizens.

The NBCC advocates believe that advocacy and science must be paired if shared goals are to be achieved—goals like life itself and quality of life. Do stakeholders in education have shared goals for learners that we believe are so critical that they must be achieved to foster a high quality of life? Could it be that, because education is not a life-or-death enterprise that clearly links actions and accountability, we feel much less urgency toward learners than physicians, medical researchers, and patients feel in their medical endeavors? An alternative response is that we lack practice in working from a moral position to identify social problems and collectively find solutions.

Pragmatists would seek to develop partnerships where engagement is central to the work, where university- and school-based educators as well as students and community members bring their respective expertise to bear during deliberations, and where all stakeholders advocate for themselves to identify educational problems and inquiry designs. Ultimately, all stakeholders would be advocates for student learning.

Dimension #2: Moral Obligation in the Selection of Research Problems

Currently, many educational researchers are stepping back from their inquiry projects and the philosophical debates about the conduct of research to ask themselves these questions: Why do I engage in educational research? How meaningful is my research? and Who benefits from my work? Chall (1998) posed a similar question to her peers in literacy research: "What is the responsibility of scholars? Is it toward searching for new knowledge about the reading process? Or should it also include the responsibility of helping to solve the grave literacy problems facing us today?" (pp. 23-24). Dewey (1938/1981) would urge literacy researchers to consider problems we face in light of the institutional, social, political, and contextual influences surrounding the problems.

The formulation of research problems. As we construct research agendas with participants and think about the ends we hope to influence, we must take more time than we have in the past to identify carefully and then outline the actual problem and its dimensions. Too often, we quickly pose research questions, spending most of our time on elegant designs or intensive analyses. As Dewey (1929/1987) warned in *The Quest for Certainty*, "The natural tendency of man is to do something at once, there is an impatience with suspense, and lust for immediate action" (p. 178). From a pragmatic perspective, more time must be spent talking about the problem with participants and other constituents, defining the contours and the ways that addressing one feature of a problem may contribute to understanding another, and thinking about the concerns and implications associated with our decisions. This stage is what Dewey characterized as "enjoying the doubtful" (p. 182). The effort at the inception of the study can result in stronger, richer efforts along the way.

Particular discernment for identifying what might be a useful focus of inquiry or a problem to solve usually rests with the researcher, or what Dewey called the expert. Campbell (1995) summarized Dewey's ideas about the role of experts: "To solve problems in our complex modern world requires us to think differently and those members of society with special experience or with special expertise may be particularly helpful in formulating problems and suggesting possible solutions" (p. 149). A pragmatic perspective requires that researchers share this power with participants; researchers come to the table with expertise, but other stakeholders also bring their knowledge and experience. Within this context, researchers are charged with teaching community members about methodological options available to understanding and solving problems. The sort of democratic dialogue Dewey envisioned in such a setting helps foster both understanding and community. Dewey (1927/1993b) observed that "the essential need...is the improvement in methods and conditions of debate, discussion, and persuasion" (p. 187). Such dialogue is an important skill, which is equally appropriate for citizens, researchers, and students. Matthew Lipman (1998) described dialogue as moving in the direction of two kinds of wholeness:

> On the one hand the mental acts form logical connections with one another. On the other hand, those who perform such acts form social relationships with one another. The first kind of wholeness is a completeness of meaning. The second kind, the interpersonal kind, moves toward a communal solidarity. (p. 208)

Within this process researchers lose some freedom in the formulation of problems, the way problems are addressed, and what is reported from the research. However, sharing of power is worthwhile when inquiry is viewed as responsive, meaningful, and credible to all participants.

Developing multiple, connected research initiatives. Along with broadening the collective of persons associated with inquiry and redefining the roles persons might assume within this process, there is a need to reconsider how we develop research agendas, identify problems, and craft studies. We propose a literacy inquiry agenda spanning three foci: (1) developing a set of critical problems, generated by a diverse group of stakeholders, that are foundational to large-scale research projects with multiple sites and community inquiry teams; (2) developing a set of critical problems generated at the local level by community inquiry teams; and (3) collectively identifying problems that interest individual researchers and that can be parsed into various facets to be addressed by individual expertise. Consistent with a pragmatic stance, we believe that on an international, national, local, and personal level researchers should consider Dewey's vision of inquiry as collectively generating research problems from actual social situations (practices) as identified by all stakeholders through practical discourse.

Researchers themselves pose the biggest challenge to taking a pragmatic stance in developing multiple, interconnected research foci. Wolcott (1992) in his discussion "Posturing in Qualitative Research" (positioning oneself strategically) illuminates the struggle researchers have when attempting to meet several, often competing, agendas, including powerful interests of their own:

> [P]osturing is not only a matter of identifying a strategy and capitalizing on research talents, it is also a personal matter influenced by the kinds of information and kinds of memberships...available to and valued by academicians individually. Prior professional commitments...and future professional aspirations...also exert an influence and extract a corresponding commitment over the problems we select.... These commitments consciously or unconsciously influence our identification of problems or lead us to redefinition of problems that make them amenable to study in some particular way rather than in others. (pp. 41-42)

To Wolcott, research is ultimately a personal matter; we research things we enjoy, believe in, or feel passionately about. Nevertheless, the problems literacy researchers typically pose and the methods they select for solving these problems are almost always mediated by the trends highlighted in professional communities such as the National Reading Conference (NRC), the Society for the Scientific Study of Reading (SSSR), the International Reading Association (IRA), and the American Educational Research Association (AERA). Individual researchers want to position themselves professionally, socially, and culturally—they want their work to fit into acknowledged trends and to be acknowledged by respectable communities. Dewey and other pragmatists oppose the perspective of research as a personal matter, noting that research agendas should be public and socially grounded in intent and process. Inquiry not so grounded fails to serve the purpose of democratic reconstruction.

Embedded within the challenge of public vs. personal research agendas is the question of how the nature of research is influenced by the way researchers are positioned by the social, cultural, and historical contexts in which they conduct inquiry. Colleagues and administrators in the university system, K-12 school-based colleagues, and local, state, and national policymakers define these contexts. For example, researchers are valued in university settings for the innovative knowledge they generate and, like it or not, productivity in the form of quantity of articles in prestigious journals. Add to this narrow conceptualization of productivity the current institutional pressures to reform teacher education programs and a situation is created in which scholars actually have little time to be scholarly. In such a climate, research is often quickly conceived; data are collected, analyzed, and interpreted in a cursory manner; and reports of research are written in bits and pieces when time permits in outlets that university promotion and tenure committees find acceptable (but persons engaged in practice may not read). Thus, much of this research may have little effect on the practices of K–12 educators or on learners' lives. There is evidence that this institutional culture is changing, but it remains a formidable force that affects the character and quality of literacy inquiry.

Literacy research agendas and designs also are shaped by commitments researchers make to commercial publishers when they sign as authors. These scholars/authors often try to balance commitments to the profession with the economic interests of their publishers/employers. Finally, many researchers have strong commitments to addressing broad issues in education (e.g, tracking, assessment, busing) that sometimes displace more immediate subtle contextual issues that uniquely inform research from site to site. Researchers, who are pulled in many different directions as they engage in their work, can disenfranchise the very practitioners and students who are at the heart of the most crucial problems that need to be addressed.

In sum, neither literacy scholars nor prospective advocates of scholarship have clearly identified a broad set of issues that deserve unified, convergent efforts, although policymakers and funding agencies have done so. Further, literacy researchers and other stakeholders currently lack a coherent plan, a process, or the leadership to initiate such efforts. Despite the identified need for a shared research agenda, most literacy researchers also believe that opportunities must be provided for innovative, unconventional research that advances the field. This tension between large-scale and local research agendas, shared and individual agendas, and the role of research paradigms can be managed productively with considerable thought, effort, dialogue, and organization. A pragmatic stance to the formation of multiple yet connected research agendas could facilitate this effort.

Keeping the end in view when designing research. In maintaining a pragmatic stance, the selection and design of studies in the literacy field should be developed with the end in view. Traditionally, this end in view is a post hoc entity we call implications or recommendations rather than an a priori design issue. Pragmatic research conversations would begin with these questions: What do we hope to achieve at the conclusion of the study? Why is this end important for learners? The conversation about the end result could help participants better define problems and improve the design of studies, and this conversation could help participants focus on the specific social, cultural, and other contextual aspects that affect a particular inquiry.

Despite its apparent usefulness, an end-in-view perspective, grounded in social responsibility and democratic purposes, presents a new challenge in conducting research. In beginning a study, researchers typically review related research, carefully crafting hypotheses or guiding research questions, developing a design that best addresses questions, collecting and analyzing data, theorizing, and interpreting the results. It is possible that the end-in-view fixation may cause researchers to lose sight of the research process, including methodological possibilities, or of certain structural considerations as a project unfolds (Thompson, 1997).

Dimension #3: Reconsidering Traditions, Methodologies, and How We Communicate Findings

The knowledge we hold and the beliefs we subscribe to dictate what research questions we ask and for whom. Polkinghorne (1983) noted that our scholarship is defined as much by the self-interrogation about why we engage in inquiry as it is in the actual conduct of research. This self-inquiry promotes the use of a broad range of designs and methods but requires that we carefully articulate the assumptions undergirding various approaches and traditions that are the basis of our inquiry.

The use of multiple traditions within a study. Technical expertise and theoretical and methodological purity have been the hallmarks of quality in paradigmatically driven research. Researchers believe that if they attend to these elements, more credible findings will result. By contrast, a pragmatic stance values communities engaged in literacy research who focus on solving problems; the selection of the theoretical frameworks and methodologies are tailored to the complexity of the problem and the promise of useful findings rather than discrete technical standards.

That said, we are not promoting the use of a-little-bit-of-this and a-little-bit-of-that inquiry. Particular frameworks or traditions and methodologies *do* have underlying assumptions, some of which are congruent with one another and some of which are not (see Jacob, 1987, for an in-depth discussion of this issue). But is it possible for literacy researchers to employ research traditions with incompatible assumptions in an attempt to explore multiple facets of a problem, to test or add depth to a primary analysis, or to offer additional, compelling evidence that appeals to wider groups of stakeholders who might then also find other less acceptable forms of data credible? We address this question in the next two sections.

The purity of traditions and methodologies versus quality of use. A pragmatic stance promotes the examination of all assumptions underlying various traditions and encourages collaborative discussion about which could be adopted and which should be rejected. But researchers, in addressing problems, understand, select, employ, and discuss the various traditions and methodologies they use to design and engage in useful research rather than taking political positions aligned with paradigms.

Pitman and Maxwell (1992) discussed the pervasiveness of paradigm wars in spite of a substantial scholarly base offering many options and broad perspectives on inquiry. They contended that philosophical debates in research have become increasingly detached from the actual conduct of research. To address this detachment, they asked researchers to reflect on their *practice* and to critique the various approaches they use within a perspective or methodology (e.g., researchers would examine the quality of research practices used within educational ethnography). In actuality, we rarely systematically critique the quality of one another's use of traditions and methodologies.

From a pragmatic stance, using a variety of methodologies can either strengthen a study or lead to its downfall. The use of multimethodologies can add breadth and depth and numerical, pictorial, and narrative data to support themes, assertions, or findings. But these studies must still evidence the tenets of quality research. Many researchers are careful to ground their work in substantive theories from the field of literacy; nevertheless, these same scholars can sometimes be criticized for neglecting to use and exhibit understanding about the theoretical frameworks undergirding their methodologies. A classic example in literacy research is the popularity of qualitative or interpretive research, specifically educational ethnography. Wolcott (1992), writing about the newly embraced qualitative research methodologies in education, observed: "Qualitative studies completed today often fail to show evidence of the disciplinary lineages that spawned them...the innovative process in educational practice tends toward adaptation rather than adoption" (p. 38). Although Wolcott acknowledged that adaptations developed by educational researchers might have admirable traits despite their hybrid nature, to adopt a methodology, he contended, one must have studied its disciplinary lineage well. Educational researchers must strengthen their theoretical knowledge base in the disciplines that inform the methodologies they wish to draw upon and articulate this knowledge in both their practice and writings. These methodologies and frameworks might include not only ideas from across educational disciplines, but also frameworks from outside the current boundaries of education such as those grounded in policy studies, political theories, literacy theories, philosophy, or even biology.

Although the title Doctor of Philosophy is reminiscent of the days in which a broad education was more valued, academe, as already noted, currently does not support the development of broadly educated researchers. Neither does the academy support the development of inquiry communities with school and community collaborators, or with the potentially diverse groups of colleagues that pragmatic inquiry needs to thrive. Again, Foucault (1975/1997, trans. 1980) reminded us that the ways in which we structure knowledge in academe serve to create regimes of truth and structures of power and authority. Thus, a pragmatic turn in inquiry provides us with compelling challenges not only to the ways in which ideas are conceived and pursued, but also to the ways in which power and authority are structured among intellectuals, and society in general. The change we suggest has both philosophical and political ramifications.

Considering new traditions and methodologies. Concurrent with the need for new knowledge is an awareness of what knowledge bases we draw upon and which ones we inadvertently overlook. For example, we believe that literacy researchers should consider Scheurich and Young's (1997) discussion of race-based paradigms constructed via cultural and historical contexts. The authors argued that all current epistemologies and accompanying tensions (e.g., issues of qualitative vs. quantitative methodologies, objective vs. subjective reality, validity and paradigmatic issues in general) rise out of the social history of the dominant white race, thus reflecting and reinforcing that social history and racial group. This white dominance has negative results for people of color and, in particular, scholars of color (cf., Collins, 1991). We need to extend paradigms to address "epistemological racism," recognizing that dominant and subordinate racial groups "do not think and interpret realities in the same way as White people because of their divergent structural positions, histories, and cultures" (Stanfield, 1985, p. 400). Scheurich and Young (1997) argued that even critical approaches (critical theory, feminism, lesbian/gay orientations, and critical postmodernism), where racism has been a focus, have been racially biased. A pragmatic perspective beckons literacy researchers to attend to how various racial groups select issues for inquiry, conceptualize research, interpret phenomena, and record results. This is a new epistemological issue that is critical to understanding literacy events in the next millennium.

Communicating the findings of research. We must consider how we relate the findings from our inquiry to other communities of inquirers, researchers within and across paradigmatic lines and disciplines, and individuals outside the research context (e.g., policymakers and the general public). Writing for multiple audiences and writing about ideas that others find useful (keeping the end in mind as one constructs a study) are important goals. Chall (1998) pointed out that literacy research is becoming more and more technical and complex, making it more difficult to translate findings in a written form that is understandable to practitioners and other researchers. From a pragmatic stance, we believe that the typical article format for sharing work should change to better illuminate complex concepts for a range of readers and to meet the needs of policymakers in terms of brevity (e.g., through the use of executive summaries), clarity, and elimination of jargon.

A shift in the expectations of journal editors and editorial review boards also will be needed to promote the publication of concise research reports while also recognizing the value of longer articles that detail theory and methodology. A pragmatic stance requires that we more carefully consider the audiences that we hope to inform with our inquiry—audiences that span far beyond our universities and research communities to local schools, communities, and state and federal agencies.

Technology also holds promise for offering new forms of representation that will display and explicate concepts that heretofore have been represented with flat text. For example, David Wray, of the University of Warwick, announced the formation of a new journal that would provide a series of abstracts of published research and other materials relating to literacy (post to the National Reading Conference listserv [nrcmail@asuvm.inre.asu.edu], February 1999). This journal, and others like it, would provide concise and accurate information for researchers and practitioners alike. Published accounts of research in new concise formats have the potential to reach a larger audience and inform practice, policy, and future inquiry efforts.

Conclusions

Many complex questions relating to how learners become and remain literate and how teachers can support this process remain uninvestigated. However, our past practices in selecting questions and formulating inquiry approaches must be adapted for the new millennium. An individual researcher's beliefs and expertise no longer can be the sole rationale for the research questions selected and pursued. Instead, the complexity of problems and social situations that affect practice and concern local constituents must be key to the creation of shared research agendas.

We have proposed the adoption of pragmatism as a new stance for academics and communities of inquirers. Pragmatism is not a paradigm adapted from those that are currently popular; rather, it is a revolutionary break in our thinking and practice relating to inquiry. As a literacy community we need to challenge ourselves to step back and think collectively and individually about the inquiry in which we are engaged. Is our research meaningful, credible, and prone to making a difference in students' learning and teachers' pedagogy? Does our inquiry work toward concrete alternatives for students and teachers? As Rorty explained, "For the pragmatists, the pattern of all inquiry—scientific as well as moral—is deliberation concerning the relative attractions of various concrete alternatives" (1982, p. 164). We see the goal of research at its best as practical rationality serving moral concerns. Pragmatic research for the new millennium can be a practical and hopeful inquiry, which avoids the arrogance of modernist empiricism and the angst of postmodern deconstructions. We can accomplish this new goal.

REFERENCES

Beach, R.L. (1994). Adopting multiple stances in conducting literacy research. In R.B. Ruddell, M.R. Ruddell, & H. Singer (Eds.), *Theoretical models and processes of reading* (4th ed., pp. 1203-1219). Newark, DE: International Reading Association.

Beach, R.L., Green, J., Kamil, M.L., & Shanahan, T. (Eds.). (1992). *Multidisciplinary perspectives on literacy research*. Urbana, IL: National Conference on Research in English and National Council of Teachers of English.

Bernstein, R. (1983). *Beyond objectivism and relativism: Science, hermeneutics and practice*. Philadelphia: University of Pennsylvania Press.

Bernstein, R. (1991). *The new constellation*. Cambridge, MA: Polity Press.

Boisvert, R.D. (1998). *John Dewey: Rethinking our time*. Albany: State University of New York Press.

Campbell, J. (1995). *Understanding John Dewey*. Chicago: Open Court.

Chall, J.S. (1998). My life in reading. In E.G. Sturtevant, J.A. Dugan, P. Linder, & W.M. Linek (Eds.), *Literacy and community* (pp. 12-24). Commerce, TX: College Reading Association.

Clay, M.M. (1994). Foreword. In R.B. Ruddell, M.R. Ruddell, & H. Singer (Eds.), *Theoretical models and processes of reading* (4th ed., pp. ix-xiii). Newark, DE: International Reading Association.

Collins, P.H. (1991). *Black feminist thought: Knowledge, consciousness, and the politics of empowerment*. New York: Routledge.

Dewey, J. (1916). *Democracy and education: An introduction to the philosophy of education.* New York: Macmillan.

Dewey, J. (1981). Social inquiry. In J.J. McDermott (Ed.), *The philosophy of John Dewey* (pp. 397–420). Chicago: University of Chicago Press. (Original work published 1938)

Dewey, J. (1982). Ethics. In J.A. Boydson (Ed.), *The middle works of John Dewey, 1925–1953* (Vol. 5). Carbondale: Southern Illinois University Press. (Original work published 1908)

Dewey, J. (1987). Ethics revisited. In J.A. Boydson (Ed.), *The later works of John Dewey, 1925–1953* (Vol. 7). Carbondale, IL: Southern Illinois University Press. (Original work published 1932)

Dewey, J. (1987). The quest for certainty. In J.A. Boydson (Ed.), *The later works of John Dewey, 1925–1953* (Vol. 4). Carbondale: Southern Illinois University Press. (Original work published 1929)

Dewey, J. (1993a). Philosophy and democracy. In D. Morris & I. Shapiro (Eds.), *John Dewey: The political writings* (pp. 38–47). Indianapolis, IN: Hackett. (Original work published 1919)

Dewey, J. (1993b). The public and its problems. In D. Morris & I. Shapiro (Eds.), *John Dewey: The political writings* (pp. 173–191). Indianapolis, IN: Hackett. (Original work published in 1927)

Dewey, J. (1993c). Creative democracy—The task before us. In D. Morris & I. Shapiro (Eds.), *John Dewey: The political writings* (pp. 240–245). Indianapolis, IN: Hackett. (Original work published in 1939)

Dickstein, M. (Ed.). (1998). *The revival of pragmatism.* Durham, NC: Duke University Press.

Donmoyer, R. (1996). Educational research in an era of paradigm proliferation: What's a journal editor to do? *Educational Researcher, 25*(2), 19–25.

Engelbreit, M. (1998, December 25–27). So the millennium is just around the corner—get over it; get on with it. *USA Today,* cover page.

Foucault, M. (1977). *Discipline and punish: The birth of the prison* (A. Sheridan, Trans.). New York: Pantheon. (Original work published 1975)

Foucault, M. (1980). Truth and power. In C. Gordon (Ed.), *Power/knowledge: Selected interviews & other writings, 1972–77* (pp. 109–133). New York: Pantheon.

Graves, M.F. (1998, October/November). Beyond balance. *Reading Today,* p. 16.

Harris, T.L. (1969). Reading. In R.L. Ebel (Ed.), *Encyclopedia of educational research* (4th ed., pp. 1069–1108). Toronto: Macmillan and the American Educational Research Association.

Hitcock, G., & Hughes, D. (1989). *Research and the teacher: A qualitative introduction to school-based research.* New York: Routledge.

Jacob, E. (1987). Qualitative traditions: A review. *Review of Educational Research, 37,* 1–50.

James, W. (1991). *Pragmatism.* Buffalo, NY: Prometheus. (Reprinted from *Pragmatism: A new name for some old ways to thinking* by W. James, 1907, Cambridge, MA: Harvard University Press)

Kellogg Commission on the Future of State and Land-Grant Universities. (1999, February). *Returning to our roots: The engaged institution.* Washington, DC: National Association of State Universities and Land-Grant Colleges.

Kuhn, T. (1970). *The structure of scientific revolutions* (2nd ed.). Chicago: University of Chicago Press.

Lincoln, Y.S., & Guba, E.G. (1985). *Naturalistic inquiry.* Newbury Park, CA: Sage.

Lipman, M. (1998, May/June). Teaching students to think reasonably: Some findings of the philosophy for children's programs. *Clearing House, 71,* 277–281.

McDermott, R.P. (1976). Achieving school failure: An anthropological approach to illiteracy and social stratification. In H. Singer & R.B. Ruddell (Eds.), *Theoretical models and processes of reading* (2nd ed., pp. 389-428). Newark, DE: International Reading Association.

Misak, C. (1998). Deflating truth: Pragmatism vs. minimalism. *Monist, 81*, 407-426.

Mosenthal, P.B. (1985). Defining progress in educational research. *Educational Researcher, 14*(9), 3-9.

Mosenthal, P.B. (1987). Research views: Defining progress in reading research and practice. *The Reading Teacher, 40*, 472-475.

Mosenthal, P.B. (1999). Critical issues: Forging conceptual unum in the literacy field of pluribus: An agenda-analytic perspective. *Journal of Literacy Research, 31*, 213-254.

Patton, M.Q. (1990). *Qualitative evaluation and research methods* (2nd ed.). Newbury Park, CA: Sage.

Pearson, P.D., & Stephens, D. (1994). Learning about literacy: A 30-year journey. In R.B. Ruddell, M.R. Ruddell, & H. Singer (Eds.), *Theoretical models and processes of reading* (4th ed., pp. 22-42). Newark, DE: International Reading Association.

Pitman, M.A., & Maxwell, J.A. (1992). Qualitative approaches to evaluation: Models and methods. In M.D. LeCompte, W.L. Millroy, & J. Preissle (Eds.), *The handbook of qualitative research in education* (pp. 729-70). New York: Academic Press.

Polkinghorne, D. (1983). *Methodology for the human sciences*. Albany, NY: State University of New York Press.

Rorty, R. (1982). *Consequences of pragmatism*. Minneapolis, MN: University of Minnesota Press.

Rorty, R. (1991). *Objectivity, relativism, and truth*. New York: Cambridge University Press.

Ruddell, M.R. (1998, December). *Of stand-up comics, statisticians, storytellers, and small girls walking backward: A new look at the discourses of literacy research*. Presidential address presented at the annual meeting of the National Reading Conference, Austin, TX.

Scheurich, J.J., & Young, M.D. (1997). Coloring epistemologies: Are our research epistemologies racially biased? *Educational Researcher, 26*(4), 4-16.

Science and research: Call to action. (1999, January/ February). *The Quarterly Newsletter of the National Breast Cancer Coalition, 5*(1), 10.

Singer, H., & Ruddell, R.B. (1970). *Theoretical models and processes of reading*. Newark, DE: International Reading Association.

Singer, H., & Ruddell, R.B. (1976). *Theoretical models and processes of reading* (2nd ed.). Newark, DE: International Reading Association.

Singer, H., & Ruddell, R.B. (1985). *Theoretical models and processes of reading* (3rd ed.). Newark, DE: International Reading Association.

Stanfield, J.H., II. (1985). The ethnocentric basis of social science knowledge production. *Review of Research in Education, 12*, 387-415.

Strickland, D.S. (1996, October/November). In search of balance: Restructuring our literacy programs. *Reading Today*, p. 32.

Taylor, C. (1994). The politics of recognition. In C. Taylor & A. Gutman (Eds.), *Multiculturalism: The politics of recognition* (pp. 25-73). Princeton, NJ: University of Princeton Press.

Thompson, A. (1997). Political pragmatism and educational inquiry. In F. Margonis (Ed.), *Philosophy of education* (pp. 425-434). Urbana, IL: Philosophy of Education Society.

Weintraub, S., & Farr, R. (1976). Introduction. In R. Farr, S. Weintraub, & B. Tone (Eds.), *Improving reading research* (pp. 1-7). Newark, DE: International Reading Association.

West, C. (1993). *Keeping faith*. New York: Routledge.

White, M. (1949). *Social thought in America: The revolt against formalism*. Boston: Beacon Press.

Wolcott, H. (1992). Posturing in qualitative research. In M.D. LeCompte, W.L. Millroy, & J. Preissle (Eds.), *The handbook of qualitative research in education* (pp. 3-52). New York: Academic Press.

Can Teachers and Policy Makers Learn to Talk to One Another?

Cathy A. Toll

Anyone who has been a new teacher in a school knows something about discourses. At every school there are unwritten rules about how to behave and act, such as how one gets supplies, who sits where in the teachers' lounge, how casually one dresses on Fridays, what terms like *Child Study Team* mean. These unwritten rules make up the discourse of that school—the "how to belong here" of a place or a group. A newcomer spends a great deal of energy, consciously and unconsciously, in deciphering these rules and assimilating them as quickly as possible in order to fit in. At the same time, and perhaps what makes this newness tolerable, the newcomer knows many things about fitting in already. For instance, there are discourses of the teaching profession that the new teacher may already know: We consider children to grow in developmental stages, the teacher is expected to be in charge of the classroom, being prepared for each day is valuable, and so on. There are discourses, too, for schools: Spaces in the building are divided into classrooms, a principal is in charge, parents participate but only in limited ways, and so on. And there are discourses about learning: It is incremental, it thrives when the learner is motivated, it requires discipline, and so on.

Perhaps you disagreed as you read the examples above. For instance, maybe you know of a school without a principal, or you believe that learning is natural and doesn't require any special discipline. As you read my statements, then, you may have felt an urge to pick a fight with me, to argue that I was making inaccurate assumptions about the discourses I was describing. This is one of the effects of discourse: One's own discourse seems so natural, so logical, and so right that it becomes difficult to see the acceptability of alternative discourses. This is also one of the dangers of discourse: It creates such a strong sense of what is normal that it often becomes impossible to think that things could be any different.

The definition of discourse that I use here comes from the sociolinguist Gee (1996), who explained that a discourse is

a socially accepted association among ways of using language, other symbolic expressions, and "artifacts," of thinking, feeling, believing, valuing,

Reprinted from *The Reading Teacher*, 55, 318–325, December 2001/January 2002.

and acting that can be used to identify oneself as a member of a socially meaningful group or "social network," or to signal (that one is playing) a socially meaningful "role." (p. 131)

I am attracted to this concept because it fits with my experiences—in schools and in life more generally—and because it has helped me make sense of some dilemmas surrounding school change, particularly in relation to literacy instruction. Discourses affect efforts to change schools. The sense of "how things are done around here"—that is, what is normal—is strong in schools, and this discourse makes change especially difficult. From this perspective, change requires a willingness to do things differently in schools, and implicit in that willingness is the requirement that one's existing sense of the way to do things may not be accurate or best. Of course, change does take place in schools, as it does elsewhere, and so we do indeed have the ability to alter our discourses, although this work is often a struggle.

What may make school change even more of a challenge, however, is that there are discourses of school change as well. I am going to give some examples of the discourses of change that I find among teachers as they talk about their literacy instruction, drawn from interviews I have conducted with them, and compare them with the discourses of change that I find among policymakers, drawn from published policy documents. This will give a sense of the competing discourses of change that can be found in education. I'll then discuss how educators might use this information in considering school change.

Teachers' Talk of Change

The discourse of teaching includes beliefs and actions that affect change. Among these are decision making based on engagement with students, concern for children's affect, and controlling one's choices. I will elaborate on each of these.

Decision Making Based on Engagement With Students

Teachers frequently express a desire to engage with their students to the extent that the teachers know what students need educationally and can provide it. For instance, Amanda Petrie (all names are pseudonyms) has changed her practice from one in which she tries to "cover the book" to one in which she tries to teach what her students seem to need next. She states that "it's important to really look at children; they're all going through different developmental steps."

Barbara Callahan, a school library specialist, has altered her approach to book selection. Her goal is no longer to have children reading certain kinds of "quality" literature but rather to have them reading at all. She explains that this change began by "just noticing the kids. You have to take the kids where they are."

Concern for Children's Affect

Teachers' discourses include frequent references to children's affect, and these concerns appear influential upon teachers' reasons for change. For instance, Alice Trimberger, a sixth-grade teacher, is delighted to report that, due to her new literature-based language arts program, "probably at least 8 out of 10 kids will say their favorite subject is language arts." She goes on to describe the "different look in the kids' eyes" that expresses the pleasure they derive from their reading. Alice is focusing on the children's personal, emotional responses to what happens in class.

Similarly, Beth Randall describes her reasons for changing to a new literacy program:

> I want them [her students] to be interested in what they're doing. I want them to be involved.... I want them to know that I care about what I'm doing here. I think that I want them to get the message that they are important, that what they do is important. I guess my expectations are high, but, you know, I am here to help them move that way. I'd like them to have goals, I'd like them to know that...what we're doing is serious, it's important, but yet I think that I like to have that attitude that this is our room, this is yours, and it's mine.... It's a happy place to be, and they're involved in things that they're learning, yet they're excited about what they're doing.

Although Beth acknowledges expectations for academic achievement, she has much more to say about her affective goals. She wants children to be happy, feel that they are valuable, and believe their school experiences are important.

Controlling One's Choices

Discourses of teaching include frequent references to controlling the choices one makes. For example, Amanda Petrie speaks with pleasure of the freedom she is given to make instructional decisions:

> This school has been wonderful. As long as we look at outcomes, as long as the children do what they need to be able to do by the end of the year,

however you get there...everybody does travel their own road.... Everybody gets there a different way, and from year to year I don't do the same thing.

On the other hand, Mary Ransom, a first-grade teacher, is critical of administrators who fail to allow for individual teachers' choices:

I think administrators...don't allow for teachers' differences in how they grow and how they teach. They say, "Well, we're gonna do this and this," and that everybody's got to do it. And then the people start resisting it, if it's not what's in them. If they don't feel good about it, they're not going to do a good job.

Clare Hansen provides a different perspective on the same idea when she explains that, as a Title I teacher charged to work with disadvantaged students, she could not make classroom teachers change their instructional practices. In her collaborations with classroom teachers, she could only "offer a little encouragement" even though she knew "they needed something different." Thus, even though Clare works closely with other teachers and has her own views about what they might do, she believes that teachers must decide for themselves. In her view, it would be an infringement on teachers' right to control their own choices if she told other teachers what to do.

Teachers' Talk and Discourse

The ways teachers have spoken to me about changes they made are reflective not just of these individual teachers' experiences but of a discourse of teaching in which they all engage. In other words, the sense these teachers have of themselves and their work reflects a discourse—a way to be, think, talk, and believe about teaching—that shapes their work and yet, on the other hand, is shaped by their participation in the discourse. When teachers speak of caring for kids, focusing on affective considerations, and controlling their own decision making, they are defining and being defined by a discourse of teaching. This is how to be a teacher, how to fit in.

I support this claim in three ways. First, I depend upon my personal experience as a teacher and as someone who has talked with many other teachers. These themes run like a thread through educators' conversations. There are other possible explanations for this, but none are convincing to me. For instance, one could consider whether all teachers are directly instructed to think in these ways as they prepare to teach, but that is not the case at my university, which has one of the largest teacher education programs in the U.S., nor is it the case at other universities with which I am familiar. Another explanation would be that these themes are communicated directly to teachers through professional journals, staff development, or administrative directives. Certainly, ideas such as control over one's choices can be found in communications to teachers, but so can contradictory messages, such as having the curriculum and standards control one's choices. To me, a much better explanation for the occurrence of similar themes of change among many teachers' views is that such themes are part of a discourse of teaching.

Beyond personal experience, I support this idea of a discourse of teaching because similar ideas about change appear in published representations of teaching. For instance, Noddings (1994) spoke of the manner in which teachers care for their students by getting to know each one's needs and responding appropriately to those needs:

> The first member of the relational dyad (the carer or "one caring") responds to the needs, wants, and initiations of the second. *Her* mode of response is characterized by *engrossment* (nonselective attention or total presence to him, the other, for the duration of the caring interval) and *displacement of motivation* (her motive energy flows in the direction of the other's needs and projects). She feels with the other and acts in his behalf. The second member (the one cared for) contributes to the relation by recognizing and responding to the caring. (p. 174; emphasis in original)

Noddings's use of gendered pronouns is notable. The carer is generally female, in the same way that teachers are still more often female than male, especially at the elementary level, which is the level of the teachers I have cited. In this way, Noddings participates in a discourse of teaching that includes the idea of teachers engaging in a gendered practice of caring for students, just as many teachers participate in the same discourse.

The media are similarly full of examples of this discourse of caring. The teacher-hero of movies is often the one who cares beyond the call of duty for her students and as a result accomplishes what no one else could on their behalf. Public service commercials on television remind us as well that teachers accomplish great things through their care for children. As a society we construct teachers as carers who engage with children, just as we construct women as people who engage with children, and teachers participate in these discourses as well when they speak of their reasons for changing practices.

My third argument for the discursive nature of teachers' beliefs and practices is based upon the contrast among documents related to school reform. Those documents aimed at teachers or written by teachers frequently use a discourse that parallels the one I have outlined. Those documents aimed at policymakers, legislators, or the public at large frequently use a very different kind of discourse.

Others' Talk of Change

The teachers I have cited were all speaking of changes in literacy instruction. Two documents, both released in the year 2000, address practices in literacy instruction as well, and the contrast between them is marked, because each uses different discourses.

The National Education Association (NEA) Report

One document is the *Report of the NEA Task Force on Reading 2000* (National Education Association, 2000). This report was issued by the NEA in February 2000 in response to a mandate from the 1999 NEA Representative Assembly that a task force of NEA members with classroom experience in teaching reading be formed to "develop comprehensive guidelines on the teaching of reading" (p. 2). The task force consisted of 11 members, all teachers.

I have carefully examined the NEA report for signs of a discourse of change, and I found in the report numerous references to themes that were discussed by the teachers I interviewed.

Decision making based on engagement with students. This report makes frequent reference to the need for a teacher to know students' individual needs. The report discusses students as individuals, noting the diverse "strengths, needs, backgrounds, interests, and ways of learning that students bring to school" (p. 7). According to the report, small class sizes are necessary in order for teachers to understand students as individuals and to provide the interaction and instruction their students need.

Concern for children's affect. The NEA report suggests that students should derive pleasure from reading and should have a positive attitude toward reading. It maintains that "learning to read should be enjoyable, attractive, and developmentally appropriate. Powerful learning experiences involve engagement, choices, success, and personal connections" (p. 23).

Controlling one's choices. The need for teachers to make their own decisions about instruction is emphasized. The report recognizes the expertise of teachers in knowing their students and the ability of teachers to develop a repertoire of classroom practices. The report also argues that teachers must influence their own professional development and the direction of programs in their buildings and districts.

The themes found in teachers' talk of change run like threads through the NEA report as well. It is perhaps unsurprising that a teachers' organization would participate to some degree in the same discourse as that of teachers themselves. However, the significance of this idea is evident after looking at a competing report.

The National Reading Panel (NRP) Report

The second document is the *Report of the National Reading Panel* (2000), which examined certain kinds of research related to reading and in April 2000 issued a report on its findings. The U.S. Congress mandated the formation of this panel in 1997 and appointed the National Institute of Child Health and Development to oversee its development. Membership on the panel consisted of 14 individuals: nine university professors, two university administrators, a middle school reading teacher, an elementary school principal, and an accountant. Thus, most members of this panel are likely to be entrenched in discourses removed from classroom teaching. What's more, the language of the report reflects this difference in discursive orientation. The themes that run through teachers' talk of change are virtually nonexistent in the NRP report.

Decision making based on engagement with students. There are two references to the need for teachers to respond to individual students' needs, but these references are outweighed by the more numerous references to the need for objective research to rule teachers' decision making. For instance, immediately after suggesting that "teachers should be able to assess the needs of the individual students and tailor instruction to meet specific needs," implying perhaps a kind of engagement with children, this report claims,

> It will also be critical to determine objectively the ways in which systematic phonics instruction can be optimally incorporated and integrated in complete and balanced programs of reading instruction. Part of this effort should be directed at preservice and inservice education to provide teachers with decisionmaking frameworks to guide their selection, integration, and implementation of phonics instruction within a complete reading program. (NICHD, 2000, p. 11)

Thus, teacher educators and staff developers are being trusted to determine what students need, rather than individual teachers who understand individual students.

Concern for children's affect. The NRP report makes one mention of student interest in books. This is the only statement that focuses on students' affective response to instruction or to engagement in literate activities. There is one mention of student motivation and one mention of the need for teachers to keep students engaged, but I would argue that these statements refer to the goal of on-task student behaviors and not to an interest in the feelings of children.

Controlling one's choices. The report discusses teachers as "consumers" of the information in the report, describing them, along with "parents, students, university faculty, educational policy experts, and scientists," as "the ultimate users and beneficiaries of the research-derived findings and determinations of the Panel" (p. 2). Thus, rather than teachers controlling their choices or creating their understandings, teachers become passive in the discourse of this report. Teachers themselves also need to be motivated, according to the report, particularly when providing phonics and phonemic awareness instruction. This discourse views teachers as the subjects of some other group's influence rather than in control of their professional work.

Summary

The discourses of change found in two national reports on reading instruction vary greatly. The report published by the NEA reflects teachers' discourses on several counts. The emphasis is on teachers' control of their work and their engagement with their own students to make instructional decisions. Consistent with teachers' own talk, this report suggests that instructional change takes place when teachers see the need in their own localized situations and act to implement the changes they desire. The report of the NRP represents a discourse of change that is markedly different from teachers' discourses. It focuses on research data removed from individual teachers' experiences and suggests that programs should change when teachers are given "objective" data and motivated to apply conclusions drawn from this data in their own classrooms.

So What?

Competing discourses. The manner in which change is talked about reflects more than just a choice of words, an opinion, or even a cultural effect. It reflects a discourse, meaning that it reflects a way of thinking, talking, and acting that signals who is in and who is out, who is in the know and who isn't, what knowledge matters and what doesn't. In other words, these discourses of change are connected to power. This is important in considering school change.

The language of the National Reading Panel report reflects a discourse of change that is rooted in a belief in objective knowledge existing outside the local context and beyond any individual teacher's awareness. It positions teachers on the receiving end of change and sees children as variables in research studies. On the other hand, the language of the National Education Association report, and the language of many teachers, reflects a discourse that positions change in the hands of individual teachers in response to their engagement with their own students, often in relation to children's affective concerns.

The discourse represented by the NRP report is a discourse found in a great deal of discussion about school change. Policymakers, administrators, and others often situate school change within the need to obtain the best science that will yield the best results and then are confused or angry when teachers don't respond favorably to these changes. On the other hand, the discourse of teachers and their union often considers the most worthy changes to be those that come from considering children's needs in particular situations, and thus they see policymakers and others as cold-hearted or out of touch when they suggest other sources of decision making. Is it any wonder that everyone in education seems frustrated by the school change puzzle?

When issues of power arise, issues of gender, class, or race are often evident. In the case of school change, gender is significant. Teaching, especially elementary school teaching, is still a gendered profession, and policymakers and administrators are still predominantly male. Engaging with children and attending to their affective needs are "womanish" concerns, and as such they are valued by many teachers. I am not suggesting that policymakers and administrators, male or female, do not value caring for children; in fact most would say, I am sure, that teachers must be caring and must engage with children. However, when one considers the discourse of change found in policy documents such as the NRP report, one finds that power is given to those who possess "clear, objective, and scientifically based information" (p. 2). Decisions are based on information other than that gathered by teachers in their own classrooms as they engage with their own students. Therefore, where does power lie? What is really important?

Implications

The practical reader looking for ways to apply these ideas might decide that these competing discourses of change indicate a need for someone's discourse to change. In other words, it may be tempting to see my argument as a call for administrators and policymakers to talk about change differently, or for teachers to do the same. However, the nature of discourses makes this idea seem unrealistic. Because discourse is so closely connected to power, the user of a discourse usually doesn't want to give it up. This is especially true when there is a lot of power associated with a discourse, as in the case of the discourse of the NRP report, which is sanctioned by the National Institute of Child Health and Development along with other government agencies, and therefore is being widely publicized and promoted. However, I would argue that teachers would not participate in their own discourse of change unless it, too, provided them with power. The power of teachers' discourse is in its elevation of teachers' own work and in the way it connects teachers with one another. This discourse provides teachers with a way of viewing teaching, learning, and change that serves as an "identity kit," in Gee's (1996) words; it is one way that teachers belong to the group called "teachers," and by privileging certain kinds of knowledge, this discourse creates a space in which only teachers can do the work as they believe it can be done.

So there may be little desire for altering one's discourse of change. Another tack would be to co-opt an alternate discourse of change. In other words, although teachers participate in a discourse unique to them, they might use the language of an alternate discourse when dealing with policymakers or administrators, say, by speaking of scientific, objective evidence while nonetheless valuing their own decision making related to individual students' needs. Conversely, policymakers might frame scientific evidence to show how it supports what teachers see in their own students' needs. These co-optations would be, in a sense, the marketing of one's discourse: One would shape the discourse of change so that it fit into an alternate discourse.

I see attempts at such marketing as likely. The history of school change efforts is one of a search for a better technology. Educators and others have manipulated the variables in school change—the innovations, the change processes, the leadership, the teachers, the larger community—in continued attempts to "get it right," despite the considerable documentation that school change efforts nearly always don't work, at least not as intended or not over the long run (e.g., see Gibboney, 1994; Hatch, 1998; Sarason, 1990; Tyack & Cuban, 1995). Some folks will no doubt see discourse as another variable to manipulate. This seems ill-advised, given the nature of discourse. Remember, discourses are not just opinions or ways of talking. As I am using the term, *discourse* refers to ways of being, reflected in words, actions, and beliefs, that are connected to power. Attempts to borrow another discourse in order to accomplish one's aims would be dishonest and manipulative, and probably not successful.

If we won't change our discourses of change, and if it is not appropriate to accommodate an alternate discourse, what can we do? I would suggest working in full awareness of competing discourses and developing a metadiscourse in school settings. Educators, policymakers, and others will benefit from open acknowledgment of the competing discourses in which they work. At minimum, this will create honesty in educational work; better, it may enable us to honor one another while preserving our sources of knowledge and power, and at best it will maximize the ability of educators to move beyond difference to a space in which the work of learning and teaching can be improved upon.

The NRP report on reading instruction provides a good example. This report has created consternation among some educators. Charges of faulty science and political positioning have been rampant (Krashen, 2000; Manzo, 1998), and it is important to consider this report from scientific and political perspectives. However, what these considerations often lead to is a kind of debate that can be reduced to, "Oh yeah?" "Yeah"—an argument in which each side claims it is more correct than the other. The public cries for an end to these debates and demands a return to the facts, which is, at least in part, what led to the formation of the NRP in the first place. Meanwhile, many educators ignore this report; in fact, one member of the NRP, who identifies herself as the only member who has spent a career in elementary education, filed a minority report that declared the NRP report to be, "to some extent, irrelevant" (NICHD, 2000).

Consideration of discourse is another way to address the report. If educators, policymakers, and others make visible the NRP's discourse of change and contrast it with teachers' discourse of change, a new kind of conversation might take place. This conversation would acknowledge that the NRP, and apparently the Congressional mandate that led to this panel, privileges evidence conducted in experimental studies outside of teachers' everyday classroom experiences, and that many teachers privilege individual knowledge garnered by teachers through engagement with their own students, often with attention to student affect. Then, if all involved can resist the urge to argue for the superiority of their own discourse, a dialogue might result about the differences between these discourses. Some questions for consideration would be the following: What are the effects of empowering certain kinds of knowledge—for example, teachers' experience or experimental evidence—over others, in schools and in classrooms? How do we make room for difference in the profession of education and in the public sphere in which educators work? Will resistance be the result of privileging one discourse over another, and what are the effects—positive or negative—of such resistance? Are there kinds of research that honor teachers' decision making in relation to their own contextualized work, yet are respected as sound according to accepted notions of science?

Let me be clear: This kind of work is extraordinarily difficult. There is a great deal of attention right now on collaborative groups among educators (and others concerned with education), and these efforts have potential. However, all too often the discourses of these groups themselves lead to power imbalances and have tremendous potential for dishonesty (Anderson, 1998; Hargreaves, 1994). For instance, some elementary school teachers, as women in U.S. society, operate within a discourse that says it is "normal" for a woman to be polite and yielding to others, and this influences their interactions in study groups. Disagreement may be a struggle for some, and participants may resort to silence or counterproductive resistance as a result.

A key consideration in shaping the success of metadiscourses about school change is how educators deal with difference. This must be an essential part of any dialogue on change. Some questions for consideration might be the following: How is difference recognized and how is it responded to? What is a "safe" difference in any group? What does a person do if her or his difference from the group is so great that she or he finds it difficult to function in that group? What does the group do when it recognizes difference between it and another group, be it a group of educators, parents, or policymakers?

This is not a cry for smoothing over points of disagreement; I am not asking, "Can't we all just get along?" Issues surrounding literacy instruction, school change, and reading research reflect broader issues about how literacy is constructed, who controls what goes on in classrooms, and the kind of world we want to have in the future (Hoffman, 2000; Shannon, 2000). We cannot afford to minimize these issues or to smooth over our disagreements. What I am arguing for is a new way to conceptualize the issues, a way that might open up new ground for debate and for moving ahead.

Better science is not going to lead us to a utopian condition in which all educators know the answers to all of education's difficult questions. The fights will continue. Power will always be at play, and some will always be privileged over others. We can improve our work as educators, though, if we continually bring these issues to the fore and create dialogue about how we work within these constraints. The arguments about how to move beyond them have not gotten us far. Perhaps it is time to open up a new discourse.

REFERENCES

Anderson, G.L. (1998). Toward authentic participation: Deconstructing the discourses of participatory reforms in education. *American Educational Research Journal, 35*, 571-603.

Gee, J.P. (1996). *Social linguistics and literacy: Ideology in discourses*. London: Taylor & Francis.

Gibboney, R. (1994). *The stone trumpet: A story of practical school reform*. Albany: State University of New York Press.

Hargreaves, A. (1994). *Changing teachers, changing times: Teachers' work and culture in the postmodern age*. New York: Teachers College Press.

Hatch, T. (1998). The differences in theory that matter in the practice of school improvement. *American Educational Research Journal, 35*, 3-31.

Hoffman, J.V. (2000). The de-democratization of schools and literacy in America. *The Reading Teacher, 53*, 616-623.

Krashen, S. (2000, May 10). Reading report: One research's "errors and omissions." *Education Week* [Online]. Available: www.edweek.org/ew/ewstory

Manzo, K.K. (1998, February 2). New national reading panel faulted before it's formed. *Education Week* [Online]. Available: www.edweek.com/ew/1998/23nichd.h17

National Education Association. (2000). *Report of the NEA Task Force on Reading 2000*. Washington, DC: Author.

National Institute of Child Health and Human Development. (2000). *Report of the National Reading Panel. Teaching children to read: An evidence-based assessment of the scientific research literature on reading and its implications for reading instruction* (NIH Publication No. 00-4769). Washington, DC: U.S. Government Printing Office.

Noddings, N. (1994). An ethic of caring and its implications for instructional arrangements. In L. Stone (Ed.), *The education feminism reader* (pp. 171-183). New York: Routledge.

Sarason, S. (1990). *The predictable failure of educational reform*. San Francisco: Jossey-Bass.

Shannon, P. (2000). "What's my name?": A politics of literacy in the latter half of the 20th century in America. *Reading Research Quarterly, 35*, 90-107.

Tyack, D., & Cuban, L. (1995). *Tinkering toward Utopia*. Cambridge, MA: Harvard University Press.

Barriers to Literacy for Language-Minority Learners: An Argument for Change in the Literacy Education Profession

Rachel A. Grant and Shelley D. Wong

oncern about the "performance chasm" in reading achievement between language-minority learners and children whose first language is English is a topic for discussion by educators, policy makers, and concerned citizens in many communities. In fact, few issues in modern education in the United States attract so much attention and controversy, yet produce so few lasting results, as the schooling of linguistically diverse learners. Why do barriers continue to restrict access to full literacy for many language-minority learners in the United States? We believe the literacy education profession is responsible for some of them. In our view, two barriers to literacy are the failure (1) of teacher-education programs to adequately prepare reading specialists to work with language-minority learners and (2) of education researchers to engage in more substantive research on English reading development for such students. The goal of this article is to point out the barriers that exist within the literacy education profession that may slow or even prevent language-minority learners from becoming fully literate in English. We use the term "full literacy" to stress not just English proficiency, but levels of achievement, especially in reading and writing, that help learners of English as a second language (ESL) to meet native-speaker norms across the curriculum (Short, 1991).

According to Thomas and Collier (1997), "at least part of the difficulty in productively discussing the education of language minority students has to do with shifting, vague, inconsistent definitions of the children" (p. 16). Here we use the terms "language minority" and "English-language learner" to refer to children, born in the United States or in other countries, who are from homes where the primary language spoken is not English. These students may have limits in their understanding, speaking, reading, and writing of English. "Limited English proficient" (LEP) has also been used to describe them. We have refrained from using the term "LEP." Others in

Reprinted from *Journal of Adolescent & Adult Literacy, 46,* 386–394, February 2003.

bilingual education and second-language learning (Chamot & O'Malley, 1994; Freeman & Freeman, 1994; Nieto, 1992) have suggested that LEP has negative connotations, and we share this feeling.

It is clear that we live in a complex and educationally competitive world and that effective formal schooling is a critical component for success in adult life in the 21st century (Thomas & Collier, 1997). Literacy is an important precondition for organizing and understanding the past, the present, and the future to determine one's role in the world. We argue that literacy professionals can help to narrow the performance gap for language-minority students. To make our case, first we highlight some of the long-standing roadblocks to literacy for English-language learners imposed by forces operating outside the literacy profession. Next we address the first barrier within the purview of literacy professionals, the preparation of literacy practitioners. Our discussion of the second barrier emphasizes problems related to the quantity and nature of English reading research. We end with several recommendations for change. We hope the following discussion will compel literacy professionals to reexamine preparatory aspects, explore new roles for literacy professionals in support of English reading for language-minority learners, and increase the levels and amount of research on ESL reading by literacy researchers.

Traditional Roadblocks

Estimates are that 30–40% of school-age English-language learners fail to reach acceptable levels of English reading by the end of their elementary schooling. For older language-minority students, failure to attain grade-level competence in reading persists well beyond high school (Thomas & Collier, 1997). In recent years, due to state-mandated testing and new standards, there has been a growing demand for higher performance levels for all students. Children at every level, even kindergarten, are now expected to meet benchmarks to demonstrate basic skills in reading and the content areas. It is unfortunate that those who would advocate for higher standards and more testing of school-age children have failed to consider what this will mean for many language-minority students (August & Hakuta, 1997). We contend that if economic, political, and social pressures deflect attention from underserved English-language learners and place these students "on the back burner," the prospect for long-term educational parity between English learners and native-English speakers is at best questionable.

Many roadblocks can derail efforts for English-language learners to attain higher levels of literacy. First, we acknowledge there are multifaceted and complex historical, social, political, and economic conditions that influence how schools respond to educating linguistically different learners. Traditionally, some of the factors that restrict access to full literacy for language-minority students have included (a) xenophobic English-only movements (Donahue, 1995); (b) limited resources and personnel within ESL (August & Hakuta, 1997); (c) controversy about bilingual education (Faltis & Hudelson, 1998; Krashen, 1996); (d) differences about the duration and type of language services children should receive (Collier, 1987); and (e) cultural and linguistic deficit models (Luke, 1986).

Factors endemic to systemic processes and institutional culture also impede efforts to address the literacy needs of language-minority children. For example, programs of study in reading education reflect state mandates and individual program philosophies. State departments of education usually dictate course requirements for endorsement and certification within a state, and reading education programs are designed so that their students meet those requirements. It is likely that unless local or state education agencies require that reading specialists take courses or receive inservice training to prepare them for meeting the needs of language-minority children, little will change. Tackling bureaucratic red tape and political maneuvering to bring about change can be labor intensive and time consuming. However, because of the indisputable importance of achievement in reading as a measure of school success, we believe that literacy professionals must assume a leadership role in the discourse for change.

It is also the case that, within universities, the organizational structures of departments and programs hamper efforts to address the needs of language-minority students. Time honored practices that determine resources and "turf protecting" can discourage faculty from developing interdisciplinary programs or establishing collaborative initiatives. Reading and ESL education programs historically have been designed to serve two distinct populations. However, concern for the achievement gap in reading between native-English speakers and children learning English dictates that, at the very least, ESL educators will need to know more about literacy development. Reading specialists also will need to know about first- and second-language acquisition and be able to employ effective strategies for helping English learners develop reading skill at levels comparable to their native-English-speaking peers.

Not surprisingly, we are not alone in our concern about the necessity for more responsive literacy professionals in meeting the needs of all students.

We want every child to learn to read and to enjoy reading for a variety of purposes. Yet much of the reform and standardization of reading education is aimed toward a select few, at the expense of a great many. It is important to consider who will benefit, and conversely who will be left out, from any given reform. (Edmondson, 2001, p. 626)

We believe language-minority students have been systematically excluded from traditional attempts to increase the reading performance levels of school-age children. Language-minority children in the United States still are overrepresented among those performing poorly in school (August & Hakuta, 1997).

Preparation of Literacy Practitioners

To begin, some background about reading-teacher and specialist training may be helpful. We have chosen to use the term *reading specialist* to refer to those who, either through number of credit hours earned, special certification, or degree status (master's in education), have received additional course work and content in literacy and reading and are considered to possess above-average knowledge of developing children's skills in reading. Traditionally, reading specialists are prepared to work with those children who are not meeting grade-level benchmarks in reading. States or local districts generally exercise considerable freedom in setting the specific requirements reading specialists will need. These can vary from as few as 9 to more than 30 credit hours or a master's degree. It is usually the case that college and university programs in reading education closely follow state or local requirements. Typical course work and content include diagnosis and evaluation, reading methods, content-area reading, writing, children's or adolescents' literature, measurement and statistics, administration and supervision, and research methodology. An additional 4 to 6 credit hours of clinical experience may be required. The clinical experience is similar to student teaching and involves working closely either one on one or with small groups of children addressing their reading difficulties. Often neither the course work nor clinical experience is designed to prepare reading specialists to meet the distinct needs of language-minority students.

We recognize that many programs in teacher education do require or have electives to address topics of diversity. However, far too often linguistic difference is nested within the context of multicultural information or even special needs. The usual response of much of teacher education is to add multicultural information to the current course curriculum (Yeo, 1997). According to Grant (1994) this effort is insufficient, ineffective, and potentially misleading—even damaging. It is done to help teachers become sensitive to individual differences. Developing awareness and sensitivity is merely a first, small step toward ensuring that teachers will have the knowledge and skills necessary to provide an equitable literacy education for language-minority learners that is based on their specific needs. Another troubling issue intrinsic to preparation is that reading specialists receive a theoretical grounding for literacy that is associated with the monolingual, meritocracy paradigm used to define literacy (Meacham, 2000–2001; Willis & Harris, 2000). In other words, the white, native-English speaker establishes the norm and sets the guidelines for literacy achievement. Course work within programs of study in reading seldom emphasizes a second paradigm on literacy that acknowledges multilingualism and multiliteracies (New London Group, 1996). Central to the second paradigm is the belief that academic success for language-minority learners can be achieved through culturally inclusive theoretical frameworks for research methods and literacy assessment as well as literacy instruction (Meacham, 2000/2001). The second framework for literacy is also characterized by emphasis on preserving children's home languages and recognizing the negative consequences of language loss (Wong-Fillmore, 2000). In addition, this paradigm promotes critical literacy and acknowledges that literacy and politics have worked hand in hand creating barriers for many language minorities, people of color, the poor, and females (Willis & Harris, 2000).

Once their preparation is complete, reading specialists move on to schools where their role is often determined by the principal or by school tradition. As a result, some reading specialists serve as diagnosticians who are largely responsible for administrating and keeping track of district- or state-mandated tests. Others may act as individual tutors working in pull-out programs with children who need more expertise and time than is available in regular classrooms. Sometimes the reading specialist may coach teachers who need help with diagnosing students who are reading below grade level and then identifying appropriate materials and instruction. Less often, the reading specialist is able to work with the regular classroom teacher or ESL teacher to collaborate on instruction for children with difficulties in reading, including language-minority students.

In their work, reading specialists usually provide instruction in a range of reading and literacy areas, including alphabet knowledge and phonemic awareness, word recognition and phonics skills, fluency, word acquisition strategies, comprehension knowledge, and vocabulary development. In terms of instructional models, reading specialists are expected to possess knowledge of a range of techniques, strategies, and approaches, as well as resources for working to improve children's reading. During their preparation, reading specialists learn about a variety of instructional frameworks such as the Directed Reading–Thinking Activity, language experience approaches, Reading Recovery, Reciprocal Teaching, traditional basal or phonics programs, and guided reading procedures. In some cases programmed instruction with highly structured manuals, computer software, or audiotapes is used. Many districts and individual schools also have their own local approaches to teaching reading. In addition to providing instruction in reading, reading specialists are expected to be familiar with aspects of writing instruction, especially writers' workshop and process writing. Overall, reading specialists are considered to be experts with well above average training in identifying reading difficulties and in teaching to meet the needs of children who have a wide range of reading abilities.

In spite of the special preparation given to reading practitioners, most do not take any courses that help them in specifically addressing the basic literacy or content-area reading needs of nonnative-English speakers. Unfortunately, when specialists in reading do begin to work in schools, usually they work exclusively with native-English-speaking students. The prevailing practice has been that ESL teachers work with English-language learners and reading specialists work with the "regular" students. Well-designed bilingual programs have English-language development, including literacy, built into the overall plan across grades (Thomas & Collier, 1997). However, only about 15% of students who need special language services are in federally funded programs, and only about one third receive any language assistance at all (Nieto, 1992). More than a quarter (26.6%) of elementary students with limited English proficiency receive no tailored education services to allow them to understand instruction (Garcia, 1992). For those English learners who do participate in language programs, many may be pushed from ESL programs when they can demonstrate oral fluency in English, not reading fluency, often after as little as one to two years. It is often the case, even when language-minority students do receive language services, that they do not achieve academic competence in English across the curriculum at levels comparable to their native-English-speaking counterparts (Collier, 1987; Cummins, 1979; Short, 1991). This suggests that many language-minority students will need help beyond ESL classes in order to develop and extend their knowledge of literacy, especially in reading and writing English.

Some literacy educators suggest that reading processes in a second language may not be significantly different from those in a first language (Fitzgerald, 1993, 1995a, 1995b). This is the "prevailing wisdom" that undergirds the preparation of U.S. reading specialists, and it marginalizes linguistic diversity as an individual difference in literacy acquisition. We believe that language-minority learners may not be best served when reading is viewed as a unitary, universal process. There are at least two aspects to consider that may make a "one size fits all" approach to teaching reading problematic. Dubin, Eskey, and Grabe (1986) indicated that the first aspect to consider is this:

> [the] linguistically constrained issue of whether the different languages in question and their different orthographic systems require different reading strategies, different learning strategies, or at least, suggest the likelihood that various universal processes interact differently for optimal processing in different languages. (p. 29)

For example, some languages, like Chinese, differ from English in that there is no alphabetic principle. (See Parry, 1996, for a discussion of the differential effects of language and culture on learning to read English and Chinese.) In some languages, like classical Chinese, punctuation is not used to signal the end of a sentence (Wong & Teuben-Rowe, 1997). In Farci, or Persian, students write most letters on a line; however, a few letters are written totally below the line, and other letters are placed through it.

Dubin et al. (1986) pointed out a second aspect that relates to sociocultural differences between U.S. assumptions about literacy and those of other societies. In the past, some research has suggested that in other societies students' reading abilities are less proficient because children simply do less reading in developing countries (Guthrie, 1981). We believe that when the practices of literacy and its functions and meaning are defined exclusively by Western standards, a deeper, more grounded understanding of the complexities of literacy is obscured (Graff, 1994; Street, 1984). The narrow, Western view of literacy often results in a deficit perspective toward non-European literacies. In our view, societies differ not just in the forms of literacy they use but also in the functions of literacy within the society, polity, culture, or economy (Graff, 1994). A pedagogy of multiliteracies suggests that "language and other modes of meaning are dynamic representational resources, constantly being remade by their users as they work to achieve their various cultural purposes" (New London Group, 1996, p. 6). When the cultural backgrounds and linguistic knowledge students bring to schools are considered "deficit models" there are often serious academic and psychological implications for teachers and students that lower expectations of what language-minority learners can achieve (Wong-Fillmore, 1992). We are encouraged that there appears to be a growing body of literature on the real and apparent differences invoked by readers of different languages and different orthographic systems (Weinstein-Shr & Quintero, 1995; Wiley, 1996). With appropriate preparation, reading practitioners will come to understand the differences and how these variations might affect learning to read English. We hope this knowledge will enable reading specialists to help students from different linguistic and educational backgrounds achieve the levels of literacy necessary to succeed in U.S. schools.

The Role for Literacy Researchers

A second barrier to full literacy for language-minority students is the modest attention devoted to investigating second-language reading. The need for more meaningful research on second-language reading has been recognized (Bernhardt, 2000; Garcia, 2000; Thomas & Collier, 1997). Still, much of the research on bilingual children's reading comes from outside the United States (Garcia, 1999). Although some improvement has occurred there still remains a lack of access to information about ESL reading for those in the literacy field (Garcia, 1999). We believe this limited access stems from attitudes within the literacy field that marginalize the role that ESL programs can play in academic achievement for language-minority learners. Fitzgerald's (1995b) review characterized research on ESL reading instruction as "having considerable breadth, but little depth" (p. 115). Both Bernhardt (2000) and Garcia (2000) have expressed their concern about similar reviews. The methodology as well as the motives for examining ESL reading research and programs have often been called into question (Bernhardt, 2000; Garcia, 2000; Thomas & Collier, 1997). According to Garcia (2000), politics rather than program evaluation findings or research has stimulated many of the federal policy changes. Bernhardt (2000) and Garcia (2000) noted that the review by Fitzgerald (1995b) of ESL reading instruction (a) focused exclusively on English programs and did not address other languages, (b) collapsed the adult and children's findings, and (c) focused on reading in English of ESL students.

Thomas and Collier (1997) expressed other concerns about effectiveness studies indicating four major limitations for typical ESL program evaluations. According to Thomas and Collier most reviews of effectiveness in ESL instruction focus on short-term, year-to-year comparison of students; lack a longitudinal view of the programs' apparent effects on students; fail to consider variations in how programs are implemented from classroom to classroom and from school to school; and use pretest scores in short-term evaluations that can typically underestimate English learners' true scores until students learn enough English to demonstrate what they really know. In terms of the research methodology used in ESL effectiveness studies, Thomas and Collier (1997) pointed out problems with the inappropriate use of random assignment, suspect statistical conclusion validity, and other issues related to external validity.

A second troubling aspect for second-language reading research is the paucity of articles and information available to the reading profession. Bernhardt (1994) observed that between 1980 and 1992, a time when the language-minority student population grew exponentially in the United States, textbooks in reading methods and language arts as well as popular journals (*Journal of Reading, Language Arts*, and *The Reading Teacher*) provided minimal treatment of the topic. Garcia (2000) indicated that "although more researchers have directed their attention to bilingual children's reading..., the level and quality of the research still have not kept pace with the numbers of bilingual children living in the United States" (p. 828). While we also have observed the increasing presence of articles about second-language literacy, still more are needed.

Although it is beyond the scope of this article to elaborate on each of the following points, we would like to conclude this section by providing a composite list of research priorities that the literacy profession should take into consideration:

- expand the scope of research on English reading to include language-minority students;
- move the research away from effectiveness studies that merely criticize ESL reading instruction without offering clear alternatives;
- develop a clear position on the danger of language loss and benefits of maintaining students' first languages;
- provide substantive information for mainstream teachers about how to help students after they have left bilingual or ESL programs;
- investigate the linguistic differences between English and other languages for literacy development;
- shift attention to students who have other native languages, especially non-European languages; and
- focus on critical literacy and teachers' attitudes toward race, poverty, language, and power.

What Next?

Gonzalez and Darling-Hammond (1997) indicated that,

> Along with an increase in sheer numbers of immigrant students who are at various stages of learning English, schools are also faced with an increasing number of students needing extra academic instruction in addition to English as a second language (ESL) classes. (p. xi)

In the past, mainstream literacy professionals have often failed to accept their role of helping language-minority learners develop skills in English reading. However, the growing numbers of students who speak other languages, as well as the demands for more standards and higher test scores in literacy and other areas, means that teachers, especially those with special knowledge about reading, must begin to address the needs of children from different language backgrounds. We hope that the issues presented here will help literacy professionals to consider the changes necessary in preparing regular teachers to work with language-minority learners, the research needed to address important questions about second-language reading, and the work required in order for literacy practitioners to gain knowledge of (and then use) effective approaches and resources to meet language-minority students' literacy needs. To this end, we hope that the literacy profession will consider the following recommendations in research, teacher preparation, and practice to help achieve educational parity for language-minority students in the United States.

1. Adjust programs of study in reading to include information about second-language acquisition, ESL methods, cross-linguistic transfer, and culture. Reading specialists must begin to understand the complex interweaving of students' cultural, linguistic, and cognitive development (Garcia, 2002). This might be accomplished through specific courses, by having ESL education faculty make presentations to students in traditional reading courses, or by offering special topic seminars for reading and ESL preservice teachers.

2. Include information about second-language literacy in all reading methods courses. Prospective teachers need to know why and how to conduct a linguistic audit of their classroom, to celebrate and know how to use the "cultural funds of knowledge" (Moll & Greenberg, 1990) within immigrant communities, to be aware of home literacy practices, and to promote first-language literacy for parents and children.

3. Provide clinical experiences for reading specialists that involve English-language learners. Reading programs offer a variety of pre-service clinical models. Although many factors are used to determine which children receive clinical services, faculty members have great latitude in setting the selection criteria. Faculty can work with local schools to be sure that language-minority children are invited to participate. The clinical experience is optimal for understanding what it will take to meet the literacy needs of language-minority learners.

4. Become strong advocates for biliteracy. A high level of literacy in the first language correlates to development of literacy in the second language (Cummins, 1991). Reading specialists need to understand the issue of language loss and that for children learning English, "limiting opportunities to learn in their first language will limit their cognitive growth and related academic achievement" (Garcia, 2002, p. 248). Parents should be encouraged to read to children in their first language (L1) and involve children in community activities where L1 or English is spoken in order to support cognitive growth and literacy development. The reading specialist can be a facilitator working with classroom teachers, parents, ESL teachers, and library personnel to make available text and videos for children and youth in a variety of languages and social contexts.

5. Work to change tests and testing practices that disadvantage children from nonnative–English-speaking backgrounds. Students need enough language proficiency to understand the language being used for the assessment. "Because language and content are intricately intertwined, it is difficult to isolate one feature from the other in the assessment process" (Carrasquillo & Rodriguez, 1996, p. 31). States and districts vary widely in policies for assessing English-language learners. Literacy professionals must begin to work with ESL educators to address at state and district levels the challenges language-minority learners encounter on high-stakes tests. Next, they should assist in developing clear guidelines for accommodations. They can add their voices to the chorus of educators who are working to ensure that assessments actually measure the knowledge or skill of particular students or groups of students.

6. Engage in collaborative research with ESL education faculty on second-language reading. Concern for the quality and quantity of research in second-language reading is clear (Bernhardt, 1994, 2000; Garcia, 1999, 2000; Thomas & Collier, 1997). Researchers in each

field can work together to answer critical questions regarding the nature of the relationships between language proficiency and literacy and between first- and second-language literacy, optimal literacy instruction, and the acquisition of content knowledge.

7. Reexamine personal and professional attitudes about teaching language-minority learners. We have not achieved educational equality for our linguistically diverse populations. The necessary change requires that "each of us must step up and be responsible" (Garcia, 2002, p. 89). Literacy professionals can no longer use history and tradition as excuses for failing to help English-language learners to improve their literacy skills. Becoming aware of our own linguistic and cultural deficit models is a critical first step.

In closing, we advocate for meaningful change at every level to ensure that children from diverse linguistic and cultural backgrounds are not left behind. If this does not happen, for these children the results will be limited school success, reduced opportunities for college and technology training, restricted access to well-paid jobs, and failure to become full participants in a democratic society.

REFERENCES

August, D., & Hakuta, K. (Eds.). (1997). *Improving schooling for language-minority children: A research agenda*. Washington, DC: National Academy Press.

Bernhardt, E.B. (1994). A context analysis of reading methods texts: What are we told about the nonnative speaker of English? *Journal of Reading Behavior, 26,* 159–189.

Bernhardt, E.B. (2000). Second-language reading as a case study of reading scholarship in the 20th century. In M.L. Kamil, P.B. Mosenthal, P.D. Pearson, & R. Barr (Eds.), *Handbook of reading research* (Vol. 3, pp. 791–811). Mahwah, NJ: Erlbaum.

Carrasquillo, A., & Rodriquez, V. (1996). *Language minority students in the mainstream classroom*. Clevedon, UK: Multilingual Matters.

Chamot, A.U., & O'Malley, J.M. (1994). *The CALLA handbook: Implementing the Cognitive Academic Language Learning Approach*. Reading, MA: Addison-Wesley.

Collier, V.P. (1987). Age and rate of acquisition of second language for academic purposes. *TESOL Quarterly, 21,* 617–641.

Cummins, J. (1979). Linguistic interdependence and the educational development of bilingual children. *Review of Educational Research, 49,* 222–251.

Cummins, J. (1991). Interdependence of first- and second-language proficiency in bilingual children. In E. Bialystok (Ed.), *Language processes in bilingual children* (pp. 70–89). Cambridge, UK: Cambridge University Press.

Donahue, T.S. (1995). American language policy and compensatory opinion. In J.W. Tollefson (Ed.), *Power and inequality in language education* (pp. 112–141). New York: Cambridge University Press.

Dubin, F., Eskey, D.E., & Grabe, W. (1986). *Teaching second language reading for academic purposes*. Reading, MA: Addison-Wesley.

Edmondson, J. (2001). Taking a broader look: Reading literacy education. *The Reading Teacher, 54*, 620–629.

Faltis, C.J., & Hudelson, S.J. (1998). *Bilingual education in elementary and secondary school communities: Towards understanding and caring*. Needham Heights, MA: Allyn & Bacon.

Fitzgerald, J. (1993). Literacy and students who are learning English as a second language. *The Reading Teacher, 46*, 638–647.

Fitzgerald, J. (1995a). English-as-a-second-language learners' cognitive reading processes: A review of research in the United States. *Review of Educational Research, 65*, 145–190.

Fitzgerald, J. (1995b). English-as-a-second-language reading instruction in the United States: A research review. *Journal of Reading Behavior, 27*, 115–152.

Freeman, D.E., & Freeman, Y.S. (1994). *Between worlds: Access to second language acquisition*. Portsmouth, NH: Heinemann.

Garcia, E. (1992). Linguistically and culturally diverse children: Effective instructional practices and related policy issues. In H.C. Waxman, J. Walker deFleix, J.E. Anderson, & H.P. Baptiste, Jr. (Eds.), *Students at risk in at-risk schools: Improving environments for learning* (pp. 65–86). Thousand Oaks, CA: Corwin.

Garcia, E. (2002). *Student cultural diversity: Understanding and meeting the challenge* (3rd ed.). Boston: Houghton Mifflin.

Garcia, G.E. (1999, Fall/Winter). Bilingual children's reading: An overview of recent research. *ERIC/CLL News Bulletin, 23*, 1–5.

Garcia, G.E. (2000). Bilingual children's reading. In M.L. Kamil, P.B. Mosenthal, P.D. Pearson, & R. Barr (Eds.), *Handbook of reading research* (Vol. 3, pp. 813–834). Mahwah, NJ: Erlbaum.

Gonzalez, J.M. & Darling-Hammond, L. (1997). *New concepts for new challenges: Professional development for teachers of immigrant youth*. Washington, DC: Center for Applied Linguistics.

Graff, H. (1994). The legacies of literacy. In J. Maybin (Ed.), *Language and literacy in social practice* (pp. 151–167). Clevedon, UK: Multilingual Matters.

Grant, C. (1994). Best practices in teacher preparation for urban schools. *Action in Teacher Education (ATE Journal), 16*, 1–18.

Guthrie, J. (1981). Reading in New Zealand: Achievement and volume. *Reading Research Quarterly, 17*, 6–17.

Krashen, S. (1996). *Under attack: The case against bilingual education*. Culver City, CA: Language Education Associates.

Luke, A. (1986). Linguistic stereotypes, the divergent speaker and the teaching of literacy. *Journal of Curriculum Studies, 18*, 397–408.

Meacham, S. (2000/2001). Literacy at the crossroads: Movement, connection, and communication within the research literature and cultural diversity. In W.G. Secada (Ed.), *Review of Research in Education, 25* (pp. 181–208). Washington, DC: American Education Research Association.

Moll, L.C., & Greenberg, J. (1990). Creating zones of possibilities: Combining social contexts for instruction. In L.C. Moll (Ed.), *Vygotsky and education: Instructional implications and applications of sociohistorical psychology* (pp. 319–348). Cambridge, UK: Cambridge University Press.

New London Group. (1996). A pedagogy of multiliteracies: Designing social futures. *Harvard Educational Review, 66*, 60–92.

Nieto, S. (1992). *Affirming diversity: The socio-political context of multicultural education.* White Plains, NY: Longman.

Parry, K. (1996). Culture, literacy and L2 reading. *TESOL Quarterly, 30,* 665–691.

Short, D.J. (1991). *How to integrate language and content instruction: A training manual* (2nd ed.). Washington, DC: Center for Applied Linguistics.

Street, B.V. (1984). *Literacy in theory and practice.* Cambridge, UK: Cambridge University Press.

Thomas, W.P., & Collier, V.P. (1997). *School effectiveness for language minority students.* Washington, DC: National Clearinghouse for Bilingual Education.

Weinstein-Shr, G., & Quintero, E. (Eds.). (1995). *Immigrant learners and their families.* Washington, DC: Center for Applied Linguistics.

Wiley, T.G. (1996). *Literacy and language diversity in the United States.* McHenry, IL, & Washington, DC: Delta Systems and Center for Applied Linguistics.

Willis, A.I., & Harris, V.J. (2000). Political acts: Literacy learning and teaching. *Reading Research Quarterly, 35,* 72–88.

Wong, S., & Teuben-Rowe, S. (1997). Honoring students' home languages and cultures in a multilingual classroom. *Sunshine State TESOL Journal, 16,* 20–26.

Wong-Fillmore, L. (1992). Language and cultural issues in the early education of language minority children. In S. Kagan (Ed.), *The care and education of America's young children: Obstacles and opportunities. Ninetieth Yearbook of the National Society for the Study of Education, Part II* (pp. 30–49). Chicago: University of Chicago Press.

Wong-Fillmore, L. (2000). Loss of languages: Should educators be concerned? *Theory Into Practice, 39*(4), 203–210.

Yeo, F. (1997). Teacher preparation and inner-city schools: Sustaining educational failure. *The Urban Review, 29,* 127–143.

What Can We Expect From a National Assessment in Reading?

Robert E. Shafer

A national assessment of education has begun. The Committee on Assessing the Progress of Education (CAPE; 1968), under joint sponsorship of the Carnegie Corporation, the Fund for the Advancement of Education, and the U.S. Office of Education is in the process of assessing achievement in 10 of the most commonly taught areas in the school program. During 1969 science, citizenship, and writing will be assessed with literature, social studies, music, mathematics, reading, art, and vocational education following in the second two years of a three-year cycle (CAPE, 1968). The history of the development of the program has been a stormy one with the proponents of the program pointing to the need for better measures of what children are learning in order to develop better educational programs and the opponents proposing that such a program would undermine local control of education and lead eventually to a more centralized federal system of education since the curriculum would tend to narrow to include only those areas assessed (Beymer, 1966).

CAPE has decided to assess the achievement of 120,000 to 140,000 individuals and to report results using the following subdivisions:

> Male and female; four geographic regions (Northeast, Southeast, Central and West); four age groups (nine, at which time children have been exposed to the basic program of education; thirteen, following elementary school education; seventeen, which is the last age at which groups are found in school in large numbers; and young adults between the ages of twenty-six and thirty-five); different types of communities (large city, urban fringe, middle-sized city, and rural small town); race (Negro, white, and other); and two socio-economic levels.

Since reading is one of the areas to be assessed and various reading skills and abilities underlie the assessment of achievement in most other areas, the project must be considered to be of crucial importance to reading teachers and specialists at all levels of instruction. How are the exercises for the assessment being developed? In what ways will they be administered? And even more importantly, what may we learn about achievement in read-

Reprinted from *Journal of Reading*, 13, 3-8, October 1969.

ing from their administration and scoring? The reading assessment like that of the other subject fields has been developed according to a carefully planned schedule. Initially, The American Institutes for Research, The Educational Testing Service, Science Research Associates, and the Psychological Corporation were asked to submit educational objectives for the areas to be assessed—objectives that would serve as the basis for developing the various exercises and questions to be used in the assessment. CAPE proposed to the agencies that

> The objectives lead to ones (1) that scholars in the field consider to be worthwhile, (2) that the schools are currently seeking to attain, and (3) that thoughtful laymen consider important for youth to learn. For each area there were objectives bearing on knowledge and skills, as well as others relating to interests and attitudes.

Statements of objectives for each of the 10 subject matter fields were developed with attention given to expectations for each of the four age levels. Eleven lay panels reviewed all objectives and further reviews were done in some instances by professional groups of consultants. Prototype exercises were then developed for each objective for each of the four age groups according to the following criteria:

> (1) Each exercise had to reflect accurately one of the objectives; (2) each exercise had to be clear in its purpose so that it would be easily understood by the individual taking it and quickly communicate information about a student's knowledge to laymen; and (3) that exercises should sample knowledges and skills at three levels—those things that practically all examinees can do, those things that an average number can do, and those things that only the ablest can do—thereby providing a picture of what is learned by the total range of students. The resulting information will be compared to that obtained in future assessments. (CAPE, 1968)

Although the objectives and sample exercises are still under development, the many difficulties inherent in developing both objectives and exercises according to the above criteria as far as reading is concerned will be apparent to many readers of this journal. The matter of objectives, certainly crucial to the entire project, presents a variety of problems in the field of reading which may not be present in other subject areas. One problem is the formulation of objectives for reading behavior at various levels of instruction when the questions concerning the definition of reading have not been resolved. As Spache (1964) has pointed out, planning the goals of an instructional program in reading necessitates a clear definition of reading. One current issue in attempts to formulate such a definition involves whether reading is defined as the translating or de-coding of print to spoken words or whether it is defined as understanding the meaning of those words. Until the advent of criticism by Fries and other linguists (Fries, 1963; Robinson, 1966) and by some advocates of systematic instructional programs in phonics such as those of Walcutt (1967) in recent years, reading, as a process, has been defined as understanding larger units of writing, such as phrases, sentences and paragraphs, and evaluating, applying, and assimilating the meanings embedded in these larger units of English structure. To those formulating objectives and developing items for a national assessment in reading, the implications of accepting or rejecting one or another of the various definitions of reading currently being propounded, are crucial. As Clymer (1968) has noted,

> If concern for understanding is eliminated from our definition of reading, obvious and sweeping changes are mandatory in our instructional programs and in the ways we evaluate our success in instruction. (p. 8)

One example may suffice to illustrate the problem. The task could be conceived as assessing reading adequacy and achievement as proposed by Fries (1963) in the following definition:

> One can read insofar as he can respond to the language signals represented by graphic shapes as fully as he has learned to respond to the same language signals of his code represented by patterns of auditory shapes.

In developing a reading assessment using the above definition, varieties of objectives and items concerned with hierarchies of learning tasks associated with learning "to respond to graphic signals represented by language shapes" for the various levels of the assessment would need to be produced. Such objectives and items could well be concerned with, but restricted to, such tasks as the following:

1. The reader's ability to recognize and identify letters, numerals, and symbols.
2. The reader's ability to recognize the spoken words symbolized by numerals, symbols, and abbreviations, as well as "sight words."
3. The reader's ability to decode printed words into spoken words on the basis of regular grapheme-phoneme relationships.
4. The reader's ability to place correct stress on the appropriate syllables in polysyllabic words.

If the definition of reading as essentially decoding is rejected and one such as the Gray–Robinson model is to be used, objectives and items for a much broader range of reading abilities would need to be developed if the assessment were to reflect adequately the more extensive outcomes proposed. Gray's model (which has been further refined by Robinson) was chiefly concerned with the categories of skills required for the various aspects of reading. He proposed that these aspects could be classified under the following four headings:

1. Word perception, including pronounciation and meaning.

2. Comprehension, which includes a "clear grasp of what is read."

3. Reaction to and evaluation of ideas the author presents.

4. Assimilation of what is read, through fusion of old ideas and information obtained through reading. (Gray, 1960)

In her refinement of Gray's original model, Robinson (1966) added "rates of reading," which she felt must be kept flexible to adjust to the reader's purpose and the type of material being read. She also demonstrated the limitless opportunities for growth in the four aspects of reading originally proposed by Gray.

A national assessment of reading based in part on the Gray–Robinson model or a similar model would necessarily reflect a more extensive variety of objectives and items. For example, if Robinson's concern for "flexibility of reading rates" was also of concern to the reading assessment, such objectives as the following would undoubtedly need to be included:

1. The reader's ability to skim a passage to determine the main idea quickly.

2. The reader's ability to scan a page or table or chart to locate needed facts efficiently.

3. The reader's ability to decide whether to skim, scan, or do careful reading of a particular passage depending on his purpose and the type of material.

A significant problem in attempting to assess those "major aspects" of reading which Gray and Robinson included in the categories "reaction to and evaluation of the ideas the author presents" and "assimilation of what is read, through fusion of old ideas and information obtained through reading," is that although we have seen a growth of secondary school reading programs, over the past several years, secondary schools, who bear the larger share of responsibility for instruction in these "aspects of reading," have not developed adequate instructional programs where such reading outcomes as those described above are systematically developed within the subject areas taught in the secondary school (Early, 1969). Early predicts what an ideal situation might be in the secondary schools if the right measures are taken:

> Ideally, there might be no reading program at all in the secondary schools, if by "program" we mean something visible on the master schedule. In a well run school system, the teaching of reading would proceed smoothly and efficiently from the primary grades where the beginning skills would be mastered by all, to the intermediate grades where basic study skills would be applied to reading in the content areas, through the junior and senior high school where reading skills, habits and attitudes would be extended and refined as students encounter increasingly complex materials. All instruction in reading would occur in the regularly scheduled subjects of the curriculum. There would be no need for extra reading classes, whether these are conceived of as "developmental" for students at every level of achievement, or as "remedial" or "corrective" since potential reading disabilities would have been diagnosed as early as primary grades and preventive measures applied. (p. 535)

Since we obviously do not have such an instructional program in reading at the present time in many schools, we may anticipate that the forthcoming national assessment of reading will reveal shortcomings in the abilities of average and above average students in such areas of flexibility of reading rates and other techniques of efficient reading providing the Gray-Robinson model, or a similar model, is used as a basis for the assessment.

Another aspect of reading instruction which seems especially essential for inclusion in a national assessment of reading concerns attitudes about and interests in reading. After an extensive summary of research concerning attitudes Squire (1969) concluded that

> Research...demonstrates that methods of teaching and conditions of teaching can affect an individual's attitudes toward reading. The attitudes which readers bring to a book and the attitudes which they derive from their reading are intimately related both of the process of reading itself and to the personal qualities of the reader. They affect preferences for reading as much as they color individual response to any selection, and they must be considered carefully by any teacher planning a literary education for students in secondary schools today. (p. 530)

The problem of measurement in these areas may be especially difficult. It might be necessary, for example, to develop objectives (and ultimately items) which will reveal not only whether a reader actually prefers reading, at particular times, but also whether he will stop reading in an interest area after one book, article, or story, or whether he will persist in seeking out additional material in the same area of interest until he has exhausted all possibilities. Such areas, though important to assess, have built-in problems for item writers. Will readers tell assessors why they choose a particular type of reading or why they choose reading over some other form of behavior? To what extent will their answers change over time? If, as Squire (1969) contends, reading preferences are highly personal, and undoubtedly change as a result of experience, what special techniques of assessment will have to be applied in order to obtain valid responses from readers? Such problems will need to be solved if an assessment of attitudes and interests is to be successful.

Once the assessment is completed, a major priority for teachers, administrators, assessors, and the general public will be the nature and meaning of the results. Since the public in particular will, unless otherwise instructed, attempt to equate the results of the assessment with those of a typical standardized testing program, it will be essential that such distinctions as the following be carefully preserved in reporting the results of the assessment:

1. No score is to be derived for an individual since each individual will receive only a portion of exercises in the various fields being assessed in his age group.

2. Individuals are not to be ranked in the reporting of results since the assessment is to describe groups and not individuals.

3. Each exercise must stand alone in the assessment; it would not be submerged as part of a test. Therefore each item must be independently defensible in terms of the objectives and capable of being reported on as to the percentage of people answering it correctly. (An extended discussion of the differences between typical testing programs and the national assessment programs can be found in McMorris, 1968.)

The reports for each age group will be released to the public in preliminary form after the assessment for each age group has been administered, evaluated and tabulated. Sample exercises will be included accompanied by percentages of those assessed who answered the exercises correctly and in some cases frequently given incorrect responses will be included. In reading, we might expect, for example:

For the sample of 17-year-old boys of higher socioeconomic status from large cities of the Northeast region it was found that

87% could identify the sequence of events in a short story;

78% could follow written directions successfully to set up an experiment in chemistry.

CAPE has noted further that the data will be published only in terms of large groups of individuals located within the four major geographic regions. The reports will be "carefully worded so as to avoid misinterpretation" and will be addressed to the educational community as well as "interested lay adults."

CAPE has also proposed that

> A series of reporting conferences be held all over the country to assure that the assessment has sufficient impact—that the results are heard, understood, and discussed by those who have the potential for implementing change and producing improvement in American education.

Such a program of professional and public attention to the results of the assessment has been called for elsewhere and should be especially important in reading because of the perennial interest of the public as well as the opportunity it gives to professionals in the field to assess their own efforts in an area like secondary reading where program development is only now seriously beginning (Moellenberg, 1969). Indeed, such program development is being hampered in a number of school systems by some teachers and school administrators, who, unaware of the recent findings of researchers concerned with reading efficiency in secondary school subjects, still contend that pupils have all the reading skills they need after finishing the sixth grade (Herman, 1969). Such teachers and administrators will need to look carefully at the results of the assessment, not only in reading, but in all those areas of the secondary school curriculum where higher levels of comprehension and techniques of reading efficiency are required.

Perhaps the greatest danger of a national assessment in reading may be found in the pleas of many who, after the results become public, will wish to restrict the curriculum to those objectives and specific areas which were included in the assessment and which they feel can successfully be measured. A further danger will be that what is considered difficult to assess will not be considered as worth having. The dangers of taking such a position have been discussed elsewhere but they remain great (Hand, 1965). Over 30 years ago Dora V. Smith (1941) assessed the value and impact of the

Regents Examinations in English in New York State. After more than a year of intensive study of these examinations, she noted, in part,

> The effect of the examinations is to put all pupils through a single program whether it is adapted to their needs and their capacities or not. With the exception of a small minority of schools, local authorities are in many instances more concerned with their pupils' making a creditable showing on the state examinations than they are with studying their own local needs and adapting instruction accordingly.... Teachers in schools are in many instances judged on the percentage of their pupils making high and low scores on the examinations.... Because of factors which might be intelligently determined by a wide variety of means, schools assume year after year relatively the same position in Regents examinations. What the local authorities need to know specifically is what are the causes leading to success or failure on these examinations.

By world standards our educational system is a relatively nonselective, open system. Although we have used statewide examinations and standardized tests for a variety of reasons, our major concern has been with the measurement of achievement in areas such as reading rather than with the uses of institutionalized testing and assessment to provide or deny educational opportunity as is done in other countries. Today our educational system finds itself in a great crisis. We are searching for ways to promote divergent thinking, to expand our concerns for all humanity in the "global village," and to make good on the basic values of our society, which reflected in the educational system, promise opportunities for the individual to maximize his potential for self-realization and self-development. We will need to begin our planning now if we are to use fully the results of a national assessment of progress in education to help us "know specifically...what are causes leading to success and failure" in reaching our past commitments and also whether our past commitments are good enough for tomorrow.

REFERENCES

Beymer, L. (1966, May). The pros and cons of the National Assessment Project. *The Clearing House.*

Clymer, T. (1968). What is "reading"? Some current concepts. In H.M. Robinson (Ed.), *Innovation and change in reading instruction* (67th yearbook of the National Society for the Study of Education, Part II, p. 8). Chicago: University of Chicago Press.

Committee on Assessing the Progress of Education (CAPE). (1968). *How much are students learning? Plan for a National Assessment of Education.* Ann Arbor, MI: Author.

Early, M.J. (1969, April). What does research in reading reveal about successful reading programs. *English Journal.*

Fries, C.C. (1963). *Linguistics and reading.* New York: Holt, Rinehart and Winston.

Gray, W.S. (1960). The major aspects of reading. In H.M. Robinson (Ed.), *Sequential development of reading abilities* (Supplementary Educational Monographs, No. 90, pp. 8-24). Chicago: University of Chicago Press.

Hand, H.C. (1965, September). National assessment viewed as the camel's nose. *Phi Delta Kappan.*

Herman, W.L., Jr. (1969). Reading and other language arts in social studies instruction. In R. Preston (Ed.), *A new look at reading in the social studies* (p. 5). Newark, DE: International Reading Association.

McMorris, R.F. (1968, Summer). Progress toward assessing progress in education. *Educational Horizons, 46,* 167-171.

Moellenberg, W.P. (1969, April). National assessment: Are we ready? *The Clearing House,* p. 453.

Robinson, H.M. (1966). The major aspects of reading. In A.H. Robinson (Ed.), *Reading: Seventy-five years of progress* (Supplementary Educational Monographs, No. 96, chapter 3). Chicago: University of Chicago Press.

Smith, D.V. (1941). *Evaluating instruction in secondary school English* (Monograph No. 11). Chicago: National Council of Teachers of English.

Spache, G.D. (1964). *Reading in the elementary school.* Boston: Bacon Company.

Squire, J.R. (1969, April). What does research in reading reveal about attitudes toward Reading? *English Journal.*

Walcutt, C.C. (1967, April). Reading—a professional definition. *The Elementary School Journal, 47,* 363-365.

High-Stakes Testing in Reading: Today in Texas, Tomorrow?

James V. Hoffman, Lori Czop Assaf, and Scott G. Paris

State-mandated achievement testing has grown at an exponential rate over the past 2 decades. Prior to 1980 fewer than a dozen states in the USA required mandated standardized testing for students, but in 2000 nearly every state used high-stakes testing. Accountability through testing, for students, teachers, and administrators, is the key leverage point for policy makers seeking to promote educational reform. Policies surrounding educational testing have become political spectacles and struggles for both publicity and control (Smith, Heinecke, & Noble, 1999/2000). State-mandated standardized tests have become the centerpiece for standards-based reform and are "high stakes" because they are often used to make decisions about tracking, promotion, and graduation of students (Heubert & Hauser, 1999). Centralized control is achieved through explicit educational standards (e.g., state curriculum frameworks, performance standards), and standardized tests that allow comparisons of students' relative performance. Educators, caught between standards and tests, are left to "align" classroom practices to meet the demands that surround them. Policy makers, and the public to this point, have judged the impact of educational reform efforts through a comparison of outcomes (i.e., changes in test scores) over time. Despite cautions and caveats from testing experts, high-stakes tests have become the public benchmark of educational quality (Linn, 2000).

This design for educational reform is conceptually elegant and seductive to those who embrace rational planning models. Many of the "results" reported by the media to date suggest positive effects for this model of change. But is this the whole story of reform? We think not. How much of the "success" is an illusion that masks an intrusion of testing into good teaching. We think a lot. We are concerned about the hidden costs of standards-based reform efforts on teachers, on the curriculum, and on teacher education. We are concerned about the negative impact on students, especially low-achieving and minority students, who may be retained in grade or denied high school promotion because of poor test performance. In an effort to explore these issues, we conducted a survey of a selected group of educators in one state—Texas. We chose Texas because the accountability system and

Reprinted from *The Reading Teacher*, *54*, 482–492, February 2001.

the standards-based reform effort there have been recognized as "a model" for other states to follow. Indeed, the press has dubbed the reform of education through accountability and high-stakes testing as the "Texas Miracle" (Haney, 2000). We begin with a brief history of the testing movement in Texas and then report the findings from our study. We conclude with suggestions to minimize the negative impact of high-stakes testing on students and teachers.

TAAS in Texas

What began in the era of minimum basic-skills testing as TABS (Texas Assessment of Basic Skills) has expanded over the past 25 years to become one of the most highly touted state education accountability systems in the United States. The main part of this accountability system is the TAAS (Texas Assessment of Academic Skills). This criterion-referenced test focuses, for the most part, on the areas of reading, writing, and mathematics and is linked directly to the state-prescribed curriculum. The TAAS test is set within a broader set of indices that feed into the total accountability system. For example, districts also monitor such factors as dropout rates, the proportion of students assigned to special education, and graduation rates. Changes in TAAS performance are examined carefully in relation to patterns on this broader set of accountability measures. These other measures are used as checks to determine if any positive changes in test performance are the result of higher levels of student learning or the result of some other factors (e.g., high levels of exemption for low-performing students). In recent years, TAAS has been expanded to include more students, more grade levels, and more subject areas. Currently, the test is administered annually in the spring to all students in Grades 3 through 8 in reading and mathematics. Students in Grades 4, 8, and 10 are tested in writing. Grade 8 students also take tests in science and social studies.

As the amount of testing has increased, so have the consequences associated with student performance on TAAS. For students, high school graduation is dependent on successful performance on TAAS. For schools and districts, accreditation is dependent in large part on TAAS performance. For principals and teachers, performance ratings and merit raises are influenced by TAAS performance of their students. The state requires the reporting of TAAS data to individual schools with school improvement plans developed in consideration of student performance patterns. The high-stakes consequences were intended to increase the quality of both teaching and learning. It is important to recognize that the identification of the "achievement problem," as well as the identification of a solution through rigorous testing, were both politically inspired and imposed on educators (Berliner & Biddle, 1997).

TAAS scores increased consistently during the last decade across all areas tested and at every grade level. For example, the proportion of students passing TAAS rose from 55% in 1994 to 74% in 1997. Further, the "gap" in performance between minority students and white students has narrowed. Only 32% of the African American students passed the tests in 1994 as compared with 56% in 1997. The passing rates for Hispanics rose from 41% to 62% in the same period. Scores rose again in 1998 with an overall passing rate of 78%. Scores for African American students rose to 63% and for Mexican American students to 68% (Texas Education Agency, 1999). In the future, TAAS may be extended into the primary grades and included as part of high school course examinations. Perhaps the most controversial proposal is to use TAAS performance as a requirement for grade-level promotion.

The apparent success of the TAAS has attracted national attention and figured prominently in Texas Governor George W. Bush's presidential campaign. Because the TAAS model of testing and accountability may be adopted by other states, it is important to examine it critically. A comprehensive review of the TAAS was conducted by Haney (2000), a testing expert who was also an expert witness in a lawsuit against the TAAS. Haney concluded that claims about Texas education have been greatly exaggerated because of five fundamental problems with the TAAS. First, the TAAS has continuing adverse effects on African American and Hispanic American students. Compared with Caucasian students, minority students have significantly lower passing rates on the TAAS; they are more likely to be retained in grade; and they are less likely to graduate from high school. Second, the use of TAAS tests to control high school graduation is contrary to professional standards regarding the use of test scores.

Third, Haney (2000) argued that the passing score set on the TAAS is arbitrary and results in racial discrimination. He conducted a small study in which randomly selected adults were asked to examine the TAAS data and set the passing scores in a way that would maximize the differences between racial groups. Their passing scores were virtually identical to the scores set by the Texas Education Authority (TEA) leading to the conclusion that the passing scores were discriminatory, whether intended or not. Fourth, analyses of the psychometric data on the TAAS, and comparisons with the National Assessment of Educational Progress (NAEP) test results, cast doubt on the validity of the TAAS test scores. The apparent increases in TAAS scores are due to factors such as teaching to the test, higher retention and dropout rates for minority students, and exemption of minority students by increased placement in special education. Fifth, there are more appropriate ways to use TAAS scores, such as in sliding combination with high school grades, that would increase the validity and decrease the negative impact of TAAS scores. The judge who presided over the TAAS lawsuit was not persuaded that these problems invalidate the TAAS. He concluded that the TAAS does have discriminatory consequences for black and Hispanic students but is not illegal because it is educationally necessary (*GI Forum Image De Tejas v. Texas Education Agency*, 87 F. Supp. 667 [W.D.Tex. 2000]).

Teachers Respond to TAAS

While the legal and political implications of the TAAS attract headlines, teachers are left to implement instruction aligned with the TAAS. What is happening at the classroom level in response to the expansion of TAAS and the pressure to perform well on tests? In an effort to explore this issue, we conducted a survey of a selected group of teachers in Texas that focused on TAAS and its effects. Our primary goal was to examine the ways in which TAAS affects teachers, students, and instruction from the perspective of the professional educators in classrooms and schools who are most affected by TAAS. Our goal is to reveal some of the ways in which the pressures of high-stakes assessments may threaten or compromise excellence in teaching.

The Participants

All of the participants in this survey were members of the Texas State Reading Association (TSRA), an affiliate of the International Reading Association. The membership of this organization includes classroom teachers, reading specialists, curriculum supervisors, and others in leadership positions. Most of the members hold advanced degrees with a specialization in reading and extensive teaching experience. The complete membership mailing list, containing approximately 4,000 names, was obtained from TSRA headquarters. Using a random selection process, 500 individuals were initially identified (20% of the total membership) and sent survey questionnaires with self-addressed and stamped return envelopes. No incentives were offered to respond. After 3 weeks, a reminder letter was sent out to those who had not responded. Additional surveys, using the random selection process, were mailed until a total of 200 usable surveys were returned. In all, 750 surveys were sent out. The 200 surveys in the sample represent an overall return rate of 27% from 5% of the total membership. No biases were detected in the response rates based on geographical areas of the state. However, the sample is a select group of educators in Texas with both expertise and experience in the teaching of reading. The sample also includes many teachers who work primarily with students in circumstances of poverty. It may be that teachers who cared most about their profession or who felt most affected by the TAAS were more likely to respond to the survey, but there is no reason to believe that the views of these 200 educators are not representative of Texas teachers.

In general, survey respondents were older and more experienced than average classroom teachers in Texas. Sixty-six percent of the sample were over the age of 30, and 33% were between the ages of 40 and 60. Likewise, 63% had more than 10 years of classroom experience and 29% had more than 20 years' experience. This is not surprising given that our selection process focused on teachers with an active affiliation with a professional organization. It is also not surprising that most respondents worked in elementary schools (78%) that have predominantly minority students (81%) and serve low-income communities (72%) where the need for reading specialists is greatest and the funding sources for reading specialists most available. Only 16% of the respondents reported working in schools where the passing rate was over 90% on TAAS. The majority of those responding (51%) were working in schools with a past passing rate for students between 70% and 90%, and 32% were working in schools where the overall passing rate was less than 70%.

The Survey

The survey consisted of 113 items about the following topics: demographic information (12 items); general attitudes of the respondent (20 items); perceived attitudes of others (22 items); test preparation and administration practices (27 items); uses of scores (16 items); effects of the TAAS on students (11 items); and overall impressions about TAAS testing (5 items). Many of the items included in the survey were exact duplicates or slightly modified versions of items that appeared on the Urdan and Paris (1994) survey of teachers in Michigan and the Nolen, Haladyna, and Haas (1989) survey of teachers in Arizona. All of the items about attitudes focused directly on TAAS testing. The majority of items about attitudes required responses on a five-point scale: 1 = Strongly Disagree, 2 = Disagree, 3 = Agree, 4 = Strongly Agree, and 5 = Don't Know. All "5" responses were treated as missing data and ignored in calculating the average responses. The last five items contained an invitation for extended responses.

The Findings

The data from the 200 returned surveys were entered into a data file for item-level analyses. Subsequently, some composite scores were constructed combining items from sections of the questionnaire (e.g., general attitudes). Items were combined based on a priori decisions about face validity rather than factor analyses of the data. In the reporting of findings that follows, we will refer to data from individual items as well as combined items. Composite scores are reported using means and standard deviations, and individual items are reported using categories of responses and percentages. Lower mean scores indicate greater disagreement with the proposition in the item; higher mean scores indicate greater agreement. The qualitative analysis of comments on the final section of the survey focused on common themes among the responses. More than 80% of the respondents offered additional comments on the five items, and their comments reveal the depth of teachers' feelings regarding TAAS testing.

General Attitudes and Perceptions of Others

To examine teachers' general attitudes about the TAAS, we created a composite score from the following four items.

- Better TAAS tests will make teachers do a better job. ($M = 1.8$; $SD = .75$)

- TAAS motivates students to learn. ($M = 1.6$; $SD = .71$)

- TAAS scores are good measures of teachers' effectiveness. ($M = 1.6$; $SD = .68$)

- TAAS test scores provide good comparisons of the quality of school from different districts. ($M = 1.9$; $SD = .76$)

Each item was asked in order to assess teachers' perceptions of the political intentions of the TAAS test. The average rating on the composite variable for these four items was 1.7, a rating between Strongly Disagree and Disagree, which suggests that teachers disagree with many of the underlying intentions of the TAAS.

Another composite variable was created with items related to the validity of TAAS as a measure of student learning. The four variables included in this analysis follow.

- TAAS tests accurately measure achievement for minority students. ($M = 1.6; SD = .73$)

- TAAS test scores accurately measure achievement for limited English-speaking students. ($M = 1.5; SD = .64$)

- Students' TAAS scores reflect what students have learned in school during the past year. ($M = 1.8; SD = .75$)

- Students' TAAS scores reflect the cumulative knowledge that students have learned during their years in school. ($M = 2.1; SD = .84$)

The average rating on the composite variable for these four items was also 1.7, suggesting that teachers challenge the basic validity of the test, especially for minority students and ESL speakers who are the majority of students in Texas public schools.

Contrast these general attitudes and beliefs regarding TAAS with the perception of the respondents that administrators believe TAAS performance is an accurate indicator of student achievement ($M = 3.1$) and the quality of teaching ($M = 3.3$). Also, contrast this with the perception of the respondents that parents feel TAAS reflects the quality of schooling ($M = 2.8$). The gaping disparity between the perceptions of teachers and their estimates of administrators' and parents' attitudes suggests an uncomfortable dissonance in attitudes about the TAAS. Although we cannot determine whether the perceptions of the respondents regarding administrators' and parents' attitudes are accurate or not, the overwhelming majority of the respondents question the assumptions, intentions, and validity of the TAAS test but believe that parents and administrators do not share their views.

A final composite variable for this section was constructed to capture additional stances toward TAAS that explore some extreme positions. This variable consisted of responses to the following four items.

- TAAS should be eliminated. ($M = 2.8; SD = .97$)

- TAAS tests take too much time from the regular curriculum. ($M = 3.2; SD = .89$)

- TAAS tests are overemphasized by administrators. ($M = 3.5; SD = .74$)

- TAAS testing is not worth the time and money spent on it. ($M = 3.0; SD = .91$)

The average rating on the composite variable for these four items was 3.0 (Agree), again reflecting a strong negative attitude toward TAAS.

Preparation and Administration of the TAAS

The questions in this section of the survey focused on the amount of time and attention that teachers devote to preparing students to take the TAAS and the kinds of strategies teachers use to prepare students to take the test. Nearly all of the respondents indicated that preparation for TAAS begins more than a month before testing. Comments from respondents suggested that preparation occurs across the entire academic year reaching its peak in the months just before TAAS is administered. The responses reveal an average of 8 to 10 hours per week spent in TAAS preparation activities. TAAS preparation is required by principals, and the majority of respondents reported that principals encourage more time than is currently devoted. Direct preparation is only one point of impact on the curriculum. Respondents reported that teachers almost always plan their curriculum for the year to emphasize those areas that will be tested on TAAS. Although some reformers may regard this planning as a positive outcome, many teachers consider it to have a negative impact on the curriculum and their instructional effectiveness.

The line between what is acceptable and what is not acceptable in standardized test preparation and administration is not always clearly delineated. Respondents were asked to rate the frequency with which teachers in their schools engaged in various testing practices related to TAAS using the following scale: 1 = Never, 2 = Sometimes, 3 = Often, and 4 = Always. The actions of teachers described in Table 1 are arranged from commonly accepted as appropriate to those that could be questioned. Although only some of these practices fall clearly into a "cheating" category, many approach an unethical stance toward testing. All are capable of affecting test performance. Haladyna, Nolen, and Haas (1991) referred to such practices on a continuum of "test pollution" because they have the potential to enhance, when present, the scores of students in unethical ways. Such practices raise test scores without actually changing students' underlying knowledge or achievement so they give the spurious impression of educational improvement.

Haladyna et al. (1991) argued that as pressures increase to raise test scores, unethical testing practices will occur more often. Our data support this hypothesis. All of the practices noted in Table 1 were reported with greater frequency in schools that had a history of low TAAS performance. For example, the practice of rewarding students for doing well occurred at a reported mean level of 3.4 (Often +) in the schools with a history of low TAAS

Table 1
Reported practices related to test preparation and administration

Practices	Means
Demonstrate how to mark the answer sheet correctly.	3.2
Give general tips on how to take tests.	3.4
Tell students how important it is to do well on the test.	3.7
Use commercial test-preparation materials.	3.4
Have students practice with tests from previous years.	3.4
Encourage student attendance.	3.7
Reduce stress and anxiety by teaching relaxation.	2.4
Teach test-taking skills.	3.5
Teach or review topics that will be on the test.	3.5
Give students hints about answers.	1.2
Point out mismarked items to students.	1.3
Give some students extra time to finish.	2.6
Provide instruction during the test.	1.2
Allow students breaks for fatigue or stress.	3.0
Directly point out to students correct responses.	1.1
Change students' answers once they have been recorded.	1.1
Award prizes to students who do well/pass the test.	2.4

scores; whereas the practice was reported at a mean level of 1.9 (Sometimes −) in the schools with a history of high performance. In the lowest performing schools, the most blatant forms of "cheating" were reported at higher levels than in the schools with a history of high performance. The practices included giving hints about answers ($M = 1.7$), pointing out mismarked items ($M = 1.7$), providing instruction during the test ($M = 1.5$), and directly pointing out correct responses ($M = 1.5$). Although the frequency of these unethical practices is low even in the low-performing schools, the rates are consistent with previous findings (e.g., Haas, Haladyna, & Nolen, 1989; Nolen et al., 1989). The total combination of practices creates a disturbing scenario of teachers succumbing to pressures to raise test scores at any cost and the TAAS scores being contaminated by factors unrelated to students' abilities.

Effects on Students

The items included in this section of the survey explored the impact of the TAAS on students and were borrowed directly from the surveys used in the Arizona and Michigan research cited earlier. The findings suggest the same

Table 2
Effects of TAAS testing on students

Behavior	Reported frequency			
	Never %	Sometimes %	Often %	Always %
Truancy	40	52	5	3
Upset stomach	7	53	32	8
Vomiting	18	53	21	8
Crying	22	60	13	5
Irritability	12	50	30	8
Increased aggression	22	43	28	7
Wetting or soiling themselves	74	23	3	0
Headaches	8	45	33	14
Refusing to take test	53	37	7	3
Increased misconduct	29	42	23	6
Freezing up	12	54	25	9

patterns for TAAS as with other standardized tests. The data from our survey are displayed in Table 2. According to teachers, many students experience headaches and stomachaches while taking the TAAS. A surprising number are anxious, irritable, or aggressive. The data are troubling because discomfort and illness during the TAAS undermine students' test performance, further polluting the scores and decreasing their validity. It seems likely that low-scoring students would be the ones most negatively affected, which puts at-risk students in more jeopardy during TAAS testing. We did not explore directly the effects of TAAS on student motivation or self-concept, although the negative effects of standardized tests, in particular on low-performing and minority students, have been clearly demonstrated (Paris, Lawton, Turner, & Roth, 1991).

Uses of TAAS

Two composite variables were created to summarize the uses of TAAS results. The first variable focused on how teachers use TAAS results by combining responses on the following items:

- To make decisions about curricula. ($M = 3.2$; $SD = .74$)
- To measure school or classroom effectiveness. ($M = 3.1$; $SD = .76$)
- To make decisions about how to group students. ($M = 2.7$; $SD = .92$)
- To identify students for remedial programs. ($M = 3.0$; $SD = .86$)

- To predict future performance. ($M = 2.8$; $SD = .76$)
- To diagnose learning problems for specific students. ($M = 2.4$; $SD = .90$)
- To assign students to low-track and basic classes. ($M = 2.3$; $SD = 1.0$)

Each of these items had been rated separately on a scale of 1 = Never, 2 = Sometimes, 3 = Often, and 4 = Always. The mean response for the composite variable for these seven items was 2.8 ($SD = .62$) suggesting that TAAS results are often used in these ways.

The second composite variable focused on the uses of TAAS results by school principals. Here we combined responses on the following items:

- To help teachers improve their instruction. ($M = 2.8$; $SD = .86$)
- To identify strengths and weaknesses of the curriculum. ($M = 3.0$; $SD = .75$)
- To evaluate teacher effectiveness. ($M = 3.0$; $SD = .80$)
- To evaluate school effectiveness. ($M = 3.3$; $SD = .73$)
- To evaluate the effectiveness of new programs. ($M = 2.9$; $SD = .82$)
- To recognize outstanding student or teacher performance. ($M = 2.8$; $SD = .98$)

The mean for the composite variable for these six items was 3.0 ($SD = .60$) suggesting that TAAS results are often used in these ways. None of the uses described in this section are surprising. What is a matter of concern is the extreme if not sole reliance on TAAS results as the data source in guiding planning, decisions, and actions.

Overall Impressions on TAAS

This final section of the survey included five questions and teachers' comments about each topic. We provide the questions and responses below.

1. The results from TAAS testing over the past several years seem to indicate that scores are on the rise. Do you think this rise in test scores reflects increased learning and higher quality teaching?

   Yes = 27%   No = 50%   Not Sure = 23%

Half of the respondents did not believe that the increases in TAAS scores were the result of higher levels of student learning. Their comments suggest that they believed the higher scores were the direct result of teaching to the test.

> "Teaching to the test and test-taking strategies."
> "Teaching to the format of the test."
> "Students know how to take the test because we practice ad nauseam."
> "Teachers are spending the school day teaching to the test."

Awareness of the objectives as well as better training and test practice materials were also given credit.

> "We have better training on how to prepare students."
> "We know what to expect on the test."

Many believed that TAAS is incapable of tapping the higher level learning that is taking place in schools.

> "TAAS does not require higher level thinking and does not allow for it."

Some teachers even suggested that the test is getting easier.

> "I think the tests are easier to make the legislators look better."

Some teachers raised the explanation of cheating.

> "There are a lot of teachers and administrators who know how to 'cheat' and get higher scores from kids...they don't want their school to score bad, so they cheat."

The results from the NAEP (Donahue, Voelkl, Campbell, & Mazzeo, 1999), as well as the results of the TEA's own national comparison study (Texas Education Agency, 1997), suggested that the improved scores in the area of reading are restricted to the TAAS test and that these increases are not reflected on the performance of Texas students on nationally standardized tests. Apparently, many respondents felt the same way because they indicated that the increases in test scores might be due to artificial causes such as teaching to the test, rather than increasing children's reading abilities.

2. It has been suggested that the areas not tested directly on the TAAS (e.g., fine arts) and other areas not tested at certain grade levels (e.g., science at the fourth-grade level) receive less and less attention in the curriculum. What do you feel about this assertion?

Very True = 49%   Somewhat True = 36%
Somewhat False = 8%   Totally False = 7%

The responses related to the second item indicate that there is considerable curriculum displacement due to TAAS because 85% of the teachers replied that "if it's not being tested, it's not being taught." These findings are consistent with those of Darling-Hammond and Wise (1985) who found that tested content was taught at the expense of untested content.

"We were told by administration if it isn't tested don't spend the bulk of your time teaching it."

"We hardly teach social studies and science."

"There is no time to teach these subject areas because of TAAS."

"At our school, third- and fourth-grade teachers are told not to teach social studies and science until March (after TAAS)."

"The test has become the curriculum."

"The principal told us not to be teaching social studies and science."

"We only teach TAAS. The rest is just fluff. My social studies and science grades come from TAAS reading passages. Everything must be done in TAAS format."

3. It has also been suggested that the emphasis on TAAS is forcing some of the best teachers to leave teaching because of the restraints the tests place on decision making and the pressures placed on them and their students. Do you agree or disagree?

Strongly Agree = 42%   Somewhat Agree = 43%
Disagree = 11%   Strongly Disagree = 4%

The third item explored the consequences of high-stakes testing on teachers. Although teachers may not value the TAAS as much as parents and administrators, they are expected to teach to the TAAS and raise test scores. This leads to frustration and a desire to escape the pressures of the TAAS. Eighty-five percent of the teachers expressed agreement with the statement that some of the best teachers are leaving the field because of the TAAS.

"People do not want to work in this type of environment."

"I know of a great many (who are leaving), and I am also."

Some teachers described efforts to flee TAAS pressure without dropping out of teaching altogether.

"I used to teach fourth grade, but now I teach first grade. I just don't want the pressure."

"This is why I teach in a specialization area where TAAS is not tested."

"It has dramatically shifted the purpose of teaching. We are 'required' to teach to the TAAS. I became a teacher to teach children."

4. TAAS is being recommended as the basis for making promotion decisions about students in some schools. What is your view regarding this policy?

Strongly Agree = 4%   Somewhat Agree = 30%
Disagree = 36%   Strongly Disagree = 30%

The use of TAAS as a requirement for high school graduation is a reality. The proposals for using TAAS to control grade-level advancement are widespread. A substantial majority (66%) of the respondents opposed the use of TAAS scores to make decisions about grade-level advancement.

"If you have a poor instrument, then you will always make poor decisions."
"TAAS + promotions = bull–."

Many commented on the logistical nightmare that would be created by such a policy.

"Fourth grade will be huge. In my class alone I suspect 40% to fail."

Some expressed general dissatisfaction with retention as a solution to anything.

"Retention doesn't work and research has shown this! We should be considering other areas to help, not the same old things that didn't work before."

Most of those responding, including those who seem to favor the use of TAAS in promotion decisions, suggest that multiple factors should be considered.

"I think it could support the decision on promotion, but it should not be the sole source for this decision."
"TAAS should be a factor in promotion decisions but not the sole criterion."

5. Do the informal assessments you currently make in your classroom provide you with a sufficient basis for good instructional decision making, or do TAAS results help you?

Informal assessments are sufficient = 43%
TAAS helps some = 52%   TAAS helps a lot = 5%

This notion of multiple measures was confirmed by the respondents' answers. Many favored a combination of measures.

Discussion

The findings from this study are consistent with research on the negative effects of "high-stakes" assessments (e.g., Airasian, 1988; Madaus, 1988; Meisels, 1989; Paris, 1998; Shepard & Dougherty, 1991). The findings from this study are also consistent with two other studies of the TAAS. In one study, Gordon and Reese (1997) surveyed 100 Texas teachers (who were apparently graduate students in their program) about the impact of TAAS on teachers and students. Twenty individuals were also interviewed. Respondents reported that preparation for the TAAS was the main activity for months before the test and that there was a de-emphasis on teaching content that was not related to the TAAS. Of the 20 interviewed, 19 teachers felt that the TAAS was not an appropriate tool for evaluating students or teachers. Teachers reported that the TAAS was culturally biased and had deleterious impact on at-risk students. A second study conducted by Haney (2000) involved two surveys of secondary teachers in Texas. He summarized four similarities among the surveys administered in his study, the survey reported in this paper, and the Gordon and Reese (1997) study. All the similarities undermine effective teaching and learning.

1. Texas schools are devoting a huge amount of time and energy preparing students specifically for the TAAS.

2. Emphasis on TAAS is hurting more than helping teaching and learning in Texas.

3. Emphasis on TAAS is particularly harmful to at-risk students.

4. Emphasis on TAAS contributes to retention in grade and dropping out of school.

This study confirms the negative impact on teachers and students in Texas. The respondents to this survey, experts in reading and close to the classroom, reported that the TAAS does not measure what it purports, is unfair to minority students, is affecting instruction in negative ways, is leading both students and teachers to "drop out," and is being used in ways that are invalid. These educators would argue that the triumph of the Texas accountability system touted by politicians, bureaucrats, and test publishers should be challenged. The extensions of TAAS into more subject areas and into earlier grade levels are disturbing. More disturbing is the prospect that many state policy makers regard the TAAS as successful and want to expand the use of TAAS results for teacher evaluation and student promotion.

Today in Texas, Tomorrow?

The impact of Texas on textbooks, curriculum, and assessment across the U.S. is enormous and continues to expand. The Texas state curriculum, The Texas Essential Knowledge and Skills, is used to guide commercial textbook development and may become the de facto reading curriculum for a large part of the U.S. As public recognition of the TAAS increases, it is likely to be emulated by other states too. When tests drive instruction, teachers become increasingly responsive to the demands of the tests and less considerate of the needs of the students in their classrooms. Instruction that conforms to high-stakes tests in content and format will become more patterned and predictable and less responsive and adaptive. Teachers and students deserve better, and the respondents to our survey recognize this. Our survey forms were filled with comments that revealed frustration, anger, and helplessness with respect to TAAS testing.

> "I am very sad that education has stooped to the low level of measuring performance with standardized testing and Texas has taken it even lower with their TAAS. We know what works in education—we just seem to ignore the research and keep on banging our heads against the 'TAAS wall' and 'retention walls.'"

> "Please support teachers more than ever. Our children are hurting more than ever. If there was ever a time to change, it is now. Give teachers back their classrooms. Let them teach and spend quality time with their students. They need us!"

> "I think TAAS is the biggest joke in Texas. I have never seen such an injustice."

> "I believe that TAAS interferes with the very nature of our job. The pressure from administrators to increase campus scores leaves teachers little time for real instruction. My heart breaks to see so many teachers 'just surviving.' I believe that our solution is just to support each other because the public has no real concept of the situation."

> "TAAS is ruining education in Texas! Help!"

What Can Be Done?

If we were totally fatalistic about the future of reading assessment, we would not have conducted this study, nor would we be writing this article. We believe there are actions to be taken within Texas and the U.S. to stem the tide of high-stakes assessments. As part of a profession of concerned reading educators, we suggest the following steps.

Provide data. Statistical claims regarding high-stakes assessments typically use data provided by those who control its design, administration, and data analysis. We are in desperate need of independent research that provides a critical analysis of the effects of high-stakes assessments on stakeholders from a variety of perspectives. Parents, teachers, and students should be surveyed about the high-stakes tests given by their districts.

Compare. There are a number of other states that have taken other paths to ensure educational accountability that are based on sound principles of assessment without the high-stakes pressure of TAAS. We need careful examination and comparison of the alternatives. Fair-Test (http://fairtest.org) offers a good example for how this kind of principled analysis can be conducted (Neill, 1999).

Advocate. Both individually and collectively, we must advocate for reasonable assessment of students in schools. The International Reading Association (1999) has taken a bold stance toward high-stakes assessment. Other national, state, and local organizations need to act similarly. We believe it is particularly important that student advocacy groups and parent groups become more active in voicing their concerns.

Challenge. The Mexican-American Legal Defense and Educational Fund (MALDEF) has taken the lead in challenging the TAAS test and its use as a graduation requirement in Texas as racially discriminatory. Despite a complex and lengthy court battle, the MALDEF suit was not successful. More challenges should be made, and the current efforts supported.

Explore alternatives. No one is opposed to accountability in education. We must demonstrate that the goals of accountability can be achieved through alternative testing. For example, states and districts could use a NAEP model in which only some sampled students are tested. This removes the onus of an individual score for students or teachers yet still provides an estimate of achievement by district or state. When high-stakes decisions are required about promotion, retention or graduation of students, or the quality of teaching, multiple measures should be used.

Don't be seduced. Silence prevails in educational circles with respect to TAAS-type testing because it is viewed as a necessary evil to achieve other goals. Recent pay raises for teachers in Texas have been negotiated in the context of accepting, if not embracing, high-stakes assessment. The words of the president of the National Education Association speak to this.

[Our] colleagues in Texas...are dealing positively and creatively with standards-based instruction...I repeat, high standards and high stakes tests are here to stay. They have thrust us into a brave new world. By all means, let us be brave and affirmative in shaping this new world in the best interests of the children we serve. (Chase, 1999)

Similarly, some minority leaders have been silent on high-stakes testing because low performance is seen as a way of increasing the flow of money to needy schools. These are indefensible positions in the light of the negative effects of such tests on education.

It is easy to get discouraged by the TAAS frenzy and the political steamrollers of standards and testing. The political and economic forces supporting the movement are formidable. TAAS is approaching a hundred-million-dollar-a-year industry in direct costs alone (Brooks, 1998). Teaching to TAAS is far easier than teaching to students. Every good teacher who drops out opens a space for someone who might be more vulnerable to the pressures of high-stakes testing. We urge teachers to stay the course. Be creatively compliant and selectively defiant as it fits the learning needs of your students. As leaders in reading and literacy education, we have an important role to play in the appropriate use of high-stakes assessment. Our professional colleagues, the voices of those responding in our survey, are crying out for assistance and guidance. Their pleas are not just about themselves and their situation but the plight of the students they serve. Will we remain silent?

REFERENCES

Airasian, P.W. (1988). Symbolic validation: The case of state-mandated, high-stakes testing. *Educational Evaluation and Policy Analysis, 10*, 301–313.

Berliner, D.C., & Biddle, B.J. (1997). *The manufactured crisis: Myths, fraud, and the attack on America's public schools*. White Plains, NY: Longman.

Brooks, P.A. (1998, December 16). Lawmaker proposes more-frequent TAAS testing. *Austin American Statesman*, p. B5.

Chase, B. (1999). Don't get mad. Get ready! *NEA Today, 17*(6), 2.

Darling-Hammond, L., & Wise, A. (1985). Beyond standardization: State standards and school improvement. *The Elementary School Journal, 85*, 315–336.

Donahue, P.L. Voelkl, K.E., Campbell, J.R., & Mazzeo, J. (1999). *NAEP 1998 reading: Report card for the nation and states*. Washington, DC: U.S. Department of Education.

Gordon, S.P., & Reese, M. (1997). High stakes testing: Worth the price? *Journal of School Leadership, 7*, 345–368.

Haas, N.S., Haladyna, T.M., & Nolen, S.B. (1989). *Standardized testing in Arizona: Interviews and written comments from teachers and administrators* (Tech. Rep. No. 89-3). Phoenix: Arizona State University, West Campus.

Haladyna, T., Nolen, S.B., & Haas, N.S. (1991). Raising standardized achievement test scores and the origins of test pollution. *Educational Researcher, 20*(5), 2–7.

Haney, W. (2000, April). *The myth of the Texas miracle in education.* Paper presented at the annual meeting of the American Educational Research Association, New Orleans, LA.

Heubert, J.P., & Hauser, R.M. (1999). *High stakes: Testing for tracking, promotion, and graduation* (A report of the National Research Council). Washington, DC: National Academy Press.

International Reading Association. (1999). *High-stakes assessments in reading: A position statement of the International Reading Association.* Newark, DE: Author.

Linn, R.L. (2000). Assessments and accountability. *Educational Researcher, 29*(2), 4–15.

Madaus, G.F. (1988). The influence of testing on curriculum. In L.N. Tanner (Ed.), *Critical issues in curriculum: 87th yearbook of the National Society for the Study of Education* (pp. 83–121). Chicago: University of Chicago Press.

Meisels, S.J. (1989). High stakes testing in kindergarten. *Educational Leadership, 46*, 16–22.

Neill, M. (1999). Is high-stakes testing fair? *NEA Today, 17*(6), 6.

Nolen, S.B., Haladyna, T.M., & Haas, N.S. (1989). *A survey of Arizona teachers and schools administrators on the uses and effects of standardized achievement testing* (Tech. Rep. No. 89-2). Phoenix: Arizona State University, West Campus.

Paris, S.G. (1998). Why learner-centered assessment is better than high-stakes testing. In N. Lambert & B. McCombs (Eds.), *Issues in school reform: A sampler of psychological perspectives on learner-centered schools* (pp. 189–209). Washington, DC: American Psychological Association.

Paris, S.G., Lawton, T.A., Turner, J.C., & Roth, J.L. (1991). A developmental perspective on standardized achievement testing. *Educational Researcher, 20*, 12–20.

Shepard, L.A., & Dougherty, K.C. (1991). *Effects of high-stakes testing on instruction.* Paper presented at the annual meeting of the American Educational Research Association, Chicago. (ERIC Document Reproduction Service No. ED337468)

Smith, M.L., Heinecke,W., & Noble, A.J. (1999/2000). State assessment becomes political spectacle: Parts I-VIII. *Teachers College Record.* Available: www.tcrecord.org. ID Number: 10454.

Texas Education Agency. (1997). *Texas Student Assessment Program: Student performance results 1995-1996.* Austin, TX: Author.

Urdan, T.C., & Paris, S.G. (1994). Teachers' perceptions of standardized achievement tests. *Educational Policy, 8*(2), 137–156.

The International Reading Association Responds to a Highly Charged Policy Environment

Cathy Roller

I n August 1998, I became the Director of Research and Policy for the International Reading Association. I wanted the position because of the volatile and explosive U.S. government policy environment confronting reading professionals. I knew that the Association, the largest literacy organization in the world, had the opportunity to influence policy directions in ways that would help all children learn to read. I also knew, because of the position announcement, that the Association's Board of Directors was ready to move in order to accomplish its goals.

I have been a member of the Association for more than 30 years, and never in that 30 years have I seen such intensity, determination, and conflict whirling through the various professional venues of reading instruction. In the period just before and since I arrived, the Association has been responding to this challenging policy environment. In this article I will touch on several of those responses. The Association has done the following:

- refocused the Research Division,
- increased its willingness to take stands on important issues,
- increased its involvement in the Title I reauthorization effort,
- monitored the National Reading Panel, and
- responded to the Reading Excellence Act.

The Current Policy Environment in the U.S.

These efforts have been necessary because teachers' and local school districts' rights to determine instructional methods used for reading instruction have been challenged. That teachers should have authority to make the decisions about how children are taught to read is central to the Association's mission. For many years that authority went relatively unchallenged. In recent years, however, legislators in the United States, at both the state and na-

Reprinted from *The Reading Teacher*, 53, 626–636, May 2000.

tional levels, have made or attempted to make decisions about reading instructional methods. Many private nonprofit groups have spent time and money encouraging legislators to mandate particular teaching approaches. In Delaware, home of the International Reading Association, the State House of Representatives Majority Leader Wayne A. Smith proposed a bill, H.B. 261, that calls for phonics as the primary form of reading instruction in Grades K–4. Smith believes his proposed legislation will improve Delaware children's reading achievement. When asked what led him to propose the legislation, he said that similar legislation had been enacted in California and that California's test scores had improved. However, California's scores on the National Assessment of Educational Progress (NAEP) in fourth-grade reading did not improve in 1998 (Donahue, Voelld, Campbell, & Mazzeo, 1998). Even if they had, there probably has not been enough time for the legislative changes to have had any effects on reading scores. Similar legislation has been introduced and in many cases passed in legislatures across the U.S.—often on the basis of such incorrect understandings.

Why are interest groups and legislators usurping reading professionals' prerogatives? This is a complex question with a complex set of possible answers. A single definitive explanation is unlikely. As the call for proposals for this issue of *The Reading Teacher* suggested, literacy failures, disenfranchised populations, and different community views have contributed to the cacophony of voices surrounding early reading instruction. Reading is very important, and parents, legislators, interest groups, and other stakeholders have a right to be heard. Their opinions should be strongly considered and attended to when teachers and local education authorities make decisions about children's reading instruction. However, it is inappropriate to dictate methodologies for teaching reading at the state and national level. Those entities are too large and too far away to consider all the relevant input that must contribute to classroom reading instructional decisions.

Literacy Failures

The media, the general public, and indeed many educators believe educators are failing to teach children to read. The perception of failure persists in the face of National Assessment of Educational Progress (NAEP) data showing that reading achievement at the Grade 4 level has remained relatively stable since the 1970s (National Center for Education Statistics, 1997), and that in 1998 reading achievement scores increased modestly and these gains were statistically significant (Donahue et al., 1998).

The perception of failure comes from several sources. Increased literacy demands in the modern economy are perhaps the most important source. Prior to the 1970s, there were still large numbers of jobs in the manufacturing sector that required minimal literacy skills and provided adequate income. With the economy's shift away from manufacturing and toward the service and information sectors, the number of such jobs has drastically declined. There simply are much greater demands for literacy. Literacy levels perceived as sufficient in the past are now insufficient.

Inequitable distribution of reading achievement across different income levels is another source of the failure perception. Poverty is one of the best predictors of reading achievement. For the U.S. as a whole, 38% of fourth-grade children scored below the basic level on NAEP; however, for children falling below the poverty line the percentage was 58%. In some urban schools, the proportion of children falling below the basic level was as high as 68% (Donahue et al., 1998). There is no way to claim that all children have access to equal opportunities to learn to read.

Wide variability in both the learning rates and the ultimate success of children learning to read also contributes to perceptions of failure. Wide variation among children in weight, height, and athletic ability is not surprising. Some children become great athletes, most engage at some point in their lives in some form of recreational sport, and others choose not to engage in sports at all. Variation in the ways that healthy children learn to read is similar. A few children learn to read before they come to school, most learn to read by second or third grade, and a few do not learn after 4 or 5 years of instruction and intensive individual tutoring. As children move through school the disparities among them increase. One study (Allington, 1983) found that the best first-grade readers read almost 2,000 words per week. Struggling first-grade children read only 16 words per week. By the intermediate grades struggling readers have read approximately 100,000 words. The average reader has read 1,000,000, and the most avid readers have read as many as 10,000,000 to 50,000,000 (Nagy & Anderson, 1984).

As a professional who worked for many years with children who struggle to learn, I am painfully aware of these differences in learning to read. There are a very few children (probably less than 1-3% of healthy children) who are extremely difficult to teach, no matter the kind and intensity of instruction provided. However, reading is more important than sports and athletic performance. It permeates all academic learning, and poor reading frequently means poor learning. Despite individual differences, parents and the public expect all children to learn to read. If we fall short of that goal, we have failed.

Statistics about the levels of adult illiteracy, the reading achievement levels of incarcerated populations, and the numbers of job applicants who cannot pass literacy tests related to the jobs they apply for also contribute to the perception of failure. Since the publication of *A Nation at Risk* (National Commission on Excellence in Education, 1983), we have been inundated with reports and reform efforts aimed at improving reading and writing skills. While reliable data suggest that reading achievement has been stable since 1970, and that 1998 NAEP scores indicated modest improvement, no one, including most educators and reading professionals, is satisfied with those levels of achievement.

Disenfranchised Populations

As noted, reading achievement is inequitably distributed across income levels in the United States. As a group, poor children do not read as well as middle class and rich children. Reading achievement also is distributed inequitably across racial and ethnic groups. African American, Hispanic, Asian/Pacific Islander, and Native American children as groups do not read as well as their white (European American) peers. While only 29% of white fourth-grade children scored below the basic level in 1998, the percentages were 67%, 56%, 41%, and 47% for African American, Hispanic, Asian/Pacific Islander, and Native American children, respectively. Cultural values, race, ethnicity, language, and poverty are all related to reading achievement levels.

Professionals and parents from these communities are rightfully concerned that the public schools are not serving their children well, and that the schools may be in fact contributing to rather than ameliorating achievement differences in reading. Children in high-poverty schools (which have disproportionately large numbers of minority children) have fewer physical resources and qualified teachers. In the schools with the highest poverty levels, in-class reading and language instruction is more likely to be provided by a teacher's aide than a certified teacher (44% in these schools compared with 17% in other schools) (Millsap, Moss, & Gamse, 1993). Less qualified personnel teach the children at highest risk for reading failure, when in fact they deserve the best teachers. In addition many persons teaching children to read are not credentialed teachers. They are working with emergency credentials and waivers, and have no formal training to teach students to read. Parents, teachers, advocates, and legislators want this problem solved.

Different Community Views

The United States does not have a homogeneous population. Its residents come in all colors, races, and religions, and have different philosophies and value systems. In any time period, various groups—environmentalists, business advocates, conservatives, liberals, the religious right, the radical left—vie for power and influence. In the recent past these groups have been more polarized. Conservative groups, religious groups, and some low-income groups—all of whom are dissatisfied with U.S. public schools—support charter schools and voucher systems, while traditional liberals, the radical left, and other groups of low-income people view charter schools and vouchers as attempts to destroy the public schools and deny disenfranchised people access to free public education. There are increasing numbers of private and religious schools and more parents are choosing to home school their children. Many U.S. parents doubt the capacity of public schools to educate their children in an appropriate moral climate. School violence and lack of discipline in some schools have contributed to these impressions. A number of special interest groups have become more vocal and waged campaigns to change the public education system. They want schools directly controlled by parents via charter schools and voucher systems, and they demand that teachers in public schools use instructional methods consistent with their views. Democracy offers the opportunity to enact these viewpoints. If we are dissatisfied with the laws being enacted, we must take action. When everyone acts it is sometimes confusing and chaotic, and we experience the voices of many actors as cacophony. Democracy in action is often discordant.

Changes at the International Reading Association

In response to this demanding political environment, the Association has changed. The title change for the Division of Research, which is now the Division of Research and Policy, is one important indicator. The change reflects the Board of Directors' concerns that legislative mandates seem to be based on no research or an unrepresentative summary of research or, worse, run counter to research findings. As a profession, reading does have a research base that can inform many instructional decisions. However, as Allington (in press) points out, it is public opinion rather than research that influences policymakers. The recognition of this influence has led the Board to focus on the importance of having the knowledge and expertise of the Association placed squarely in the public arena. The change in the title of the division is concrete evidence of the Board's emphasis on influencing policy that affects reading instruction and reading professionals.

A second important change indicator is the willingness of the Board to take stands in position statements. Prior to 1995, there were very few position statements. Since 1997, the Board of Directors has developed and adopted six such statements: *The Role of Phonics in Reading Instruction* (1997); *Phonemic Awareness and the Teaching of Reading* (1998); *Learning to Read and Write* (A joint statement with the National Assocation for the Education of Young Children, 1998); *Using Multiple Methods of Beginning Reading Instruction* (1999); *Adolescent Literacy: A Position Statement* (1999); and *High-Stakes Assessments in Reading* (1999). These position statements are available online at www.reading.org. The Association is developing several other statements on teacher effectiveness, reading instruction for speakers of English as a second language, provision of adequate resources for reading, and social promotion.

In a very short time, the Association has gone from regarding beginning reading instruction as the prerogative of reading professionals to realizing that if that prerogative is to be maintained, the Association as the representative of over 90,000 individual and institutional members needs to take strong stands. This was very explicitly stated in the 1998 resolution on policy mandates (see sidebar); four of the recent position statements are directly related to beginning reading instruction.

A third indication of changes at the Association is the use of Board-approved principles to guide the reauthorization of Title I of the U.S. Elementary and Secondary Education Act. While the Association has been involved with Title I since its inception, and its Washington office has monitored and influenced previous reauthorizations, this is the first time Association committees (Title I and Government Relations) have worked with the Board and the Washington representative to produce principles to guide reauthorization efforts. Those principles with explanations and supporting citations are available from pubinfo@reading.org.

A fourth manifestation of the change is our careful monitoring of the National Reading Panel. This panel was created by legislation passed prior to the Reading Excellence Act and was envisioned as a group that would summarize reading research and thus make it easier to determine what practices were supported by scientifically based research. In essence, the government panel would determine practices eligible for federal funding. The panel was originally supposed to complete its task by January 1999. However, once

On policy mandates

Background

We, the International Reading Association, believe that student learning is most
likely to be maximized under conditions of local control; and that an open
intellectual marketplace for ideas and a competitive economic marketplace for
materials must be valued and protected as the basis for the improvement of
reading instruction. Policymakers at the state and national levels play an
important role in the conduct and improvement of reading instruction, and have
the potential to make a positive impact on reading education, research, and
teacher education.

We are concerned, therefore, with the trend for policymakers to mandate specific
instruction practices, programs or materials, classroom reading assessments, and
narrowly restrictive content knowledge requirements for pre- and inservice
preparation of reading teachers. If we are to be successful in improving reading
achievement we must locate decision making at the point of service to students.
Broad mandates can intrude on or even replace professional decision making,
resulting in instruction that is less responsive to student needs. Ultimately, the
effects of such mandates are to reduce the quality of instruction in schools and
classrooms and to limit the potential for all students to be successful in learning
to read.

Resolution

Be it resolved, therefore, that the International Reading Association urges
policymakers to promote policies that allow publishers and developers to create
materials and programs that are responsive to the needs of all students.

Adopted by the Delegates Assembly, May 1998

convened, the panel petitioned the government for an extension because it
simply was not possible to do the task in the time originally allotted.

The Association was active in nominating members for the panel, and
5 of the 14 panelists are Association members. The panel has engaged in a
number of activities including conducting regional hearings at which many
Association members and Board members testified. It has also conducted a
series of open meetings, most of which either the Association's Executive
Director Alan Farstrup or I attended.

The panel published an interim report, available online at www.
nationalreadingpanel.org. This report gives the background information about
the panel, summarizes the regional hearings, and gives a detailed explanation
of the methodology the panel will use in evaluating research evidence for its reports. The Association Board and headquarters staff are following the work of
the panel closely so that the Association will be in a position to provide appropriate and needed information at the time of the report's release.

A fifth manifestation of change is the Association's involvement with the Reading Excellence Act legislation that the U.S. Congress passed in final form in fall 1998. More than any other situation the activity around this act represents the cacophony of voices contesting reading instruction. In the next section, I will provide a narrative (clearly one that reflects my personal experiences and opinions) of the Association's involvement with the Reading Excellence Act.

The Reading Excellence Act

The Reading Excellence Act began its life as H.B. 2416. This original version, sponsored by U.S. Congressman William Goodling of Pennsylvania and introduced to the U.S. House of Representatives on November 7, 1997, contained many elements that were unacceptable to reading and language arts professionals. The purpose of the act was to funnel funds to high-poverty districts for (a) professional development for teachers, (b) tutoring programs, and (c) family literacy initiatives. While some applauded the use of federal dollars for professional development and family literacy efforts, many were less certain about the possible uses of public dollars to support private vendors for tutoring.

However, there were three features of the bill that were particularly troublesome to the reading community—the definition of reading, the definition of research, and the constitution of the panel to review and recommend the most meritorious applications for funding. In the early versions of the bill, reading was defined as follows:

> The term "reading" means the process of comprehending the meaning of written text by depending on—
>
> (a) the ability to use phonics skills, that is the knowledge of letters and sounds, to decode printed words quickly and effortlessly, both silently and aloud;
>
> (b) the ability to use previously learned strategies for reading comprehension; and
>
> (c) the ability to think critically about the meaning, message, and aesthetic value of the text.

In addition the original bill defined reading readiness:

> The term "reading readiness" means activities that—
>
> (a) provide experience and opportunity for language development;
>
> (b) create an appreciation of the written word;

(c) develop an awareness of printed language, the alphabet, and phonemic awareness; and

(d) develop an understanding that spoken and written language is made up of phonemes, syllables, and words.

Reliable, replicable research was also defined:

The term "reliable replicable research" means objective, valid, scientific studies that—

(a) include rigorously defined samples of subjects that are sufficiently large and representative to support the general conclusions drawn;

(b) rely on measurements that meet established standards of reliability and validity;

(c) test competing theories where multiple theories exist;

(d) are subjected to peer review before their results are published; and

(e) discover effective strategies for improving reading skills.

Many reading professionals found the definitions of reading and reading readiness incomplete and too heavily focused on word recognition. They found the definition of research eliminated much educational research. The phrase *reliable, replicable research* was repeated more than 20 times throughout the bill, and at every opportunity the bill restricted activities funded only to those that were supported by reliable, replicable research. The phrase and the definition it invoked were associated with particular forms of both research and instruction substantially narrower than those existing in the field as a whole. The intent was to restrict the types of instruction and professional development funded by the bill.

The reading community also objected to the panel because panel membership was determined mainly by government agencies that had not traditionally been involved in classroom-based reading research. There was no participation from the Office of Educational Research and Improvement (OERI)—the agency that funds most classroom research by reading educators. The inclusion of the National Institute for Child Health and Human Development (NICHD) intensified fears that only instruction and professional development that was consistent with a narrow range of research and practice would be funded. The ultimate fear was that the federal government, having been effectively manipulated by a few special interest groups, would dictate practice. This was an unacceptable precedent.

Both the Association and the National Council of Teachers of English (NCTE) instructed our Washington representative, Richard Long, to work for substantial changes in the bill. Although we were unsuccessful in changing the language on H.R. 2614, Long and representatives from IRA, NCTE, and several other literacy organizations were able to work with Senator Jim Jeffords of Vermont in introducing an amended version of the Reading Excellence Act (Jeffords Amendment No. 3740, Senate, October 6, 1998). The amended version of the act substantially changed definitions, although the changes to the panel were less substantial.

The Jeffords amendment defined reading as follows:

The term "reading" means a complex system of deriving meaning from print that requires all of the following:

(a) The skills and knowledge to understand how phonemes, or speech sounds, are connected to print;

(b) The ability to decode unfamiliar words;

(c) The ability to read fluently;

(d) Sufficient background information and vocabulary to foster reading comprehension;

(e) The development of appropriate active strategies to construct meaning from print; and

(f) The development and maintenance of a motivation to read.

The term *reliable replicable research* was replaced with the term *scientifically based reading research* and defined:

The term "scientifically based reading research"

(a) means the application of rigorous, systematic, and objective procedures to obtain valid knowledge relevant to reading development, reading instruction, and reading difficulties; and

(b) shall include research that—
   (i) employs systematic, empirical methods that draw on observation or experiment;
   (ii) involves rigorous data analyses that are adequate to test the stated hypotheses and justify the general conclusion drawn;
   (iii) relies on measurements or observational methods that provide valid data across evaluations and observers and across multiple measurements and observations; and
   (iv) has been accepted by a peer-reviewed journal or approved by a panel of independent experts through a comparably rigorous, objective, and scientific review.

Both these definitions were broader than the original definitions. The definitions of reading and reading readiness contained three of seven items that were focused on phonics and word identification. In the Jeffords version that ultimately passed only two of six focused at that level, but more important was that the definition was far more inclusive and more representative of our understanding of the complexity of the reading process and the extent to which prior knowledge, comprehension, and motivation are important components.

There were bigger changes in the definition of research. The original definition seemed to restrict acceptable research to large methods experiments. The Jeffords definitions made it clear that observational research was included in the definition. The phrase *established standards of reliability and validity*, which might have been construed to refer only to quantitative measures, was reworded to "relies on measurements or observational methods that provide valid data across evaluations and observers and across multiple measures and observations." The new wording clearly included qualitative research. The Association's view was that these changes were crucial. They made it clear that no one research paradigm could claim to be "scientific" and relegate others to the category "unscientific."

We were not able to change the composition of the panel, and we were unhappy with the idea that it would not contain representatives nominated by OERI. We were worried because ultimately it would be the panel that decided whether a state application was supported by scientifically based research, and that the panel could possibly be biased toward particular research paradigms and instructional practices. However, the Jeffords version of the bill passed and became law.

What to do? Should we oppose the bill and encourage the states not to apply for the money? Or could the bill work in a way that benefited the field? The Board concluded that if properly implemented the Reading Excellence Act could benefit children and teachers in high-poverty schools, and so the Association decided to do what we could to ensure a quality implementation. In a news release (Butler, 1998) the Association noted that it supported the purposes of the act and was pleased with the broader definitions. However, it also noted some areas of concern:

> Despite its positive response to the overall bill, the Association is concerned about the following issues:
> - Allocation of funding—There is not enough total funding to make a significant impact at the local district level.
> - Control of education—A national panel advises the Secretary of Education on funding or disapproval of state applications. This is a cumbersome process which may undermine local control of education and may implement a too narrow vision of effective reading instruction.
> - Tutorial assistance—Grants may provide voucher-like funding for nonprofit agencies that could be hastily created and poorly qualified for providing the services needed by children who are already having problems.

Farstrup commented on some of these concerns, "We are still not satisfied with the heavy representation of federal employees on the peer review panel and call for the appointment of experienced, field-based reading professionals, not federal employees." On another point he noted, "If the after-school program is to be effective, it should be coordinated by a school-based, professionally qualified reading specialist."

Subsequently, the Board's Executive Committee met with Joseph Conaty, the official in charge of Reading Excellence Act implementation, to make it clear that we wanted to be helpful and wanted the legislation implemented in ways that helped children learn to read. When Conaty made requests for scientific research that supported good reading instruction Carol Santa (then president-elect of the Association) and I (as Director of the Research and Policy Division) drafted a document that would represent a broad range of research findings, which we forwarded to Conaty.

We were pleased with the outcomes of our efforts because *Learning to Read and Write*, the Association's joint position paper with the National Association for the Education of Young Children (NAEYC), was listed in the Reading Excellence Act guidelines for applications as one of the references that could be used to support applications. In addition we posted on the Association Web site a list of research studies that could be used to support the applications. This was much narrower than the one forwarded to Conaty because of our uncertainty about the constitution of the panel that would judge the applications. We felt that by narrowing the list we would decrease the possibility that a state application would be eliminated from the competition because it cited one of the studies on our list. In addition the Association gave permission for the Center for the Improvement of Early Reading Achievement (CIERA) to copy and distribute to the states a set of *Reading Research Quarterly* articles that would be useful for supporting applications. Those articles were also available in downloadable form on the Association Web site. Conaty spoke at the Association's 1999 convention in San Diego, California, to explain the act and the application process and to answer questions. In addition we have worked with the National Institute for Literacy—charged with disseminating information related to the act—to assure that the Association will be seen as a resource. As the implementation of the act continues we will continue to do what we can to ensure its success.

Different people will have different takes on this narrative. Some individuals and groups have taken the stance that we should work against the implementation and have it repealed. My personal take is that the Association, working in concert with other literacy organizations, did reasonably well. We were successful in changing the most onerous sections of the bill. We participated effectively in a democratic process that will fund activities to help children in some of the nation's poorest schools learn to read. In a democracy where many individuals and groups vie for power, it is rare that any particular group accomplishes all that it wishes in any piece of legislation. It is always a judgment call to decide which features of the legislation are crucial and which less so.

What the Association Must Continue to Do

The Association's basic position, that teachers should make the decisions about how children are taught to read, is in jeopardy. It is increasingly likely that instructional methodologies for reading instruction in the U.S. will be circumscribed by legislation and strongly influenced by federal funding sources. For any number of reasons, the public is not convinced that teachers are the best decision makers. What must we (the Association's 90,000+ individual and institutional members and the over 350,000 affiliates worldwide) do to assure that every child has access to excellent reading instruction?

There are two basic goals we must achieve. First, we as professionals must be capable of providing excellent reading instruction. Second, we must communicate our expertise effectively to various stakeholders such as parents, the media, legislators, and policymakers. Four critical objectives will move us toward the first goal.

1. Every primary classroom must have a well-qualified teacher who has the knowledge and capacities requisite for teaching reading.

This is the first recommendation in the Title I reauthorization document (available from pubinfo@reading.org). In many cases unqualified and unsupervised aides are teaching reading. This must stop. We know that in some schools, particularly those serving high-poverty communities, the failure rates in reading are simply unacceptable. Often these schools are struggling with inexperienced or unqualified teachers hired through emergency certification programs.

2. Every teacher preparation program graduate must be able to teach reading well.

Many entry-level teachers begin with only three to six semester hour credits related to teaching reading. This is not enough. While excellent models exist for preparing beginning teachers to teach reading, most beginning teachers do not go through these programs. For example, at many universities one option for undergraduates is to take a reading specialization, which involves up to 20 extra hours in reading-related courses and practicums. Students who go through these programs are more confident and skilled at reading instruction as they begin their teaching.

On May 5, 1999, at its annual convention in San Diego the International Reading Association announced the formation of the National Commission for Excellence in Teacher Preparation for Reading Instruction (Commission on Teacher Preparation, CTP). The long-term goal of the CTP is to provide sound research-based recommendations for the preparation of reading teachers. While the Association's Standards for Reading Professionals (revised in 1998) are research based, the individual standards have never been explicitly linked to particular pieces of research. CTP will initiate the effort to provide such links. The CTP is a 3-year effort devoted to the study of excellent 4-year undergraduate teacher preparation programs. In choosing the undergraduate program as our starting point, we are recognizing that the majority of teachers in the United States are prepared in such programs.

The eight members of the CTP were chosen through a competitive application process that included providing descriptions of the program, the faculty, a brief vignette of a beginning teacher from the program teaching reading, and commentaries by various stakeholders on that vignette. The members are as follows:

James V. Hoffman (Chair)	University of Texas at Austin, USA
Joyce C. Fine	Florida International University, Miami, USA
Deborah Eldridge	Hunter College, New York, New York, USA
Amy Seely Flint	Indiana University, Bloomington and Indianapolis, USA
Denise Littleton	Norfolk State University, Norfolk, Virginia, USA
Shane Templeton	University of Nevada at Reno, USA
Diane Barone	University of Nevada at Reno, USA
Miriam Martinez	University of Texas at San Antonio, USA
Rachelle Loven	University of Sioux Falls, South Dakota, USA

The CTP will conduct a series of three studies: features of excellence (to identify common features of programs selected for the CTP), a study of beginning teachers (to describe reading instruction of first-year graduates in relation to a comparison group of similar graduates from programs not emphasizing reading instruction), and a national survey (to describe teacher education programs nationwide in relation to features of excellence). The CTP will seek funding to conduct a large-scale excellence study (a coordinated set of studies across sites that systematically varies the excellence factors, program structures, and other important variables).

3. We must promote conditions of practice that allow good teachers to achieve optimal results.

This means making sure that teachers have reasonable class sizes, adequate instructional materials, and enough planning time. We must join with associations and partners who have similar concerns and support efforts to achieve these ends. We must carefully orchestrate efforts that include developing resolutions and position papers, collaborating with legislators, and supporting the efforts of other organizations with similar goals.

4. Finally, we must be sure that we know what we know and what we do not know and support research to answer our questions.

There is an extensive research base underlying reading instruction. In the last decade we have learned a lot about the reading process, and there have been many studies of various aspects of reading instruction. The major problem here is in defining the term works. Everyone expects the field to be able to identify what works and to use methods that work. The field as a whole must either agree to a general definition or be very clear and explicit at all times when using the term.

I raise this issue because there has been so much rhetoric with statements like, "30 years of research support direct explicit phonics instruction." Much of the rhetoric has been encouraged by a paper, *30 Years of Research: What We Now Know About How Children Learn to Read*, which has been published in various forms but is usually attributed to Bonnie Grossen (1997) of the Center for the Future of Teaching and Learning. The paper claims to summarize the NICHD research, and was featured prominently in the California and Texas legislation of phonics instruction. It has been subsequently discredited (Allington & Woodside-Jiron, 1998). Reid Lyon, Director of the NICHD reading research program, has made it clear in recent publications that the NICHD research does not support a beginning reading program focused primarily on phonics. He has said that NICHD research

> is consistent with the larger body of research in showing that explicitly teaching phonics and awareness skills is an important part of early reading instruction. Gains in early reading skills are mediated by the effect of the intervention on phonological processing abilities. The interventions used in the NICHD studies, however, involve more than explicit teaching of phonics. They also include good literature, reading for enjoyment, and other practices believed to facilitate the development of reading skills and literacy. Hence the NICHD studies are consistent with educational research highlighting the importance of balanced approaches to reading instruction. (Fletcher & Lyon, 1998, p. 50)

Researchers and materials developers must be cautious in their claims and work to fund research that has the potential to support strong claims about what works.

Achieving the second goal, communicating with stakeholders, is also crucial. Parents, the media, legislators, and policymakers are important constituencies who must consider us knowledgeable and competent. Earlier I cited an article by Richard Allington (in press) about the influence of research on policy. He analyzed three recent legislative examples: class size, phonics, and bilingual instruction. There is a strong body of research that supports the effects of smaller class sizes on children's achievement. The research surrounding phonics is contested. Professionals who define reading as the ability to pronounce words point out that systematic phonics instruction results in children's increased ability to pronounce lists of pseudowords and real words. Professionals who define reading more comprehensively suggest that there is no clear evidence that children who have systematic phonics instruction become more fluent and comprehend better than children who learned to read using other methods. In the case of bilingual instruction there is a clear research consensus that bilingual instruction leads to better achievement; however, the legislation passed in California outlawed such instruction.

There were clear differences in the level of research consensus in these areas. In one area the research supported the legislation, in one the research was equivocal, and in one the research was clearly against the legislation. Despite the differences in research support, legislation reducing class sizes, mandating phonics instruction, and dictating English only rather than bilingual education passed in California, and similar legislation has been proposed and passed in other states. In each case, however, opinion polls showed that the public supported the legislation.

If we want research to influence policy, we must communicate the findings of research effectively to the general public as tapped by opinion polls. Several important objectives will help us meet this goal.

- We must all be clear about our definitions for the word works.

Often in studies we have multiple dependent measures, and the effects are different for different measures. For example, if comparisons find that there is an advantage for method A on two measures, and a clear advantage for method B on another measure, and on two other measures there is no clear advantage for either, which method "works"?

- Researchers must communicate findings in ways that preserve scholarly integrity and convey the importance and usefulness of the findings.

They must be clear on when they are talking from data and when they are giving considered opinions. They must constantly respect the limits of the operationalized definitions of their studies. They must be very clear regarding the context, relative value, ramifications, and, especially, the limitations of the data.

- Teachers must understand and be able to communicate the influences that research, theory and practice have on the instructional decisions they make.

Teachers have daily contact with the children of the public. They are in a strategic position to communicate the important findings of the extant research base in terms related to specific children. Teachers can communicate their instructional decisions in terms that clearly mark how research findings have been implemented and how their own classroom research has guided their decisions. They should also communicate what influences their decisions when research findings are unclear. The field as a whole will gain substantial credibility when teachers are able to do this. Substantial increases in training for both inservice and preservice teachers will be necessary.

- The Association must systematically communicate with media and policy audiences.

We are the largest literacy organization in the world, and we have access to impressive expertise. We must be sure that anyone considering policy related to literacy thinks of us first.

Throughout the article I have referred to Association efforts to increase our communication capacities. We have added a staff member in our Washington office to improve our ability to follow legislative efforts in the states; we have focused on placing the Association's expertise squarely in the public arena; we have increased our publications efforts; we have increased the number of position papers, resolutions, press releases, and press conferences; and we have held one-day forums across the U.S. to highlight crucial issues such as beginning reading instruction and early childhood literacy development. Other efforts are in the planning stages.

I conclude this article with both hope and trepidation—hope because I know that within the organization we have both the talent and the will to achieve these goals, and trepidation because I know that moving an Association that is 90,000 members strong and growing is no small task. Taking proactive stands and placing our expertise squarely in the public arena will not happen without considerable work and some anguish. There are many issues for which 90,000 members cannot find agreement. Inevitably there will be conflict. It is also difficult to perform effectively all of the time, and each time we take a stand, we increase the number of opportunities for mistakes. However, reading is simply too important for the Association to observe at a distance as other stakeholders with less knowledge and expertise set policy. We want the world to know that the International Reading Association is the place to come for credible information on reading instruction.

REFERENCES

Allington, R.L. (1983). The reading instruction provided readers of differing ability. *The Elementary School Journal, 83*, 548-559.

Allington, R.L. (in press). Crafting state educational policy: The slippery role of research and researchers. *Journal of Literacy Research.*

Allington, R.L., & Woodside-Jiron, H. (1998). Decodable text in beginning reading: Are mandates and policy based on research? *Journal of Research and Information, 16*(2), 3-11.

Butler, J. (1998, October 28). International Reading Association responds to new Reading Excellence Act [Press release]. Newark, DE: International Reading Association.

Donahue, P.L., Voelld, K.E., Campbell, J.R., & Mazzeo, J. (1998). *National Assessment of Educational Progress 1998 reading report card for the nation and the states.* Washington, DC: U.S. Government Printing Office.

Fletcher, J.M., & Lyon, G.R. (1998). Reading a research-based approach. In W.M. Evers (Ed.), *What's gone wrong in America's schools* (pp. 49-90). Stanford, CA: Hoover Institution Press.

Grossen, B. (1997). *30 years of research: What we now know about how children learn to read.* Santa Cruz, CA: Center for the Future of Teaching and Learning.

Millsap, M.A., Moss, M., & Gamse, B. (1993). *The Chapter 1 implementation study: Chapter 1 in public schools*. Washington, DC: U.S. Department of Education, Office of Elementary and Secondary Education.

Nagy, W., & Anderson, R.C. (1984). How many words are there in printed English? *Reading Research Quarterly, 19,* 304–330.

National Center for Education Statistics. (1997). *The condition of education, 1997.* Washington, DC: U.S. Department of Education.

National Commission on Excellence in Education. (1983). *A nation at risk.* Washington, DC: U.S. Department of Education.

The Voices of Researchers: Conflict and Consensus in Reading Research and Policy

Claude Goldenberg

That great social philosopher, Dilbert, tells the story of Tod, who makes a presentation on behalf of the research department one day. Tod distributes a handout and tells the audience that the research department has done a study to assess the value of their previous research. "Sadly," Tod reports, "all of our past work was either ignored or totally misinterpreted by idiots." Tod is unsparing: "Such as yourselves." So, Tod continues, the research department has decided that instead of doing more research, "we'll just lie." Now for the carrot: "Play along," Tod says, his eyes narrowing, "and we'll make sure the 'industry salaries' study goes your way." Tod looks at his watch: "Well, it's 2:00, and that's quitting time in the research department." Wally, the little bespectacled bald guy with tufts for hair, looks at Dilbert: "You're not my role model anymore. I've found another."

It is easy to understand the contempt with which the public sometimes regards researchers, particularly researchers who till the behavioral and social science fields. Social research often seems to produce trivia masquerading as deep insight. Or else researchers themselves seem to be manipulative and self-serving, as suggested by the famous saying that there are three kinds of lies: big ones, little ones, and statistics. How many times have we heard teachers and others comment cynically (if incorrectly) that you can find a study to prove either side of any issue? Former Assistant Secretary of the U.S. Department of Education Christopher Cross called it Cross's Corollary: "For every study in education research, there are an equal or greater number of opposing studies." He was quoted in an article by Carl Kaestle entitled "The Awful Reputation of Educational Research" (1993).

There are many reasons for this awful reputation, but researchers themselves seem to take pleasure in needlessly undermining one another. I recently came across a *Baltimore Sun* article (Lally & Price, 1998) about reading that contained this exchange: Siegfried Engelmann of direct instruction fame called whole language proponents "brain dead," while Kenneth

---

Reprinted from *The Reading Teacher, 53,* 640–641, May 2000.

Goodman observed that phonics represents a "flat-earth view of the world." So much for civil discourse.

What started out as a "great debate" about how children learn to read at some point erupted into the "reading wars." The release of every new study or report from the National Assessment of Educational Progress (NAEP) or new legislative proposal signals a battle on the horizon. There is widespread disagreement, fueled by mutual antagonism, ideological fervor, and deep suspicion, over the best way or ways to help students become successful readers and writers. The accusations and recriminations sometimes fly fast and furious, partisans for each side often declaring that they are the true last best hope for children and teachers. Policymakers, the public, and even some educators might be forgiven for looking elsewhere for answers.

And it is this elsewhere that worries me. When the research seems to cancel itself out, you can be sure of one thing: People will use research—if they use it all—to support what they already believe. We are seeing precisely this in many places around the U.S. Policymakers and the public will instead rely on some version of common sense, personal experience, and prejudice. I am a big fan of common sense, but it's often not a good guide for determining policy. If we relied only on common sense we would still think the sun revolves around the earth. Personal experience is also a good thing but by definition is idiosyncratic and simply inadequate to form a knowledge base (even if combined with common sense). As for prejudice—it will always lurk. But researchers who are forever nullifying one another are simply providing more room for prejudice to take root and spread its influence.

Let me be clear about this: I do not wish to obscure or minimize the importance of real differences and issues in reading research and policy. My concern is with the zealous focus on differences that creates the impression of utter, unrepentant chaos in our field, chaos that contributes to the "awful reputation" of our research and that poorly serves students, teachers, and the public. In fact, I don't believe the field is nearly as chaotic as many believe or would like to portray. There is actually considerable agreement, for example, on the importance of phonological awareness, learning the systematic relationships between letters and sounds, and meaningful and authentic literacy experiences. Whether there is an optimal "balance" and what that actually looks like for different learners is far from resolved. But we do have reasonable research-based consensus on some key ingredients of a healthy literacy diet.

Whose voices matter in our great conversation about how best to help children learn to read? Educators', parents', and students' voices matter; so too do the voices of the public and of policymakers and political leaders.

Researchers' voices should count as well, since they—we—have an important contribution to make. But we must take care that research and researchers not become just background noise, an incoherent thicket filled with little more than sound and fury.

REFERENCES

Kaestle, C. (1993). The awful reputation of education research. *Educational Researcher, 22,* 23, 26-31.

Lally, K., & Price, D. (1998, September 30). The brain reads sound by sound. *Baltimore Sun.* Available online: www.baltimoresun.com.

Educators Influencing Legislators: Commentary and the Kentucky Case

Shirley C. Raines

athy Roller's article "The International Reading Association Responds to a Highly Charged Policy Environment" is a case study in advocacy. Voices of professional educators have become the other voices in the controversy over legislating educational practice. The decision of the Association's Board of Directors to write position papers is a first step; however, position papers are easily ignored without expert educators' direct interactions with legislators to help construct better policies. Roller's account of the passing of the Reading Excellence Act in the U.S. is a good example of these dynamics.

In Kentucky, high-stakes accountability with rewards and sanctions for schools has been in place since the inception of KERA, the Kentucky Education Reform Act of 1990. Many educators were teaching students successfully long before KERA, but it took an act of the legislature and the state courts to get the attention of other educators to define the state school system as dysfunctional, and to emphasize that student failure was no longer acceptable. The legislative act was necessary before substantial change in education occurred.

Why are federal and state legislatures setting policies and restructuring entire state school systems? The answer to this question is that achievement gaps in educational attainment alarm legislators and the citizens they represent. Despite the slight increase in National Assessment of Educational Progress reading scores in 1998, we are failing to teach the children of the poor beyond basic literacy, with 58–68% of poor children at or below this level (Donahue, Voelkl, Campbell, & Mazzeo, 1998). The phrase *achievement gap* is now in the rhetoric of school board meetings, educational media, grassroots advocacy organizations, and in state and federal legislatures.

I could not agree more with James Hoffman's argument in this issue against centralization and control, reductionist curricula, and groups attempting to silence professional dialogue and debate. However, whether or not policy makers should legislate educational practice is no longer the question. They are doing so. The issue has become whether professional educa-

---

Reprinted from *The Reading Teacher*, 53, 642–643, May 2000.

tors can use research and effective practice to influence policy makers' decisions. We must make our voices heard.

A case study of the Kentucky experience of working with legislators in passing Senate Bill 186, the literacy bill, is an example of how to bring professional voices to the dialogue. Like many other bills introduced in state legislatures around the U.S., the early version of the Kentucky bill contained a narrow definition of reading and reading instruction. However, state Senators Jack Westwood and Dan Kelly sought information from several sources before filing the Kentucky bill. They asked for assistance from a Reading Recovery teacher, an education reform researcher, university reading faculty, and me. Senator Westwood even traveled to Arkansas to learn about a statewide literacy initiative. Working with legislative staff and with us, Senator Westwood redrafted the bill. Passing the bill required support from both Democrats and Republicans, as well as designation of resources for the various constituencies of the public schools, higher education, and the Kentucky Department of Education.

A key turning point in the success of the bill was a legislative field trip. Speaker of the House Jody Richardson, key leaders from both parties, and Governor Paul Patton visited an elementary school to see a demonstration lesson. During the legislative committee hearings, International Reading Association members, school district superintendents, and Reading Recovery teachers inundated their representatives with support for the main concepts of the bill.

The enacted bill presently provides funds for a Collaborative Center on Literacy Development, where courses, follow-up, staff development, and research are conducted. Eight state universities formed a partnership to provide these services throughout the state. In addition, a clearinghouse of research information is provided for schools to determine the changes they want to make in reading instruction. Schools apply for reading incentive grants, administered by the Kentucky Department of Education, for teams of teachers to improve instruction in the primary levels.

The negotiated bill would not have been successful without Senator Westwood's passion for education, the reading teachers who were the voices of Senator Kelly's constituency, Governor Patton, and leaders from both parties. Without the dedicated legislative staff members who counseled our team of educators, arranged for our testimony, and cut through the legislative and educational jargon, the negotiations would have broken down. Working with this one bill required literally hundreds of hours, extreme patience, and the willingness to keep the dialogue open. I am convinced that without the commitment of educators, the availability of experts, and a great deal of trust in working together our voices would not have been heard.

The Association should be applauded for influencing the Reading Excellence Act, as should state councils for their work with state legislatures throughout the U.S. The remaining challenge is to devote the time and mount the resources for effective advocacy. The achievement gap is real in Kentucky for poor and minority children, just as it is throughout the world. The next round of legislation will not be as kind to educators if we do not close the gap.

REFERENCE

Donahue, P.L., Voelkl, K.E., Campbell, J.R., & Mazzeo, J. (1998). *National Assessment of Educational Progress 1998 reading report card for the nation and the states*. Washington, DC: U.S. Government Printing Office.

Critical Policy Action

Policy negotiations take place among groups with unequal power, and therefore, the benefits of policies are distributed unequally among affected parties. In this way, the advocates of policy communications concerns do not carry their analyses of interaction patterns among participants far enough to determine why and how dominant groups' definitions and rules prevent open and free communication and, therefore, prevent good policy. Because the current relationships among groups are based on the social relations of the past, participants understand the inequalities in participation and benefits to be "just the way things are." Critical educators and researchers attempt to illuminate the past and current relationships surrounding policies, to document policy consequences for various groups, to identify the contradictions between the rhetoric of equity of policies with the limits of their benefits, and to bring their findings before the disadvantaged groups to develop strategies in order to effect the conditions for just policies (Edmondson, 2004).

Critical policy action rejects the policy-driven assumption that science provides the only legitimate knowledge and is not satisfied to accept the prevailing ideas, actions, or social conditions unthinkingly or from habit. Rather, advocates engage in relentless criticism of all existing conditions in order to address the questions, Why are things the way they are? How did they become this way? Who benefits from their continuation? and How can we distribute those benefits more widely? These questions require critical educators and researchers to delve into the histories of the intentions, interests, and values of groups participating in policy decisions, to listen to the individuals and groups affected by policy to understand its consequences psychologically and socially, and to examine the social structures that enable policymaking and institutional behaviors. Unlike policy-driven or policy communication approaches, critical policy action requires an advocacy position for change in the status quo.

Critical policy action has four tenets:

1. Policy is the authoritative allocation of values to maintain social, economic, and/or political status quo.

2. Policymaking is a political negotiation among groups of unequal power.

3. Policy decisions are expressions of power in which advantages are maintained.

4. Policy is the product of historically conditioned social relations that are often hidden from view by common-sense understandings of "the way things are," which can be overcome through self-reflective social action.

In her response to policy-driven work, Edmondson lays out the tenets of critical action research in more detail. She begins with a critique of functionalist thought that attempts to preserve the status quo as if it were the best that people can hope for. Concluding that the present is not the best of all possible worlds, Edmondson explains how asking simple questions about why things are the way they are can have profound effects on what we come to notice and know. She states, "Critical analyses allow us to consider the consequences of particular research [and policy] for the children, teachers, schools, and communities that are implicated as we consider broader contexts and ideological visions for the future of schools."

The next five articles are examples of how the simple question of why things are the way they are has been posed to great advantage in developing a critical understanding of reading education policy. Shannon proposes a critical model of reading education in order to explain why elementary school teachers in his study relied so heavily on commercial reading materials during reading instruction. Although administrators' interest in one best method required them to use the materials, classroom teachers in Shannon's study confused the science of reading instruction with the technology of reading instruction and defined their jobs as applying the materials. These objective and subjective factors separated them from their reading instruction bringing feelings of anxiety and loss. Smith, Jiménez, and Martínez-León use interviews with children and teachers as well as classroom observation to understand the literacy knowledge and practices that recent immigrants bring to classrooms in U.S. schools. Their work questions current state and federal policy to supplant this rich knowledge with abstract notions of U.S. literacies. Paul examines the consequences of No Child Left Behind policies for black and Latino students throughout the grades. She fears that the increased emphasis on school accountability without the original social supports of the Elementary and Secondary Education Act from the 1960s (health care, job programs, food aid, and public housing) will make minority students pariahs in schools required to demonstrate adequate yearly progress. Weiner describes his efforts to turn the structural biases of a college developmental reading program on its head in order to help "contingent" college students to acquire multiple literacies to interrogate their schooling and lives. Finally, in a brief piece, Shannon uses the metaphor of the movement to control and eliminate corporate hog farms in Pennsylvania to suggest strategies for how teachers might address the forces that are taking over the control of their reading instruction in schools.

In the last article, Luke expands the scope of these arguments to highlight the challenges of schooling in the 21st century. He writes,

> The problem, then, is this. The selection, codification, and differential transmission of a dominant set of literate and linguistic practices via institutions like schooling must contend with unprecedented and increasing diversity of background knowledge and competence, linguistic and cultural resources, available discourses and textual practices brought to and through classrooms and schools.

In this short passage, Luke undermines the project of policy-driven work ("transmission of a dominant set..."), exposes the unequal negotiations ("the selection...of a dominant set..."), and subverts the notion of the problem of schooling. From Luke's critical vantage point, the problem is the intent to impose one set of literate and linguistic practices in a world exploding with new literacies.

REFERENCE

Edmondson, J. (2004). *Understanding and applying critical policy study: Reading educators advocating for change.* Newark, DE: International Reading Association.

Asking Different Questions: Critical Analyses and Reading Research

Jacqueline Edmondson

n a recent study published in *Reading Research Quarterly*, Jill Fitzgerald (2001) asked, "Can minimally trained college student volunteers help young at-risk children read better?" In a within-group comparison of at-risk first- and second-grade students' reading growth as they were tutored by minimally trained America Reads tutors, Fitzgerald found the following:

1. At-risk first- and second-grade students improved their reading achievement an average of 1.19 grade levels when tutored for a full term by minimally trained college student volunteers.

2. While students made gains in letter knowledge, knowing sounds in isolation, and knowing letters for sounds in context, the greatest gain was in their ability to read words.

3. Growth in reading words was the factor that distinguished low- and high-gains groups of children.

4. Tutors and supervisors responded positively to the program, conveying that it was beneficial to the children.

Fitzgerald concluded her study provided evidence that minimally trained college student volunteers can help at-risk readers.

Fitzgerald's study is timely, particularly given the political attention to young children's reading achievement in the United States begun with renewed vigor during the Clinton administration and continuing into the new Bush administration. College students working as individual reading tutors seem a viable solution to ensuring that no child is left behind, even though the federal office for Clinton's America Reads Challenge Program has officially closed. Presently, provisions for volunteer tutors, particularly college-age students, to teach at-risk children to read are available through the Reading Excellence Act. The pending reauthorization of the Elementary and Secondary Education Act (the Educational Excellence for All Children Act of 1999) and Bush's new legislative proposals in reading likewise hold potential for funding directed toward reading tutors.

Reprinted from *Reading Research Quarterly*, 37, 113–119, January/February/March 2002.

Fitzgerald's work is an example of policy-driven research (Shannon, 1991) that addresses functionalist questions with a goal of confirming or disconfirming a phenomenon as it exists within the current system. While policy-driven research and functionalist questions are commonplace in reading research, different questions can and should be asked, particularly if we are to understand the pragmatic implications (Cherryholmes, 1999; Young, 1999) of our work as reading researchers. With this in mind, I describe two research frames, functionalist research and critical analyses, focusing on the different questions they raise in and around Fitzgerald's study. My hope is to suggest that, as reading researchers, we must extend our tendency to conduct policy-driven research toward critical and pragmatic questions about reading education, research, and policy.

Functionalist Research

Much research begins and ends with functionalist questions concerning what works. Functionalism avoids ideological considerations (Marcuse, 1964), reflecting a positivist view that facts are separate from human values, thus avoiding explicit linkages between education and politics. Typically this research is policy driven, an attempt by reading researchers "to find the answers to the questions current policymakers pose in order to become recognized as the primary source of valued information" (Shannon, 1991, p. 164).

Much of the policy-driven research in reading education has focused on functionalist, methodological issues (see the National Reading Panel Report as one recent example), contributing to our understandings of autonomous aspects of literacy (Street, 1995). However, some of this work has been conducted at the expense of addressing matters of social inequalities and injustices (Siegel & Fernandez, 2000) in relation to literacy, as well as the issues of culture and power that influence multiple literacies (Cope & Kalantzis, 2000; Street, 1995). Emphasis on the seemingly neutral and psychological aspects of reading and research and the search for one right method has left much unsaid with regard to literacy learning and use, particularly as it pertains to the broader historical and societal contexts and relations of power that are brought to bear on literacy learning and use (see the draft of the Rand Reading Study Group, 2001, as one example). With functionalist analyses, the role of the researcher is to instead assess the policy within the current structures of schools and society to determine its goodness of fit.

Consistent with this line of reasoning, Fitzgerald examined college-age federal work study tutors in the America Reads program. The question "Can minimally trained college student volunteers help young at-risk children to read better?" assumes a functionalist stance. Without questioning the broader contexts that would make relatively untrained college students responsible for the reading instruction of at-risk children, this study offers reasonable evidence to support the claim that tutors work to help the reading achievement of these children. Children's reading achievement is the central point of analysis; therefore, Fitzgerald carefully defined reading, detailed the methods, procedures, and measurements employed in the study, and closely aligned them with her initial definitions. Some additional information is offered, including an explanation of how college students as reading tutors are more cost efficient than Reading Recovery programs.

Fitzgerald offered an affirmative answer to those policymakers and others who hope to better understand the potential for relatively untrained tutors to work with young children to improve reading achievement. Fitzgerald's suggestions for further study remain consistent with functionalist, policy-driven research, never straying from the initial definitions, assumptions, and findings of her work. Similarly, the findings do not acknowledge that different definitions of reading would raise different questions, use different research designs, and most likely elicit different conclusions. Nor does the study consider the complex social and cultural conditions in schools and communities that complicate the work of literacy instruction for even carefully trained reading tutors (see Dozier et al., 2000). Not acknowledging different questions or research frames is a limitation of policy-driven research that needs to be carefully considered.

Functionalist research may offer a starting place for discussion and analyses; however, these analyses are insufficient in and of themselves, particularly if we are to truly understand a phenomenon. In fact, sociologist Max Weber considered relying solely on functional analyses to be "highly dangerous" (1947, p. 107). The reduction of reading research to questions of efficiency, management, and prediction inhibits its capacity to question and challenge important issues such as ideology, race, class struggles, and power as they relate to literacy research, education, and schooling. For these reasons, I'd like to extend Fitzgerald's work by considering an alternative analysis.

Critical Policy Analyses

Critical analyses, grounded in the work of Marx, Kant, and the Frankfurt School, historicize policy, considering the broader economic and social conditions that shape its initial viability, formulation, and implementation (see Apple, 2000). As Siegel and Fernandez (2000) described it, these origins of critical theory focused on two major thrusts: a critique of positivism and a concern for the relationship between theory and society. Since the time of the Frankfurt School, critical theory has evolved and been influenced by feminism, postmodernism, and poststructuralism (see Siegel & Fernandez, 2000), resulting in a broadly drawn theory that considers issues of race, class, and gender (see Schneider & Ingram, 1997). In general, critical policy analysts recognize that work in and around schools is unavoidably political, and for this reason, values cannot be separated from facts or choices. Instead, ideology, particularly the ways in which choices are "historically constructed and limited" (Giroux, 1981, p. 25), works in concert with broader cultural influences to dialectically shape research and policy.

Policy is the crystallization of values (Ball, 1990), therefore power is the central point of analysis in critical policy work as analysts acknowledge how power is used to produce different meanings and practices in society and schools, often reproducing power structures embedded in the status quo (Giroux, 1989). Rather than focusing solely on the question of *what is*, the critical policy analyst asks, among others, *what has been, why*, and *what might be*. In what follows, I'll briefly consider each of these questions.

What Has Been?

Historicizing a phenomenon is an important consideration of critical analysts. Social phenomena do not exist isolated from a past, present, or future, and knowing where particular events or issues have come from, both their essence and appearance, contributes much to our understanding of current circumstances (Marcuse, 1964). For example, considering the history of America Reads and the beginning of the employment of minimally trained college-age students as reading tutors allows a critical understanding of the neoliberal origins and influences that helped to shape it as policy. Neoliberalism, an ideology that "maximizes the role of markets and profit-making and minimizes the role of non-market institutions" (McChesney, 1999, p. 6), gained unprecedented dominance during Bill Clinton's two terms as president as this policy extended to traditionally nonmarket sectors of American society. As a result, economic investment took priority over social investments as hypercommercialism increased and social safety nets for the poor and disadvantaged were whittled away (Connelly, 2000; Giroux, 1999; Greider, 2000).

Because neoliberalism endorses the belief that people's freedom and prosperity are best left to the marketplace (Chomsky, 1999), the influence of neoliberalism and the marketplace on education has manifest itself in at least two education arenas. On the one hand, there is increased emphasis on competition and self-interest, particularly through school choice and vouchers where parents are education consumers (Gewirtz, Ball, & Bowe, 1995). Additionally, the emphasis on efficiency, particularly in the form of standards and high-stakes testing, provides evidence of a school's increased market value for public consumption. Although there has been increasing centralization in education, much of the responsibilities of this trend have been relegated to state and local arenas as a new corporate federalism (Lingard, 1993), similar to that in Australia, emerges. Corporate federalism reflects the federal government's moves toward centralized policies imbued with a human capital agenda (Smith & Scoll, 1995) that are directed by a corporate managerialism (i.e., the tendency for elites to act as decision makers).

When Bill Clinton first entered the White House in 1992, he was the first U.S. president to openly embrace neoliberal ideologies (Fowler, 1995). Up to this time, in his capacity as Arkansas governor, Clinton placed core neoliberal values central to education reform efforts (Clinton, 1992; Smith & Scoll, 1995). While Clinton passed education legislation, the Goals 2000: Educate America Act, within his first 100 days in office, 1994 National Assessment of Education Progress (NAEP) results showed little to no improvement in children's test scores. Secretary of Education Richard Riley's Third Annual State of America Education Address (1996) reported little evidence that the administration's reform efforts were producing gains in student achievement. As a result, Clinton proposed in his 1997 State of the Union Address that a call to action for American education was needed. Included in this address was a provision to ensure that all American children were reading well and independently by the end of the third grade, and Clinton proposed sending an army of a million tutors into schools and communities to accomplish this goal. Subsequently, the America Reads Challenge formalized Clinton's plan. The program began in the spring of 1997 when, due to a robust economy, the U.S. Congress allowed for some of the US$225 billion windfall from extra tax revenues to go to a few of the promises Clinton made during the campaign.

America Reads seemed viable to the public at large, due in part to a widely held belief that U.S. children were not reading well enough, and that reading well was necessary for a good education and later success in life. At the time America Reads was conceptualized, the nation was in the throes of what was largely perceived to be a literacy crisis (see Aronowitz & Giroux, 1993; Chall, 1996; Hirsch, 1987; Kozol, 1985; McQuillan, 1998; Shannon, 1998; Smith, 1995, for different perspectives on this crisis). What is interesting about this so-called crisis is that, although there are certainly some children who experience a crisis in their encounters with print and schools (see Allington & Walmsley, 1995), most Americans do not experience a literacy crisis in their personal lives (Shannon, 1998). Indeed, most parents are happy with the public schools their children attend (Ascher, Fruchter, & Berne, 1996). Aronowitz and Giroux (1993) noted that the attention devoted to the literacy crisis is a misplaced emphasis that generates fear and anxiety in order to introduce new school policies, America Reads being one of the more recent.

Contextualizing the use of minimally trained college students as tutors for at-risk readers gives insight into the broader structures and relations of power that make it feasible in a particular time and place. In this way, educational issues can be conceptualized "as part of the social, political, cultural and economic patterns by which schooling is formed" (Siegel & Fernandez, 2000, p. 143). This disrupts the tendency to view educational policy as a natural evolution of scientific progress, devoid of values and interests, and allows us to consider the implications of our research as it supports or disconfirms the ideological vision for schools that is embedded in policy proposals.

Why Should Minimally Trained College Students Be Expected to Tutor At-Risk Children?

To answer this question, we would need to deliberate about broader societal influences, particularly the influence of neoliberalism on American schools and schooling. The employment of college students as volunteer tutors for children who are considered at-risk readers is well aligned with neoliberal ideology, particularly as it corresponds with overt neoliberal values of economy, efficiency, community, and equality (Fowler, 1995). In other words, America Reads has as its primary goal the development of a literate citizenry that can in turn maintain the economic competitiveness of the United States in the context of a global market and global economy. Reading well is seen as the first step in this *reading success equation* (Edmondson & Shannon, 1999). Meanwhile, there is an emphasis placed on *community*, or developing a shared citizenry (see Edmondson, 2000) that helps *them* (the downtrodden, poor, and illiterate) become more like *us* (dominant, typically white middle class Americans enjoying the success of the bull market in the 1990s). This is accomplished through volunteer tutors helping all citizens learn to read and share in the common values of "our America" (Clinton, 1996, August 28). At the same time, America Reads, by attending to the children who struggle with reading, could help increase the move toward efficiency in schools, more commonly referred to as standards and accountability, by emphasizing early reading achievement. This was carried out in the midst of broader messages of perceived social justice and fairness, including a sharing of social benefits.

Closer examination of these neoliberal values points to less obvious aims. At one level, the emphasis on the economy and marketization, reflecting the surrender of social services, including schooling, to the whims of the market, has not benefited all (see Bourdieu, 1999). Meanwhile, not only is reading a commodity that is marketed and sold (Shannon, 2001), but so are children, who are considered value-added products, as evidenced by improvement in their test scores (see Peterson, 2000). At the same time, community, as used by neoliberals, could be seen and understood as an effort toward normalization; that is, there is a push to ensure that all Americans share common values, abilities, and goals. However, this neglects different uses and conceptualizations of language and literacy as every child is expected to learn in "the same way, at the same time" in a common language of English (Clinton, 1997). Correspondingly, as the federal centralization of education increases (Kaestle & Smith, 1982; Kirst & Guthrie, 1994), evidenced in part as standards and testing become increasingly influenced by the National Assessment of Educational Progress and other federal incentives, college-age tutors can be seen as one way to move children and schools more quickly toward these efforts. Yet, this rhetoric of standardization and equality largely masks the personal interests and agendas that are forwarded through America Reads (see Edmondson, 2000) and other education legislation (see Stone, 1997), as more children become marginalized from public schools (see Sacks, 1999, as one example). In other words, particular issues, such as reading, rise on political agendas as developments in the political sphere (influenced by perceptions of national mood, new administrations, elections, interest groups, and others) facilitate the consideration of particular policy proposals (Kingdon, 1995).

Engaging critical questions about these issues of power causes us to consider who may be marginalized by these political agendas. For example, if we place race at the center of questions about volunteer tutors working with at-risk children, many unanswered questions about the meaning of the term *at-risk* in relation to America Reads and other educational policies can be raised (see Crenshaw, Gotanda, Peller, & Thomas, 1995; Roithmayr, 1999, for explanations of critical race analyses). To some critical race theorists, the term at-risk is read as African American, reflecting a deficit model that casts African American students "in a language of failure" (Ladson-Billings, 1999, p. 22). One consequence of this term and its corresponding deficit model is remediation instruction for African American students, instruction which is often limited in scope and based on skill-and-drill exercises that do little to move these students toward a powerful literacy (Finn, 1999). From a critical race perspective, it becomes necessary to ask what at-risk means, who it defines, and what the implications might be in relation to a program such as America Reads. In other words, does such a program increase the likelihood that children of color will have less access to highly skilled teachers? Whom will this program truly serve?

Meanwhile, the federal work study component of America Reads channeled millions of dollars to university federal work study students rather than public schools. This occurred during a time when marked variations in school and community resources and attitudes toward education were commonplace throughout the United States. In fact, recent studies have noted vast differences in literacy that reflect race, gender, and economic and class issues, including disparate attitudes toward students based on cultural, ethnic, or gender differences, differential resources and access to print, and differentiated instruction. It is worth briefly summarizing research in these areas to demonstrate the different questions that can and should be asked in and around literacy education.

Villenas, Deyhle, and Parker (1999) employed a critical race analysis to consider the struggles of Chicana(o), Latina(o) and Navajo students as the researchers attempted to move understandings of race away from deficit views to "a critical view of discriminatory social practices that limit people's educational and life opportunities" (p. 42). By encouraging their readers to see the lives of their students through the students' eyes, the researchers hoped for educational practices that embraced the language and culture, indeed the dignity of these groups. Similar questions could be raised pertaining to volunteer tutors; in other words, whom do the tutors serve? Might this be considered a discriminatory social practice? What are the students' perceptions of their work with tutors?

Meanwhile, Marshall (1997) encouraged readers to dismantle traditional policy analyses, and to culturally reconstruct policy analyses around views of power, language, discourse, politics, and others. Marshall encouraged a new feminist critical policy analysis that put women at the center. In this spirit, Hollingsworth (1997) argued for feminist praxis that would turn attention toward the lived experiences of practicing teachers. Based on her engagement with pre- and inservice teachers, as well as her understandings and interests in feminist scholarship and action research, Hollingsworth raised questions concerning how feminist educators may contribute to the conservative nature of schooling and correspondingly how schooling, and inservice teacher education, may be different. If we direct Marshall and Hollingsworth's concerns to policies such as America Reads, we could explore questions about how such programs contribute to the deprofession-alization of primary-grade (mostly female) educators through an implica-tion that relatively untrained college-age volunteers can successfully teach young children to read. Further, we could raise questions about how this pro-gram perpetuates the status quo in education by leaving literacy education relatively unchanged (see Edmondson, 2000).

More recently, Neuman and Celano (2001) pointed out the deprived text/print encounters for populations of children living in poor communities in Philadelphia. Meanwhile, Duke (2000), in her comparison of print envi-ronments for low- and high-socieconomic status (SES) first-grade students, concluded that "print environments and experiences run wide and deep" (p. 458) and that schools themselves foster lower levels of literacy achieve-ment among low SES students, contributing to differential curricula and so-cial reproduction through schooling. Similarly, McQuillan (1998) has noted the limited access to texts in public and school libraries for children from poor communities. While President Bush's new education proposals con-tained provisions for volunteer reading tutors (see *No Child Left Behind*, 2001), access to books seemed in jeopardy as significant budget cuts to Reading Is Fundamental, a program that places millions of texts in children's hands, were proposed (Masterson, 2001, April 26). Will volunteer tutors help to compensate for these gaps?

What these studies point to, I hope, is that there are many questions that remain unexplored regarding the use of volunteer tutors. Critical analy-ses engage alternative questions that help us to more fully understand this phenomenon. If we consider race, gender, and class issues, different ques-tions and different consequences remain unresolved.

What Might Be

Critical analyses allow us to consider the consequences of particular research for the children, teachers, schools, and communities that are implicated as we consider broader contexts and ideological visions for the future of schools. In fact, in asking what might be, perhaps the most important con-versation reading educators and researchers should have around Fitzgerald's study is how it will be read by different communities. In other words, how will politicians and policymakers, journalists, teachers, university adminis-trators, parents, and others use the findings of this study? How might the findings, coupled with the appearance and language of science (Coles, 2000; Marcuse, 1964), prevent these different groups from asking different ques-tions about this issue? These pragmatic matters (Cherryholmes, 1999) need to be contemplated as we consider the mainstream groups who will take up the findings of our research. More specifically, during this time of increased public accountability and high-stakes consequences for teachers and children, do we hope to forward the message that minimally trained college students can accomplish what many perceive trained teachers cannot? We need to be increasingly careful of the questions we raise, particularly given the uses of research by journalists (Mathews, 2000) and policymakers. This is not to suggest that our research should be shaped to accommodate these audiences; however, the consequences of our work and the vision it forwards must be taken into account. Shannon (1999) has reminded us:

> [E]ducation always presupposes a vision of the future. Regardless of who defines the way, why, and how of education, it is someone's plan for how we will live together. (p. 95)

As educators and researchers, it seems important for us to consider our visions for the future of reading education in schools, and to articulate that to others. Whether we imagine minimally trained college students teaching at-risk readers, or whether we imagine highly skilled inservice teachers gaining specialization in the teaching of reading, we must work knowledgeably toward our broader vision (Simon, 1992). Most importantly, we must imagine this vision within a broader context of the purposes for public education in a participatory democracy (Sehr, 1997).

This brief consideration of alternative questions about minimally trained tutors raises several issues. In particular, it seems important to consider how subscription to America Reads or the use of volunteer college-age tutors as part of other legislation to teach reading to at-risk students as a viable option for schools perpetuates a status quo ideology. For example, while some educators may find no harm in neoliberalism as a dominant political ideology, others have raised significant and important questions about its consequences (see Aronowitz, 2000; Chomsky, 2000; Giroux, 1999; Shannon, 1998; to name a few). Additionally, we need to consider the implications of such programs in relation to race and gender issues, particularly as it pertains to the possibility of perpetuating inequities in and around education. Before concluding affirmatively that tutors can improve reading achievement, it seems that these other points must be carefully considered.

Asking Different Questions

> Not asking certain questions is pregnant with more dangers than failing to answer the questions already on the official agenda; while asking the wrong kind of questions all too often helps to avert eyes from the truly important

issues. The price of silence is paid in the hard currency of human suffering. Asking the right questions makes, after all, all the difference between fate and destination, drifting and travelling. Questioning the ostensibly unquestionable premises of our way of life is arguably the most urgent of the service we owe our fellow humans and ourselves. (Bauman, 1998, p. 5)

Fitzgerald's work contributes to our understanding of college student tutors and their capacity to work with at-risk readers. Indeed, functionalist questions are important and have contributed to our understanding of educational matters (Young, 1999). Yet, Fitzgerald's policy-driven research should not stand alone. Other questions reflecting other research frames must be considered (Young, 1999), and as a community, reading researchers need to extend questions and conclusions beyond policy-driven research. In other words, educational policy and educational practices are never objective, technical matters. Instead, they are always valuative and political, involving competing definitions. As such, educational policy and practice merit "our very best thought" (Apple, 2000, p. xii). Critical analyses offer the potential to engage such thought as complex issues of race, class, and gender compel researchers to consider how power is used to define the parameters of particular questions, to set the rules for particular practices, and to shape particular agendas.

REFERENCES

Allington, R., & Walmsley, S. (Eds.). (1995). *No quick fix: Rethinking literacy programs in America's elementary schools.* New York: Teachers College Press; Newark, DE: International Reading Association

Apple, M. (2000). *Official knowledge: Democratic education in a conservative age.* New York: Routledge.

Aronowitz, S. (2000). *The knowledge factory.* New York: Beacon Press.

Aronowitz, S., & Giroux, H. (1993). *Education still under siege.* Westport, CT: Bergin & Garvey.

Ascher, C., Fruchter, N., & Berne, R. (1996). *Hard lessons: Public schools and privatization.* New York: Twentieth Century Fund Press.

Ball, S. (1990). *Politics and policymaking in education.* New York: Routledge.

Bauman, Z. (1998). *Globalization: The human consequences.* New York: Columbia University Press.

Bourdieu, P. (1999). *The weight of the world: Social suffering in contemporary society.* Stanford, CA: Stanford University Press.

Chall, J. (1996). *Learning to read: The great debate* (3rd ed.). Orlando, FL: Harcourt Brace Jovanovich.

Cherryholmes, C. (1999). *Reading pragmatism.* New York: Teachers College Press.

Chomsky, N. (1999). *Profit over people.* New York: Seven Stories Press.

Chomsky, N. (2000). *Miseducation.* New York: Rowman & Littlefield.

Clinton, B. (1992). The Clinton plan for excellence in education. *Phi Delta Kappan, 74*, 131, 134–139.

Clinton, B. (1996, August 28). Speech at Wyandotte, MI. Washington, DC: Democratic Party Press Release.

Clinton, B. (1997, June 23). 65th Annual Conference of Mayors [Online]. Available: www.whitehouse.gov/WH/library.html

Coles, G. (2000). *Misreading reading: The bad science that hurts children*. Portsmouth, NH: Heinemann.

Connelly, D. (2000). *Homeless mothers*. Minneapolis: University of Minnesota Press.

Cope, B., & Kalantzis, M. (2000). *Multiliteracies: Literacy learning and the design of social futures*. London: Routledge.

Crenshaw, K., Gotanda, N., Peller, G., & Thomas, K. (1995). *Critical race theory: The key writings that formed the movement*. New York: The New Press.

Dozier, C., Collins, J., Johnston, P., Jury, M., Grand, J., Delsant, D., et al. (2000, November). *A multi-layered study of middle school struggling readers in the University Literacy Lab*. Symposium presented at the 50th annual meeting of the National Reading Conference, Scottsdale, AZ.

Duke, N. (2000). Print environments and experiences offered to first-grade students in very low- and very high-SES school districts. *Reading Research Quarterly, 35*, 456–457.

Edmondson, J. (2000). *America Reads: A critical policy analysis*. Newark, DE: International Reading Association; Chicago: National Reading Conference.

Edmondson, J., & Shannon, P. (1999). Reading education in the 21st century: Questioning the reading success equation. *Peabody Journal of Education, 73*, 104–126.

Finn, P. (1999). *Literacy with an attitude: Educating working-class children in their own self-interest*. Albany: State University of New York Press.

Fitzgerald, J. (2001). Can minimally trained college student volunteers help young at-risk children read better? *Reading Research Quarterly, 36*, 28–47.

Fowler, F. (1995). The neoliberal value shift and its implications for federal education policy under Clinton. *Education and Administration Quarterly, 31*, 38–60.

Gewirtz, S., Ball, S., & Bowe, R. (1995). *Markets, choice, and equity in education*. Buckingham, UK: Open University Press.

Giroux, H. (1981). *Ideology, culture, and the process of schooling*. Philadelphia: Temple University Press.

Giroux, H. (1989). *Schooling and the struggle for public life: Critical pedagogy in the modern age*. Minneapolis: University of Minnesota Press.

Giroux, H. (1999). *Corporate culture and the attack on higher education and public schooling*. Bloomington, IN: Phi Delta Kappa Educational Foundation.

Greider, W. (2000, November 20). The last farm crisis. *The Nation, 271*(16), 11–18.

Hirsch, E.D. (1987). *Cultural literacy: What every American needs to know*. Boston: Houghton Mifflin.

Hollingsworth, S. (1997). Feminist praxis as the basis for teacher education: A critical challenge. In C. Marshall (Ed.), *Feminist critical policy analysis: A from primary and secondary schooling* (pp. 165–182). London: Falmer.

Kaestle, C., & Smith, M. (1982). The federal role in elementary and secondary education: 1940–1980. *Harvard Education Review, 52*, 384–408.

Kingdon, J. (1995). *Agendas, alternatives, and public policies*. New York: HarperCollins.

Kirst, M., & Guthrie, J. (1994). Goals 2000 and a reauthorized ESEA. In N. Cobb (Ed.), *The future of education: Perspectives on national standards in America* (pp. 157–174). New York: Doubleday.

Kozol, J. (1985). *Illiterate America*. Garden City, NY: Anchor Press/Doubleday.

Ladson-Billings, G. (1999). Just what is critical race theory, and what's it doing in a nice field like education? In L. Parker, D. Deyhle, & S. Villenas. (Eds.), *Race is...race isn't: Critical race theory and qualitative studies in education* (pp. 7–30). Boulder, CO: Westview.

Lingard, B. (1993). Corporate federalism: The emerging approach to policy-making for Australian schools. In B. Lingard, J. Knight, & P. Porter (Eds.), *Schooling reform in hard times* (pp. 24–35). London: Falmer.

Marcuse, H. (1964). *One-dimensional man*. Boston: Beacon.

Marshall, C. (1997). *Feminist critical policy analysis: A perspective from primary and secondary schooling*. London: Falmer.

Masterson, K. (2001, April 26). Book to close on literacy program. *Houston Chronicle* [Online]. Available: www.chron.com/cs/CDA/story.hts/metropolitan/889976

Mathews, J. (2000). Writing for Rosie: How a journalist uses (and doesn't use) research. *Journal of Literacy Research, 32,* 449–456.

McChesney, R. (1999). *Rich media, poor democracy*. Champaign: University of Illinois Press.

McQuillan, J. (1998). *The literacy crisis: False claims, real solutions*. Portsmouth, NH: Heinemann.

Neuman, S., & Celano, D. (2001). Access to print in low-income and middle-income communities: An ecological study of four neighborhoods. *Reading Research Quarterly, 36,* 8–26.

No Child Left Behind Act of 2001. Pub. L. No. 107-110, 115 Stat. 1425 (2002).

Peterson, B. (2000). Is there value in value-added testing? *Rethinking Schools, 14*(4), pp. 1, 14.

RAND Reading Study Group. (2001). *Reading for understanding: Towards an R & D program in reading comprehension*. Washington, DC: U.S. Department of Education.

Riley, R. (1996). *Third annual State of American Education Address* [Online]. Available: www.ed.gov/pressrelease/02-1996/state96.html

Roithmayr, D. (1999). Introduction to critical race theory in educational research and praxis. In L. Parker, D. Deyhle, & S. Villenas (Eds.), *Race is...race isn't: Critical race theory and qualitative studies in education* (pp. 1–6). Boulder, CO: Westview.

Sacks, P. (1999). *Standardized minds: The high price of America's testing culture and what we can do to change it*. Cambridge, MA: Perseus Press.

Schneider, A., & Ingram, H. (1997). *Policy design for democracy*. Lawrence: University Press of Kansas.

Sehr, D. (1997). *Education for public democracy*. Albany: State University of New York Press.

Shannon, P. (1991). Politics, policy, and reading research. In R. Barr, M.L. Kamil, P.B. Mosenthal, & P.D. Pearson (Eds.), *Handbook of reading research* (Vol. 2, pp. 147–167). White Plains, NY: Longman.

Shannon, P. (1998). *Reading poverty*. Portsmouth, NH: Heinemann.

Shannon, P. (1999). Daydreams believer. In E. Clinchy (Ed.), *Reforming American education from the bottom to the top* (pp. 94–109). Portsmouth, NH: Heinemann.

Shannon, P. (2001). *iSHOP, you shop*. Portsmouth, NH: Heinemann.

Siegel, M., & Fernandez, S. (2000). Critical approaches. In M.L. Kamil, P.B. Mosenthal, P.D. Pearson, & R. Barr (Eds.), *Handbook of reading research* (Vol. 3, pp. 141–151). Mahwah, NJ: Erlbaum.

Simon, R. (1992). *Teaching against the grain*. New York: Bergin & Garvey.

Smith, H. (1995). *Rethinking America: A new game plan from the American innovators: Schools, business, people, work.* New York: Random House.

Smith, M., & Scoll, B. (1995). The Clinton human capital agenda. *Teachers College Record, 96,* 389-404.

Stone, D. (1997). *Policy paradox: The art of political decision making.* New York: W.W. Norton.

Street, B. (1995). *Social literacies: Critical approaches to literacy in development, ethnography and education.* London: Longman.

Villenas, S., Deyhle, D. & Parker, L. (1999). Critical race theory and praxis: Chicana(o), Latina(o), and Navajo struggles for dignity, educational equity, and social justice. In L. Parker, D. Deyhle, & S. Villenas (Eds.), *Race is...race isn't: Critical race theory and qualitative studies in education* (pp. 31-52). Boulder, CO: Westview.

Weber, M. (1947). *The theory of economic and social organization.* New York: Oxford University Press.

Young, M. (1999). Multifocal education policy research: Toward a method for enhancing traditional educational policy studies. *American Educational Research Journal, 36,* 677-714.

The Use of Commercial Reading Materials in American Elementary Schools

Patrick Shannon

M any researchers describe elementary-grade teachers' behavior during reading instruction as the application of commercial materials (Artley, 1980; Barton & Wilder, 1964; Duffy, 1982; Durkin, 1978/1979). While researchers do not object to the thoughtful use of the materials, they find this overreliance unfortunate for three reasons: it precludes attention to students' individual needs (Austin & Morrison, 1963; Goodlad, 1970); it stymies attempts at instructional innovation (Chall, 1967; Rosecky, 1978; Singer, 1977); and it predetermines teachers' instructional decisions (Duffy & McIntyre, 1980). Despite these criticisms, researchers have not adequately explained rationales for teachers' overreliance on commercial materials. This study presents a model to explain possible contributing factors to teachers' overreliance and reports a test of that model in one school district.

The model is composed of three tenets based loosely on Lukacs's (1971) theory of reification, which explains "instructional behavior" as a dialectic among formal rationality, reification and alienation. First, reading programs are organized according to the principles of formal rationality. They operate, as bureaucracies. Second, rationalized reading programs are predicated on reification of reading instruction. Participants treat reading instruction as the strict application of commercial materials. Third, the combination of rationalization and reification forces the alienation of teachers from their reading instruction. Teachers are separated and accept their separation from the control of the content, method, and pace of their instruction. According to this model teachers' overreliance on commercial materials results from subjective factors, psychological factors within their control, and objective factors, social factors beyond their control.

Tenet One: Reading Programs Are Organized According to the Principles of Formal Rationality

Several organizational theorists maintain that schools are "loosely coupled" organizations based on public confidence in the certification of teachers, stu-

---

Reprinted from *Reading Research Quarterly, 19,* 68–85, October/November/December 1983.

dents, and curricula (Lortie, 1975; Meyer, 1978; Meyers & Associates, 1978; Weich, 1976). Meyers and Rowan (1978) report that within schools which enjoy public confidence, "structure is disconnected from technical (work) activity, and activity is disconnected from its effects" (p. 79). "Education comes to be understood by corporate actors according to the 'school rule': Education is a certified teacher teaching a standardized curricular topic to a registered student in an accredited school" (p. 94). While the notion of "loose coupling" may be accurate when schools are examined in total, it does not explain the organization of sub-systems which fail to inspire public confidence. Reading instruction is such a sub-system (Gallop, 1980; Gratiot, 1980; Postman, 1979; Wise, 1979).

In order to regain public confidence in reading programs, schools seek mechanisms to assure the public that their standards are high, and that all students who graduate meet those standards (Good, 1980; Hannon & Katims, 1979). This search has affected reading programs profoundly (Wise, 1979). First, it has reduced the goals of reading instruction from the development of students who love and analyze literature to a standard identifiable level of reading competence (Artley, 1980; Brown, 1978). Second, the search has increased the importance placed on testing in the reading program (House, 1978; Rivilin, 1971). Often reading test results are published in local newspapers, notifying the public of the relative success of area reading programs and assuring them that all school graduates reach the identified literacy end point.

While many tested ways to teach reading exist (Bond & Dykstra, 1967), schools have reacted in an historically predictable way (Apple, 1972; Callahan, 1962; James, 1969). The reduction of goals and the apparatus to certify students' reading competence has allowed schools to conceptualize reading instruction as a managerial concern. Schools seek increased control over reading instruction through formal rationality in order to establish a predictable and standard way to reach the goal of reading competence. For standardization, decisions on goals, methods, and pace must be separated from the practice of reading instruction, and these decisions must be made at a level of authority higher than the individual practitioner. Commercial reading materials afford a mechanism for standardization: they supply a hierarchical set of testable goals, directions to teachers on how to reach those goals, and tests to certify students attainment of those goals (Aukerman, 1981). Because success on these tests is often predicated on students' familiarity with the materials rather than their ability to read (Johnson & Pearson, 1975), schools can standardize teachers' reading instruction with a systematic review of the test results. Thus, both the product, test results, and the process, teaching methods, come under administrative scrutiny

(Samuels, 1970). Consequently, application of the commercial materials becomes the primary method to ensure students' reading competence and to increase public, confidence in the reading program.

Tenet Two: Rationalized Reading Programs Are Predicated on the Reification of Reading Instruction

Researchers conclude that teachers treat reading instruction as the application of commercial materials; that is, teachers reify reading instruction (Austin & Morrison, 1963; Durkin, 1978/1979; Goodlad, 1970). Teachers use the materials uncritically (Rosecky, 1978); often, they apply the materials regardless of the instructional situation (EPIE, 1977). Distribution and explanation of the materials fills the majority of time designated for reading instruction (Durkin, 1978/1979); teachers maintain that these behaviors constitute reading instruction (Duffy & McIntyre, 1980). However, teachers' reification of reading instruction is not sufficient evidence to conclude that rationalized reading programs are based on reification. For that conclusion, administrators and students must also reify reading instruction.

Barton and Wilder (1964) reported that administrators consult commercial guidebooks to form their opinions on reading instruction. Chall (1967) and Durkin (1974/1975) offered anecdotal accounts of the influence commercial materials made on administrators' decisions about reading instruction. Recent literature concerning teachers' accountability and student competence also lends insight into administrators' perceptions of exemplary reading instruction (Artley, 1980; Wise, 1979). Emphasis in this literature is placed on the sanctity of the reading curriculum and the management system to deliver that curriculum (Hyman & Cohen, 1979; Schoephoerster, 1980). However, since Austin and Morrison (1963), Chall (1967), and EPIE (1977) report that the reading curricula in over 90% of American schools come from the scope and sequence of goals in commercial materials, it appears that administrators have reified the notion of reading curricula and management systems as the ones supplied by commercial publishers and have reified reading instruction as the application of those materials.

If teachers and administrators treat reading instruction as the application of commercial materials, then students should reify reading as the completion of those materials (Deford & Harste, 1982). Johns and Ellis (1976) found this to be the case during interviews with 1600 students and reported that "(students') views of reading were restricted and often described reading as an activity occurring in classrooms using textbooks, workbooks, and reading groups" (p. 115). In response to the question "What is reading?" 36% of the 1600 students responded that reading is an activity using commercial materials, 33% said "I don't know," 16% stated that reading is solely a decoding process, and less than 10% stated that reading is a meaning-getting process.

The reification of reading instruction seems to be based on a general misunderstanding of science and reality in Western Society. Habermas (1970) suggests that since the Industrial Revolution, science has played an increasing role in daily life until it is now considered the sole problem-solving agent. To solve the problem of teaching students to read, schools seek a solution in science. However, according to Habermas (1970), outside the actual practice of scientific research, science is understood as technology. People understand the practical results technology delivers—increased quantity, standard means, and time savings—but they do not comprehend the underlying human activity required within the scientific process to develop that technology. So perceived, technology transcends human activity; it becomes a purposeful creature without need of human action or judgment. Technology, then, becomes the solution to the problem of teaching students to read.

According to Barton and Wilder (1964), over 80% of teachers and administrators considered commercial materials the technology of the scientific study of reading instruction. Several factors might have led them to this conclusion: most college methods textbooks advocate their use (Shannon, in press); they are used as treatments in major experiments (Bond & Dykstra, 1967); and their publishers promote them as scientific and technological (Bowler, 1978; Chall, 1967; Goodman, 1979).

Tenet Three: The Combination of Rationalization and Reification Force the Alienation of Teachers From Their Reading Instruction

Since rationalization limits teachers' instructional behaviors, and reification freezes instruction as a standard procedure, teachers are objectively alienated from their reading instruction. They control only the level of precision with which they apply commercial materials. Within a rationalized reading program with the acceptance of the application of commercial materials as scientific reading instruction, the use of commercial materials becomes the end of classroom reading instruction rather than its means.

It is debatable whether or not teachers recognize either their objective separation from their reading instruction or the inversion of the means and the ends of that instruction. While the separation and inversion are clear to the observer, professionalism may shelter teachers from this reality. "Apparently, teachers are committed to the notion that they are professionals who should be free to decide how to teach in their classroom (93%

agreed), but when one considers their heavy dependence on basal readers this commitment to professionalism and autonomy appears to be an expression more of ideology than of reality" (Barton & Wilder, 1964, p. 384).

In summary, stimulated by a loss of public confidence and society's reification of science as technology, schools attempt to tighten the organization of reading programs by actualizing the principles of formal rationality. This attempt requires the reduction of literacy goals, the acceptance of tests as the arbiter of reading competence, a standard technology to meet those goals, and the acquiescence of participants to the notion that a "scientific" organization is the proper solution. The stringent application of commercial materials accepted as scientific reading instruction meets each of these requirements and becomes the unquestionable method to produce literate students. The implementation of the rationalized program and reification of reading instruction objectively alienates teachers from their reading instruction, but the ideology of professionalism may shield them from recognizing the fact.

Method

The test of the model was limited to one school district for two reasons. A comparison of teachers' behavior across districts would yield redundant information since researchers have already found that 90% of all elementary teachers use commercial, materials during 90% of their instruction (EPIE, 1977). Second, the model suggests that both objective and subjective factors contribute to teachers' overreliance. Since these factors combine in various ways for different school districts, an investigation in one district should present the clearest picture of a combination of factors and disclose why teachers overrely on the materials. The investigation of objective factors was a n attempt to describe the organization and procedures of the reading program. Toward that end, a comparison of the perceptions of teachers, reading teachers, and administrators concerning the reading program was made; the interactions among personnel were observed informally over a one-year period; and an examination was made of the school district's printed explanations of their reading program. Survey instruments were used to investigate subjective factors—teachers' conscious perceptions of the reading program. Analysis of the results should suggest whether or not teachers recognize their alienation from their instruction, their reification of reading instruction and science, and the limits rationalization places on their behavior. However, the results of the survey should not be accepted as confirmation or rejection of alienation, reification, or rationalization because teachers may be inaccurate in their perceptions. Rather, the survey data must be examined in light of the investigation of objective factors.

Development and Distribution of the Survey Instruments

The survey instruments were designed to test four subjective hypotheses.

1. Teachers are not involved with their reading instruction (Durkin, 1978/1979).
2. Teachers believe the commercial materials can teach a student to read (Austin & Morrison, 1963).
3. Teachers believe that the materials embody scientific truth (Barton & Wilder, 1964).
4. Teachers think they are fulfilling administrative expectations when they use the materials (Chall, 1967).

After two pilot studies, 20 forced-choice items were selected for the final version of the questionnaire. Five items tested each of the four hypotheses. (See Table 1 in the results section for a list of items by hypothesis.) Additionally, three open-ended questions were included to allow teachers to elaborate on their perceptions and to provide rationales that had not been considered previously. These questions asked teachers to explain "why," "how," and "when" they used the materials. Alternate forms of the questionnaire were prepared for reading teachers and administrators to allow comparison of perspectives on the four hypotheses.

Interview schedules were developed to check the stability of the information gathered by questionnaire. One forced-choice item for each hypothesis was selected randomly and included in the interview schedule to meet this concern. The three open-ended questions from the questionnaire were used as the initial portion of the interviews to relax the respondents and to probe the depth of their responses to the "why" question.

Appropriate questionnaires and biographic information sheets were distributed to 539 teachers, 26 reading teachers, and 26 administrators in a large midwestern suburban school district, which served previously as a model for the Right to Read Program. Subsequent to the collection of questionnaires, interviews were held with 26 teachers, three reading teachers, three administrators, and the reading coordinator.

Scoring the Responses

The forced-choice items used a five point Likert-type response format. A score was assigned for each response according to its corresponding hypothesis. For example, respondents were asked to consider the following item which was written to test hypothesis 3: "The sequence of goals for teaching

Table 1
Means and standard deviations for responses to forced-choice items listed by hypothesis

Hypothesis 1: Teachers are not involved with their reading instruction.

	Teachers		Reading Teachers		Administrators	
	M	SD	M	SD	M	SD
Reading lessons are-never boring to me.	2.68	1.31	3.82	.98	3.88	.90
Each day my reading lessons contain something unique.	3.00	1.10	3.43	1.08	2.18	.70
Often I wish I could cancel reading instruction for a day and pursue something more interesting.	2.98	1.40	3.34	1.19	3.28	1.40
When I am teaching reading I often think of other things.	2.72	1.25	3.48	1.20	3.33	1.24
No one could teach reading in the same way I do.	3.65	1.15	2.09	1.15	3.17	.92
GROUP	3.00	1.46	3.23	1.21	3.17	1.26

Hypothesis 2: Teachers believe commercial materials can teach reading.

	Teachers		Reading Teachers		Administrators	
Basal workbooks and worksheets are necessary reading instruction.	4.42	.96	3.96	1.30	4.33	.77
I usually try different workbook materials if my students are having difficulty with a, particular reading skill.	3.34	1.39	2.95	1.30	3.05	1.41
The materials that make up the basal program are the most important part of my reading instruction.	3.79	1.16	.3.43	1.27	3.83	1.35
Materials that can teach a student to read are called instructional materials.	3.16	1.32	4.08	.73	3.61	1.07
When discussing reading instruction with teachers from other districts, the first question I ask is "Which basal do you use?"	3.53	1.31	3.87	.81	4.28	.82
GROUP	3.65	1.30	3.66	1.19	3.82	1.10

(*continued*)

reading is scientifically valid within basal reading programs." A score of five meant strong agreement, three suggested moderate agreement, and one was interpreted as strong disagreement with the hypothesis.

The open-ended questions were scored in three ways by three independent scorers. (A .90 interscorer reliability coefficient was set as the acceptable level of agreement among scorers.) First, responses to the "why" and

Table 1 (continued)

Hypothesis 3: Teachers believe that commercial materials embody scientific truth.

	Teachers		Reading Teachers		Administrators	
	M	SD	M	SD	M	SD
The readability of stories within a basal text is systematically controlled.	3.68	1.15	3.30	1.12	4.16	.92
Basal reading programs are scientifically tested.	3.78	1.07	3.83	.98	4.33	.98
The sequence of goals for teaching reading is scientifically valid within a basal reading program.	3.39	1.17	3.23	1.08	3.83	.86
Educational publishers suggest that basal reading programs are scientifically tested.	4.06	.76	3.96	.88	4.33	.68
Basal reading programs are the product of scientific investigations of the reading process.	3.73	1.04	3.21	1.24	4.06	.54
GROUP	3.76	1.04	3.52	1.08	4.12	.88

Hypothesis 4: Teachers think they are fulfilling the instructional expectations of administrators and parents.

	Teachers		Reading Teachers		Administrators	
Administrators outlined the immediate and long range goals for my reading instruction.	4.15	1.08	3.96	.93	4.17	1.20
If I decided to teach reading without the basal Workbooks and worksheets, it would be acceptable to the administration.	4.62	.91	4.22	1.13	4.22	.88
The administration selected the basal reading series that I use in my classroom.	4.24	1.29	2.52	1.34	1.61	1.24
I do feel pressure from administration concerning the use of commercial materials.	3.76	1.19	3.26	1.32	3.94	.80
Parents expect me to follow the basal procedures for reading instruction.	4.28	.86	3.86	1.06	4.00	1.08
GROUP	4.21	.97	3.57	1.30	3.60	1.45

the "how" questions were sorted according to whether or not respondents provided different information for each of the questions. Respondents who did not provide distinct information were expected to be stronger in their belief that the materials can teach reading (hypothesis 2) than respondents who did separate that information. That is, because they have not articulated the thought which provides direction for their actions (separated the why from the how), they would be more likely to attribute that direction to commercial materials, ultimately imbuing them with instructional powers. Second, respondents were sorted according to the gist of their responses to the "why" question. After reading short descriptions of the four hypotheses, scorers were asked to score responses holistically by assigning the number of the appropriate hypothesis. Third, the number and the type of subordinate reasons in the response were recorded by assigning the numbers of the hypotheses. (See the chapter Appendix for examples of scoring procedures.)

Survey Results

Eighty-two percent of the questionnaires were completed and returned (445 teachers, 23 reading teachers, and 18 administrators). Teachers who responded were relatively young (69% less than 40 years old), inexperienced (55% less than 10 years experience), and female (80%). While these teachers had completed few college reading courses ($M = 1.54$), most (66%) were strongly confident in their abilities to teach reading. The distribution across grade levels of the responding teachers was representative for the district, $\chi^2(5) = 7.26, p < .05$. Reading teachers were also young (52% less than 40 years old), inexperienced (52% less than 10 years), and female (91%). They were slightly less confident in teachers' ability (52% strongly confident) and had completed remarkably more reading courses ($M = 5.70$). Administrators were older (28% less than 40), more experienced (no one less than 10 years school experience), and male (89%). They averaged 1.89 reading courses, and 61% of them were strongly confident in teachers' ability to teach reading. Despite each group's strong confidence, teachers (66%), reading teachers (65%), and administrators (78%) thought most instructional decisions should be made outside individual classrooms. While teachers (47%) and reading teachers (48%) were split concerning direct administrative intervention into classroom reading instruction, administrators (94%) were strongly in favor of such action.

Table 1 displays the individual items, means, and standard deviations from the returned questionnaires. The ANOVA comparing teachers, reading teachers, and administrators on hypothesis 1 was not significant, $F(2, 483) = 1.61, p > .05$; nor was it significant for hypothesis 2, $F(2, 483) = .64, p > .05$. Differences were significant for hypothesis 3, $F(2, 483) = 4.12, p < .05$. Administrators agreed more strongly than reading teachers that commercial materials embody scientific truth (Dunn, 1961, multiple comparison procedure, $p < .05$). For hypothesis 4, the means were also significantly different, $F(2, 483) = 18.97, p < .01$. Teachers agreed more strongly than reading teachers or administrators that teachers use commercial materials because they believe they are fulfilling administrative expectations (Dunn, $p < .05$).

The ANOVA comparing strength of agreement with hypotheses within groups was significant for teachers, $F(1, 482) = 228.16$, $p < .01$, and administrators, $F(1, 54) = 14.28$, $p < .01$, using Geisser–Greenhouse (Winer, 1977) conservative F test. Teachers agreed more strongly with hypothesis 4 than with the other hypotheses (Dunn, $p < .05$). Administrators agreed more strongly with hypotheses 2 and 3 than they did with hypotheses 1 or 4 (Dunn, $p < .05$). Reading teachers agreed equally with each hypothesis, $F(1, 63)$ M 3.65, $p < .05$.

Open-Ended Questions

Respondents were sorted according to whether or not they provided different information for the questions: "Why do you use commercial materials?" and "How do you use commercial materials?" (see Table 2). Sixty-two percent of the teachers and nearly half of the reading teachers (47%) and administrators (44%) did not answer each question explicitly; rather they described how they (teachers) use the materials in response to both questions. The ANOVA was significant for a comparison of agreement with hypothesis 2 for respondents who did not provide separate information and those who did, $F(1, 480) = 20.5$, $p < 0$ 1. Teachers and administrators who did not separate the information were stronger in their agreement that commercial materials can teach (Dunn, $p < .05$). The difference was not significant for reading teachers (see Table 2).

In response to the "why" question, seventy percent of the teachers emphasized that they used materials because of administrators' expectations (hypothesis 4) (see Table 3). The majority of administrators (56%) argued that teachers use commercial materials because the materials can teach reading (hypothesis 2). Reading teachers were spread evenly across three hypotheses.

Table 2
Means and standard deviation for hypothesis 2 grouped by separation of information in response to the "why" and "how" questions

Respondent	Teachers			Reading Teachers			Administrators		
	N	M	SD	N	M	SD	N	M	SD
Did not separate	277	3.94	.56	11	3.813	.42	8	4.09	.5
Did separate	168	3.18	.57	12	3.51	.49	10	3.61	.4

Table 3
Distribution of respondents by gist of their response to "Why do you use commercial materials?"

Hypothesis	Teachers	Reading Teachers	Administrators
1	20	7	3
2	110	9	10
3	5	0	0
4	310	8	5

Table 4
Distribution of respondents by type of subordinate reasons (hypothesis) mentioned in response to "Why do you use commercial materials?" listed by gist score

Gist	Sub-hypothesis	Teachers	Reading Teachers	Administrators
1	2	2	4	2
1	3	0	0	0
1	4	5	2	0
2	1	3	0	0
2	3	0	0	0
2	4	1	1	1
4	1	20	0	1
4	2	60	2	0
4	3	1	0	0
	Total	92	9	4

The five respondents who offered hypothesis 3 as the gist of their response did not offer a subordinate hypothesis.

The majority of teachers (77%), reading teachers (61%), and administrators (78%) supplied only one reason for teachers' reliance on commercial materials in response to the "why" question. (Only two respondents supplied more than two reasons.) Scorers categorized these subordinate reasons according to the appropriate hypothesis (see Table 4). Two-thirds of the subordinate reasons suggested that commercial materials can teach reading (hypothesis 2).

The results from the interviews corroborated the findings from the questionnaires. The responses to the forced-choice items were correlated significantly with the questionnaire items, $r = .83, p < .01$. The responses to the open-ended questions were scored only for gist because the interviewer was instructed to probe during the interviews until the respondents said they had nothing more to say. The gist of these responses corresponded with those from the questionnaires; 84% of the 26 teachers emphasized hypothesis 4, two of the three administrators offered hypothesis 2 as the primary reason teachers use commercial materials, and reading teachers were split between two hypotheses.

Results From the Investigation of Objective Factors

The investigation of objective factors was an attempt to describe the reading program accurately using a composite of the survey results, observations of meetings between faculty and administrators, and examination of the district's printed descriptions of the program.

Organization of Personnel

During the interviews, respondents (5% of each group) were asked to sketch "the line of command" which they would consult in order to bring about change in the district reading program. Allowing for different symbols and terminology, each respondent drew the same structure (see Figure 1). As can be seen, the district's personnel were organized hierarchically. The reading coordinator for the district described the organization for personnel most succinctly:

> Central administrators are responsible for decisions. This is a large district and the coordination of efforts is a big job...principals decisions. This a large district and the coordination of efforts is a big job.... Principals are instructional leaders in the (school) buildings. They are responsible for carrying out district policy. They carry it out and interpret it to an extent. Reading teachers are there to help the program run smoothly. They meet classes but also coordinate the building program.... They explain the policy to teachers and facilitate the classroom instruction.... Teachers are the strength of the program. They provide the instruction on the basic skills of reading that all children need to know.

The Scope and Sequence of Goals for Reading Instruction

The textbook selection committee reviewed the district's reading goals in 1977 as the beginning of a five-year review cycle. According to a reading teacher who served on the committee, "the charge to the committee was to select a basal (type of commercial reading materials) that matched our needs.

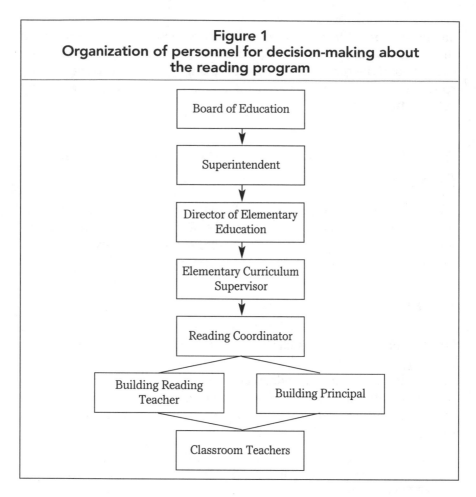

**Figure 1
Organization of personnel for decision-making about
the reading program**

Board of Education

Superintendent

Director of Elementary
Education

Elementary Curriculum
Supervisor

Reading Coordinator

Building Reading
Teacher

Building Principal

Classroom Teachers

That meant, we looked at how they taught the skills, then the goals of our program became the scope and sequence of goals in the basal." The criteria for selection of the commercial materials were presented in the objectives section of "A Course of Study to Guide Reading Instruction," a printed description of the district's reading program.

Objective 2: There is a commitment to the use of a single scope and sequence for teaching basic reading skills.

Objective 3: The skills program is complete. That is, it includes all those skills which are generally considered to be essential to the development of people who can read efficiently for information and pleasure.

According to the reading coordinator, once the commercial materials were adopted, "a review of the scope and sequence of objectives is impossible before the next textbook adoption is considered." "Notes on Pacing Instruction," a pamphlet about the reading program, reported that: "Teachers cannot change the pupils, or the materials, or the scope and sequence of skills..."

Assumptions of Proper Reading Instruction

Reading instruction, in this district, was based on an idea of mastery learning.

> Objective 4: There is a commitment on the part of staff to teach for mastery of reading skills.

All teachers, during the interview, stated that they agreed with the concept of mastery learning. The 26 teachers defined mastery learning as, "a student reaching the critical score on the book tests." That is, a student will answer correctly more than 80% of the questions on the criterion-referenced tests that commercial publishers supply. One reading teacher described mastery learning as "a philosophy...it means that all students can learn to read...the method of how everyone will learn is supplied by the basal."

The Pace of Instruction

According to the district's printed descriptions, teachers controlled the pace of reading instruction.

> Objective 7: Provisions for individual differences that exist in the rates at which children learn is built into the organizational structure and the underlying philosophy of the reading program.

"Teachers can change the pace at which they present materials. The rate at which teachers move through the program is one variable over which teachers have complete control" ("Notes on Pacing Instruction"). However, the declared goals for pacing did not seem to be clearly related to the perceptions of the personnel interviewed. Twenty-one teachers (of 26) suggested that the goals and procedures to meet those goals were "inappropriate at any pace for some of (their) students."

Eighteen teachers suggested that there was pressure within their schools to cover a certain amount of the commercial materials in a specified amount of time. One teacher described the primary sources of this pressure: "We are required to record the criterion test scores and the dates that the test was taken on student file cards. These cards are reviewed every other week by (our reading teacher). Sometimes the principal looks at them and announces whose class is doing well over the loud speaker." During each interview, this internal reporting system was described. One principal explained, "Pacing is crucial for mastery learning. The student records are kept because the pace (of reading instruction) was not always under control. It's not because we don't have confidence in our teachers. We do."

Use of the Commercial Materials

According to all personnel, teachers were expected to use commercial materials, and they did use them. Five of six reading teachers and administrators interviewed stated that teachers follow the commercial guidebook "more or less like a Bible." The strict adherence was appreciated; one administrator related that "the systematic use of the commercial materials insures the continuity of the program." The reading coordinator explained that "because of the size and mobility of the student population, it is necessary to use one set of goals and procedures."

Teachers recognized the administrators' expectations. In response to the questionnaire item, "If I decided to teach reading without the basal workbooks and worksheets, it would be acceptable to the administration," 93% of the classroom teachers strongly disagreed with the statement. Furthermore, teachers' most frequent response to the question "why do you use the commercial materials" was "because I want to keep my job."

Selection of the Commercial Reading Materials

District personnel disagreed concerning the manner in which the commercial materials were selected. Eighty-five percent of the teachers agreed strongly with the questionnaire item suggesting that administrators selected the commercial materials. Three-quarters of the reading teachers and administrators disagreed with that statement. When asked to elaborate on her position, one teacher, who had worked with the committee, stated,

> First, teachers were underrepresented on the committee and those who were on the committee were selected by administrators. Second, I feel, and others agree with me, that the major decisions were made before the committee was called together. We did pick the same materials as the last time, you know. Most teachers' would like a choice of materials, so that they can match the students to the materials.

The reading coordinator, a member of the textbook selection committee, explained the position of the administration.

The selection process was an open one. Anyone had an opportunity to provide input. The committee studied the literature for one year. It was a knowledgeable group. We narrowed the choices down to three series easily. We distributed those materials to every school and sought teacher input. We did not take a democratic vote. But we did try to reach consensus. (The set of commercial materials) was the most acceptable program to everyone concerned.

Assessment Procedures

According to "Notes on Assessment," another pamphlet of the school district I assessment took place in three ways: students, daily work was examined; their oral reading was analyzed; and test scores were reviewed. Several teachers suggested that priorities for assessment differed among levels of personnel. All teachers interviewed thought that oral reading and daily work were primary methods of assessment. Only one teacher suggested that administrators shared her priority for assessment. The rest of the teachers suggested that administrators were interested primarily in criterion-referenced test scores. The test scores were, indeed, the basis for several administrative decisions: grouping for instruction, placement of students in remedial programs, and reporting student progress to parents. Finally, the criterion-reference tests were the only testing device used for every pupa. Norm-referenced tests were administered only to a random sample of third- and sixth-grade students. The reading coordinator explained, "The information from the (norm-referenced tests) is used by (central administrators) to judge the adequacy of the district reading program."

Discussion

The model of reading programs rests on three tenets: reading programs are organized and function according to the principles of formal rationality; these programs are based on the reification of reading instruction as the application of commercial materials; and this rationalization and reification forces the alienation of teachers from their reading instruction. To a degree, each of these tenets was supported by the data gathered.

Formal Rationality

The survey, observation, and published documents provided evidence that the reading program was an attempt to implement the principles of formal rationality. Each of the four main components of formal rationality was exhibited. First, the sketches of the organization of personnel and the reading coordinator's role description delineated clearly a hierarchy of authority. Second, a separation was made between the planning and implementation of reading instruction. This separation was demonstrated in each groups agreement that, "Administrators outlined the immediate and long range goals for (teachers') reading instruction," by the edict "Teachers cannot change...the scope and sequence of skills," and with each group's agreement that most instructional decisions should be made outside individual classrooms.

Standard procedures, a third principle of formal rationality, were also attempted in the district. According to all personnel interviewed, the goals for reading instruction were supplied by the commercial materials without addition or deletion. The reading coordinator suggested that "a review of the scope and sequence of objectives is impossible before the next textbook adoption is considered." Administrators made a conscious effort to have teachers use the same set of commercial materials to reach those goals. For example, administrators ($M = 4.22$) found reading instruction without commercial workbooks and worksheets unacceptable, and "Notes on Pacing Instruction" stated that "Teachers cannot change...the materials." One administrator suggested that "systematic use of (commercial materials) ensures the continuity of the program." Teachers were well aware that administrators expected them to use the materials ($M = 4.21$, hypothesis 4).

Perhaps the strongest evidence of formal rationality was found in the monitoring system of instructional results (the fourth principle of formal rationality). The reading program was designed and functioned as a closed system. The commercial materials supplied the only recognized goals, methods, and tests used during formal instruction, and a periodic review of students' scores on criterion-referenced tests was employed to ensure that students progressed through the materials. Many teachers (18 of 26) interpreted this administrative review as pressure to maintain at least a standard "pace at which they present materials" ("Notes on Pacing Instruction"). One teacher described succinctly the faculty's position on the close relationship between the use of the commercial materials and success on the criterion-referenced tests:

> I took several tests home and asked my husband to take them. He's a vice president of his company and has a degree in engineering. I can vouch for his ability to read. Anyway, there were at least three tests on which he failed to reach mastery because he couldn't pass the sub-tests. The funny part is that our fourth grade son who goes to school in this district.... Well, the funny part is that my son could pass all the tests.

The idea that the rationalization of the reading program was a reaction to a lack of public confidence was not clearly demonstrated in the investigation. When asked, most personnel stated that "the community was confident in the program," that "the program was highly successful," and that everyone was concerned "only with the best possible reading instruction." There were, however, several ways the district kept the public informed about the organization and functioning of the program. Several pamphlets were published to describe the policy and procedure of various aspects of the program (three of these pamphlets have been quoted in the results section). The major pamphlet, "A Course of Study to Guide Reading Instruction," included the objectives of the program and a lengthy (20 of 29 pages) explanation of the commercial reading materials and their use in the district program. Finally, the reading coordinator reported that "a random sample of third- and sixth-grade students are selected to take (a norm-referenced reading achievement test) each year." The results were published in local newspapers to demonstrate the competence of the reading program.

The rationalization of the reading program was not without conflict. For example, a majority of teachers agreed strongly that administrators selected the commercial materials ($M = 4.24$). Reading teachers ($M = 2.52$) and administrators ($M = 1.61$) disagreed and stated that the process was democratic. This disagreement explains the difference among group means concerning hypothesis 4 on the questionnaire. A second area of conflict was assessment of student progress and administrative monitoring of that assessment. Many teachers criticized administrators' emphasis on test scores and remarked that the frequent review decreased their ability to provide appropriate instruction. Finally, there was some resistance to the scope and sequence of goals which the commercial materials provided or the reading program. Nine of the 26 teachers related the same example during interviews. They suggested that several third-grade teachers requested a postponement of some objectives because most students, "even the good ones," had difficulty passing the tests. Central administrators rejected their request because "with proper instruction any objective can be reached. It is not the objectives' fault when students fail a test." The teachers appealed to an author of the commercial materials who explained that their complaint was common among third-grade teachers and that the objectives had been moved to a higher level in the soon to be published edition. With this information, the teachers renewed their request, which administrators accepted with the stipulation that the change be predicated on the adoption of the new edition. Until that time, the teachers were to continue as before.

Reification

The discussion of the rationalization of the reading program demonstrates that administrators reified reading instruction. That is, they treated reading instruction as the systematic application of one set of commercial materials and attempted to exclude all other forms of instruction. For these administrators, the materials defined reading; they supplied the content for teaching reading; and they decided whether or not a student could read. While administrators took every opportunity to affirm their confidence in their teachers, most wanted teachers to follow the materials "like a Bible" to ensure that they provided continuous and standard instruction for the mobile student population. Moreover, administrators designed the reading program to make sure that teachers followed the materials. Their confidence appeared to be more in teachers' use of the commercial materials rather than in the teachers themselves.

The survey results suggest that adminis-trators recognized that they reified reading instruction. They agreed strongly that the materials embody scientific truth ($M = 4.12$, hypothesis 3) and at the same time agreed that the materials can teach reading ($M = 3.82$, hypothesis 2). The means for these hypotheses were statistically equal, and the items testing the two hypotheses were significantly correlated, $r = .54$, $p < .05$, which was the only significant correlation among items testing different hypotheses for any group. Two-thirds of the administrators offered instructional powers (hypothesis 2) in response to the open-ended question asking "Why (teachers) use commercial materials?" However, administrators did not mention hypothesis 3 in response to that question. This omission should have been anticipated because it is consistent with Habermas's (1970) notion that science is understood as technology. The majority of administrators acknowledged that commercial materials are the technology of reading instruction when they offered hypothesis 2 in response to the open-ended questions. However, they did not find it necessary to mention the presumed scientific foundation of the commercial materials (hypothesis 3) because "everybody knows" that technology is scientific. On the other hand, when asked to consider hypothesis 3 in the forced-choice section of the questionnaire, administrators agreed that the materials were based on science.

Administrators ($M = 4.12$) agreed more strongly than reading teachers ($M = 3.52$) that the materials embodied science (hypothesis 3). Educational background may explain this difference. On average, reading teachers completed three more reading courses than administrators. The coursework seemed to have had an opposite effect on these groups. Reading teachers with more reading courses were less likely to accept the scientific validity of commercial materials, $r = -.50, p < .05$. Administrators displayed the opposite tendency, $r = .59, p < .05$. Teachers did not follow either tendency, $r = .06, p < .05$, and their level of agreement with hypothesis 3 was statistically equal to both groups ($M = 3.76$). It may be that the accumulation of coursework confirms the biases of school personnel. Reading teachers who have daily contact with students who fail in the district's reading program begin to doubt the possibility of scientific validity of the materials. Teachers, however, see most of their students successfully complete the commercial materials, and they acknowledge the results of the technology. Yet, they recognize the limitations of using only one set of materials. This ambivalence was not resolved through coursework. Administrators who have little direct contact with reading instruction and the use of commercial materials see only the managerial opportunities available. Apparently, coursework in reading did not disconfirm their beliefs.

At first glance, teachers' reason for using commercial materials appears to be administrators' expectations (hypothesis 4). Certainly, there is strong evidence to support such a conclusion. They preferred hypothesis 4 to the other hypotheses when forced to consider each, and the majority (70%) offered it as the gist of their answer when they were allowed to respond openly. In fact, some teachers wrote notes on the questionnaires to ridicule the naiveté of the investigator for even considering other hypotheses. However, teachers' concerns about administrators' expectations were limited primarily to the selection of commercial materials and the rigidity of the monitoring process. The intensity of teachers' expression of their concerns obscures easy identification of the essence of their reliance on commercial materials.

While administrators' expectations appear to explain the stringency with which teachers applied the materials, teachers' belief that commercial materials provide instruction contributed significantly to their reliance on the materials. Several factors led to this conclusion. Teachers never rejected the organization of the program, the commercial materials, or their use. In fact during interviews, most teachers (22 of 26) stated that they would continue to provide reading instruction in almost the same way without administrative directives. (The change would be to increase the number of sets of materials available.) All 26 teachers interviewed said that commercial materials were needed to supply the continuity of instruction among classrooms and grade levels.

Additionally, the questionnaire results suggest that most teachers thought the materials could teach reading, $M = 3.65$, hypothesis 2. Their agreement did not appear to be dependent on their perceptions of administrators' expectations; the correlation coefficient for hypotheses 2 and 4 was

$r = .17, p > .05$. For example, while teachers recognized that administrators would not accept reading instruction without the use of workbooks and worksheets from the commercial materials ($M = 4.62$), they were equally certain that these commercial materials were necessary for reading instruction ($M = 4.42$). The majority of teachers (those 277 who did not separate clearly their response to the "why" and "how" open-ended questions) implied that an explanation of how they used the commercial materials was sufficient to explain why they used them. In other words, they thought their use of the materials spoke for itself.

Alienation

The rationalization of the reading program forced the objective alienation of teachers from their instruction. That is, the organization of the program to deliver standard instruction separated teachers from the control of their reading instruction. Most decisions usually associated with reading instruction (goals, method, materials, and assessment) were made at a higher level of authority and were beyond teachers' control. Even the pace at which teachers guided their students through the materials was influenced by administrators. The periodic review of test results allowed administrators to identify and to react to the relative speed with which students, classes, and even schools progressed. For example, the reading coordinator related that an author of the commercial materials was hired to provide inservice training concerning the appropriate use of the commercial materials for the teachers from a "slow moving school."

Teachers' reification of reading instruction and their agreement that the materials can teach reading suggest some recognition of their alienation from their instruction. Indeed, 81% disagreed with the questionnaire item, "No one can teach reading in the same way I do." During interviews, teachers explained this response by stating "anyone can use the (commercial materials)." All considered however, there is very little evidence from the investigation to conclude that teachers were alienated subjectively from their reading instruction. To arrive at such a conclusion, teachers would have had to indicate that they felt less like teachers because of the rationalization of the reading program and their reification of reading instruction. However, such an occurrence is unlikely. Since teachers reified reading instruction as the application of commercial materials, the rationalization which afforded teachers a program based on the application of commercial materials made them feel more like teachers rather than less like them.

Teachers' reification decreased the likelihood of the recognition of their alienation from instruction in a rationalized reading program.

Conclusion

The model proposed to explain teachers' overreliance on commercial materials during their reading instruction did account for most of the data gathered during the examination of one reading program. The investigation of rationalization, reification, and alienation from objective and subjective perspectives afforded insight beyond description of the program. Rationalization and reification formed a dialectical relationship to direct teachers' use of the materials. That is, the relationship was not causal, in which one element determines the other; rather, reification of reading instruction as the application of commercial materials affected the rationalization; and the organization of the reading program according to the principles of formal rationality contributed to the reification. Teachers' alienation from their reading instruction was an objective fact of the program, but it did not appear to contribute significantly to teachers' overreliance on commercial materials.

This finding runs counter to the suggestions in previous descriptions of teachers' use of commercial materials (Austin& Morrison, 1963; Durkin, 1978/1979). Several researchers suggest that teachers use the materials because it is an easy way to conduct school and that teachers' overreliance would disappear if teachers were more involved with their reading instruction (Barton & Wilder, 1964; Durkin, 1978/1979; Goodlad, 1970). Some researchers maintain that the only way to change teachers' instruction is to alter commercial guidebooks (Chall, 1967; Rosecky, 1978). These somewhat cynical suggestions may be true, but it is not because teachers are not involved with their instruction that they are correct. Rather, it is the type of involvement that teachers and administrators exhibit which makes this prediction correct. Teachers and administrators believe that the materials can teach reading, and they treat reading instruction as the application of the materials. These beliefs and actions, and not lack of involvement, explain why teachers would change to accommodate new materials.

This finding raises two related questions: Should something be done concerning teachers' reliance on commercial materials? If so, what might that be? By consensus, reading researchers answer the first question "yes." However, there does not seem to be agreement concerning the second. Some researchers advocate the production and use of more scientific materials (e.g., Becker, 1977), others suggest structured modification of existing materials (e.g., Beck, Omanson, & McKeown, 1982), and still others call for better training of teachers (e.g., Anderson, Evertson, & Brophy, 1979). While these researchers offer different solutions, they justify their suggestions primarily on increased achievement test scores. This is unfortunate because the reduction of reading to test scores and the use of those scores as determiners of instructional methodology are first steps toward rationalization of programs, reification of instruction, and alienation of teachers. These researchers appear to wish only to substitute another standard method for the present reified practice. Those who wish to change teachers' reading instruction from the application of commercial materials to a more thoughtful mode will have to find ways to defeat this reification of reading and instruction before they will evoke permanent and thoughtful change. There may not be simple solutions since the reification may be based on educators' sense of science, and solutions may seem contradictory with common sense notions of reality.

Limitations of the Model/Further Research

The model may be simplistic in several ways. First, several social and classroom factors have been excluded which might alter teachers' reasons for relying on commercial materials. Further investigation should be initiated to determine the relative effect of the training teachers receive concerning reading instruction (Bartholomew, 1977), the types of students and communities in which the instruction is delivered (Shannon & Fernie, 1982), the types of commercial materials used (Goodman, 1919), the sizes of the school districts and levels of rationalization of the reading programs (Samuels, 1970), and the ideology of professionalism (Barton & Wilder, 1964). Second, the model may not be sensitive enough to account for subtle differences in reasons for teachers' reliance in various contexts. That is, it may not explain possible differences concerning why personnel reify reading instruction or seek rationality in their reading program. Finally, the model minimizes the contribution of teachers' alienation. While the data from this investigation confirmed this subordinate role, that may be an artifact of the investigation rather than an accurate description. Teachers' separation from their reading instruction may play a greater role than the model suggests.

REFERENCES

Anderson, L., Evertson, C., & Brophy, J. (1979). An experimental study of effective teaching in first-grade reading groups. *The Elementary School Journal, 79*, 193-223.

Apple, M. (1972). The adequacy of systems management procedures in education. *Journal of Educational Research, 66*, 321-338.

Artley, A. (1980). Reading—Skills or competencies? *Language Arts, 57*, 546-549.

Aukerman, R. (1981). *The basal reader approach to reading.* New York: Wiley.

Austin, M. & Morrison, C. *The first R.* New York: Wiley.

Bartholomew, J. (1977). Schooling teachers: The myths of the liberal college. In G. Whitty & M. Young (Eds.), *Explorations in the politics of school knowledge.* Driffield, England: Nafferton Books.

Barton, A., & Wilder, D. (1964). Research and practice in the teaching of reading. In M. Miles (Ed.), *Innovations in education.* New York: Teachers College Press.

Beck, I., Omanson, R., & McKeown, M. (1982). An instructional redesign of reading lessons: Effects on comprehension. *Reading Research Quarterly, 17*, 462-481.

Becker, W. (1977). Teaching reading and language to the disadvantaged. What we learned from field research. *Harvard Educational Review, 47*, 518-543.

Bond, G., & Dykstra, R. (1967). The cooperative research program in first-grade reading. *Reading Research Quarterly, 2*, 5-142.

Bowler, M. (1978). Textbook publishers try to please all, but first they woo the heart of Texas. *The Reading Teacher, 31*, 514-519.

Brown, R. (1978). Response to John Bormuth. In R. Beach & P.D. Pearson (Eds.), *Perspectives on literacy.* Minneapolis: University of Minnesota Press.

Callahan, R. (1962). *Education and the cult of efficiency.* Chicago: University of Chicago Press.

Chall, J. (1967). *Learning to read: The great debate.* New York: McGraw-Hill.

DeFord, D., & Harste, J. (1982). Child language research and curriculum. *Language Arts, 59*, 590-600.

Duffy, G. (1982). Commentary: Response to Borko, Shavelson, and Stern: There's more to instructional decisionmaking in reading than the "empty classroom." *Reading Research Quarterly, 17*, 295-300.

Duffy, G., & McIntyre, L. (1980). *A qualitative analysis of how var ious primary grade teachers employ the structured learning component of the direct instruction model when teaching reading* (Research Series No. 80). East Lansing: Institute for Research on Teaching, Michigan State University.

Dunn, O.J. (1961). Multiple comparisons among means. *Journal of the American Statistical Association, 56*, 52-64.

Durkin, D. (1974/1975). A six year study of children who learned to read in school at the age of four. *Reading Research Quarterly, 10*, 9-61.

Durkin, D. (1978/1979). What classroom observation reveals about reading comprehension instruction. *Reading Research Quarterly, 14*, 481-533.

Educational Products Information Exchange. (1977). *Report on a national study of the nature and the quality, of instructional materials most used by teachers and learners* (Tech. Rep. No. 76). New York: EPIE Institute.

Gallup, G. (1980). The 12th annual Gallup Poll of the public's attitudes toward the public school. *Phi Delta Kappan, 62*, 33-46.

Good, C. (1980). Organizing reading management systems in urban districts. *The Reading Teacher, 33*, 816-818.

Goodland, J. (1970). *Behind the classroom door.* Worthington, OH: Charles Jones.

Goodman, K. (1979). The know-more and the know-nothing movements in reading. *Language Arts, 56*, 657-663.

Gratiot, M. (1980). Research reveals why parents choose nonpublic schools. *Momentum, 11*, 18-19.

Habermas, J. (1970). *Toward a rational society*. Boston: Beacon Press.

Hannon, J., & Katims, M. (1979). The Chicago Plan: Mastery learning in the Chicago Public Schools. *Educational Leadership, 37*, 120–122.

House, E. (1978). Evaluation as scientific management in United States school reform. *Comparative Education Review, 22*, 388–401.

Hyman, J., & Cohen, S. (1979). Learning for mastery: Ten conclusions after 15 years and 3,000 schools. *Educational Leadership, 37*, 104–109.

James, H.T. (1969). *The new cult of efficiency and education*. Pittsburgh, PA: University of Pittsburgh Press.

Johns, I., & Ellis, D. (1976). Reading. Children tell it like it is. *Reading World, 16*, 115–128.

Johnson, D., & Pearson, P.D. (1975). Skills management system: A critique. *The Reading Teacher, 28*, 757–764.

Lortie, D. (1975). *Schoolteachers: A sociological study*. Chicago: University of Chicago Press.

Lukacs, G. (1971). *History and class consciousness*. Boston: The MIT Press.

Meyers, J. (1978). Strategies for further research: Varieties of environmental variation. In M. Meyers (Ed.), *Environments and organizations*. San Francisco: Jossey-Bass.

Meyers, M., & Rowan, A. (1978). The structure of educational organization. In M. Meyers (Ed.), *Environments and organizations*. San Francisco: Jossey-Bass.

Meyers, M., & Associates. (1978). *Environments and organizations*. San Francisco: Jossey-Bass.

Postman, N. (1979). *Teaching as a conserving activity*. New York: Delta Books.

Rivilin, A. (1971). *Systematic thinking for social action*. Washington, DC: Brookings Institute.

Rosecky, M. (1978). Are teachers selective when using basal guidebooks? *The Reading Teacher, 32*, 381–385.

Samuels, J. (1970). Impingments on teacher autonomy. *Urban Education, 5*, 152–171.

Schoephoerster, H. (1980). *Building a failure-proof reading program*. Boston: Houghton Mifflin.

Shannon, P. (in press). The treatment of elementary-grade commercial reading materials in college developmental reading textbooks. *Reading World*.

Shannon, P., & Fernie, D. (1982). Commentary—Grounds for divorce: A critique of Au and Mason's research. *Reading Research Quarterly, 17*, 596–599.

Singer, H. (1977). Resolving curriculum conflicts in the 1970's. *Language Arts, 54*, 158–163.

Welch, K. (1976). Educational organizations as loosely coupled systems. *Administrative Science Quarterly, 21*, 1–16.

Winer, B. (1971). *Statistical principles in experimental design* (2nd ed.). New York: McGraw-Hill.

Wise, A. (1979). *Legislated learning*. Berkeley: University of California Press.

Appendix

Examples of Scoring Procedures of Responses to the Open-Ended Questions

One example was selected randomly from each group to demonstrate the techniques used in scoring. Fifteen percent of all responses were scored by three scorers with an overall interscorer reliability coefficient of $r = .94$. The scores and scorers' comments are included in the examples (they have not been edited).

Teacher:

Why do you use these materials?	"I use workbooks to teach a student a skill and to check that skill. Readers are interesting and at the reading level.
How do you use these materials?	"Not all time should be just spent on skills and reading stories. Creative writing and other such aspects are very important."

Scoring:

Separation:	The respondent did not separate information. Information for the why question deals primarily, if not solely, with how this teacher uses the materials.
Gist:	The gist of the answer is that the materials can teach (hypothesis 2). For example, "workbooks to teach"
Subordinate hypotheses:	There's really only one hypothesis mentioned. She implies scientific development with statement, "readers...at the reading level" but it is not developed enough.

Reading Teacher:

Why do teachers use basal materials?	"To insure that basal words (vocabulary) and skills are taught as suggested by the basal reader company."
How do teachers use basal materials?	"As the core of the reading program, to teacher vocabulary, practice it; teach and practice skills."

Scoring:

Separation:	It's a tautology. Teachers use materials because they use them. The materials teach what they teach.

Appendix

Examples of Scoring Procedures of Responses to the Open-Ended Questions (continued)

Gist: Materials can teach what they suggest should be taught (hypothesis 2).

Number: Only hypothesis 2 is mentioned.

Administrator:

Why do teachers use basal materials?   "As one would use a set of instructions to build something."

How do teachers use basal materials?   "To guide; to provide practice; as a group discussion; as evaluative tools."

Scoring:

Separation: Only tells how materials are used.

Gist: The most reasonable interpretation is that the directions teach someone how to build something, and so the materials can teach (hypothesis 2).

Number: One statement.

Other Countries' Literacies: What U.S. Educators Can Learn From Mexican Schools

Patrick H. Smith, Robert T. Jiménez, and Natalia Martínez-León

Until fairly recently, instruction and research on literacy development in U.S. schools paid little attention to the language and literacy practices ethnic- and linguistic-minority students bring to the classroom. Where mentioned, these practices were often considered barriers to development of the types of literacy valued in schools (Weber, 1991). In the past two decades, paralleling landmark studies by Au and Jordan (1981), Heath (1983/1999), Moll and Diaz (1985), Philips (1982), and Valdés (1996), teachers have discovered the substantial benefits of incorporating linguistic and other aspects of nonmainstream cultures with instruction. Much of this work has focused, for obvious reasons, on the benefits to language-minority learners of reducing the cultural mismatch between students' lives and the ways U.S. schools have traditionally been organized to create what Reese (2002) and others have called culturally relevant pedagogy.

More recently, advocates for dual-language and second-language immersion programs have made strong claims about educational enrichment for language-majority and language-minority students alike (Cloud, Genesee, & Hamayan, 2000; Lindholm-Leary, 2001). In this article, we explore a third, complementary possibility, namely that educators can expand their own understanding of reading and writing—and how to teach them—by considering the literacy practices of other countries. We have chosen Mexico, the country of origin of many students and families in U.S. schools, as a case example to illustrate our ideas.

Why Mexican Literacies Matter in U.S. Schools

As Spanish-speaking children in U.S. schools continue to increase in number, we are excited about their influence on what Halcon (2001) has described as "mainstream ideologies" about education, language, and literacy. Despite the current popularity of English-only and antibilingual education referenda with

Reprinted from *The Reading Teacher*, 56, 772–781, May 2003.

many voters, a parallel countertrend can be seen in the rapid growth in the number of Spanish-English dual-language or two-way immersion programs across the United States (Smith, 2001). Although it is difficult to predict which of these trends will ultimately gain the upper hand (indeed, it seems likely that they will continue to coexist for the foreseeable future), the prospect of adding the worldview and command of language of, say, Sergio Galindo, Juan Rulfo, Elena Poniatowska, Gabriel García Márquez, Isabel Allende, Julio Cortázar, and other distinguished Spanish language writers to the literate worlds of U.S. readers is indeed exciting. In a more immediate sense, however, the findings of this study are most relevant to U.S. classrooms through the stakeholders: students, families, and teachers. As Miller (2001, p. 706) put it in his overview of literacy instruction in Mexico, "Many of the students in our schools are from Mexico, and it is important to find out what they have been taught." We would add that it is perhaps equally important to know *how* they have been taught about literacy, both in and out of school.

Globalization and Access to Knowledge About Mexican Schools

Spanish translations of English language books, textbooks, and other teaching materials are part of a larger "invasion" of U.S. mainstream and popular culture in Mexico and throughout Latin America. Although this is hardly a new phenomenon—Dorfman and Mattelart (1971/1991) began writing about the "Disneyfication" of children's literature in Latin America more than 30 years ago—television, movies, music, music videos, and other media products created primarily for U.S. audiences have become so widely available that students from all but the most isolated rural communities have regular contact with aspects of U.S. culture. We make this observation to point out that while the virtual presence (there are relatively few Anglos living in Mexico) of U.S. culture is commonplace in Mexico, it is almost entirely a one-way street. The millions of Mexicans who consume U.S.-produced materials do so with little opportunity to modify their content. In contrast, despite the historical and rapidly increasing numerical presence of Mexicans in the United States, mainstream culture here remains largely untouched by Mexico in ways that are meaningful for education. To give an example from popular culture, during the writing of this article television viewers in Mexico were able to watch movies and television comedies that depict students and teachers in U.S. classrooms. There are such programs produced in Mexico (although their numbers are much reduced because it is cheaper to broadcast dubbed versions of U.S. favorites), but they are generally available in the United States only on cable television and are not dubbed into English. Presumably, few non–Spanish-speaking viewers watch them. With an important exception (books donated by Mexican educators to bilingual education programs in the United States), which we will discuss later, the same is true for children's literature. Many of the titles available in Mexican bookstores are Spanish translations of stories originally written in English and dealing with life in the United States or Europe. Thus, and in contrast to the supply of labor and raw materials, the flow of information in education, as in many intellectual areas, is generally from north to south, from producers in the United States to consumers in Mexico (Bonfil Batalla, 1996; Herrera Beltrán, 2002).

There have been other attempts to draw on Mexican knowledge and practices around the area of literacy to improve reading instruction for Spanish-speaking students in the United States. In our view, such efforts have tended to focus on the procedures or methods used in literacy instruction in Mexican classrooms in the hope that these procedures can be successfully implemented with Mexican students in U.S. classrooms. Herbert's study (1971) is an early example of a study in which techniques developed to teach initial literacy in Mexico were closely implemented in bilingual programs in Texas. More recently, Miller (2001) documented instructional trends and practices on a macroscale, using teacher response to a survey.

Although valuable background knowledge—about grade-level equivalencies between the Mexican and U.S. systems and the nature of instructional materials, for example—has been shared in this way, there are also important limitations. First, because these studies are typically based on data from Mexico City schools, they tell us little about the poorer, rural schools that characterize much of the *provincia*, the regions from which international migration typically begins. Also, because these studies include few hours of observation, the results indicate what teachers say they do, with little opportunity to assess whether reported practices are actually used in classrooms. In our investigation we have chosen a somewhat different approach; rather than identifying specific procedures for the teaching of reading and writing, we attempt to make sense of the views of language and literacy that sustain and legitimize classroom practices. Instead of documenting procedures in order to transplant them to U.S. classrooms, we seek to explain the ideas and ideologies about the uses of written and spoken language in Mexican schools and communities.

We have chosen this approach for several reasons. First, we wish to avoid romanticizing Mexican schools or presenting a simplistic and thus inadequate picture of what they are like. As in our previous work in schools in Mexico, Spain, and the United States, we observed literacy practices that made much sense to us, as well as aspects that we believe should probably be changed. In addition to sharing our observations and recommendations directly with teachers in the participating schools, we have also shared them with Mexican literacy educators through presentations and publications in Spanish (Jiménez et al., 2002). In this article, our goal is to present the implications of this research for U.S. teachers who work with children of Mexican origin. We believe that this discussion has particular relevance for educators who teach reading or language arts in Spanish or English. Second, as research in literacy and bilingualism amply demonstrates, transporting methods across contexts seldom works as expected. Third, we believe that the one-way flow of information from the United States to other countries is unfortunate because it may inhibit creation of new, indigenous instructional practices outside the United States. With a few notable exceptions such as the work of Marie Clay and Paulo Freire, U.S. teachers cannot easily gain exposure to new and possibly empowering ideas about literacy from other countries, due to unfamiliarity with and perhaps perceptions of inferiority of other countries' literacies. Thus, the homogenizing effects of globalization limit the possible intellectual and pedagogical tools available to educators in the United States and around the world.

Research Context and Methods

We conducted this qualitative study in a small city in central Mexico, approximately equidistant between Mexico City and the Atlantic port city of Veracruz. Over a period of six months we collected data in first- and fourth-grade classrooms in two neighboring primary schools with very different socioeconomic populations. The first school, established in the 1980s with the vision of empowering poor children of indigenous heritage, is attended primarily by children of working class parents. The first author (Patrick Smith) spent six months there in the early 1990s as a volunteer literacy teacher. The second site, a private Montessori school attended primarily by children of middle class and professional parents, served as a point of comparison. Our contact with both schools as researchers, and more recently as parents, dates back to 1993.

In addition to some 34 classroom observations, we conducted formal, audiotaped interviews with the principals and first- and fourth-grade teachers at each school, as well as analysis of student-produced texts and other documents created at the school. Data were collected and analyzed by the authors, with support from graduate students studying literacy research as part of a master's program in applied linguistics at a local university. The bilingual, bicultural nature of the research team, including members educated in Mexican and U.S. schools, enabled us to conduct ongoing cross-cultural analysis of the data, in a sense to "view schooling from both near and far simultaneously" (Anderson-Levitt, 2002, p. 19). Besides working with multiple observers, sometimes in the same lesson, we also had many opportunities to "hang around" in different school domains and at different times of the day. Finally, to understand how the school-based literacy practices we observed fit with those in the surrounding community, we studied many samples of school- and locally produced texts (e.g., signs, advertisements, announcements, banners). For a full description of research context and method, see Jiménez, Smith, and Martínez-León (2002).

In the following sections we present a summary of our major findings. We discuss differences in the uses of oral and written language, with emphasis on the degree of freedom and control Mexican students are accorded to express themselves in the modalities of reading, writing, and speaking. Next, we examine differences between the forms of literacy produced in school and those visible in the community. We conclude with a discussion of parents' and teachers' views as important factors in shaping the language and literacy practices we observed.

Differences in the Uses of Oral and Written Language

As Figure 1 suggests, writing was generally highly controlled in both schools. During our observations in all four classrooms, student writing centered on short, discrete texts, typically dictation or copying of teacher-produced models. Students were rarely given the opportunity to write texts longer than the sentence level, with notable exceptions including paragraph-length texts

---

Figure 1
Degree of control and freedom in three language modalities

Control		Freedom
←		→
Writing	Reading	Speaking

---

copied off the chalkboard. Significantly, we think, we observed no examples of students writing for communicative purposes, or what Barton (1999) has described as the "authoring" function of writing.

Perhaps the most striking feature of the use of written language had to do with an overall concern for correctness of form, in spelling, accent marks, and punctuation, as well as in the actual quality of student handwriting, the "scribal" aspect of written language in Barton's (1999) terms. Editing of students' written work was usually done immediately and on an individual basis, either as the teacher circulated in the classroom or as students brought their work to be checked. Literacy lessons tended to be self-contained, with little overlap of activities or themes from one day to the next. When work was redone, often rewritten in students' *libretas* [notebooks], students and teachers alike seemed more concerned with the form of the work than the content or meaning it conveyed. Perhaps for this reason, we saw very few examples of student-produced text on display in either school.

Interestingly, spoken language was at the other end of the continuum, as we observed very few restrictions on what students were allowed to say or how they said it. For example, during a group reading of the African folktale *Las bellas hijas de Mufaro* [Mufaro's Beautiful Daughters], a first-grade boy yelled out, "¡Son lesbianas!" [They're lesbians!] on seeing an illustration of two women embracing. Although the U.S.-educated members of the research team felt the volume in the classrooms was quite high, neither the teachers nor the students appeared to be distracted by the noise levels. Indeed, our observations revealed that much of the talk was directly related to the lesson at hand, as students enthusiastically commented to seatmates and called out answers to the teacher. Generally, our findings for spoken language are consistent with Herbert's (1971) comment about first-grade reading instruction that "there appears to be an interesting and warm interaction between the teachers and the students in Mexican schools" (p. 261).

On the basis of our observations, we concluded that reading occupies an intermediate position in that it is neither as controlled as students' writing nor as free as oral language. First of all, we observed few instances of free reading at either school. Teachers confirmed that there was no equivalent of Drop Everything And Read time, the group sustained silent reading practiced in many U.S. schools. In part, this may have been due to the relative lack of books in the classrooms where we conducted our observations. When free reading did occur, it was a solitary activity rather than a collective one and was almost always reserved for the end of lessons or for occasions when the teacher was absent. These moments, although obviously pleasurable to the child readers we observed, were apparently regarded as outside the curriculum; children were never asked to comment on or write about what they had been reading. We have some evidence that the idea of reading for extended periods of time is considered somewhat odd, even antisocial, behavior. In fact, our observations of students being chided for reading too much in school may be evidence of very different notions of what "readers" should look like.

In contrast, oral reading was treated like written language in that it was highly monitored for form. As students read aloud to the group, control was exerted through corrections of student mispronunciations or their inability to vocalize a particular word. We observed a similar emphasis on form over meaning during a lesson in which first graders acted out the story of *"Ricitos de Oro"* [Goldilocks and the Three Bears] as presented in their textbook. When student actors "read" their lines, they occasionally made miscues of form (e.g., reading *cold* instead of *freezing*), which were immediately noted and energetically corrected by the teacher and several students following along in the book. Thus, oral reading was treated much like written work: a public display of literacy performed with the expectation that it be free of error.

Differences in School and Community Uses of Written Language

In order to more fully understand literacy in the focus community, we also surveyed and analyzed examples of text on public display. These included many commercially produced banners advertising businesses and services; walls of homes and other buildings painted with the names and slogans of political candidates or promoting an upcoming concert or community event; and handwritten signs to announce help wanted, land for sale, and apartments for rent. These texts were different from the written language used at school in three important ways. First, unlike the texts that we saw students and teachers producing, these texts were produced for communicative purposes, to convey information of potential benefit to the writer to the largest possible audience. Although the aesthetics of some of these texts was apparently an important feature in their production, their primary function was communicative. Second, there seemed to be little control of the content and language represented on these public texts, which sometimes bordered on profanity. Finally, we found numerous examples, particularly in the handwritten and handpainted signs, of nonconventional spellings and nonnormative use of capital letters, accent marks, and other forms of punctuation. Figure 2 presents an example from a sign at the annual *Feria de Nopal* [Prickly Pear Festival] in a neighboring community.

Figure 2
Todo echo con nopal: An example of publicly displayed text

A loose English translation of this sign reads "TUrNoVERS CUS-TARDS JELLIES CUPCAKES ALL MADE WITH PRICKLY PEAR." In addition to the inconsistent use of capital letters (*EmPaNADAS*) and lack of commas or end punctuation, note the nonconventional spelling of the word *hecho* (echo) [made], reflecting the writer's level of knowledge of the Spanish silent letter *h*. Such characteristics suggest that written language in these community texts is seen very differently from the ways literacy is viewed in classrooms. Rather, it is treated more like spoken language in the classroom: largely unmonitored for form and content. This disparity leads us to speculate that similar differences may exist in parts of the United States and other developed countries.

It was also very interesting to us that these community texts were not analyzed or discussed in the schools, even though many of the miscues in orthography were examples of the same features teachers and students were dealing with in the classroom. We have borrowed and extended Ferguson's (1959/1972) notion of diglossia, the coexistence of two varieties of a spoken language within the same speech community, as a useful one for capturing the essence of the differences between the ways writing is used inside and outside school domains. In this "digraphic" context, writing done inside schools and for the purposes of schooling is expected to be tightly controlled for form, with less attention placed on the content of the message. Writing done outside schools is typically not held to such high standards for form, but the communicative value is much higher.

Parents' Views of Reading and Writing

Throughout the study, during formal interviews, parent meetings, and in informal contexts, parents expressed concern for the form of children's writing. From parents at both schools we heard numerous comments about students' "*mala ortografia*" [poor handwriting]. One parent described how, as a young girl in Mexico City, she received a 10 (Mexican schools typically grade on a 10-point scale) for a story she had written. The teacher, recently graduated and enthusiastic about applying new ideas, responded to the story by writing words of encouragement and posing questions about the story. In contrast, this parent recalled, her own mother did not comment on the meaning of the story but was highly critical of misspellings that the teacher had chosen to ignore.

Somewhat to our surprise, parents voiced less concern about their children's reading. Some reported reading to and with their children, and some parents wanted us to know that they had purchased books specifically for children. Although we are still in the process of interviewing parents, we learned of one case in which a university professor parent (a literacy specialist) removed her child from one of the schools because she felt children did not read enough there. Overall, however, parents' views of reading seemed to match a self-critical discourse, which has been widely circulated in the national media, that Mexico is not a country of readers. During our fieldwork we collected numerous expressions of this belief, including this rather plaintive headline in a Monterey newspaper: "*Cada vez se lee menos*" [People are reading less and less] (Reyes Calderon, 2002).

Because we expected to find differences in the views middle- and lower socioeconomic status parents held with regard to written language, it is important to point out that we heard comments of this sort from parents at both schools and from across a range of social classes.

Teachers' Views of Reading and Writing

The teachers we interviewed and observed face a dual and sometimes conflicting set of discourses with regard to the teaching of written language. Parents, the media, and their own school experiences and professional training encourage teachers to focus on form in the ways that we have just described. On the other hand, more recent teacher training stresses instruction to promote written and oral language for communicative purposes. For example, through the recently announced *Programa Nacional de Lectura* [National Reading Program] the Mexican government has invested considerable effort and resources into commissioning authors to produce a new series of authentic reading materials (Secretaría de Educación Pública, 2001). Teacher training programs based on this model are designed to promote "amor a la lectura" [love of reading]. However, the philosophy underlying these moves has yet to guide instruction. One of the clearest examples in our study comes from the area of assessment. During a language arts test prepared by the Secretaría de Educación Pública (SEP), Marina (pseudonym), one of the participating first graders, answered, *"von vero"* to a question that asked who extinguishes fires. Her response was marked incorrect because she had not spelled the target word *bombero* [firefighter] conventionally. In the example *"La enfermera cuida a los ____"* [The nurse cares for the ____], Marina's response (*en fermos*) shows not only that she has read and understood the question, but that she can spell the target word *enfermos* [the sick]. Although she did not receive credit for this answer, Marina also demonstrates her knowledge of principles of syllabification by writing the word as *en* (on/in) and *fermos* (not an attested word in Spanish but certainly a phonologically and morphologically viable combination).

We want to make it clear that this test was neither created nor graded by the classroom teacher. Indeed, it was Marina's teacher who brought these examples to our attention, pointing out that the person who graded the test, an SEP official at another school, had missed the essential features of the answers—that Marina fully understood the questions and had responded in a meaningful if nonconventional form.

Implications for Research

We are in the process of expanding the investigation by conducting interviews with children and their family members at both schools in order to learn how these constituents and stakeholders view the literacy practices we observed in classrooms. With help from graduate student researchers we also plan a similar project in a nearby public school to determine whether the practices we observed do indeed cut across social class lines as we have speculated. There are obviously many other sites that could be considered. While the national curriculum works to homogenize many aspects of education in Mexico more than in the United States, the slow but definite trend toward school autonomy suggests that local literacy conceptions and practices in other regions of Mexico may differ from the picture we have painted here (Schmelkes, 2001). Decentralization of authority to regional and local levels will presumably lead to increased variation in the nexus between literacy and power relations related to indigenous learners (Cifuentes, 1998), gender (Cortina & Stromquist, 2000), and the historic imbalance between Mexico's urban and rural schools (Rockwell, 1996). And students and families may question the need for advanced levels of academic literacy in regions where many adolescents leave school by the end of *secundaria* (approximately equivalent to junior high school in the U.S. system), at age 14 or so, to work in the United States (Levinson, 2001). For this reason we would like to see similar literacy research conducted in other Mexican communities.

We are particularly interested in why written language looks the way it does in Mexican schools. Considering that developmental notions of literacy such as invented spelling have become widely accepted in the United States and other countries, what accounts for Mexican literacy teachers' focus on form at the apparent expense of meaningful expression? How is it that "correctness" has become paramount over meaning? We believe that the answers to these questions may be rooted in what we have called a "layered colonialism" that characterizes contemporary Mexican society. Briefly, the various layers include (a) the continued importance of aesthetic dimensions of text found in preconquest and later indigenous writing (King, 1994); (b) the fact that the indigenous cultures borrowed from one another or had practices imposed by conquest; (c) the linguistic effects of the Spanish conquest, described as *letras sobre voces* [letters over voices] (Cifuentes, 1998); (d) the influence on language and literacy of the French occupation in the mid-19th century, still apparent today in the SEP's approach to the training of reading teachers (see Petit, 2001); (e) the prescriptivist influence of the Real Academia Española [Spanish Royal Academy] on language choice and orthography, including the 1999 change stipulating that accent marks be placed on uppercase letters; and (f) the more recent and rapidly accelerating economic dominance of the United States. Although it is probably true that, by almost any standard, a greater percentage of Mexicans can read and write today than at any other point in the nation's history, it is also true that what is regarded as skillful use of written language is often determined by non-Mexicans.

Implications for U.S. Classrooms

Knowing that we have more to learn about the uses of reading and writing in Mexico, we offer the following ideas for U.S. educators to consider in their work with Mexican students. In the most basic sense, teachers should understand that students' notions about the appropriate uses of oral and written language may be very different from the norms of U.S. classrooms. Teachers can create opportunities for children to talk—in terms of volume, interaction patterns, and topics—in ways that fit with the ways of speaking developed in Mexico (Bean, 1997). In terms of written language, teachers should be aware that concern for form is a valuable component of writing in any language, while encouraging students to explore meaningful self-expression via written language. Teachers who become aware of these cultural differences around language are thus enabled to take advantage of what Smith (2001) has described as "funds of linguistic knowledge" (p. 381), collectively held resources that educators can tap in designing relevant instructional practices and materials.

Asking students directly can be one of the most effective means of getting at this knowledge. Our interviews with transnational learners, children who have been schooled on both sides of the border, reveal that language differences, smaller class sizes, teacher aides, more books, and physically more attractive classrooms are among the most distinguishing characteristics of U.S. schools, according to newcomer students from Mexico (Smith & Martínez-León, in press). Reading and writing teachers can take this investigation a step further by getting their students to talk directly about comparative literacy practices in the two countries, including their reaction to locally produced and community texts in the target language. We have recently noticed such texts at Mexican *tienditas* [small grocery stores] in the United States, an indication that these practices are being imported—and most likely ignored by U.S. schools.

Educators can also analyze academic texts produced for use in Mexican schools. At the beginning of this article, we compared the virtual presence of aspects of U.S. education inside Mexico with the absence of similar images of Mexican schools inside the United States. An exception to this rule is the SEP's annual donations of textbooks and other teaching materials to bilingual education programs and schools and libraries serving large Mexican populations. The intent is to provide linguistically and culturally relevant literature for child readers, but these books and the companion teacher texts also highlight the preferred literacy practices of thousands of Mexican classrooms. Teachers seeking to improve their Spanish during summer study, home stays, and other language-learning experiences in Mexico can also see for themselves by observing these literacy practices in the context of Mexican classrooms.

Finally, the notion of other countries' literacies can also be seen as evidence supporting the literacy component of minority-language and native-language programs. Programs that use written Spanish primarily as a bridge to English literacy are unlikely to incorporate the views of literacy that we have illuminated in this article. Indeed, as we have argued, due to the powerful effects of mainstream ideologies of literacy (Halcón, 2001), educators in the U.S. would find it difficult to see the value of these practices or even to know that they exist. In contrast, programs that stress the development of Spanish as an academic language would seem to offer richer opportunities for children to become advanced biliterates, capable of reading and writing in Spanish in ways that make sense on both sides of the border. To name just a few examples of transnational literacies, letter writing (Guerra, 1998), translation and interpretation of documents (Jiménez, 2001; McQuillan & Tse, 1995), and the invention of new systems of notation (Kalmar, 2001) are extensions and applications of some of the practices we documented.

Reexamining Language and Literacy

We have been concerned here with the language and literacy practices of Mexican schools and how these shape and are shaped by the ideologies of students, families, and teachers. We have also described possible areas for awareness and action by literacy educators in the United States who work with Mexican students. What has yet to be done, of course, is for readers to test the value of these ideas in their classrooms and as they think about their own teaching.

It is likely that some of the beliefs about language and literacy described here are already making themselves felt in U.S. schools via the instructional practices of Mexican-educated and Mexican-trained teachers. With thousands living in the United States, many of them working in jobs outside education, it makes sense that schools turn to this underutilized resource to help meet the growing need for Spanish-fluent teachers (García & González, 2000; Riojas Clark & Flores, 2001). However, as school districts recruit Spanish-speaking educators from outside the United States, it is important to remember that ideas about literacy in Spanish-speaking countries are not monolithic. Despite certain common colonial and postcolonial experiences, including national educational systems and the relatively high price of books throughout much of Latin America, there are almost certainly important differences between the literacy experiences of Mexicans and, say, those of Colombians or Salvadorans. John Baugh, a sociolinguist whose work focuses particularly on African American Vernacular English (perhaps better known to readers as Black English), has observed that the spoken language of Mexican Americans is considerably more varied among individuals than that spoken by African Americans (Baugh, 1998). We speculate that the spoken and written varieties of Spanish that have developed in the Americas—and that are increasingly present in the United States—may be similarly diverse.

In this article we have tried to describe aspects of that richness and to outline possible responses. Other responses are certainly possible. The field of literacy research has advanced to the point that it should be obvious to all that expecting children from other countries to flourish under approaches based on only U.S. mainstream culture is naive, unjust, and ultimately unproductive. Accommodating this linguistic and literate diversity does indeed represent a serious challenge for U.S. educators, but it is also an invitation to reexamine the language and literacy practices found within local schools and communities and, thus, to grow as literacy teachers and responsible members of an increasingly global society. *Todo el mundo es bienvenido en este viaje*. We welcome everyone on the journey.

REFERENCES

Anderson-Levitt, K.M. (2002). Teaching culture as national and transnational: A response to teachers' work. *Educational Researcher, 31*(3), 19-21.

Au, K.H., & Jordan, C. (1981). Teaching reading to Hawaiian children: Finding a culturally appropriate solution. In H.T. Trueba, G.P. Guthrie, & K.H. Au (Eds.), *Culture and the bilingual classroom: Studies in classroom ethnography* (pp. 139-152). New York: Newbury House.

Barton, D. (1999). *Literacy: An introduction to the ecology of written language.* Oxford, UK: Blackwell.

Baugh, J. (1998, November). *Linguistic variation: Discriminating speech in social context.* Paper presented in honor of Letticia Galindo at the meeting of the American Anthropological Association, Tempe, AZ.

Bean, M.S. (1997). Talking with Benny: Suppressing or supporting learner themes and learner worlds? *Anthropology & Education Quarterly, 28*(1), 50-69.

Bonfil Batalla, G. (1996). *México profundo: Reclaiming a civilization* [P.A. Dennis, Trans.]. Austin: University of Texas Press.

Cifuentes, B. (1998). *Letras sobre voces* (Letters over words/voices). Mexico City: Centro de Investigación y Estudios Superiores en Antropología Social.

Cloud, N., Genesee, F., & Hamayan, E. (2000). *Dual language instruction: A handbook for enriched education.* Boston: Heinle & Heinle.

Cortina, R., & Stromquist, N.P. (2000). *Distant alliances: Promoting education for girls and women in Latin America.* New York: RoutledgeFalmer.

Dorfman, A., & Mattelart, A. (1991). *How to read Donald Duck: Imperialist ideology in the Disney comic.* New York: International General. (Original work published 1971)

Ferguson, C. (1972). Diglossia. In P.P. Giglioli (Ed.), *Language and social context* (pp. 237-251). London: Penguin. (Original work published 1959)

García, A.G., & González, J.M. (2000). *The views of Mexican Normalista and U.S. bilingual education teachers: An exploratory study of perceptions, beliefs, and attitudes* (CBER Explorations in Bi-national Education No. 3). Tempe: Arizona State University, Center for Bilingual Education and Research.

Guerra, J.C. (1998). *Close to home: Oral and literate practices in a transnational Mexicano community.* New York: Teachers College Press.

Halcón, J.J. (2001). Mainstream ideology and literacy instruction for Spanish-speaking children. In M. de la Luz Reyes & J.J. Halcón (Eds.), *The best for our children: Critical perspectives on literacy for Latino students* (pp. 65-77). New York: Teachers College Press.

Heath, S.B. (1999). *Ways with words: Language, life, and work in communities and classrooms.* Cambridge, UK: Cambridge University Press. (Original work published 1983)

Herbert, C.H., Jr. (1971). Initial reading in Spanish for bilinguals. In W.F. Mackey & T. Andersson (Eds.), *Bilingualism in early childhood* (pp. 259-271). Rowley, MA: Newbury House.

Herrera Beltrán, C. (2002, July 29). ONU: México calca el modelo educativo de EU (UN: Mexico copies U.S. education model). *La Jornada,* pp. A1, A7.

Jiménez, R.T. (2001). Literacy and the identity development of Latina/o students. *American Educational Research Journal, 37,* 971-1000.

Jiménez, R.T., Smith, P.H., & Martínez-León, N. (2002). *Freedom and form: The language and literacy practices of two Mexican schools.* Manuscript submitted for publication.

Jiménez, R.T., Smith, P.H., Martínez-León, N., Ballesteros, R.M., Ceballos, M., & Kimbrough, J. (2002, October). *Language and literacy practices in two Mexican schools.* Paper presented at the Seventh Latin American Congress on Reading and Writing Development, Puebla, Mexico.

Kalmar, T.M. (2001). *Illegal alphabets and adult biliteracy: Latino migrants crossing the linguistic border.* Mahwah, NJ: Erlbaum.

King, L. (1994). *Roots of identity: Language and literacy in Mexico.* Stanford, CA: Stanford University Press.

Levinson, B.A.U. (2001). *We are all equal: Student culture and identity at a Mexican secondary school, 1988-1998.* Durham, NC: Duke University Press.

Lindholm-Leary, K.J. (2001). *Dual language education.* Clevedon, UK: Multilingual Matters.

McQuillan, J., & Tse, L. (1995). Child language brokering in linguistic minority communities: Effects on culture, cognition, and literacy. *Language and Education, 9,* 195-215.

Miller, R. (2001). A 20-year update on reading instruction and primary school education in Mexico: Mexican teachers' viewpoints. *The Reading Teacher, 54,* 704-716.

Moll, L.C., & Diaz, S. (1985). Ethnographic pedagogy: Promoting effective bilingual instruction. In E. García & R. Padilla (Eds.), *Advances in bilingual education research* (pp. 127-149). Tucson: University of Arizona Press.

Petit, M. (2001). *Nuevos acercamientos a los jóvenes y la lectura* (New understandings of youth and reading). Mexico City: Fondo de Cultura Económica/Secretaría de Educación Pública.

Philips, S.U. (1982). *The invisible culture: Communication in the classroom and community on the Warm Springs Indian Reservation.* New York: Longman.

Reese, L. (2002). Parental strategies in contrasting cultural settings: Families in México and "El Norte." *Anthropology & Education Quarterly, 33*(1), 30-59.

Reyes Calderón, G.S. (2002, April 12). Cada vez se lee menos [People are reading less and less]. *El Norte*, p. B2.

Riojas Clark, E., & Flores, B. (2001). Is Spanish proficiency simply enough? An examination of Normalistas' attitudes toward Spanish, bilingualism, and bilingual education pedagogy. *Mextesol Journal, 25*(3), 13-27.

Rockwell, E. (1996). Keys to appropriation: Rural schooling in Mexico. In B.A.U. Levinson, D.E. Foley, & D.C. Holland (Eds.), *The cultural production of the educated person: Critical ethnographies of schooling and local practice* (pp. 301-324). Albany: State University of New York Press.

Schmelkes, S. (2001). School autonomy and assessment in Mexico. *Prospects, 31*, 575-586.

Secretaría de Educación Pública. (2001). *Programa Nacional de Lectura* (National Reading Program). Mexico City: Secretaría de Educación Pública. Retrieved from http://lectura.ILCE.edu.mx/documentos/pnl/html

Smith, P.H. (2001). Community language resources in dual language schooling. *Bilingual Research Journal* [Special issue on recently completed dissertations], *25*, 375-404.

Smith, P.H., & Martínez-León, N. (in press). Transnationalism and language-in-education planning in Mexico: Response to Robert B. Kaplan's "Language Teaching and Language Policy." *Applied Language Learning.*

Valdés, G. (1996). *Con respeto: Bridging the distance between culturally diverse families and schools.* New York: Teachers College Press.

Weber, R.M. (1991). Linguistic diversity and reading in American society. In R. Barr, M.L. Kamil, P.B. Mosenthal, & P.D. Pearson (Eds.), *Handbook of reading research* (Vol. 2, pp. 97-119). White Plains, NY: Longman.

The Train Has Left: The No Child Left Behind Act Leaves Black and Latino Literacy Learners Waiting at the Station

Dierdre Glenn Paul

A number of distinguished analysts have stepped forward in the past two years to critique the No Child Left Behind Act (NCLBA), a reauthorization of the Elementary and Secondary Education Act of 1965, and its corresponding Reading First guidelines. Among those notable critics are Allington (2002b), Coles (2002), and Garan (2002). Their much needed analyses and commentaries focus, primarily, on the broad implications of "junk" science dictating classroom literacy practice. Specifically, the critics address flaws in the research reviewed by the National Reading Panel, which serves as the basis for Reading First. Those flaws primarily pertain to issues regarding sampling, research methodology, and a broader relevance of the findings. These analysts' critiques have revitalized professional debate and moved many teachers toward reflection and contemplation about what is best for school-age children in the United States. Noticeably absent from these critiques of the 670-page document has been the inclusive exploration of the NCLBA and Reading First implications as they directly relate to black and Latino student populations. In addition, a number of opportunities have been missed to comprehensively probe the ways in which this legislation serves to exacerbate the existing achievement gap between black and Latino students and their white counterparts.

The Civil Rights Project (2001) of Harvard University has prepared a report entitled *A Multiracial Society With Segregated Schools: Are We Losing the Dream?* (Frankenburg, Lee, & Orfield, 2003). The study's most pointed finding indicates that approximately 2.3 million U.S. public school students attend what the authors of the report called "apartheid" schools. In those schools, all students are racial "minorities." Yet the schools must be viewed within a broader societal context that is equivalently segregated (especially in relation to residential patterns). Black and Latino students who attend "apartheid" schools are more likely to receive "dis-education," which can be

---

Reprinted from *Journal of Adolescent & Adult Literacy*, 47, 648–656, May 2004.

characterized as "the experience of pervasive, persistent, and disproportionate underachievement [of black and Latino masses] in comparison with their white counterparts" (Carruthers, 1994, p. 45).

Black and Latino students who attend such schools are also more likely to be affected by lower rates of per-pupil expenditure, less experienced or less qualified teachers, and less challenging curricula. While there is a clear understanding that black and Latino students are not the only minority groups affected by racist schooling, they are the primary groups discussed in respect to the achievement gap prevalent throughout the U.S. public school system.

Where Are the Solutions?

The sole remedy that the NCLBA presents for dealing with the problem of pervasive and deep-seated racism (which manifests itself in the form of inequitable rates of per-pupil expenditure and widespread neglect of urban schools amongst other such forms) is to increase accountability through mandatory testing (Paul, in press). Without a doubt, the challenges most public school districts face are numerous and vast. Relatively few people would quarrel with the premise that the U.S. public education system, especially in its service to poor children and students of color, is in need of an overhaul. Issues of poverty and race are often inextricably linked, and child poverty for blacks and Latinos remains at approximately 30% and 28%, respectively. The public should challenge, however, whether the NCLBA is the solution.

When one ponders the plausibility of any real reform occurring in the near future, the outlook is concomitantly bleak and debatable. Funding for the NCLBA simply doesn't exist; the costs of military defense and wars on terrorism leave very little currency for domestic priorities.

> The relationship between militarism and education is evident. The current Department of Education budget proposal for 2003 [was] $56.5 billion. The recently-approved Department of Defense budget is $396 billion, nearly seven times what is allocated for education, and more than three times the combined military budgets of Russia, China, Iraq, Iran, North Korea, Libya, Cuba, Sudan and Syria. (Wells, 2003, p. 2)

Within the context of this article, I examine the ways in which the NCLBA, generally, and Reading First, in particular, can be considered socially and morally unjust. The focus on increased accountability through testing and the stronger emphasis on reading in grades K–3 pose the greatest threats and place black and Latino students in imminent educational danger. In many ways, this legislation has the potential to maintain a system in which the majority of blacks and Latinos never achieve full economic or sociopolitical parity. Throughout, I discuss the ways in which the NCLBA has offered false hope to poor parents through school vouchers and bolstered the numbers of black and Latino youngsters referred to and placed in special education. Finally, I discuss the lifelong consequences of the NCLBA on black and Latino literacy learners as they apply to the workforce, the prison industrial complex, and higher education.

In this article, I use the terms *black* and *white* rather than *African American* and *Euro-American* as racial descriptors. My desire is to be inclusive and acknowledge the deep connection among all of the African diaspora. Globally, white skin still bestows privilege. The term *Latino* is used purposefully to convey "the deep connections among all of us in the Americas who are descendants of native inhabitants, Spanish and other European colonizers, and enslaved Africans or any combination of these groups" (Nieto, 1992, p. 177).

The Illusion of School Vouchers

When the press first caught hold of the No Child Left Behind Act, the hot topic was school vouchers. These vouchers were to be used to subsidize the costs of moving a child from a failing public school to a parochial or private school. This facet of the NCLBA garnered the most media attention. It was also the most controversial and gave critics the ammunition needed to effectively argue that the principal education goal of the U.S. federal government under the current administration of President George W. Bush was to decimate the public school system.

In its present form, the NCLBA allows parents or caregivers to remove their children from low-performing public schools (after those schools have received sufficient time to improve) and place them in better *public* schools. Funds can also be used to provide children with supplementary education that includes tutoring, after-school services, and summer school programs offered by private schools and faith-based contractors.

When I first learned of the NCLBA, my thoughts were with the many parents and caregivers of color (especially the poor and those residing in urban centers) who would be duped into believing that the NCLBA could improve the quality of education for their children. My thoughts gravitated to this group for many reasons. Before becoming a teacher educator, I spent six years in an intermediate school classroom and a year as a communication arts teacher trainer. All of my public school teaching experience occurred in the South Bronx, New York, and much of it took place in the community where I grew up. I felt and continue to feel a tremendous sense of connection to the black and Latino children I taught, as well as to their respective families and that community.

I initially considered the most pernicious aspects of the NCLBA to be those that centered on the use of Title I funds to subsidize private schools. I was beguiled by press events where the media trotted out parents of color who passionately expressed their support for school vouchers. The media claimed that these vouchers would either put public education out of its misery or give it a much needed reality check. What I found most striking about these media spectacles in which such claims were made was the apparent desperation and lack of confidence (in the public schools) that led to the acceptance of this modern-day snake oil.

The parents and caregivers of color who rallied behind school vouchers failed to understand that private schools are frequently more successful in their efforts to educate because they have the ability to select in and select out. They do not admit "problem" students (however they might be defined) or keep them, once discovered. Many private schools also require parental involvement in the forms of financial commitment and support of school activities. Public schools have no such mandates. They cannot deny certain children access to schooling or coerce parents to support their children's education (in a legally protected manner, at least). For those reasons and others, public schools in the most poverty-stricken areas of the United States continue to poorly educate their students. In some instances, where school funds have been cut as a consequence of poor standardized test scores, such students have been denied the resources that might have helped them to improve.

But, in the midst of all this talk about vouchers, many of us missed the features of the NCLBA that would do the most damage to public education, especially as they pertain to educating black and Latino youngsters.

Harmful Consequences

The following are cornerstones of the No Child Left Behind Act:

- increased accountability for states, school districts, and schools;
- greater choice for parents and students, particularly those attending low-performing schools;
- more flexibility for states and local educational agencies in the use of federal education dollars; and

- a stronger emphasis on reading, especially for the country's youngest children (U.S. Department of Education, 2002a).

A number of the NCLBA's components are based upon a formula used "successfully" by President Bush and his Secretary of Education Rod Paige during Bush's tenure as governor of Texas and Paige's stint as Houston's superintendent of schools. Unfortunately, the good results yielded in Houston have been exaggerated. For example, while the number of Houston students who passed statewide achievement tests went from 44% to 64%, the gains were boosted by an "abysmal dropout rate" (Winters, 2001). Low-performing students, under constant pressure, simply surrendered and left school prematurely. A report published in 2001 by Johns Hopkins University in Baltimore, Maryland, ranked Houston 28th in school completion out of the 35 largest U.S. school districts. Almost half of the ninth graders in most of Houston's school systems failed to reach graduation (Winters, 2001).

Another compelling point to explore in regard to the "successes" of which Houston boasted is that *academic success* is defined quite narrowly as one's ability to score well on standardized tests. Yet much of the research literature indicates that a student's ability to perform well on standardized tests is most closely correlated with parental income, the level of maternal education, and the quality of the classroom teacher. The degree to which each of these factors influences performance is arguable. For example, some researchers focus on the role of the classroom teacher, characterizing the quality of the teacher as the single most important factor for achieving excellence in education (Michelli, 2001). Others emphasize family literacy and providing parents or caregivers with opportunities to develop children's personal and community literacies in the hope of boosting their school literacies, which include testing and evaluation (Gallego & Hollingsworth, 2000; Taylor & Dorsey-Gaines, 1998).

The NCLBA is deceptive with its stress on accountability through testing in other ways as well. It fails to acknowledge that most U.S. schoolchildren are tested each year anyway, especially those children attending schools in poor communities. According to Allington (2002a), "the children most likely to be tested frequently are poor children, who attend schools that are eligible for that smorgasbord of federal education program dollars" (p. 236). The NCLBA merely "expands the testing requirement to the few schools that didn't already test for federal programs compliance, primarily schools serving an almost exclusively middle class population of students" (p. 236).

This testing requirement also enhances the possibility that black and Latino children will be further disenfranchised through special education. In

2000, although African American children represented only 15% of the U.S. school population (ages 6–21), they represented

20 percent of students referred into special education and over 26 percent of youth identified by schools as emotionally and behaviorally disturbed. Nationally, black students are identified as emotionally disturbed at over one and one-half times the rate of white students. (Osher, Woodruff, & Sims, 2002, p. 93)

Black youngsters are overrepresented in each category of special education services and in every U.S. state. "States with a history of racial apartheid under de jure segregation...account for five of the seven states with the highest overrepresentation of African Americans labeled mentally retarded—Mississippi, South Carolina, North Carolina, Florida, and Alabama" (Losen & Orfield, 2002, p. xxiii). Furthermore, it has become increasingly difficult for black students to extricate themselves from special education placements (which are supposedly temporary).

Latino children, on the other hand, are overidentified in some states and underidentified in others (Parrish, 2002). Yet, the ways in which these identifications are affected by second-language acquisition factors should be explored and further studied. The designation of "being learning disabled" is difficult to determine for students who are native speakers of a language; but that difficulty is compounded for students who are learners of English as a second language (Gunderson & Siegel, 2001). In many instances, learning disability is determined by assessing the difference between the student's performance on IQ tests and achievement tests. A significant discrepancy is characterized as indicative of a learning disability. Yet one must possess English-language facility with both the IQ test and the achievement tests. So how does the evaluator truly distinguish between the lack of English facility and a difficulty in learning if such a distinction is made at all?

Difficulties in the referral process, assessment bias, and a lack of cultural synchronization all contribute to the rise in special education placements among black children and youth. People of color compose approximately 13% of the extant teaching corps and an even smaller percentage of school psychologists and administrators (National Center for Education Statistics, 1993). Conversely, "Blacks and Hispanics are the two largest minority groups in the United States, together accounting for 32 percent of the 1998 U.S. student population" (Fierros & Conroy, 2002, p. 47). My own educated conjecture would be that the majority of such placements are based upon observations and evaluations made by white teachers, school psychologists, and other school professionals who may be culturally out of synch with black student cultures and needs.

Cultural synchronization is a harmony established between the cultural systems of schools, diverse groups of learners, and the communities from which those learners come (Gay, 1993; Irvine, 1991). School professionals who

> are often cultural outsiders in the communities where they work may misunderstand or misinterpret the cultural nuances present.... [T]his lack of cultural continuity can result in cultural misunderstanding, student resistance, low expectation for student success, and self-fulfilling prophecies of student failure. (Paul, 2000, p. 247)

"The biases of school personnel...come from many sources and go in many directions, and within-group bias is as likely to exist as intergroup bias" (Harry, Klingner, Sturges, & Moore, 2002, p. 75).

One also needs to consider hypotheses regarding the adverse links between poverty, cognitive development, and "soft" disorders. Children of color (who are disproportionately represented with respect to poverty) could also be at greater risk for exposure to factors that have a negative effect on cognitive development and processing ability—like lack of prenatal care, low birth weight, exposure to lead, and so forth (Books, 2000). Yet poverty alone stands as an insufficient explanation.

> Comparisons of identification levels have shown that the degree of racial disparity in rates of identification of black children with "hard" disabilities that are easy to diagnose medically, such as visual and hearing impairment, is significantly smaller than the degree of racial disparity in rates of identification for the soft, subjective categories. (Parrish, 2002, p. 16)

The potential for an increase in referrals to special education for black and Latino children and youth becomes even greater when the following consideration is taken into account. An inverse correlation has been established between decreased federal funding for remedial reading programs and concomitant increases in funding for special education programs (Allington, 2002). Thus, students who may not be eligible for assistance through Title I reading programs do become eligible once they are diagnosed as learning disabled—a distinction for which there is no standard or universally accepted definition (Allington, 2002).

The Effect on Older Literacy Learners

According to the Reading First Guidance Draft, "by effectively teaching children to read well by the end of the third grade, we ensure that all students advance later to grades well prepared to achieve their full academic potential"

(U.S. Department of Education, 2002b, p. 1). I have no doubt that the presage of this focal point was the National Research Council's *Preventing Reading Difficulties in Young Children* (Snow, Burns, & Griffin, 1998), in which the various authors emphasized the importance of early intervention. Whereas a number of research studies suggest that early intervention correlates with positive reading achievement, the availability of such programs proves problematic (especially for the most disadvantaged students).

The point I want to make here is that an "inoculation approach" (McPartland, as citied in McCabe, 2003, p. 227) to reading difficulties does not do much to ameliorate the present problem. Further, the NCLBA seems to focus on a single aspect of a complex dilemma when there are more practical responses to a call for early intervention. Although there is wholehearted support (amongst many literacy professionals) regarding the importance of building an early foundation of literacy,

> it often comes at the price of a lack of resources and attention to the needs of adolescent literacy learners. An early literacy emphasis assumes that once children learn to read and write, they will be able to use reading and writing to learn for the rest of their lives. From a developmental perspective, such an assumption is tenuous at best. (Vacca, 2002, p. 9)

Too many adolescents and adults who are literate choose not to read. "Unfortunately, as students move into the middle grades and high school, they often receive little or no instruction in how to use reading and writing strategies to learn with texts" (Vacca, 2002). Furthermore, they do not possess the kinds of higher-order literacy skills needed to attain gainful employment in a sagging U.S. economy.

"Current difficulties in reading largely originate from rising demands for literacy, not from declining absolute levels of literacy" (Snow, Burns, & Griffin, 1998, p. 1). The information age

> places higher order literacy demands on all of us.... These demands include synthesizing and evaluating information from multiple sources. These multiple sources have fewer editorial controls and fewer filters through which the information is sifted for accuracy, reliability, and civility. (Allington, 1998, p. 7)

If students continue on a path of disengagement from texts, they will not achieve true sociopolitical empowerment that can enhance the quality of their lives. In National Adult Literacy Survey (NALS) data collected in 1992 by the National Center for Education Statistics (Reder, 2003), it was reported that 75–80% of black adults in the United States were functioning at the two lowest proficiency levels, in contrast with 38–43% of whites. The NALS assessment consisted of simulated functional or authentic tasks such as form completion, use of graphic organizers, and newspaper reading.

What are the implications here for black and Latino adult populations with respect to quality of life and sociopolitical parity? They are vast and numerous, but let's start by examining some unemployment figures. The unemployment rate for blacks jumped from 9.8% in October to 11% in November of 2002. In January 2003, there was a slight decline in black unemployment to 10.3%. Latino unemployment rates remained steady at 7.8%, and unemployment among whites was maintained at 5.1%. It is far from incidental that black unemployment is double that of white and that Latino unemployment is not lagging far behind.

Another implication that needs discussion is the prison industrial complex. I use the term *prison industrial complex* with premeditation. The term was made popular because it questions the existence of a system in which the containment of black and brown bodies has become an industry—one that bolsters capitalism with its modern-day form of chattel slavery (Paul, 2000). With 14 million people entangled in the penal system, the rate of imprisonment in the United States is the highest on the planet, surpassing even that of Russia (Cose, 2000). As of June 30, 2002, there were 2,470 per 100,000 blacks and 895 per 100,000 Latinos incarcerated, in comparison with 353 per 100,000 whites (PrisonSucks.com, 2003). It is consequential to note that there has also been a 126% increase in the number of black women arrested. In 1991, the largest racial group of women in state prison was black (46%), and that group's number has increased significantly since then. Seven of 10 prisoners perform in the two lowest levels of literacy (Weiner, 2003).

It would be safe to say that a significant number of these prisoners have been adversely affected by poverty, unemployment, and a need for the highly sophisticated literacy skills required for successful competition in the current job market. Coupled with those factors are sentencing disparities, the inability of many defendants to secure competent counsel, a lack of comprehension of judicial processes, and a concomitant failure to understand systems employing a bureaucratic literacy that proves disempowering (Taylor, 1996).

Finally, the conjecture can be made that people who are chronically unemployed or incarcerated are not likely to be in a position to attend institutions of higher education. At present, high school dropout rates appear greatest for Latino males at around 50%, and a mere 25% of black males go to college (in contrast to 35% of black females). The high-stakes testing associated with the NCLBA can only exacerbate this situation as "it remains the case that far more states sanction individual students for poor test performance than impose sanctions on individual adults, be they teachers, administrators, school board members, legislators, parents, or taxpayers" (Heubert, 2002, pp. 138-139).

Casualties of the NCLBA

This article was originally cast as my personal response to the dissolution of a department I chaired, Literacy and Educational Media, situated within the College of Education and Human Services of a large university in the eastern United States. The department, traditionally small (up to 10 members), had contributed to the university community in two distinctive and important ways. One way was to serve as an essential component of the preservice and inservice teacher education programs. We had envisioned our raison d'être as preparing literacy educators and media specialists to meet highly sophisticated literacy and technological demands. The increasing need for public school students to demonstrate facility with print and nonprint texts has intensified the demand for skilled educators with sound knowledge of their respective content areas, as well as the dispositions necessary to facilitate the processes of learning and teaching.

The second way was that the department played a significant role in serving the campus's Basic Reading Skills population. Many of us were dissatisfied that students usually failed in the basic skills class and frequently demonstrated resistance to the content because they viewed it within the contexts of deficit and failure. Yet we were actively engaged in revising the program and had changed the name of the Reading Center to the Literacy Enrichment Center.

With the dissolution of the department, the remaining members, with one exception, were awkwardly integrated with the department of Early Childhood and Elementary Education. At times my heart and pride dictate that the department's dissolution was purely personal and malicious, but more reasoned justifications also present themselves when my calmer head prevails. For instance, I think about college administrators' desires to keep the institution solvent. One way to accomplish that task is to align the institutional goals with those of the federal government. The need to secure higher education funding may have significantly affected the decision to skew the departmental focus to early literacy.

While the dissolution was painful on professional and personal levels, I was most angered because the administrative decision seemed to uphold flawed educational policy (the NCLBA and Reading First) that proves morally and socially unjust. Prior to the dissolution, our department members (individually and collectively) were invited to meet more than once with college administrators, who emphasized the need for the department to focus more on "teaching children to read" (via phonemic awareness strategies and so forth) in addition to specifically addressing the core curriculum standards. Many of us already addressed these issues; yet we chose to have students problematize them, reflect on their practice, and make pedagogical decisions that centered on best practice and knowledge of individual students' needs first. For many of us, effective pedagogy should have driven the standards rather than the standards driving the pedagogy.

Furthermore, we were encouraged to familiarize ourselves with the Reading First guidelines, paying particular attention to the focus on primary grades, and to discuss these guidelines with our students. Many of us clung to the belief that, just because political policy mandated a back-to-basics approach to literacy development, it didn't mean that we should cave in to equivalently flawed science and unsound practice.

Yet, in my estimation, our department was a casualty of the NCLBA and Reading First. People who hear this story usually display various signs of bemusement and seem to have as much difficulty as I do in determining the logic in a decision to dissolve a department of literacy education during these troubled times for education. But the decision has forced me to focus on the values that I hold dear and come to the stark realization that many education decisions are more about money than about what is best for students. In the process, my resolve to resist unjust policy has grown even stronger, and some might say it has come at the cost of my future in college administration. Nevertheless, I am at peace with that outcome.

I believe teachers and teacher educators have a responsibility to resist socially unjust education policy like the NCLBA and to make the public aware of the threats it poses. I also believe society has a responsibility to do something about the students who have already fallen and to prevent future students from falling behind. Through this article, I hope to have made it clear that the creation of flawed education policy does not alleviate the academic distress experienced by far too many black and Latino students in U.S. public schools. Instead, a shared understanding about what is best for children and young people should direct our steps, our thoughts, and our hearts.

REFERENCES

Allington, R.L. (1998). *What really matters for struggling readers: Designing research-based programs.* New York: Longman.

Allington, R.L. (2002a). Accelerating in the wrong direction: Why thirty years of federal testing and accountability hasn't worked yet and what we might do instead. In R.L. Allington (Ed.), *Big brother and the national reading curriculum* (pp. 235-263). Portsmouth, NH: Heinemann.

Allington, R.L. (2002b). *Big brother and the national reading curriculum.* Portsmouth, NH: Heinemann.

Books, S. (2000). Poverty and environmentally induced damage to children. In V. Polakow (Ed.), *The public assault on America's children: Poverty, violence, and juvenile injustice* (pp. 188-210). New York: Teachers College Press.

Carruthers, J.H. (1994). Black intellectuals and the crisis in black education. In M.J. Shujaa (Ed.), *Too much schooling, too little education: A paradox of black life in white societies* (pp. 37-55). Trenton, NJ: Africa World Press.

Civil Rights Project. (2001). *Community and school predictors of over representation of minority children in special education.* Cambridge, MA: Harvard University Press.

Coles, G. (2002). *Great unmentionables: What national reading reports and reading legislation don't tell you.* Portsmouth, NH: Heinemann.

Cose, E. (2000, November 13). America's prison generation. *Newsweek*, 42-49.

Fierros, E.G., & Conroy, J.W. (2002). Double jeopardy: An exploration of restrictiveness and race in special education. In D.J. Losen & G. Orfield (Eds.), *Racial inequity in special education* (pp. 39-70). Cambridge, MA: Harvard Education Press.

Frankenburg, E., Lee, C., & Orfield, G. (2003). *A multiracial society with segregated schools: Are we losing the dream?* Retrieved January 2, 2004, from www.civilrightsproject.harvard.edu/research/reseg03/finalexec.pdf

Gallego, M.A., & Hollingsworth, S. (2000). Introduction: The idea of multiple literacies. In M.A. Gallego & S. Hollingsworth (Eds.), *What counts as literacy: Challenging the school standard* (pp. 1-23). New York: Teachers College Press.

Garan, E. (2002). *Resisting reading mandates: How to triumph with the truth.* Portsmouth, NH: Heinemann.

Gay, G. (1993). Building cultural bridges: A bold proposal for teacher education. In F. Schulz (Ed.), *Annual editions: Multicultural education 95/96* (pp. 34-40). Guilford, CT: Dushkin/Brown & Benchmark.

Gunderson, L., & Siegel, L.S. (2001). The evils of the use of IQ tests to define learning disabilities in first- and second-language learners. *The Reading Teacher, 55*, 48-55.

Harry, B., Klingner, J.K., Sturges, K.M., & Moore, R.F. (2002). Of rocks and soft places: Using qualitative methods to investigate disproportionality. In D.J. Losen & G. Orfield (Eds.), *Racial inequity in special education* (pp. 71-92). Cambridge, MA: Harvard Education Press.

Heubert, J. (2002). Disability, race, and high-stakes testing of students. In D.J. Losen & G. Orfield (Eds.), *Racial inequity in special education* (pp. 137-165). Cambridge, MA: Harvard Education Press.

Irvine, J.J. (1991). *Black students and school failure: Policies, practices, and prescriptions.* New York: Praeger.

Losen, D.J., & Orfield, G. (2002). Racial inequity in special education. In D.J. Losen & G. Orfield (Eds.), *Racial inequity in special education* (pp. xv-xxxvii). Cambridge, MA: Harvard Education Press.

McCabe, J. (2003). *The wasted years: American youth, race, and the literacy gap.* Lanham, MD: Scarecrow.

Michelli, N. (2001, January/February). Teacher education in the new millennium: The view from New York City. *The College Board Review*, No. 197.

National Center for Education Statistics. (1993). *America's teachers: Profile of a profession*. Washington, DC: U.S. Department of Education, Office of Educational Research and Improvement.

Nieto, S. (1992). We have stories to tell: A case study of Puerto Ricans in children's books. In V.J. Harris (Ed.), *Teaching multicultural literature in grades K–8* (pp. 171-201). Norwood, MA: Christopher-Gordon.

Osher, D., Woodruff, D., & Sims, A.E. (2002). Schools make a difference: The overrepresentation of African American youth in special education and the juvenile justice system. In D.J. Losen & G. Orfield (Eds.), *Racial inequity in special education* (pp. 93-116). Cambridge, MA: Harvard Education Press.

Parrish, T. (2002). Racial disparities in the identification, funding, and provision of special education. In D.J. Losen & G. Orfield (Eds.), *Racial inequity in special education* (pp. 15-37). Cambridge, MA: Harvard Education Press.

Paul, D.G. (2000). *Raising black children who love reading and writing: A guide from birth to grade six*. Westport, CT: Bergin & Garvey.

Paul, D.G. (in press). *Talkin' back: Raising and educating resilient black girls*. Westport, CT: Praeger.

PrisonSucks.com. (2003). *Research on the crime control industry*. Retrieved May 20, 2003, from www.prisonsucks.com

Reder, S. (2003). *NALS raises vital equity issues*. Retrieved May 20, 2003, from www.nald.ca/fulltext/report2/rep16-01.htm

Snow, C.E., Burns, M.S., & Griffin, P. (Eds.). (1998). *Preventing reading difficulties in young children*. Washington, DC: National Academy Press.

Taylor, D. (1996). *Toxic literacies: Exposing the injustices of bureaucratic texts*. Portsmouth, NH: Heinemann.

Taylor, D., & Dorsey-Gaines, C. (1988). *Growing up literate: Learning from inner-city families*. Portsmouth, NH: Heinemann.

U.S. Department of Education. (2002a). *No Child Left Behind Act of 2001: Executive summary*. Retrieved January 2, 2004, from www.ed.gov/nclb/overview/intro/exec-summ.html

U.S. Department of Education. (2002b). *Reading First guidance*. Washington, DC: U.S. Department of Education.

Vacca, R.T. (2002). From efficient decoders to strategic readers. *Educational Leadership*, *60*(3), 7-11.

Weiner, E.J. (2003). *Leaving adults behind: The conservative and neoliberal attack on adult learners*. Manuscript submitted for publication.

Wells, L.C. (2003). *No child left alone by military recruiters*. Retrieved April 3, 2003, from www.commondreams.org/views02/1206-08.htm

Winters, R. (2001). *Teacher in chief*. Retrieved February 7, 2003, from www.time.com/education/article/0,8599,98013,00.html

Beyond Remediation: Ideological Literacies of Learning in Developmental Classrooms

Eric J. Weiner

> [R]emedial education is one of the thorniest issues in higher education to-day. Many students sail through their K–12 education and arrive confidently on campus, only to find that they are academically unprepared. Universities provide costly assistance to these students, only to face internal and external pressure to tighten standards. And parents and community members everywhere are left bewildered: How could the public education system have shortchanged these students so completely in the past, and how can it fail them now? (Reed, 2001, p. B9)

> But, of course, we know perfectly well that people can know how to read, in the sense of decode and engage in word recognition, and even achieve basic comprehension, and still not know how to read to learn. (Gee, 1999, p. 342)

> The illiteracy to which we refer can only be addressed in the context of social movements that wish to make serious social changes. The other model of rapid learning for whole populations is the ideological model. In a country lacking the conditions for rapid economic growth or the motivating force to accept a highly militarized educational process as grounds for learning, the only alternative is to argue for literacy on radical foundations. (Aronowitz & Giroux, 1993, p. 62)

Remedial or developmental academic programs generally, and reading and literacy programs specifically, are in high demand in colleges and universities. However, they are threatened by a number of different social and political forces. From the call to privatize remedial services and bill high schools for the cost of remediation ("Remedial Ed," 2001), to passing the buck to community colleges and blaming teachers for their students' struggles, remedial education and those that it serves are under siege. Striving to survive in an academic climate dominated by a discourse of high-stakes testing, standardization, and "excellence," remedial programs have felt pressured to respond to these demands, regardless of whether it is in the best interest of the students, democracy, or transforming society's inequities. In New York City, "Mayor Rudolph Giuliani...threatened to withhold millions from the City University system unless steps were taken to privatize remedial education training for incoming students and to hire a pri-

Reprinted from *Journal of Adolescent & Adult Literacy, 46*, 150–168, October 2002.

vate company to review testing standards" (Taylor, 2001, p. A06). Charles B. Reed, chancellor of the California State University system, argued that "eliminating the need for remedial education begins not in high school or elementary school, but with the preparation of high-quality classroom teachers. Understanding that the quality of students we receive depends on the quality of teachers we prepare" (2001, p. B9).

The problem with Reed's approach is that it embraces a debilitating contradiction; that is, while he claimed to want to better prepare teachers to teach, he simultaneously embraced the logic of standards and testing, two of the major conditions that prevent teachers from teaching and students from learning. To teach is more than managing a packaged curriculum, overseeing practice tests, and drilling students on material that might not have any meaning to them. Likewise, to learn is more than rote memorization and the regurgitation of information. Stating the devastating effects of standardized testing, Miner (2000) wrote, "It leads to a dumbed-down curriculum that values rote memorization over in-depth thinking, exacerbates inequities for low-income students and students of color, and undermines true accountability among schools, parents, and community" (p. 40). In the face of Miner's research, to subject remedial studies to the logic of standardization and testing is to doubly bind the teaching and learning process. Because many of the students who need or are placed in remedial classes have low incomes and are from cultural and linguistic minority groups, the ability of remediation to address academic inequities is seriously compromised by the exacerbating effects that standards and testing have on socioeconomic and cultural power inequities.

In this context, the discourse of "accountability" so prevalent in the conservative view of schooling—evident in Giuliani's and Reed's approaches to remedial education—and how strategies of remediation are deployed obscures the social, cultural, and economic conditions that have at least as much to do with failing schools and academically struggling students as any other variable (see Aronowitz & Giroux, 1993; Gee, 1999; Kozol, 1991; Paul, 2000). Obviously, both Giuliani and Reed want to limit the need for remedial education. But without acknowledging and working on the vast inequalities that plague our cities and schools, we will fail to alleviate the need for remediation. The most vulnerable in our society, as well as the most victimized, are made, on some level, responsible for their own "substandard" conditions. Thus, the need for remediation (and the monies that it necessitates) is seen as an effect of a personal or cultural failure as opposed to (from one perspective) a systemic failure or (from another) a natural outcome of an educational system that is racist, sexist, and class biased (see Marable, 1996;

Willis, 1977). Ignoring, as Kohn (2000) pointed out, "the very real obstacles [that limit learning and teaching opportunities in schools] such as racism, poverty, fear of crime, low teacher salaries, inadequate facilities, and language barriers" (p. 60) increases the likelihood that those suffering are blamed for their own predicaments. From this perspective, "standards of outcome rather than standards of opportunity" (Kohn, 2000, p. 60) become the register of accountability. In the context of remedial literacy education, this is especially true (Daniels, Zemelman, & Bizar, 1999; Edmondson & Shannon, 1998; Gee, 1999).

Unfortunately, as more high school students enter college ill-prepared to tackle the kind of literacies that will be asked of them, more universities and colleges have offered remedial or developmental reading and writing classes guided by the assumption that literacy can be mastered through methodological proscriptions and high-stakes testing on decontextualized generic texts. This is a mistake. On the contrary, *literacy* is a term that signifies an investment in a complex matrix of language, learning, culture, identity, knowledge/power, and political ideology. At the minimum, to be literate means, in Gee's (1992) terms, to develop "control over secondary uses of language" (p. 25). Thus, to become literate in the multiple discourses of the academy, students must be introduced to an array of texts and the politics that inform them, while being exposed to the theoretical tools that can help them link these discourses to larger formations of power. Literacy, in this context, must be linked to social engagement. For example, the "savage inequalities" that Kozol (1991) spoke of could become both a text and context to read, engage, and transform. In other words, the conditions that exacerbate schooling that Kohn mentioned would be taken up as texts to be read, with the understanding that to be literate—going beyond Gee's definition—is to be able to learn about, engage, and transform the oppressive social, economic, and cultural conditions that have exacerbated inequities and sanctioned ideological illiteracy.

Although advocates of traditional remediation would most likely balk at this approach to literacy, believing that it is either too rigorous or that it is outside what it means to teach people to read, in what follows I will argue, through an interpretation and discursive analysis of my experiences teaching developmental reading, that this kind of literacy project not only teaches students multiple literacies, but also radically intervenes with the debilitating effects that the standardization and testing movements continue to have on economically, culturally, and linguistically marginalized populations. I will discuss how remediation can be more—must be more—than phonetic decoding, literal comprehension, and a generic engagement with language and written texts. I will also discuss how strategies of critical pedagogy can help break down the boundaries of traditional remediation and the methodologies that support it. Neither a method nor a technique, critical pedagogy provides a theoretical map of power relationships, curriculum, and ideology in which to develop culturally and politically responsive practices that encourage ideological literacies of learning and social engagement.

Implicit in this approach to literacy is the notion that teachers should always begin with the understanding that students who need remediation are not stupid and have an array of literacies to draw upon that can help them interrogate, interpret, and revise dominating discourses—those same discourses that have often been at the heart of exacerbating retrograde social and economic policies. In my work with developmental readers, I tried to learn what these literacies were and how to use them in the service of a project of possibility (see Simon, 1992). I created remedial projects that taught ideological literacies of learning. These are literacies that not only prepare students to read the word and the world, but also give them the tools "to read to learn" (Gee, 1999, p. 342), and transform the world. Those who read to learn in order to transform are social agents—students and citizens of the word and the world—teaching as they learn and learning as they teach (Freire, 1998). As such, they act upon the world, transforming it, just as they are transformed themselves.

Developmental Reading and the Politics of Literacy: Moving Beyond Basic Skills

The College Assistance Migrant Program (CAMP)—a federally funded educational initiative—originated at Pennsylvania State University's main campus in State College, Pennsylvania, to provide students of migrant and seasonal farm workers with access to postsecondary education. CAMP offers its students academic, personal, and financial support. A large part of the academic support comes in the form of two "developmental" reading classes: LLED 05 and LLED 297A. Before I became involved in the CAMP program, these classes were undergirded by an investment in generic language learning, a back-to-basics program that resulted in the students scoring worse on reading tests than before they took the classes. In this context, I was asked to develop a literacy project that respected the students, taught them how to read, and prepared them for a successful university career.

It should be noted at the outset that, according to my personal conversations with many CAMP students, the acronym CAMP has some unfortunate effects on their sense of themselves as university students. Students who are accepted into CAMP sometimes feel that they are not part of a vibrant intellectual experience, but are rather going to camp. The association can be demeaning simply because of its name. Moreover, as Macedo has pointed out on numerous occasions, the tag *migrant* connotes negative images and is an ideologically loaded word. As an example, he correctly points out that European immigrants are never referred to as migrants, but are called settlers (see Macedo, 1994).

CAMP students must take LLED 05 in their first semester and LLED 297A in their second semester. Together, I wanted these two courses to offer students the opportunity to read more effectively across the many different academic disciplines that they would encounter at Penn State. From comprehension and critique to interpretation and interrogation, these two courses were designed to prepare students for the rigorous reading and research schedule that they could expect from a research-oriented university.

At Montclair State University in New Jersey where I currently teach, students are tested before entering the university. Those who don't fare well on the test are required to take READ-053, a course that has traditionally been taught by adjuncts and non-Ph.D. faculty members. Both whole language and phonetic practices have been used, as is the Nelson-Denny Test as a measure of students' reading ability. My students are African American, white, Latino/Latina, Asian, and Arab. All are from working class or poor neighborhoods, and the majority are women, facts that trouble the widely held belief that schools are providing equal opportunity and access for all students.

My approach to these classes diverges considerably from the norm, rooted in the belief that, "We must first read the world—the cultural, social, and political practices that constitute it—before we can make sense of the word-level description of reality" (Macedo, 2000, p. 11). But as Chomsky (1999) documented, an established antidemocratic ideological system of indoctrination has been "teaching" our students in a way that consistently privileges and reinforces dominant power:

> Because they don't teach the truth about the world, schools have to rely on beating students over the head with propaganda about democracy.... This is well known by those who make policy, and sometimes they don't even try to hide it. The Trilateral Commission referred to schools as "institutions" responsible for the indoctrination of the young. The indoctrination is necessary because schools are, by and large, designed to support the interests of the dominant segment of society, those people who have wealth and power.... And schools succeed by operating within a propaganda framework that has the effect of distorting or suppressing unwanted ideas and information. (p. 17)

In order for students to break out of this debilitating system of schooling, I introduce them to different academic and social texts, offering strategies of ideological comprehension and interpretation. This is quite different, and more difficult, than reading to memorize or to pass a test. It suggests that there is a relationship not only between the world and the words that help construct our understanding of it, but also between language—written, oral, visual, and technological—and the ideological systems that, in part, structure our ability to participate in a democracy. Students are challenged to engage academic and social texts critically, which means that they learn to situate texts ideologically and in terms of race, class, and gender. At the same time, they are introduced to a number of different theoretical tools that encourage questioning how these texts fit within the political assumptions of larger social and cultural institutions, such as schools, the workplace, home, and media. Reading critically also means being able to discern what these texts teach us about ourselves and the world in which we live, while being able to register the implications—social, cultural, political—of their pedagogical lessons. Last, students are asked to produce new knowledge in light of the various literacies that they learned to exercise throughout the year.

Framing both of these programs is a concern with critical inquiry and the responsibilities of citizenship in a public democracy. Critical inquiry is the ability to mediate, interrogate, interpret, intervene, and revise multiple texts. Students educated in the art of critical inquiry are less likely to be victimized by exclusionary practices and more likely to be the authors of their own experiences, histories, and ideas. Having critical inquiry skills will help prepare students to govern thoughtfully and effectively in a multicultural world and to respond to a rapidly evolving economic environment. Critical inquiry will assist students in negotiating the challenges of a rigorous academic schedule, while remaining cognizant of the extracurricular messages embedded within the social, written, and oral texts that they will be asked to read and learn. Because developmental readers often come from communities that have struggled to be heard in political and academic life, they will sometimes find that the texts that they are assigned in their classes do not represent their experiences, memories, or social realities. Critical inquiry affords them the opportunity not only to acknowledge what is in the texts, but also to be aware of what is absent. Reading the absences—historical, cultural, and economic—offers developmental readers the opportunity to interpret and "revise" these texts so that their invalidating absences become potent presences. Through critical thinking, reading, and writing, they can begin to use "interpretation as intervention, as interrogation, as relocation, and revision" (Homi Bhabha, quoted in Worsham & Olson, 1998,

p. 11). In these terms, critical inquiry is a key principle in the development of democratic citizens prepared to govern.

My approach to ideological literacies of learning is rooted and informed by a central premise (and promise) of a social or public democracy, which states that each citizen must not only be governable but, more important, be prepared to govern. A government by and for the people demands a "people" competent in certain skills and abilities, possessing certain attributes and capacities, and committed to a value system undergirded by a commitment to equity, political struggle, human rights, and social justice. Building upon the work of Jefferson, Dewey, and Rousseau, David Sehr, an English teacher to new immigrants and former Director for Educational Change at Brooklyn College in New York, mapped out five major elements of a public democracy that inform this literacy project.

A public democracy

> sees people's participation in public life as the essential ingredient in democratic government. Public participation arises out of an ethic of care and responsibility, not only for one's self as an isolated individual, but for one's fellow citizens as co-builders and co-beneficiaries of the public good. (Sehr, 1997, p. 5)

In the context of a literacy project, we might also add as "coauthors" as well as "cointerpreters" of public texts.

Beginning with "an ethic of care and responsibility," Sehr suggested that social citizens must value and accept the view that we are "individuals-in-relation." As such, we neither give up our individuality nor deny our social responsibilities. In this formulation, it is quite possible to see how our sense of ourselves as individuals rests, in part, on how we see and treat others. Second, a public democracy demands "respect for the equal right of everyone to the conditions necessary for their self-development" (p. 79). In this context, a notion of difference is not linked simply to a notion of democratic tolerance, but rather articulates with the "fundamental equality of all social groups" (p. 79), not including those that threaten the rights of others. Third, Sehr argued for the "appreciation of the importance of the public" (p. 79). Given the recent tendency to privilege the forces of privatization over the public trust, his call for a renewed sense of the public is not only timely, it is imperative. The creation of public spheres where citizens can go to debate and discuss the most pressing social issues of our times must be developed with as much abandon, if not more, as the proliferation of strip malls and designer coffee chains. In these public spheres, the public nature of certain private troubles can become manifest, illustrating what it means to be individuals-in-relation, conscious of our responsibilities as social citizens. Fourth, a public democracy demands a citizenry capable of "examining underlying relations of power in any given social situation" (p. 79). The connection between literacy/language and power is profound, undergirding these literacy projects while, at the same time, providing trajectories of inquiry for both the students and teacher to explore. Last, citizens should be able to "learn more about any issue that arises," through either public disclosure or self-guided research (Sehr, 1997, p. 5). These points provide markers, not so much dictating curricular decisions as influencing my pedagogy as I construct a classroom environment that encourages a range of literacies in the service of bringing into being democratic institutions and a sense of social responsibility.

Critical Strategies and Generative Themes

Two important curricular features are part of these literacy projects. First, I introduce my students to the approach to reading and language just discussed, through what I hope is a provocative description of literacy as a process—cultural, ideological, political, and pedagogical:

> This is a course designed to help improve your reading. But unlike many other literacy courses, we are going to learn about reading in many different ways: We will talk about reading in relation to books, magazines, newspapers, and scholarly articles; we will learn what it means to "read" films, television, advertisements, murals, art, and music videos; we will learn what it means to "read" the culture of this university, U.S. culture, and the culture of academia; we will learn what it means to "read" political events, such as the presidential election and political commercials; we will learn what it means to "read" and do research on the Internet. In short, we will discuss and learn what it means to be literate in the 21st century.
>
> This approach to literacy will help you develop cross-disciplinary reading skills that are invaluable in college. From literature and philosophy to biology and physics, this literacy strategy will help prepare you for a successful college career.
>
> In addition to reading these "texts," we will be writing about them also. We will write "essays," "compare/contrast" papers, "critiques," "summaries," and "discussion" papers. We will be writing about these texts in a way that asks them questions and responds to their messages.
>
> How do their messages relate to our personal experiences? What do their messages say about the role of schools? What do they teach us about the world that we live in? How do they influence us to think in particular ways about each other? How are women portrayed differently than men in music videos? Should we care? How are nonnative speakers of English represented in movies, television, and news reports?

All of these different "texts" provide us as a class and individually with challenging and timely material. We will find, I think, that we might "read" the same text differently. Because of our different experiences, we often have a different understanding of the same text.

Second, I include a somewhat lengthy "letter" to my students, which I read aloud. Although I do not have the space to include the letter here, in summary it talks to them as intellectuals and future leaders. I speak with them about the importance of their experiences and interests in the development of the course. I speak with them about their limitless capabilities. I speak with them about how they deserve to be at Penn State or Montclair State University and how reading ability has nothing to do with intelligence. Finally, I speak with them about their own personal and community literacies and the significance of those literacies within an academic context. It is of utmost importance that these students understand that their experiences and their reading of those experiences matter.

Following this introduction, my syllabus is designed to be open enough to be responsive to my students' needs and experiences, while at the same time it shapes the direction of our literacy project. For example, every two weeks we would read a different text. In the CAMP program, the first two weeks focused on Penn State. Beginning in the library, the students were introduced to the "official" culture of Penn State via an overview of the collections, databases, scholarly journals, and so on. Quite unexpectedly, they were also introduced to the "unofficial" culture of Penn State via racist attitudes expressed "innocently" by the white woman who was conducting the workshops. Two examples will suffice. As my students made their way into the library—with baggy jeans, bandannas, and a determined swagger—this woman said cheerfully, "Wow, ya'll look like you're in a gang." My students just looked at her, aware of the comment but unsure what to do in the face of it. The second incident occurred moments later while we were in the computer lab. "Ya'll have such difficult names to pronounce," she said, proceeding to mispronounce names, as though it was my students' fault that she must now contend with names other than Michael, Robert, and Jennifer.

Back in the classroom, I simply asked my students whether they thought the woman's attitudes were problematic. They didn't hesitate to speak of her attitude as "racial," demeaning, and hurtful. I tried to move this "reading" of her attitude into a discussion about racism. Moving the conversation from the personal to the public, means, in part, drawing connections between larger formations of power and privilege and the attitudes and ideas that they reward and legitimize. In other words, it is often the unofficial discourse that gives us insight on the underlying logic and ideology of the official discourse. If the responsibility for the dissemination of the official discourse is conveyed by people who embody a discursive position that, for example, is racist, then we must be diligent in our interrogation of the *relationship* between the two. Complicating matters, of course, is that my students must feel comfortable not only going to the library, but also asking for help when they need it. In the face of this experience, it was a real challenge to get my students back into the library, even though they had engaged in a complex and critical reading of the culture of Penn State along racial lines.

But it would be false to suggest that all my students came to the same conclusions about the racist discourse that they had experienced at Penn State. They all "read" the situation as racial, but their feelings about the implications of that discourse varied. For example, one student said he understood that the woman was prejudiced, but he didn't believe that her bigotry was articulated institutionally. Another student was concerned that by naming racism as a hindrance to opportunity, he was making excuses for himself. Rather than suggesting racism as a reason for the difficulty many students of color have in places like Penn State, he was thinking of it as an excuse. Both of these comments provoked a conversation in which I wanted my students to make a distinction on one hand between opportunity and capability, and on the other between cause and effect. In the context of a dialogical pedagogy, it is less important that students are convinced or persuaded by my arguments (and vice versa), and more important that they are provoked to interrogate ideas, attitudes, and institutions that have become the norm under the influence of established power. In the end, the strength of this practice is not in its immediacy, but in its relevancy; that is, it provides an environment for students to develop more complex understandings of the world and the word, while also honing their ability to defend their ideas in a public forum.

Another two-week section was entitled "News and Perspective: Reading Between the Lines." I picked *The New York Times* as the primary text for three reasons. First, the students receive it for free. Second, I felt it offered a more advanced reading level for my students, and third, it dealt with international and national issues in a way that is authoritative and seemingly objective. The combination offered a pedagogical opportunity to, as I wrote in my syllabus, "discuss layout, photography, design, advertising, content, context, perspective, and tone."

Many of my students had never read a newspaper and brought to the class the dominant assumptions that "news" meant unbiased reporting of an event. As we began to discuss the paper, I depended heavily on Gee's (1992) notion of discourse to begin to interrogate what the newspaper represented.

He wrote, "By a 'discourse' I...mean a socially accepted association among ways of using language, of thinking, and of acting that can be used to identify oneself as a member of a socially meaningful group or 'social network'" (p. 21). Some of the questions I asked my students to consider regarding the newspaper articles that we read were these: What group did the newspaper represent? What ways of thinking and acting did the newspaper's messages articulate? What future does the newspaper's discourse imply, and how can we begin to break into the dominant meanings that the "text" connotes? What relations of power are legitimated in the texts? These questions were difficult for my students to understand at first. It is not that they failed to get the "right" answer (as I will discuss later in the article), but rather that the very politics that drive these types of questions were, for the most part, foreign to my students, which made them difficult to grasp. By beginning with my students' experiences, we slowly began to make some headway into considering the implications of these questions for making meaning, producing knowledge, and disrupting the consensus of commonsense that news often manufactures and legitimates.

In more strategic terms, when we had a text that we were struggling to read and understand, I would not begin with the text. Rather, I would begin with my students' experiences and then pull them, and be pulled by them, through the text. In this way, we can begin to see how reading is a political process of translation, explication, interpretation, and construction. We can then begin to link the products of these processes to larger social formations, revealing the intertextual nature of reading, and on a much larger scale, life itself. On the other hand, if I was to begin with the text as an isolated moment, as a product to be reified, as an objectified fact, I not only would be privileging text over context, but also reinforcing the validity of dominant social structures that teach us to believe that language is nonideological, history is singular, and facts are meaningful outside of our interpretation of them. Even if I was sensitive to my students' experiences and at some point wanted to address them in relation to the text, if I didn't begin by understanding the text as meaningless outside of a particular social and political discourse then I simply reproduced the dominant traditions of those who privilege the importance of the text over the context that gives it meaning in the first place.

A couple of examples will make these ideas more concrete. Because African Americans and Hispanics are often portrayed in the news as criminals, the commonsense assumption is that most African Americans and Hispanics are criminals. In my CAMP class, a Hispanic male student argued that this portrayal was accurate; after all, he reasoned, if you rounded up the drug dealers he knew in New York City, they would be primarily black and Hispanic men. For him, the representations that he saw and read in the media were reflective and not constructive of a reality that he knew all too well. But more to the point, his critique failed to consider that the representations and their immediate source constituted a network of cultural practices that are "always linked together with specific social formations and have specific effects" (Gunster, 2000, pp. 245-246). As Boggs (2000) wrote,

> while blacks constitute only 13 percent of the total population and 13 percent of regular drug users, they account for 35 percent of those arrested for possession, 55 percent of those convicted, and 74 percent of those jailed.... As Diana Gordon argues, U.S. drug policy is at heart an attack on poor urban minorities. (pp. 55-56)

My response was that the student should measure the percentage of representations that he sees in the media of African Americans and Hispanics as criminals against those that are not portrayed as criminals, and the percentage of the African American and Hispanic population in New York City that are drug dealers against those that are not.

Pedagogically this intervention is meant to instigate a political economy of representations that focuses not just on what we see, but (maybe more important to the literacy project) on what we do not see, why we do not see, and the political, social, corporeal, and pedagogical implications of those absences. More to the point, it is vital that students begin to interrogate how representations help to exacerbate the "attack on poor urban minorities," exemplified by the recent exposure of the practice of racial profiling by a number of different law enforcement agencies. As Stuart Hall cogently remarked, "what is 'out there' is, in part, constituted by how it is represented" (quoted in Giroux, 1999, pp. 298-299).

At Montclair, a student discussed his experiences with racial profiling, and from there the class began to interrogate the recent profiling of Muslim people in the United States. Reading articles from different news sources, like *The New York Times* and *The Nation*, students were able to identify the different logics that informed the news articles that they read. Seeing his own experiences similarly articulated (read *validated*) in alternative news sources throws into relief not only the ideological perspective that informs such perspectives, but also presents the dominant discourse as ideological. No longer invisible behind the veil of truth and objectivity, dominant news is read as a cultural practice; that is, as an ideological activity that inscribes and legitimates specific relationships of power, cultural norms, and economic practices.

For the last example, at Montclair we read about the September 11, 2001, attacks on the World Trade Center. In an effort to provoke my students into thinking about the construction of meaning, even in relation to such a horrific event, I assigned them a writing and research project that asked them to find two news sources—mainstream and alternative—that discussed some aspect of the bombings. This was immediately a problem for my students because most didn't know what "alternative" news meant. How do you speak about ideology when one of its major principles is hegemony? Mainstream news I described as that to which we have easy access, such as *The New York Times*. I described alternative media as that which is not part of the popular media and often takes a very different view from the mainstream. Most students came back the next class and said they couldn't find any alternative news sources in the library. Part of this, of course, was the fact that they were not looking in the right places. But more significantly, it says something about the almost complete domination through saturation of dominant media. In response, I told them to find articles in *The Nation*, because it comes out every week and is also available online. As students compared the different reports of the same event, they began to get an idea of how meaning gets constructed through our interpretations of facts. Many students also found articles from other countries, some of which addressed questions that had not even been posed by the U.S. media at that point. Although we were not speaking about these differences as ideological per se, the students were being introduced to a major principle of ideological literacy; that is, they were being made aware of the power of language to construct reality. As I will discuss in a moment, we eventually took up issues of power, presenting a more complete picture of how these constructions become truths and commonsense, and hence, ideological.

Honesty, Respect, and Accountability: Three Principles of Pedagogical Engagement

I conduct my classes as seminars, dialogical as I mentioned, and therefore reading assignments are relatively short, although our discussions of the texts read are intense and rigorous. But for this process to be effective we needed to develop a sense of trust and respect. It is these issues of trust and respect that are often overlooked as major barriers to radical pedagogies. In my class, I found that a combination of blunt honesty, holding students accountable for what they say, and a process of questioning that stayed consistent to my project of expanding political agency through ideological literacies began to establish a modicum of trust and eventually a level of mutual respect. As Chomsky (2000) suggested, we must speak *with* our students, not *to* them.

A few examples will suffice in illustrating how this process developed. My "blunt honesty" was exemplified by both an intellectual and emotional commitment to take a position, however contestable and provisional, about something that I might have heard on the radio or seen on television. When a telephone strike had paralyzed many students' phone service at Penn State, I was not hesitant to voice my opinions about how the management of the company had presented the conflict as a "labor problem." I suggested to my students that I felt that with the overwhelming profits and mergers that big corporations were enjoying unmolested by antitrust laws, it was unfair that labor was being blamed for the problems. As Freire (1998) and other critical pedagogues have written, it is unethical for a teacher to try to hide her or his own perspective, just as it is unethical to deny others the right to reject it. Freire (1998) went on to say, "In the name of respect I should have toward my students, I do not see why I should omit or hide my political stance by proclaiming a neutral position that does not exist. On the contrary, my role as teacher is to assent to the student's right to compare, to choose, to rupture, to decide" (p. 68). Because this strike was being reported in *The New York Times*, we were able, as a class, to interrogate the written reports as a cultural practice. Of course, many of my students did blame the workers for their lack of phone service. Why wouldn't they? But as we read through the articles, and I filled in some of the epistemological gaps with relevant labor history—referencing Marx, whom many students had never heard of—the "discourse" of *The New York Times* began to come into relief. When students are offered even a small bit of a secondary discourse, like labor history, the dominant discourse looks a little different than it did before; it makes the invisible visible, "desublimating" a discourse, ostensibly revealing it as a discourse.

But what is the role of the teacher in this kind of literacy project? It should be to lead the class through the articulatory relationships of these discourses in an effort to reveal their associations and disassociations to larger social formations. Discourses need to be rubbed up against each other in an effort to reveal what they teach, the history that they imply, and the future that they suggest. In this way, students begin to get a sense of how discourses create subject positions for them to inhabit that are part of a social network. It is less important that students agree with my beliefs than that they have the discourses and the power to disagree.

Whether they agree or not, I find that holding them accountable for what they say establishes a certain amount of respect by showing them, on one hand, that what they think matters and, on the other, that what they think is always already caught in the web of social and political relations. Too often I hear of teachers who agree with everything their students say, simply because they want to validate their experiences, avoid confrontation, and refrain from decision making. This makes no sense to me. How does offering students facile validation for the thoughts they have, and the experiences they draw upon, do anything more than create docility and apathy? If it is all just about having an opinion, then what is the point of teaching? This is not to say that as critical teachers we should deny the validity of students' experiences; it simply means that we complicate them, move them out of the domain of the private, personal, and psychological and into the arena of the systemic, political, and sociological. By validating experiences without linking those experiences to larger social formations, we do a great disservice to students. By failing to show how experience is inevitably caught up in a web of power relationships, we help perpetuate a discourse of individualism and self-blame. It is incorrect to assume that students won't make the connection between what it means to be validated individually as well as blamed individually. In other words, if students' experiences are not seen as part of a larger network of beliefs, attitudes, behaviors, and expectations, those students will learn that their struggles and failures are also theirs alone. This does little to advance the student's political agency and only reinforces what it means to make the mistake to think that private accomplishments as well as "private agonies and anxieties...turn into public issues just for being on public display" (Bauman, 1999, pp. 2–3).

A Pedagogy of Critical Questioning: Bridging the Gap Between Acquisition and Learning

In the service of these literacy projects, I have taken up a strategy, as I illustrated, of critical questioning. These questions attempt to organize what Ernesto Laclau would call a new discursive field (see Worsham & Olsen, 1999, p. 10), developed to motivate counterhegemonic ideas, attitudes, and actions. Whether my students have answers to these questions matters little. In fact, some of the questions are strictly rhetorical in that they are advanced to highlight absences in texts, contradictions in experiences, and possibilities that lie dormant at the bottom of the epistemological barrel. But don't get me wrong, these questions are not innocent. They are leading (although not Socratic because I don't necessarily know where), designed to make my students think about the relation of things, and as Foucault has showed, the order of things as well.

Sometimes I'll attempt to answer my own questions if I find that they have failed to stir the curiosity of my students. Sometimes I will try to pose my questions differently. This is not a case in which I always know the answers to the questions I ask. It is the indeterminate and contingent aspect of this strategy that is important. Depending upon my students' experiences with the topic that we are discussing, or the text that we have read, the answers to my questions and the questioning of my answers are always caught in the web of identity, ideology, and power/knowledge. The questions are asked in an effort to engage my students in a critical dialogue, to get them to think creatively about the topic we are discussing, and eventually, to get them to create linkages between what is said, what they see, and how they understand the network of discourses that locates them as bodies and minds and the identifications they make ideologically. In the final analysis, one central goal of critical literacy and pedagogy "that wishes to force a shift in ways of seeing, feeling, and perceiving [must] begin by questioning established power" (Stanley Aronowitz, as cited in Giroux, 1997, p. 52).

This pedagogy of questioning is aligned with Gee's (1992) important distinction between acquisition and learning. "Acquisition is a process of acquiring something subconsciously by exposure to models and a process of trial and error, without a process of formal teaching" (p. 23). On the other hand, "Learning is a process that involves conscious knowledge gained through teaching, though not necessarily from someone officially designated a teacher" (p. 23). By initiating the strategies in my literacy classes that I have just discussed, I am trying, in a sense, to create a hybrid pedagogy of acquisition and learning. This hybrid, if held up against Gee's definitions, would appear not as a hybrid at all, but as an example of "learning." But by loosening the definitions a bit, I think that it is possible and fruitful to conceptualize and enact a pedagogy that attempts to make the relationship between learning and acquisition more porous.

For example, when I ask questions about established power in class, it is a pedagogy that begins in the domain of learning. When students struggle to respond to these questions based upon their experiences and the texts being read, either with answers or more questions, they are making a transition from learning to acquisition. When they respond with questions of their own, they are advancing their ideas from the domain of acquisition. Again, these distinctions are analytical. In the context of the classroom it would be impossible to make any clear distinctions between one or the other.

But it is helpful in beginning to think more critically about what schools and teachers can do to disrupt, validate, and complicate knowledges that have been strictly acquired or learned and that have come to occupy the realm of commonsense. A hybrid pedagogy that blends the knowledge domains of acquisition and learning attempts to make the classroom an extension of the world and the world an extension of the classroom.

In both programs, creating a hybrid space of acquisition and learning means asking and addressing some fundamental pedagogical questions. First, how can "critical" authority—that is, the authority of a teacher who is responsive to the link between social formations and power/knowledge—be made operational in a way that subverts the mistrust that students, especially those from oppressed classes and cultures, generally have of educational institutions? Second, how can counterhegemonic knowledge be presented so that it disrupts and disturbs without terrorizing and disrespecting students' vernacular understanding of the world? Third, how can teachers begin to conceptualize the literacy process as it functions as part of a primary and secondary social network? In other words, teachers not only need to address the distinction between acquisition and learning, but also need to pay attention to the distinction between what it means to know or to be knowledgeable in different sociopolitical contexts. Pedagogically, the implications of recognizing such distinctions lead toward the realization that knowledge, whether it is acquired or learned, often means two or more entirely different things depending upon where and when it is deployed.

For example, when a working class student has acquired the knowledge that he or she is outside the domain of "official knowledge"—that is, outside the discourse of capital, both cultural and material—while at the same time victimized by it, the student can still deploy that knowledge in a way that gives him or her some power. As Willis (1977) has shown, from a working-class student's perspective, to be in the elite is to be weak and unknowing in the things that count in working-class life. But, of course, in the context of the elite, working class knowledge is not only subordinated, but its resistant functions work against working class people's own political agency. The point here is that critical teachers must be responsive to how "secondary discourses" and "primary discourses" are taken up inside the classroom, because they often act upon and in the social reality outside the classroom in unexpected ways.

For another example, if I incorporate rap music in my curriculum, or a popular film, I must be aware of how the school might be seen as a threat to the resistant functions of popular culture. For students, this can be an affront to their sense of power. If they get some of their power from acts

and products of cultural subversion and resistance, then bringing the sub-
versive material into the classroom as part of the curriculum is to say that
nothing is sacred and that the power of the institution can reach even the
most intimate places. But I do think it is imperative to include popular culture in the literacy classroom, because it does often necessitate dealing with
the intimate and affective investments people make. As Stuart Hall
remarked,

> One should not forget why one went to the popular in the first instance. It's
> not just an indulgence and an affirmation; it's a political, intellectual, peda-
> gogical commitment. Everybody now inhabits the popular, whether they
> like it or not, so that does create a set of common languages. To ignore the
> pedagogical possibilities of common languages is extremely political. (quoted
> in Drew, 1998, p. 198)

The role of the literacy teacher would be to include these materials in
a way that complicates them, holds them accountable to the worlds they
imagine, and recognizes the power they have in mobilizing desire and passion. By complicating these materials, the teacher "de-reifies" them, while
respecting their power. The combination of effects illustrates what it might
mean to be conscious of the pedagogical fusion of acquisition and learning in
regards to secondary and primary discourses.

But it is important to understand two things about acquisition and
learning as they get taken up in the service of an ideological literacy project.
First, acquisition, as Gee (1992) said, is a powerful force in the learning
process; it is a conditioning of the intellectual, subconscious, and corporeal
dimensions of social and private life. This includes deeply held myths of the
human condition, history, and knowledge and the invisible or normalizing
power of the social formations that mythologize these conditions in the
first place. When conditions are ingrained in the subconscious as traditions, they move into the mythological sphere of determined outcomes. A
pedagogy that hopes to dislodge ideas stuck in the fatalistic sphere of determination must attempt to harness and understand the "differential sources
of power" (Gee, 1992, p. 24) that learning and acquisition represent.

Second, the relationship between teaching and ideological literacy is indeterminate. This means that there is not going to be a necessary or immediate response to pedagogies that attempt to dislodge what has been
acquired. Dislodging or transforming acquired knowledge is like removing
the color blue from a complicated, multicolored weave. It is not impossible,
but it takes perseverance, dedication, and the understanding that the weave
itself will be unlikely to call attention to the nooks and spaces in which the
blue has been spun. Unlike advocates for standardized testing who believe

that the relationship between learning and teaching can be measured, critical literacy educators must be aware of the indeterminancy of their pedagogies and hence the inability of their pedagogies to create a direct trajectory of literacy and ideological consciousness. In light of this, creating multiple trajectories of possibility by leading students through the complex associations of learning, doing, knowing, and understanding should be, strategically, the broadly conceived goal as it relates to teaching and learning in the remedial literacy classroom. In effect, an ideological literacy project prepares students for a life of learning and political participation minus the oversimplified certainty that standardizing outcomes promote.

On the other hand, indeterminacy does not mean that the contingent nature of knowledge/power and experience should be discarded for a laissez-faire pedagogy in which all relationships are seen as arbitrary or all meanings relative. What might it mean pedagogically to say that contingency is a force that contextualizes, and hence politicizes, the indeterminacy of teaching and learning? It means that teachers must take seriously the experiences of their students and that they need to occupy the space of leadership in their classrooms; that is, teachers must take back control of their classrooms from administrators and corporate overseers so that they can be responsive to their students' needs. It also means that social formations have a powerful effect on how individuals think about their experiences and the world around them. Thus, social formations must be linked historically, epistemologically, and politically to students' experiences. Moreover, it suggests that the formation of political agency is a consequence of indeterminacy in that political agents must be able to respond to the unexpected in a manner that is empowering, ethical, and effective. In this context, political agency represents a condition of humanity that is antithetical to the standardizing effects that standards-based education has on students, when standards education is understood as an essentializing process of teaching and learning that separates knowledge from power and politics from education. This notion of political agency celebrates diversity and difference and thrives on the indeterminacy that must obviously follow.

The Praxis of Political Discriminations: Literacy of Ideology

In my literacy classes, I tried to encourage my students to engage structures of power by first suggesting that they existed. The most powerful thing about structures and systems of power are their invisibility. My students had acquired an understanding of language in its most one-dimensional form; that is, they understood language and reading as a way to describe and explain reality, what they observed and thought as individuals. But even after my introduction to literacy, it was still very difficult to enter into a dialogue about discourses and the knowledges that they produced. As far as my students were concerned, there was only one "discourse," that being the words, images, and ideas that circulated through dominant society every day, although "dominant society" wasn't a concept anyone was prepared to easily accept. It's not that they did not know that many of their experiences and opinions, as I have said before, were inconsistent with a certain societal logic. Rather, they didn't have a language that could begin to make ideological distinctions between discourses. Having a language of critique and a language of discrimination is more than just being aware of and fluent in primary and secondary discourses. If a language of critique suggests the critical function of theoretical discourses on one hand, and the potency of inquiry to disrupt the normalizing processes of dominant ideological formations on the other, then a language of discrimination suggests the need to make distinctions between ideological spheres as part of the literacy process.

Having a language of critique and discrimination at the earliest stages of literacy is to be able to ideologically situate discourses. In short, this process reflects a literacy of ideology, a powerful first step in the reading–learning–transforming process. Moreover, becoming ideologically literate doesn't just mean that students are able to discern one ideology from another, it also means that ideological spaces open up for them to consciously inhabit.

One way I tried to instigate a literacy of ideology was to teach students what it means to be on the political "left" or on the political "right." Although these political designations float freely within the theoretical discourses of academia, especially within educational and cultural theory, my students in both institutions didn't know what it meant to be on the right or on the left. I found Derrida's (2000) distinction between the right and the left particularly helpful in getting students to begin to think about ideological perspective in relation to the meaning of the texts they read. "On the left there is the desire to affirm what is to come, to change, and to do so in the greatest possible justice...[the right] never makes justice the first resort or axiom of its action" (Derrida, 2000). In our present conjunction, the right affirms the rule of capital and the market to fairly determine the social and political outcomes of daily life. Moreover, the right tends to celebrate individual competition while at the same time denying the value of social and political struggle. Last, the right can be discerned by its mistrust of government outside of its role as handmaiden to corporate activities. Thus, material values more than social values take precedent. In Chomsky's (1999) famously direct language, the right generally puts "profit over people," with the implication that a free market is the same thing as a democratic republic.

With these guideposts, my students had a "language" to begin to critique what they read. This is not to say that they immediately knew whether they were on the right or the left, but at least they were able to begin a process of discrimination in which issues of power as well as meaning were part of the learning process. By offering them the admittedly simplistic dichotomies of right and left ideologies, the notion of perspective moved from a quality and an effect of character and individuality to one that suggested a condition of power. These broad political designations acted generatively in the service of political classification that is "the basis for all social discrimination, and discrimination...is no less a constituent element of the social realm than equality is a constituent element of the political" (Arendt, 1968, p. 3). These political discriminations offered students a vantage point from which to build a vocabulary of distinctions. From here, they were able to rub "texts" against each other, measuring the limitations and possibilities of their truths within the parameters of power.

For example, I first gave the CAMP students an article to read in *Newsweek* entitled the "The New Face of Race in America" (Campo-Flores, 2000). After a week of discussion, I gave them an article from *The Nation* entitled "The Real World of Race" (Geiger, 1997). In retrospect, I should have assigned them the articles together, because they so explicitly present two different ideological perspectives about race and power in America. The *Newsweek* article argues that we are in an "Age of Color" and that the "ancient divisions of black and white" are no longer relevant in a time when "an entire generation [of youth of color] have grown up in prosperity, attending schools with people of mixed backgrounds and set out to work in the New Economy, where there are few walls and little hierarchy" (Campo-Flores, 2000, p. 40). The implication, of course, is that we are in a state of integration in which opportunity does not discriminate, power is perfunctory, and, although "there is no question that African-Americans still bear heavy burdens, disproportionately suffering from poverty, imprisonment, and racial profiling" that "old dualities have given way to a multiplicity of ethnic forces" (Campo-Flores, 2000, p. 40). The article seems to suggest that multiculturalism has replaced the white/black dichotomy, and thus power can no longer be delineated in racial terms. Power is not mentioned in the article, but the implication is that it now runs along multiple trajectories of color, deflecting attention away from the unequal power whites have over all other ethnic minorities. What the article does on the one hand is make whiteness invisible, declaring a laissez-faire multiculturalism in which opportunity exists outside the sphere of power, while on the other it admits to power struggles within the ranks of ethnic minorities. This strategy is effective in a pedagogical sense because it addresses the visibility of the multicultural "other" in the New Economy, while making invisible the formations of white power that limit the opportunities for the "other." Half-truths are always more convincing than complete lies.

In Geiger's review of David Shipler's *A Country of Strangers*, he began by outlining the right-wing ideology of reactionary intellectuals who announce, resonating with the dominant public discourse on race, "Racism is dead!" "How then," Geiger (1997) wrote, rhetorically responding to this conservative declaration and the one ostensibly articulated in the *Newsweek* article, "to explain the overwhelming realities of desperate inner cities, soaring back unemployment, crumbling housing, failing schools, increasing segregation and family disintegration, crime and drugs if white racism is not their root cause?" (p. 27). Again echoing the right's response,

> Black people did it, did it to the country, did it to themselves. Black behavior, not white racism, became the reason why Blacks and whites lived in separate worlds...the failure of the lesser breeds to enjoy society's fruits became their fault alone. (Geiger, 1997, p. 27)

At the heart of Geiger's review of Shipler's book is the notion that "true integration means power sharing," an absence in our present multicultural conjunction, often ignored by the right and one that should define the struggle of the left.

What occurred as a consequence of the *Newsweek* article standing alone was that my students had no language to discriminate this perspective from any other, and therefore no language of critique to interrogate the parameters of power that informed such a reading of the world. When I gave them the article from *The Nation* to read, and even before our discussion of left and right, they not only recognized a difference of perspective, but almost all were incredibly "jazzed" about the perspective itself. One woman who had not yet spoken in class enthusiastically yelled out when I asked what people thought of Geiger's article. She said that she liked it much, much better than the *Newsweek* article because it described the way she had experienced race in America. In short, when provided with a countertext, they not only began to read intertextually, but also began to conceptualize what it means to make distinctions and discriminations between texts.

But again, it would be misleading to suggest that all my students agreed with Geiger's statements. In fact, when asked to engage these ideas at the level of their experiences, many of them shared stories of interethnic racism. My students had been victimized by other ethnic minorities, just like the *Newsweek* article suggested. This provoked me to address the issue of whiteness. It also provoked me to ask them about their experiences with white people. As I came to find out, they had plenty of experiences with white racism, but because I was white they felt hesitant to share their experiences with me. To digress for a moment, this is why trust and respect must be seen as principles of pedagogy that are under constant negotiation. Just because a level of trust was established under one set of circumstances it does not automatically mean that it will carry over into another set.

As I gained their trust anew in the context of white racism by discussing white privilege, we discussed both the validity of their experiences with interethnic racism and its limitations to address the invisible and often anonymous power of white racism. In other words, we discussed how, when ethnic minorities participate in racist ideologies, it pushes them down and lifts the white race up. Likewise, whites are elevated under the regime of white supremacy, while ethnic minorities (the majority) are pushed down (see Wah, 1994).

Moving beyond the texts toward an engagement with the political and social formations in which these texts articulated was a small step. Concrete examples taken from the material of the urban landscape provided sufficient illustrations for my students to begin interrogating the texts. The CAMP students' questions dug at the roots of poverty by beginning in the fields of migrant workers, shedding light on how *Newsweek*'s portrayal of race and ethnicity victimized the victims of poverty and racism by failing to consider how "social power and transforming discourses, institutions, and social practices of privilege" normalize whiteness in a "liberal swirl of diversity" (McLaren, 1997, p. 282). As Geiger asked rhetorically, how else to explain overwhelming poverty and urban decay in minority neighbhorhoods if one does not consider formative structures of racism and oppression, but by blaming those who live there? My students began to understand that reading the word did in fact mean reading the world. How, they asked, could Newsweek print such an article? How indeed. This question completed the hermeneutical gesture by acknowledging not only the authority and power that the text had to teach and persuade, even when the lessons contradicted the experiences of my students, but also by initiating a relational process of reading in which the link between source, message, social construction, social formations, and pedagogical implications were understood as interrelated parts of the "literacy" whole.

The CAMP students also began to make connections between the politics of the *Newsweek* piece and personal interactions they experienced at Penn State regarding their status as CAMP students, in effect an affirmative action program. If everything is equal and opportunity has nothing to do with resources, if integration means diversity and not the democratization of power, then what is the defense of CAMP and programs like it? The defense, if it comes at all, is that minority students are incapable of succeeding without help due to their own individual problems or character traits and not that we live in a racist society in which the distribution of wealth is iniquitous, and power and white privilege are made invisible. As Geiger (1997) wrote, "Affirmative action is such a threat because it challenges unseen and unacknowledged privileges of whiteness" (p. 29) thereby exposing the symbolic violence of "white" power in the form of a pedagogy of invisibility and normalization. Moreover, programs like CAMP are identified as giving minorities an unfair advantage over whites, tipping the scales in favor of the "other." My students had been subjected to this kind of racism at Penn State and had felt defeated and diminished by it. After reading these two articles against each other, they were better able to articulate a defense of their right to an education on the basis of social justice.

At Montclair, I gave my students an article to read from *The New York Times* entitled "Counterpoint to Unity: Dissent" (Bernstein, 2001). We first discussed any personal experiences that my students had with dissent. One was involved in a class in which students were discussing school tracking, and he was the only person arguing against the practice. Another student found herself quietly dissenting from the ideas of one of her professors. Interestingly, after speaking with her classmates, she found solidarity. This generated a conversation about the notion of dissent and power, for if dissent is a "minority" opinion, then could this student's dissent actually be dissent? After all, she and her classmates outnumbered the professor. Students began to question power's ability to create a consensus, or a perceived consensus.

I then asked the students if "dissent," as it was situated in the title of the article, indicated the opposite of unity. They said yes. I then asked them how they understood unity. They responded with phrases like "coming together," "unified," and "agreeing." I then asked them what Americans were coming together around. Answer: the war in Afghanistan. Yes, but what larger principles were being discussed in relation to the war? What unifies Americans politically, whether one is on the right or the left? A commitment to what? Some said "freedom." Freedom of what, I asked. "Freedom of speech," many said because earlier in the class we had discussed free speech and access to media. And why is free speech important? We struggled and eventually found "democracy." Yes, we are unified to a greater or lesser degree around the tenets of democracy, the most urgent, some would argue, being free speech. Is dissent a necessary outcome of free speech? If so, why is it set up as a counterpoint to "unity"? In this context, wouldn't dissent be a natural and necessary element of a democratic republic unified by its commitment to free speech? Is there a commitment to free speech given the unequal access to media and the public ear that the wealthy have in the U.S. and around the world in comparison with the poor? Is there a commitment to free speech given the recent call to ban certain songs from the radio? Is there a commitment to free speech given President Bush's displeasure at the media for allowing the Taliban to communicate their ideological position on the ideology of the U.S.? These questions were posed and discussed. Again, answers varied. But the point, it seems, is that we created a pedagogical space in which these questions could be asked and grappled with.

As a consequence of these questions, the Montclair students began to interrogate the very notion of unity in relation to difference. Some questioned why people were not asking why so many countries "hated" the U.S. Others challenged their fellow classmates when they presented the popular view, becoming dissenters in the process. In the face of these interactions, I again brought attention to the "unity" of the class in spite of the dissension. This unity is established by a belief and corresponding pedagogy that encourages dialogue and critical engagement. They also began to ask why the dissenting opinions didn't get as much coverage in the mainstream press, leading them to further problematize the relationship between knowledge and power. They then began to make links between power and right and left ideologies, understanding quickly that, as the article states, the dissenters are on the left, minus significant power and access to the mechanisms of public disclosure. It should be made very clear that this whole process is a literacy process, one in which students are learning about power, ideology, and their place in the world. Thus, they are being prepared to act upon the world, to govern, to have power, to lead.

Critiquing Power

What has become evident for me in these classes is that, in the end, when we talk about the relationship between pedagogy and knowledges, and especially when we talk about ideological literacies of learning, we are talking about "relations of power, not relations of meaning" (Foucault, 1977, p. 114). These relations of power, lived out pedagogically in the literacy classroom through the battles between acquired and learned knowledges, suggest that educators must be aware, as Foucault (1977) has argued, of how "power produces knowledge" (p. 59). Certainly in the context of expanding political agency and democratic relations, destructive knowledges, both acquired and learned, as products of a "'general politics' of truth" (Foucault, p. 131) must be interrogated as part of the literacy process, if learning how to read means, in part, developing a "critical" stance toward society's dominating discourses. As Foucault (1977) stated,

> Each society has its regime of truth: that is, the types of discourse which it accepts and makes function as true; the mechanisms and instances which enable one to distinguish true and false statements, the means by which each is sanctioned; the techniques and procedures accorded value in acquisition of truth; the status of those who are charged with saying what counts as true. (p. 131)

In other words, literacy education not only must be involved in a pedagogical process of "translation," but also must encourage an engagement with structures of power and the knowledges that they produce. This is one of the reasons why a "critical" pedagogy is not, in fact, an indoctrination but, at its best, is an intervention into oppressive regimes of truth. When the accusation of indoctrination is applied to "critical" practices, it is often the case that a critique of power relationships is missing. Certainly beyond the scope of this article, it is nevertheless important to realize that without a critique of power relations and the knowledges that they legitimate and invalidate, an analysis of pedagogy as either indoctrination or intervention will lack substance.

Educating people to read and act upon the world is quite different than training them to pass a test. The former produces citizens prepared to govern, while the latter has the real potential to produce students "who have successfully passed basic reading tests by the third grade and yet cannot use language (oral or written) to learn, to master content, to work in the new economy, or to think critically about social and political affairs" (Gee, 1999, p. 356). Considering the overwhelming need for remediation and the contradictions that I discussed in the beginning of this article that bind traditional remedial programs, ideological literacies of learning provide a comprehensive and effective alternative. Moreover, the general principles of evaluation are well tested in other progressive literacy projects of the past, including Dewey's experimental schools, Highlander Folk School, the

Citizenship Schools, and the Quincy schools to name only a few (see Shannon, 1990).

But it would be wrong to suggest that all that needs to happen to improve the conditions in schools, remedial reading programs, and impoverished neighborhoods is to teach ideological literacies of learning. Without a significant redistribution of power in our schools, neighborhoods, and governmental institutions, without a commitment to democratizing our most important social institutions, progressive projects and the citizens that they produce will continue to exist at the margins of political and educational discourses, or worse, their ideas and practices will disappear into the shallow grave of history that established power and privilege quietly dig.

REFERENCES

Arendt, H. (1968). Introduction. In H. Arendt (Ed.), *Walter Benjamin's illuminations* (pp. 1–29). New York: Schocken.

Aronowitz, S., & Giroux, H. (1993). *Education still under siege*. Westport, CT: Bergin & Garvey.

Bauman, Z. (1999). *In search of politics*. Stanford, CA: Stanford University Press.

Bernstein, R. (2001, October 6). Counterpoint to unity: Dissent. *The New York Times*, pp. A13, A15.

Boggs, C. (2000). *The end of politics*. New York: Guilford.

Campo-Flores, A. (2000, September 18). The new face of race in America. *Newsweek*, pp. 38–41.

Chomsky, N. (1999). *Profit over people*. New York: Seven Stories Press.

Chomsky, N. (2000). *Chomsky on miseducation*. New York: Rowman and Littlefield.

Daniels, H., Zemelman, S., & Bizar, M. (1999, October). Whole language works. *Educational Leadership*, pp. 32–37.

Derrida, J. (2000). Intellectual courage: An interview. *Culture Machine*. Available online: http://culturemachine.tees.ac.uk/journal.htm.

Drew, J. (1998). Cultural composition: Stuart Hall on ethnicity and the discursive turn. *Journal of Composition Theory*, *18*, 183.

Edmondson, J., & Shannon, P. (1998). Reading education and poverty. *Peabody Journal of Education*, *73*, 104–126.

Foucault, M. (1977). *Power/knowledge*. New York: Pantheon.

Freire, P. (1998). *Pedagogy of freedom*. New York: Rowman and Littlefield.

Gee, J.P. (1992). What is literacy. In P. Shannon (Ed.), *Becoming political* (pp. 21–28). Portsmouth, NH: Heinemann.

Gee, J.P. (1999). Reading and the new literacy studies: Reframing the National Academy of Sciences Report on Reading. *Journal of Literacy Research*, *31*, 355–368.

Geiger, H.J. (1997, December 1). The real world of race. *The Nation*, pp. 27–29.

Giroux, H.A. (1999). Doing cultural studies: Youth and the challenge of pedagogy. *Harvard Educational Review*, *6*, 278–308.

Gunster, S. (2000). Gramsci, organic intellectuals, and cultural studies. In J.A. Frank & J.T. Borino (Eds.), *Vocations of political theory* (pp. 238–259). Minneapolis: University of Minnesota Press.

Kohn, A. (2000, March-April). The real threat to American schools. *Tikkun*, p. 60.

Kozol, J. (1991). *Savage inequalities*. New York: Crown.

Macedo, D. (1994). *Literacies of power*. Boulder, CO: Westview.

Macedo, D. (2000). Introduction. In *Chomsky on miseducation* (pp. 1-18). New York: Rowman and Littlefield.

Marable, M. (1996). *Speaking truth to power: Essays on race, resistance, and radicalism*. Boulder, CO: Westview.

McLaren, P. (1997). *Revolutionary multiculturalism*. Boulder, CO: Westview.

Miner, B. (2000, August). Making the grade. *The Progressive*, pp. 40-43.

Olson, G.A., & Worsham, L. (1998). Staging the politics of difference: Homi Bhaba's critical literacy. *Journal of Advanced Composition, 18*(3), 1-29.

Paul, D.G. (2000). Rap and orality. *Journal of Adolescent & Adult Literacy, 44*, 246-252.

Reed, C.B. (2001, February 23). Remediating college level students. *The San Diego Union-Tribune*, p. B9.

Remedial ed. (2001, May 12). *Minneapolis Star Tribune*, p. 22A.

Sehr, D.T. (1997). *Education for public democracy*. Albany: State University of New York Press.

Shannon, P. (1990). *The struggle to continue*. Portsmouth, NH: Heinemann.

Simon, R. (1992). Empowerment as a pedagogy of possibility. In P. Shannon (Ed.), *Becoming political* (pp. 142-155). Portsmouth, NH: Heinemann.

Taylor, C.L. (2001, April 26). CUNY funds threatened. *Newsday*, p. A06.

Wah, L.M. (1994). *The color of fear* [Videorecording]. Berkeley, CA: Stir-Fry Productions.

Willis, P. (1977). *Learning to labor*. New York: Columbia University Press.

Worsham, L., & Olson, G.A. (1999). Hegemony and the future of democracy: Ernesto Laclau's political philosophy. *Journal of Advanced Composition, 19*(1), 1-27.

Hog Farms in Pennsylvania

Patrick Shannon

A remote sign of hope for a sane and harmonious future has shown up in the struggle over Pennsylvania's interest in attracting corporate hog farms to the state. The public rhetoric behind this interest is to bring new jobs and new taxes to impoverished communities and to make Pennsylvania a player in the global agricultural economy. As I understand it from local newspaper accounts, the corporate hog farms in question are mainstays in the production of pork for public consumption. As James Adams, president of Penn Agris (a farm-industry trade organization) explained, "the corporate system is designed to get large quantities of high quality meat to dinner tables at the least cost" (in Avril, 2002, March 18, Mass pig pens: Good farming or bad practice, *Philadelphia Inquirer*, p. A01).

To accomplish this goal, agricultural corporations buy land, hire a manager, and then ship 7,000–10,000 piglets from corporate breeding farms to the fattening farms in order to raise each hog's weight from 10 to 250 pounds. At that weight, it does not matter if the hogs are as cute as Wilbur—they are shipped to the next step on the production line before heading to U.S. grocery stores. In order to increase the hogs' weight, the farm manager loads the hogs with considerable amounts of grain. Anyone who has read Taro Gomi's classic *Everyone Poops* (1993, Kane/Miller) knows what happens next. But in this case, we are talking about thousands of pigs whose only job it is to eat.

The potential neighbors for all these hogs are not eager to deal with this "residue," and in 10 townships across Pennsylvania coalitions of environmentalists, conservatives, traditional liberals, and farmers of all political stripes have banded together to fight the possible invasion of corporate hog farms. Together these groups have bypassed the usual scientific strategies that limit hog farming to minimize the consequent smell and water contamination. Rather, the community members have passed zoning laws in their townships to prohibit corporate farms. In Franklin Township, one family farmer presented the locals' complaint this way:

> I don't like the way they treat the animals. I don't like the conditions for the farmer. I don't like the smell. There is no escape from that. I don't like the potential to damage the water supply. I don't like the amount of antibiotics they use to keep the animals alive. (in Avril, 2002)

Reprinted from *The Reading Teacher*, 56, 688–690, April 2003.

The state, corporations, and even the Pennsylvania Farm Bureau have responded that the citizens in these townships have no right to ban corporations from farming in their communities. Moreover, they argue that corporations know more about how to farm and about what is good for the economy than do the locals. For example, the pending state Senate Bill 826 calls for the repeal of township control of zoning in rural areas, and Penn Agris has filed a lawsuit claiming that the zoning laws in the 10 townships discriminate against corporations. Each of these responses seems to have stiffened the citizens' resolve.

On April 16, 2002, during their annual convention, 300 Pennsylvania township supervisors voted overwhelmingly to sustain the townships' right to ban corporate farms. These supervisors were determined to demonstrate that community members have the authority to define what goes on in their jurisdiction when it does not inflict pain or hardship on any class of people. "I just want to be able to sleep through the night without that smell in the house that my grandparents built on the land that we have farmed for over 100 years," said Eleanor Strict (personal communication, April 17, 2002). "This will go all the way to the Supreme Court of the Commonwealth," she said.

Where Is the Hope?

For me, the hope of this struggle lies in the vivid demonstration of literacy in these communities. Citizens are pouring through texts—printed and lived—in order to learn more about themselves, which has tested their understanding of their history, cultures, and values. They are relating this new awareness to the lives of others and the guiding social structures put in place to guide those lives. During these literate practices, the people have become aware that they can control their own destiny, and this awareness and their continued reading have caused them to act.

This example is sophisticated literacy at its best, and it belies the rhetoric of a literacy crisis. These citizens are using their literacy as political agents—just like we were taught to do in our civics classes in high school—in order to participate in the decisions that affect their lives. Too often, people retreat from civic confrontation because they believe that "you can't fight city hall."

What makes this use of literacy unique in contemporary political discourse is the citizens' choice to rely on ethics, history, and culture—rather than science or the economic market—in order to direct their work. That is, the citizens in these townships have judged the rightness or wrongness of the actions to start corporate hog farming in their communities on the basis of the virtue or vice of the motives that prompted the actions, the moral character of the agents who would perform those actions, and the resulting good or bad consequences.

To set these ethical judgments in context, the citizens have taken inventory of the history of their townships and the cultures that are present or might come into being because of the actions and reactions of the corporate hog farms. They acknowledge that hogs can be fattened more efficiently on such farms, that additional taxes might help their communities, and that scientists from outside their community could establish "acceptable" levels of smell and water contamination. However, after weighing these scientific and economic "facts" against the consequent effects on community health, history, and culture in these 10 townships, the citizens have concluded that the whole thing stinks too much to allow it to happen, and they have not allowed it to happen—at least, not yet.

So What?

It may seem odd to think about corporate hog farms as a metaphor for reading education in the United States. But I think there are important lessons for all of us to consider within the civic courage demonstrated in these rural Pennsylvania townships. Many of us face similar dilemmas in different packages: We're told that others know better about our work and how to do it and about our lives and how to live them. For example, educational publishers tell us what materials we need for instruction. Educational scientists explain how we must teach. And now state and federal governments define when and how to assess our teaching and students' learning.

The first lesson the story of Pennsylvania's hog farm struggle has made me consider is the developing courage the people of these communities had to question science and the commercial market. I don't mean that these citizens doubted the scientists' conclusions or the economists' predictions about corporate hog farms: They conceded those as facts. The majority of citizens in the 10 communities, however, refused to elevate those facts above what they knew about their lives and community. Through their literacy practices they decided that they didn't want to live their lives as science and the market told them they should. And the town supervisors agreed with them.

Acting on that decision blurs the distinction often drawn between objectivity and subjectivity. These people did not automatically accept the modern tradition that objectivity is always preferable to subjectivity. Rather, they sought and continue to seek to subordinate science and the economic market to their subjective and ethical analyses of the situation. To take this step, they have realized that science and economics are social constructions similar to ethics, history, and culture. They know that people have developed science and the market over time and work to maintain them as disciplines of authority in life. In fact, the idea of the market is only 400 years old, and the scientific experimental method (the foundation of scientific objectivity) isn't much older than Eleanor Strict's house, which she's trying to save in Franklin County, Pennsylvania.

Statistician Karl Pearson is often credited with the elaboration of the scientific method at the turn of the last century. His construction of science, however, bears little resemblance to the science that Copernicus, Newton, Darwin, or Einstein practiced. Although some scientists approximate the method, their work is always more complex, subjective, and messy than the myth of the scientific method allows. At its best, science is a human endeavor that requires a combination of imagination, creativity, speculation, prior knowledge, library research, perseverance, and, often, blind luck—the same combinations of intellectual resources available to all in differing amounts when trying to solve problems. Members of the coalitions in these 10 Pennsylvania townships used all of these capacities in defense of their communities.

Recognizing that science is anthropomorphic brought me the second lesson from the hog farm story. These rural citizens identified ties between the science of hog farming and the money in the hog farming industry. This is science at its worst. In the struggle over hog farming in Pennsylvania we have learned that science has social entailments just like ethics, history, and culture. This knowledge was obvious to the citizens when contradictory scientific facts appeared on both sides of the hog farm issue. The Community Environmental Legal Defense Fund (which is based in Chambersburg and provides financial support for Franklin Township residents to defend themselves against the Penn Agris lawsuit) provided scientific reports and experts who attested to the negative environmental impact of corporate hog farms. Penn Agris supplied experts and reports that "prove" the smell and the water contamination produced by the farms are manageable and can be tolerated.

This example does not suggest that all scientific research is tainted. One of the most dramatic trends influencing the direction of science during the past century has been the increasing dependence on funding from government and industry. Today, mainstream scientists engage in expensive research that requires considerable financial support from grant agencies. This trend is noticeable in the soft, as well as the hard, sciences—and the education field is not immune. It would be easy to track the variation in reading research topics during the last three decades to the ones mentioned in federal proposals for research. The smell of money, then, contradicts the scientific method—or, in other words, the collective interest created by the concerns of the funding agencies competes with the individual objectivity promoted by the scientific method.

What's It Going to Be?

When we read events like the struggle over hog farms as texts, we have the opportunity to ask questions about the present and the future that such events offer us. Each event contains the history of the activities that brought it about and carries the promises and values of a "better" future. The corporations, professional organizations, and government officials who promote corporate hog farms promise more pork on our tables and value efficiency and profits most highly. Rather than accept this promotion, the citizens of these 10 Pennsylvania townships have decided that they are willing to eat less pork and to pay more for it. They have established a different set of criteria on which to base their present and to work for their desired future.

This power to develop the criteria—not just to choose among the options others set for us—is a freedom seldom mentioned in the current talk about reading and reading education in the United States. We must ask ourselves: Do we share the values of those who are telling us what materials to use, how to teach, and when to test as if they know the answers better than we do? If we do share their values, then we should accept the corporate logic, which flows through these sources, and step enthusiastically in whatever direction they point us. If we do not share those values, however, then we must seek others within our communities who share our own values and begin to develop our criteria to judge the present and to work for the future.

Literacy and the Other: A Sociological Approach to Literacy Research and Policy in Multilingual Societies

Allan Luke

An Australian Standpoint on Literacy Policy

In multicultural nations the issues of language rights and loss and the equitable redistribution of textual and discourse resources through literacy education are test cases for democratic education. The *RRQ* invitation to write about the future of literacy research in multilingual societies was timely. As I write this piece, a team of us are undertaking policy research on the teaching of language and literacy education for Aboriginal and Torres Strait Islander students in the Queensland state system, working with Aboriginal teachers, principals, elders, and senior state bureaucrats. We are reviewing data on these communities' language and literacy achievement, current system and school-level interventions, and the adequacy and cultural bases of existing performance measures and reporting systems (Luke, Land, Christie, & Kolatsis, in press). We are drawing upon a wide range of disciplinary, empirical, and interpretive evidence.

Whatever pretences we may have about the scientific formation of government policy, it is inevitably both socially and culturally normative and regulative. In this case, we are developing an overarching "language-in-education" policy (Kaplan & Baldauf, 1999) and literacy strategy for indigenous schools and communities. Policymaking is not simply subjective, and it need not be at the whims of partisan politics, constituency expediency, and so forth. It can indeed be based on powerful, rigorously theorised, grounded, and documented observations and analysis of the contexts for language, literacy, and education. But exactly how and with what intellectual, discursive, disciplinary, and governmental resources we do such analyses are the hard questions.

One of the binary divides that has emerged in the ongoing U.S. debate over "evidence-based" policy is between a narrowly circumscribed version of "pure," objective science and a Hobbesian universe of arbitrary, subjective,

Reprinted from *Reading Research Quarterly*, 38, 132–141, January/February/March 2003.

and politically contaminated decision making (see commentary by Cunningham, 2001). Yet the making of literacy policy is—in actual practice and social fact—hermeneutic, interpretive, discourse constructive, case based, and highly contextual. Because it is tied up with the normative allocation of resources, policy is by definition and necessarily political. Hence, it is not simply a matter of whether we use contextual, sociocultural research to make policy—we should, and I will argue that case momentarily. My starting point is the view that policymaking itself is discourse constructive, interpretive, and contextual, made in those strange textual monocultures that we call bureaucracies (Luke, 1997).

Educational policies are bids to centrally regulate and govern flows of discourse, fiscal capital, and physical and human resources across the time and space boundaries of educational systems. Policies and policymakers set out to achieve estimable educational, cultural, social, and economic goals and outcomes. In outlining a scenario for literacy research in multilingual societies and communities, my case is that, if indeed there is to be a critical science of literacy policy development and intervention, it must be multidisciplinary. It must also draw from a range of sources and kinds of data (sociological, demographic, social geographic, economic, and, of course, linguistic as well as data on individual or institutional performativity). It needs to be reliant on interpretive debate and analysis at the most sophisticated levels and be socially and culturally contextual in the most fine-grained ways. Such a policy challenges governments—politicians and civil servants alike—senior educational administrators, and researchers to actually engage in new coalitions and to create new critical fora, new zones of proximal development for the articulation and implementation of educational policy.

So my particular standpoint and interest in writing this piece is as a researcher and bureaucrat trying to come to grips with the unreconciled issue of redistributive social justice in Australian education: the educational achievement and life pathways of Aborigine and Torres Strait Islander children and youth. I'll take this as an illustrative case for the kinds of research we would need for proper evidence-based policy formation and as a lead to current and possible directions of literacy research in multilingual societies.

A More Formal Introduction

The perennial questions of literacy education are only subordinately about method. First, the *lingua franca* question: Whose languages should be the media of instruction in schools, and also civic domains, workplaces, mass media, and other institutions? Second, the curriculum questions: Which selective traditions should shape what will count as literacy; which texts and discourses, literacy practices, and events will be codified and transmitted in schools; in whose interests and with what material and discourse consequences will it be done?

Over the second half of the 20th century, state school systems struggled to address the challenges of cultural and linguistic diversity—tenacious and ongoing problems in the educational participation and achievement of students from cultural and religious minority and second-language-speaking communities. More specifically, the educational systems in what are termed "advanced" and "postindustrial" countries of the North and West confront the educational needs of not only longstanding diasporic communities and their indigenous peoples but also the recent waves of migrants, refugees, guest workers, and postcolonial subjects of their own making. The legacies of these efforts are ongoing debates about the extent to which mainstream schooling systems are and should be agents of cultural assimilation or pluralism, how these same systems serve to enhance or deny minority language rights (May, 2001), and, centrally, the redress of differential and unequal access to educationally acquired cultural and linguistic capital. These debates sit within the contexts of geopolitical conflict and warfare, resurgent nationalism, emergent issues around economic globalisation and the "spatial redistribution" of wealth and privilege (Harvey, 2000), and the politics of racism and religious intolerance.

These new economic and cultural conditions, complicated by the emergence of digital technologies, have made educational policy and practice more complex and more contingent, rather than less. It is worth noting sociologist Manuel Castells's (1996) observation that one of the emergent responses to globalisation is fundamentalism of all orders: the harkening for a simplicity, reductionism, and literalism. In literacy debates, back to the "basics" movements are modes of educational fundamentalism. What counts as literacy itself is in historical transition: How will literacy practices be redefined in relation not only to the emergence of digital technologies but also to the emergent, blended forms of social identity, work, civic and institutional life, and the redistributions of wealth and power that accompany economic and cultural globalisation?

Further, the "Others" of mainstream literacy education are not the selfsame populations that we identified as "disadvantaged" or "at risk" or "underserved" or "underperforming" in the postwar period. What counts as a "minority," "diasporic," "linguistically marginal," or disadvantaged group in postindustrial economies is, of course, a matter for debate and definition beyond the scope of this piece. For my purposes here, I provisionally note three defining characteristics, all of which define historically marginalised communities in relation to dominant fields of power: (1) minorities are communities whose characteristic forms of cultural capital—embodied discourse practices and skills—are of lesser immediate exchange value in dominant social fields and linguistic markets; (2) they develop "minority discourses" (JanMohamad & Lloyd, 1990), ways of talking back against power, modes of critique, voice, and speaking positions that may or may not "entitle" them to access or break the strangleholds that mainstream markets hold over that access; while (3) they remain pressed to master dominant forms of cultural practice in order to achieve degrees and kinds of access to and mobility across mainstream political and economic institutions—some of these dominant forms of practice are arbitrary forms of symbolic power; others are requisite for technical and espistemological mastery of particular forms of life in capitalist economies.

One of the consequences of economic globalisation is the relative permeability of borders and accelerated, though uneven, flows of bodies across geographical and political boundaries. New population demographics threaten the stability of large-scale educational systems as linguistic and ethnic monocultures, and they have destabilised longstanding curriculum settlements. Schools now include those groups that have historically struggled with access and participation in mainstream economies—new and recent migrants, as well as emergent "underclasses" of new poor and geographically marginalised communities.

In light of these conditions, it is not surprising that how best to educate ethnic and linguistic minorities in current contexts is straining the boundaries and the credibility of discourses of multiculturalism and compensatory education—the terms of which were set over 30 years ago by U.S. civil rights and school desegregation legislation, framed by the Bernstein/Labov debate and Cazden, Johns, and Hymes's (1972) prototypical work on the ethnography of speaking. We are now dealing with the social and demographic impacts of postcolonialism and economic globalisation, with culturally and linguistically diverse student bodies having become the norm in many educational jurisdictions. At the same time, the actual practices and demands of literacy are in historical transition (Alvermann, 2002).

How adequate are our disciplinary, policy, and pedagogy toolkits for addressing new times? All of the discussion pieces in this edition of *RRQ* are, to some extent, normative and ameliorative. Whatever our epistemological standpoint or "scientific" basis, all of these pieces speak to longstanding patterns of inequality. Yet the educational solutions on offer are very much those of the last three decades. These run across a broad theoretical, scientific, and political landscape to include mainstream compensatory programs that attempt to identify and remediate ostensive early literacy or language problems experienced by minority students; transitional bilingual, English as a Second Language and English as a Second Dialect programs; programs that focus on multicultural content and culturally appropriate pedagogy to address cultural and linguistic mismatch; and critical and postcolonial pedagogies that focus on the need for student and community voice and identity politics.

There is emergent social science research that documents new configurations of "difference" and "diversity" in literate identities, practices, and pathways. This work includes studies using hermeneutic, sociocultural, and critical or interpretivist approaches to redefine second-language acquisition (e.g., Miller, in press; Norton, 1999; Norton & Toohey, in press; Pavlenko, Blackledge, Piller, & Teutsch-Dwyer, 2001; Toohey, 2000) and to set the grounds for a "critical applied linguistics" (Pennycook, 2001).

Extending Hymesian traditions, such approaches have refocused second-language teaching and learning towards issues of identity and subjectivity and turned attention to the embedded relationships of schools and learning in community and home contexts (e.g., Lin, Wang, Akamatsu, & Riazi, in press). At the same time, other approaches to literacy research have moved from traditional anthropological definitions of culture to plural redefinitions of cultures that draw from poststructuralist feminist and postcolonial theory (for a recent, more general review, see Foley, Levinson, & Hurtig, 2001). They have moved in ways that have begun to blur the once clear paradigmatic distinctions between traditional reading research, literacy research, and, indeed the aforementioned second-language and multicultural research. This corpus of work includes the following: Studies of the new patterns of development and use of spoken language, print literacy, and digital multiliteracies in the formation of social and cultural identities, as children begin to blend languages and cultures—ethnic and popular and gendered—in new and novel ways. Researchers draw upon a broad range of disciplinary and theoretical resources, including sociocultural psychology, cultural studies, postcolonial and feminist studies, the ethnography of literacy, and critical discourse analysis (e.g., Alvermann, Moon, & Hagood, 1999; Buckingham & Sefton-Green, 1994; Comber & Thompson, 2001; Dyson, 1997; Moje, 2000).

This work documents and describes how language, discourse, and literacy are media for the construction and negotiation of identity and power in all of their dynamic forms (e.g., sociocultural, economic, libidinal) and in relation to local collocations of social class, race, and gender. It also has begun to broaden its focus beyond schools and other educational institutions to examine the new and volatile life pathways to and through social fields (both informal and formal, community and corporate, traditional and modern) in relation to economic globalisation and its new, oscillating formations of capital, discourse, and power. Such studies work both at the microethnographic level, examining institutional sites and relations, and via a macrosociological analysis, tracing globalised flows of language, discourse, texts, and power. These include (a) studies of diversity and multilingualism in workplaces and other social institutions, which have begun to document new patterns of textual and identity work, the impacts of new technologies, and emergent power relations (e.g., Goldstein, 1997; Hull, 1997) and (b) studies of national and regional, local and "glocal" cultural and linguistic, social, and economic responses to the hegemony of world-language English (e.g., Pennycook, 1996, 1998).

A research agenda around multilingualism so conceived marks an epistemological shift that is far more intricate than a simple expansion from psychological to social foundations or from reading research to new literacy studies (Barton, Hamilton, & Ivanic, 1999). It moves first from postwar, modern "culturalisations" of language pedagogy, psychology, and learning heralded near mid-century by Hymes (1996) and sustained by current U.S. neo-Vygotskian work, to an explicit engagement with new ways of theorising and studying culture, identity, and discourse. Encouraged by new social theory on globalisation and social movements of the past five years, this agenda has begun to move from a focus on identity and subjectivity motivated strongly by feminist poststructuralist and postcolonial theory towards a regrounded socioeconomic analysis of globalised patterns and configurations of language, literacy, power, and capital (e.g., Burbules & Torres, 2000).

It is not particularly surprising that this work has not factored into U.S. policy debates on pedagogical method, given the continued sublimation of social class analysis in literacy research, despite the extensive and continued sociological research on the impact of class on school achievement since Coleman. Likewise, much of the literature on multiculturalism tends to treat all multilingual "ethnicities" of a piece, without due attention to social class, location, and history. It is impossible to understand relative socioeconomic power and networks of, for example, diasporic Chinese communities without an analysis of class and economic globalisation that, for many of these communities, began over 100 years ago (Luke & Luke, 1999). In the face of the new social facts of diversity and difference, I here want to ask how it is that, in countries like the United States, United Kingdom, and Australia (each with over a quarter of their population non-English-speaking in background), literacy and language education continues to routinely categorise the multilingual subject as "Other," as afterthought, exception, anomaly, and "lack." Because of the Treaty of Watangi, New Zealand is a remarkable exception, where all educational and language policy and intervention is responsible for addressing indigenous language and cultural rights (McNaughton, 2002).

On a related subject, I want to ask what is missing from the current debates over scientific approaches to reading, especially to the degree to which their affiliated funding and policy agendas have direct impact on these same marginal communities. Do the current debates around method, alphabetics, and phonics become a de facto strategy, regardless of researcher good faith and scientific intent, for further deferring the *lingua franca* and the curriculum questions above? If they do not, then we must ask how they address and frame the multilingual subject.

What is needed is an historical and sociological perspective on literacy and educational policy in multilingual societies. Here I want to build a case for a broader language and literacy in education approach to policy that draws upon rich sociological, ethnographic, and economic evidence about emergent literacies, economies, and cultural practices across increasingly multilingual communities and stratified educational systems. In so doing, I draw from the work of Pierre Bourdieu (1991, 1998) to argue that we need a rigorous sociological, demographic, and economic analysis of how literacy makes a difference in communities and institutions in relation to other forms of available economic and social capital.

Literacy, Nation, Globalisation

The linguistic, cultural, and educational calculus of European and Asian colonialism was inescapably simple: One nation = one race = one language (Hall, 1992; Willinsky, 1998; Young, 1995). To this, Benedict Anderson's (1991) *Imagined Communities* adds one further element to the equation: "print capitalism" as a core component of the modern nation state. A common stock of literate practices has been crucial for the building of national culture and identity. Universal print literacy has been a widely documented precursor for the expansion, distribution, and consolidation of capital, though obviously not in equitable ways.

Since its initiation in Reformation Germany, the official governmental support for universal literacy via mass public schooling has been, as well, a push towards linguistic and cultural homogeneity, and via the selective traditions of schooling, towards political and social hegemony. In instances, literacy education has been remoulded by governments to accommodate and facilitate linguistic and cultural diversity and, indeed, to enable the progressive or revolutionary redistribution of power and capital. Numerous postcolonial literacy campaigns have shaped literacy education in ways that run counter to the simple assertion of colonial or imperial power, knowledge, and language relations (e.g., Arnove & Graff, 1987). In several postcolonial contexts in the Americas and Asia, literacy education has been redesigned for the economic enfranchisement of rural classes and for the extension of franchise and social participation to women and diasporic ethnic communities. Further, throughout Asia and the Pacific literacy education has been used as a postcolonial vehicle for language policies that promote cultural nationalism and solidarity and ethnic identity and essentialism. These policies tend to be based on the choice and, in instances, construction of an indigenous *lingua franca* such as Maori, Bahasa Indonesian, Bahasa Malay, or Putonghua (e.g., Kaplan & Baldauf, 1999).

Contrast this situation with current approaches and debates in economically and geopolitically focal countries like the United States and United Kingdom, where questions about literacy remain focused principally on pedagogic method and systems reform, seemingly divorced from larger issues of blended cultural identity, linguistic diversity, and economic enfranchisement. Government literacy policy, where it exists, has been deployed as an adjunct to the neoliberal rationalisation of schooling systems through the development and deployment of discourses of school-based management, "quality assurance," and accountability via standardised testing—often without any powerful normative positions on the social and cultural consequences of literacy.

Policy interventions are, by definition, synergistic and potentially countersynergistic in local effects, both across government silos (e.g., education, health, social welfare, urban planning, policing) and within a particular department or ministry such as education. That is, educational policies are never stand-alone phenomena. In order to be effective they must orchestrate a series of intertextual "embeddings" in relation to other extant educational and social policies.

How often, any policy analytic perspective on literacy must ask, do those who pursue "pure" and scientific literacy policy query the larger suite of systemic and strategic policy interventions and reforms incorporating any policy on literacy? State and national policies are divorced from the explicit development of larger language policies, which in turn (the extensive work in the field of language planning tells us) must be articulated in relation to other social policies (e.g., health, child care, employment, immigration). My point is that most advanced or "late" capitalist countries have proceeded to make literacy policy as if existing social contracts around literacy, cultural identity, and language rights have been reconciled and solved—even in the face of new waves of migrants, the facts of *majority* second-language populations in many educational jurisdictions, or the absence of treaty with indigenous peoples. At the same time, a further operational assumption is that literacy itself—its functions and uses—is a relatively stable phenomenon that can be assessed, transmitted, acquired, and used accordingly—even in the face of new digital multiliteracies and hybrid textual practices. Another assumption is that its initial acquisition has field-universal effects, regardless of the rules of exchange in particular linguistic markets and the relative availability and nonavailability of other forms of capital (e.g., social infrastructure, nondiscriminatory social institutions, meaningful and gainful labour)—even in the face of rapidly shifting "linguistic markets" driven by rapid economic change and restratification of material and discourse resources. All are broad assumptions about the contexts where language and literacy are acquired and used. To understand them and factor them into the planning of curriculum and instruction would require rigorous documentation of changing domains of use (e.g., "status planning"; Fishman, 1989), within which educationally acquired competence is actually negotiated, used, and, indeed, often lost.

To proceed without such planning is to assume, as many post-National Reading Panel federal and state policies in the United States have done, that there can indeed be free-standing pedagogical and psychological decisions around the official classification and framing of literacy as school knowledge independent of broader sociological, linguistic, and ethnographic analyses of the functions and uses of literacy in multilingual and, indeed, multiliterate societies increasingly characterised by cultural and linguistic diversity and dynamic, hybrid textual and semiotic systems, and volatile flows of capital and discourse. Such a position is sociologically and historically, indeed social scientifically, naïve. It is destined as well, from the public policy perspective I have described here, to have limited, accidental, and contradictory effects.

Of course, in some ways, we look to print literacy, face-to-face literacy education, and canonical cultural texts and genres as moral, epistemological, and political anchors in the face of socioeconomic change. The 20th-century shaping of literacy in industrial countries has entailed the institutional construction of literate workers, citizens, and consumers with a powerful desire and will towards capital via textual work (e.g., Gee, Hull, & Lankshear, 1997) and the establishment through education of a homogeneous linguistic and cultural nationalism (Luke, 1988; Shannon, 1987). Current conditions of economic and cultural globalisation, of transnational flows of capital, information, and bodies, make it extremely tempting to simply re-frame these industrial discourses for the production of literate workers into "new narratives of human capital" (Luke, 2000). But these new conditions also raise two new defining challenges to literacy education.

First, postindustrial nation states of the North and West are increasingly built on what we could term semiotic economies. For many, labour in these societies has become increasingly service- and information-based, with an increasing proportion of the overall employment (and consumption) via text work. This type of work requires cognitive engagement and social interaction around spoken language, traditional print texts and records, and digital and online communications. Whether workers are involved in knowledge constituent, symbolic analyst roles or as new proletarian end users, automaticity and innovative capacity with a range of linguistic, semiotic, digital, and analogue codes make gainful and willful participation in economic fields tighter, more complex, and, across one's life trajectory, more volatile than in industrial economies of the last two centuries. In the emergent industrial and transitional peasant economies in postcolonial countries, the principal laboring classes did not engage in such wholly language-dependent or text-saturated labour. If class stratification is contingent on access to material and discourse resources and if access to different kinds and levels of print literacy (*qua* cultural capital) is a major regulatory gatekeeper in "print capitalist" societies, that mix becomes complicated, more volatile, and releveled by the emergence of digital literacies. How these new blends of knowledge, skill, and identity count in economies in transition is a pressing empirical question with which governments and educational planners are struggling.

Second, these same societies have become increasingly multilingual and multicultural in population demographics and in the cultural and textual practices of everyday life. The social and demographic facts of cultural and linguistic diversity are inescapable both in English-dominant, postindustrial countries like the United States and United Kingdom, in the European Union countries described by Charles Berg earlier in this issue of *RRQ*, and in postcolonial countries in East and West Asia, Africa, and the Middle East as well. Social structure in the North and West remains characterised by class stratification linked strongly to ethnic and religious and linguistic background, with indigenous and vernacular speakers, guest workers and refugees, and longstanding diasporic cultural minorities still struggling to gain access and power in mainstream economies and their text-based institutions. Any serious policy effort to alter or ameliorate these patterns may require something more than tinkering with industrial-era, monocultural school systems; token inclusion of ethnic content in mainstream curriculum; teacher consciousness raising; or the adjustment of classroom methods.

The problem, then, is this. The selection, codification, and differential transmission of a dominant set of literate and linguistic practices via institutions like schooling must contend with unprecedented and increasing diversity of background knowledge and competence, linguistic and cultural resources, available discourses and textual practices brought to and through classrooms and schools. (For a recent review of U.S. work, argued from a multiculturalist perspective, see Meecham, 2001; for a series of insightful U.K. studies on multilingualism and cultural diversity in U.K. contexts, see Gregory, 1997; for a very useful New Zealand-based introductory synthesis of sociocultural work, see McNaughton, 2002.) This situation is at least in part a challenge for the adjustment of curriculum and pedagogy; to a significant but not exclusive extent, questions of minority achievement fall within the ambit of educational policy and practices. At the same time, any educational system with democratic and egalitarian aspirations that go beyond the language/culture stratified production of literate workers must visibly enable multiple pathways and equitable access to the languages, texts, and discourses of power in these emergent semiotic economies and globalised cultures, where biographical lifelines through communities, workplaces, and civic institutions are taking risky, different patterns that governments and social scientists are struggling to document and understand. This is only partly within the capture of educational policies, systems, and practices, for the alteration and improvement of life pathways to and from educational institutions into other social and economic fields depend only in part on the contingent educational provision of literacy, whether conceived as print or digital, behaviour or practice. The use and value of literacy for learners—the available discourses, background knowledges, repertoires of practices and motivation structures for learning and using literacy—are as contingent on those extraeducational social relations and linguistic markets that they inhabit before, during, and after schooling.

Traditionally, reading researchers have framed this issue as one of transfer of training, a perennial empirical problem since Thorndike's time. But it is also a more complex sociological problem: how social subjects embody educationally acquired skill and competence and put them to work in variable social fields, in complex combinations of other kinds of available social, economic, and cultural resources, with differential payoffs in their life trajectories (Luke, 1996; Olneck, 2000). It is axiomatic in the literature on migrant language retention and language planning that, unless powerful functional domains for everyday practical language use in the target language exist, pedagogical efforts to maintain, preserve, or retain language will be less than effective. It has been a salutary lesson since the United Nations World Experimental Literacy Program that the effectiveness of pedagogical delivery is contingent on its ready deployment in functional, powerful, and necessary everyday domains of use (Arnove & Graff, 1987). In order to build effective literacy programs to respond to the *lingua franca* and the curriculum questions, we cannot simply focus narrowly on what experimental research on variable pedagogic method tells us. The achievement of automaticity of skill cannot be the sole or driving focus of a language and literacy-in-education policy. We need a rigorous understanding of the places and spaces; the "social fields" and "linguistic markets" (Bourdieu, 1991); the zones of sociocultural and political power where language and literacy are acquired and used, gained and lost outside of schools.

Towards a Sociological Analysis of Literacy as Capital

In multilingual societies, specific modes and genres of linguistic and literate practice constitute forms of cultural capital with variable and field-specific exchange value. But they never have freestanding effects independent of the availability and use of other forms of economic, social, and cultural capital. The work of the late French sociologist Pierre Bourdieu (1989, 1991, 1998) provides a template for the analysis of class-based available resources in communities and institutions. He argued that human subjects' trajectories take them through a range of institutional fields that shape their discourse and linguistic resources. Each of these fields forms a distinctive linguistic market. Students bear acquired, embodied, and structured "dispositions"— the sum total of their skills, competences, and knowledges—into these fields, where they are valued and exchanged. By this account, community culture, ethnicity, race, gender, and identity are embodied in a social class-based "habitus." Forces and relations within the field position each habitus in particular relations of power and status, and individuals can actively "position take" in such fields (Bourdieu, 1998), attempting to alter their positions, relative power, and the rules of exchange within them.

To illustrate, a Torres Strait Islander girl might enter Thursday Island Primary School (in a remote indigenous Islander community off Australia's northern coast) with trilingual linguistic competence (typically one of three vernaculars, plus Torres Strait Creole and English) but limited early print knowledge (embodied capital), access to family networks and community infrastructure (social capital), and limited family material wealth (economic capital). The state school, operating as a mainstream Australian institution, endeavours to exchange and transform her capital into other forms of cultural capital. This would set up optimal zones and environments for the conversion through social relations and linguistic interaction for the student to further develop English-language reading and speech. She would then transform this into a visible portfolio of artefacts of writing and other literate practice as demonstration of competence (objectified capital) and degrees/diplomas/grades (institutional capital) that might enhance her traverse through both Islander community life and mainstream Australian and Queensland institutions and economies. These in turn are re/mediated and exchanged in other institutional settings (other educational organisations, communities local and "glocal," face-to-face and virtual, workplaces) with differential field-specific cachet (Luke & Carrington, 2002). Some of these institutions will be more friendly and welcoming than others in terms of the ways they structurally position and enable Islander women.

To make inclusive and enabling educational policies for multilingual societies, we must see and know and understand as much as possible about the totality and interrelationships of social fields and linguistic markets and of people's lateral traverse of them. I have here tabled a somewhat different perspective on the various pedagogical and technical solutions on offer in the current version of the "great debate" on reading, literacy, and education. The game has changed. Even the baseline discourses and tenets of multiculturalism, as it struggles to become policy in the face of backlash, have been destablised by cultural and economic globalisation. The research and policy questions about language and literacy in multilingual societies are now about language and literacy in globalised economies. At the same time, the persistent questions of local language maintenance and the hegemony of English and other dominant languages are no longer, if they ever were, solely juridical matters of nation states, regions, or regional educational authorities. They too are embedded in the complex fields of multinational economies, flows of human subjects, globalising media, and their attendant world cultures. Finally, the actual populations and communities have shifted in ways that make minority-majority distinctions at the least locally variable and unstable.

The continuing parochialism of literacy research debates may be in their viewing of the problem in now traditional dichotomies that oscillate between neodeficit, neoliberal models of minority failure and liberal, romantic models of minority voice and linguistic rights and between narrow technocratic skills approaches and child-centred, progressivist pedagogies. There must be a more sociologically trenchant way of theorising and studying linguistic minorities and literacy in multilingual societies. If we are serious about building the kinds of literacy that will have visible and transformative impacts on communities' futures and life pathways, this must involve a more complex analysis of the availability and flows of capital in globalised and globalising economic contexts of localities, regions, and states.

In these contexts of global flows, it should not be surprising that language and literacy education are explicitly political matters. In the current U.S. context, this is usually meant in the pejorative sense that somehow literacy education is political because of unwarranted and conspiratorial interference of elected officials or state governments. But it was Freire's (1970) initial point that literacy is political, inasmuch as its use and deployment are acts of power in complex political economies where language, literacy, and affiliated systems of representation are used for purposes of economic and social power. If we take literacy and literacy education to be political in this sense, the imperative would be to develop strategies—whole-school, classroom-based pedagogic strategies—curriculum selective traditions, and literacy and language education policies that sit well and dovetail with other kinds of overarching state strategies, interventions, and schooling policies to concentrate and coordinate discourse, material, and human resources. The lesson of the Bourdieu model is that just fixing pedagogy one way or another might be necessary but is never sufficient for such a difference to be made. The consequences of literacy—and its ever present radical potential for altering life pathways and inequitable access to discourse, knowledge, and power—depend at least in part on the availability of other kinds of capital—social, economic, and symbolic—both within the school and across other social fields.

By accepting as scientific fact that the pedagogic delivery of basic skill with automaticity is the bare and baseline solution, we leave educational research, school systems, and teaching professionals vulnerable to the most sophisticated form of victim blaming in social policy: where governments and systems and public and private sectors make available to community ineffective or dysfunctional combinations of capital. It is all too easy for systems to deliver, for example, economic capital in the form of social welfare or charity but not jobs or education, education but not health or jobs, jobs but no welfare and health infrastructure. In the case of Australian indigenous communities, it is easy to deliver education and, indeed, alphabetics on the one hand while running policies that actually accelerate the deterioration of the communities' kinship structure, traditional values, and forms of work, private sector investment, and community social infrastructure on the other.

In such scenarios, indigenous communities, linguistic minorities, diasporic communities, and others are often blamed for having squandered or abused government "handouts" and other resources made available.

A research agenda that focuses on the relationships between language and other forms of capital in social fields opens the fields of research and policymaking. We can focus on how schools shape variable repertoires of practices with specific texts and discourses that have potential combinatory power with other kinds of capital available in students' lived communities. This means that shaping a selective tradition is done optimally with an eye on the changing social fields where students live and work. It also means that the redefined function of governments (and other non-government organisations, as well as private sector, traditional, and community bodies) is to provide access to combinatory forms of enabling capital that enhance students' possibilities of putting the kinds of practices, texts, and discourses acquired in schools to work in consequential ways that enable active position taking in social fields. These ways should enable some control on the part of these people over the shapes of their life pathways and, ultimately, over the shapes and rules of exchange of the places where they will put their cultural capital to work.

Hence, a new set of questions for literacy research in multilingual communities might underpin language and literacy-in-education policy:

> Which linguistic competences, discourses and textual resources, and multiliteracies are accessible? How, in what blended and separate domains and to what ends, are different languages used? How do people use languages, texts, discourses, and literacies as convertible and transformative resources in homes, communities, and schools?
>
> How are these resources recognised and misrecognised, re-mediated and converted in school-based literacy instruction?
>
> How are these resources taken into communities and recombined with other kinds of social, economic, and ecological capital in consequential ways in which social fields and linguistic markets? Which children's and adolescents' pathways through and across social fields will be affected?
>
> How can government policies, including (but not exclusively) language, literacy, and educational policy, be coordinated to enable the "just in time" access and delivery of the requisite kinds of educationally acquired capital, health and social resources, jobs, and work to enhance communities and individuals' lives?

Such an agenda need not be restricted to ethnographic, discourse analytic, observational, and other forms of case-based research—a great deal of which is in hand. Powerful forms of social statistical analysis, and a rigorous modelling of how multiple sociodemographic factors and available capital optimise literate cultural capital as a convertible resource, are crucial. These would be needed for cross-government and locally effective social policy development.

For a simpler universe and science of literacy it would, indeed, be easier if we had verifiable evidence of decontextualised skills that could be inculcated (with precision and alacrity and at reasonable economies of scale); acquired with automaticity by all; and then predictably redeployed regardless of the demands, rules of exchange, linguistic norms, and symbolic power available in any and every social field. This has been the object of 100 years of reading research. The caveat here is that such a science provides a very small and highly contingent part of a larger evidence base about language, about literacy, and about the life worlds where they are won and lost.

While the Bourdieu model underlines the sociological contingency of literacy practice, it also provides new grounds for analysing the intrapsychological contingency and locality of practice. Literate practice is situated, constructed, and intrapsychologically negotiated through an (artificial) social field called the school, with rules of exchange denoted in scaffolded social activities around particular selected texts. But any acquired skills, whether basic or higher order, are reconstituted and remediated in relation to variable fields of power and practice in the larger community. These, indeed, constitute political economies (see work by Engestrom and colleagues at the Centre for Activity Theory and Developmental Work Research: www.edu.Helsinki.fi/activity/).

A science of literacy education that restricts itself to the efficacy of classroom method and that attempts to control against the variance of these economies and cultures is, indeed, a naïve science—at best decontextualised, at worst part of a long ideological effort to remove reading and literacy forcefully from its complex social, cultural, and economic contexts. To move forward both in research and policy towards a more inclusive literacy in multilingual societies is a task that will require broader, more complex forms of social science, not reductionist ones.

REFERENCES

Alvermann, D.E. (Ed.). (2002). *Adolescents and literacies in a digital world*. New York: Peter Lang.

Alvermann, D.E., Moon, J.S., & Hagood, M.C. (1999). *Popular culture in the classroom: Teaching and researching critical media literacy*. Newark, DE: International Reading Association; Chicago: National Reading Conference.

Anderson, B. (1991). *Imagined communities* (2nd ed.). Minneapolis: University of Minnesota Press.

Arnove, R., & Graff, H.J. (Eds.). (1987). *National literacy campaigns: Historical and comparative perspectives.* New York: Plenum.

Barton, D., Hamilton, M., & Ivanic, R. (Eds.). (1999). *Situated literacies.* London: Routledge.

Bourdieu, P. (1989). Social space and symbolic power. *Sociological Theory, 7,* 14–25.

Bourdieu, P. (1991). *Language and symbolic power.* Cambridge, MA: Harvard University Press.

Bourdieu, P. (1998). *Practical reason: On the theory of action.* London: Polity Press.

Buckingham, D., & Sefton-Green, J. (1994). *Cultural studies goes to school.* London: Taylor & Francis.

Burbules, N., & Torres, C.A. (Eds.). (2000). *Globalisation and education.* New York: Routledge.

Castells, M. (1996). *Rise of the network society.* Cambridge, UK: Blackwell.

Cazden, C.B., Johns, V., & Hymes, D. (Eds.). (1972). *Functions of language in the classroom.* New York: Teachers College Press.

Comber, B., & Thompson, P. (with Wells, M.). (2001). Critical literacy finds a "place": Writing and social action in a neighbourhood school. *The Elementary School Journal, 101,* 451–464.

Cunningham, J.W. (2001). Essay book review: The National Reading Panel Report. *Reading Research Quarterly, 36,* 326–345.

Dyson, A.H. (1997). *Writing superheroes: Contemporary childhood, popular culture, and classroom literacy.* New York: Teachers College Press.

Fishman, J.A. (1989). *Language and ethnicity in minority sociolinguistic perspective.* Clevedon, UK: Multilingual Matters.

Foley, D.A., Levison, B.A., & Hurtig, J. (2001). Anthropology goes inside: The new educational ethnography of ethnicity and gender. *Review of Research in Education, 25,* 37–98.

Freire, P. (1970). *Pedagogy of the oppressed.* New York: Seabury.

Gee, J.P., Hull, G., & Lankshear, C. (1997). *The new work order.* Boulder, CO: Westview.

Goldstein, T. (1997). *Two languages at work: Bilingual life on the production floor.* Berlin: Mouton de Gruyter.

Gregory, E. (Ed.). (1997). *One child, many worlds: Early learning in multicultural communities.* New York: Teachers College Press.

Hall, S. (1992). Culture, community, nation. *Cultural Studies, 7,* 349–363.

Harvey, D. (2000). *Spaces of hope.* Edinburgh, Scotland: Edinburgh University Press.

Hull, G. (Ed.). (1997). *Changing work, changing literacies.* Albany: State University of New York Press.

Hymes, D. (1996). *Ethnography, linguistics, narrative inequality.* London: Taylor & Francis.

Janmohamed, A.R., & Lloyd, D. (1990). *The nature and context of minority discourses.* Oxford, UK: Oxford University Press.

Kaplan, R.B., & Baldauf, R.B. (1999). *Language planning: From practice to theory.* Clevedon, UK: Multilingual Matters.

Lin, A.M.Y., Wang, W., Akamatsu, N., & Riazi, A.M. (in press). Appropriating English, expanding identities, and re-visioning the field: From TESOL to teaching English for glocalized communication. *Journal of Language, Identity and Education.*

Luke, A. (1988). *Literacy, textbooks and ideology.* London: Falmer.

Luke, A. (1996). Genres of power? In R. Hasan & G. Williams (Eds.), *Literacy in power* (pp. 308–338). London: Longman.

Luke, A. (1997). The material effects of the word: Apologies, stolen children and public speech. *Discourse, 23,* 151–180.

Luke, A. (2000). New narratives of human capital. In S. Ball (Ed.), *Sociology of education: Major themes. Vol. 4: Policies and politics* (pp. 326-340). London: Routledge.

Luke, A., & Carrington, V. (2002). Globalisation, literacy, curriculum practice. In R. Fisher, M. Lewis, & G. Brooks (Eds.), *Language and literacy in action* (pp. 231-250). London: Routledge/Falmer.

Luke, A., Land, R., Christie, P., & Kolatsis, A. (in press). *Standard Australian English and language education for Aboriginal and Torres Strait Islander students.* Brisbane, QLD, Australia: Indigenous Education Consultative Board.

Luke, C., & Luke, A. (1999) Theorising interracial families and hybrid identity: An Australian perspective. *Educational Theory, 49,* 223-249.

May, S. (2001). *Language and minority rights.* London: Longman.

McNaughton, S. (2002). *Meeting of minds.* Wellington, New Zealand: Learning Media.

Meecham, S.J. (2001). Literacy at the crossroads: Movement, connection and communication within the research literature on literacy and cultural diversity. *Review of Research in Education, 25,* 181-208.

Miller, J. (in press). *Audible difference.* Clevedon, UK: Multilingual Matters.

Moje, E.B. (2000). "To be part of the story": The literacy practices of "gangsta" adolescents. *Teachers College Record, 102,* 652-690.

Norton, B. (1999). *Language and identity.* London: Longman.

Norton, B., & Toohey, K. (in press). *Critical pedagogies and language learning.* Cambridge, UK: Cambridge University Press.

Olneck, M. (2000). Can multicultural education change what counts as cultural capital? *American Educational Research Journal, 37,* 317-348.

Pavlenko, A., Blackledge, A., Piller, I., & Teutsch-Dwyer, M. (Eds.). (2001). *Multilingualism, second language learning and gender.* Berlin: Mouton de Gruyter.

Pennycook, A. (1996). *The cultural politics of English as an international language.* London: Longman.

Pennycook, A. (1998). *English and the discourses of colonialism.* New York: Routledge.

Pennycook, A. (2001). *Critical applied linguistics: A critical introduction.* Mahwah, NJ: Erlbaum.

Shannon, P. (1987). *Broken promises: Reading instruction in Twentieth-Century America.* South Hadley, MA: Bergin & Garvey.

Toohey, K. (2000). *Learning English at school.* Clevedon, UK: Multilingual Matters.

Willinsky, J. (1998). *Learning to divide the world: Education at empire's end.* Minneapolis: University of Minnesota Press.

Young, R.J.C. (1995). *Colonial desire: Hybridity in theory, culture, and race.* New York: Routledge.

Conclusion: The Policy Culture of Reading Education and Research: Places We Might Go

Jacqueline Edmondson

The diverse views on policy presented by authors across these articles demonstrate important aspects of policy research and study in literacy education that span three general categories: policy-driven research, policy communications research, and critical policy research. In part, the efforts of researchers that cross these categories show the priority that policy study has assumed in the field of reading, opening much-needed possibilities for discussion and debate concerning the politics of reading education (see Shannon, 1991).

Across the articles in the section on policy-driven research, there is evidence of experiments and program evaluations whereby researchers have sought out empirically based answers to complex problems facing reading educators. This research is typically aligned with the definitions and problems offered by policymakers, and effort is made to confirm or disconfirm solutions to policy problems. Such research seeks out objective, law-like generalizations that can be readily used by policymakers, educators, and the general public.

Policy communications research acknowledges the political aspects of literacy problems, and it recognizes that there are differences in approaches and solutions to policy problems. Policy communications researchers offer opportunities for reading researchers and educators to understand these differences as the need for quality research, and participation in the policy process is emphasized. Proposed solutions to communications research typically suggest a change in discourse for one group, usually leaving the initial assumptions and definitions of the policy proposal intact.

Critical policy study moves away from the functionalist assumptions of policy-driven and policy communications research to immanent critiques of why things are the way they are. Critical policy study begins with a different set of assumptions than functionalist study. First is an understanding that educational policy is historical and political, and it always involves values and relations of power. As such, there is a belief that policy negotiations are not constructed among equals because "social, economic, and political circumstances have given certain segments of society license to assert greater influence over the outcomes" (Shannon, 1991, p. 164). Because of this inequality, critical policy analysts tend to ask questions of policy that illuminate inequalities and injustices, particularly as these questions lead them to expose contradictions. This questioning, in turn, allows policy analysts to strategically advocate for change for teachers and students. Such study considers what policies offer as well as what they deny and, in turn, allows those who study policy to engage in strategic advocacy for change.

The research that spans the categories in this volume gives us a glimpse into the policy culture of reading research and education at this particular point in time. Studying this culture involves understanding the shared and cumulative values, beliefs, understandings, and artifacts that a group holds in common. Yet, using such a classification scheme or framework can be dangerous because such categories are never complete; instead, there are always questions and areas that are omitted. More than a decade ago, Shannon (1991) noted that "we have few sophisticated answers to even the most basic policy questions that could be posed about federal, state, and citizen influences on the organization and process of reading instruction" (p. 159). He raised important questions that still remain largely unanswered today. Specifically, Shannon asked who the policy insiders were and why they had particular influence, why reading policies had attention from policymakers, which agencies and organizations held sway over policy, and what the consequences of reading policies might be for teachers, students, and researchers. In particular, it seems beneficial if we understand more fully the role of local, state, and federal governments, the workings of professional organizations in relation to policy, and the possibilities that exist for literacy researchers and educators as we consider international governments and transnational organizations such as the United Nations. As we broaden our inquiries in policy, the cultural aspects of the ways meanings and our lives are shaped through, by, and with these groups are essential. As reading educators, we need policy research that helps to untangle these influences and, in turn, provide possible direction for researchers and educators who hope to understand and participate in policy. In part, such research could help reading educators to be proactive in the creation of policy, rather than reactive to policies and legislation that have already been enacted. It also seems that such research could work to open policy research to participation from many individuals and groups so that policy is more representative of those it is intended to serve.

The aspects of policy not considered in this volume can be extended by turning toward cultural theories, particularly the critical work of researchers Miller and Yúdice (2002), who suggest that culture is connected to policy through two overlapping registers: (1) the aesthetic, which involves decisions about agreeableness, and (2) the anthropological, which concerns choices about the ways in which we hope to live together. Policy study can reveal important aspects of a culture by illuminating the values, beliefs, and ideologies inherent in and missing from policy texts and contexts. While the pieces in this volume demonstrate in part the importance of policy in the reading education and research community, this final chapter suggests some of the "places we can go" in order to further the depth and breadth of work that can be done in reading policy. To begin, we will consider some of the aesthetic aspects of policy study.

Aesthetic Judgments and Creativity

Aesthetic judgments are not often associated with policy study, as many who study policy consider it and questions of governance to concern social sciences rather than the arts (see Foucault, 2000). Yet aesthetics necessarily involve judgments about what is acceptable or agreeable among or across groups of people, embracing a kind of ambiguity that is not easily mapped out or defined in prescriptive ways. Policy is located in a similar space where circumstances and conditions of policy development and implementation are not always well-defined or clear, and decisions must be made concerning purposes, interpretations, and uses of policy. In other words, policy texts, like literary texts, have indeterminancies or gaps that must be filled and interpreted (see Iser, 1978, 2000) by those reading, implementing, and studying policy. Such interpretation requires judgments that rely in part on readers' repertoires of familiar themes and allusions that policies contain. For example, former U.S. President Bill Clinton's America Reads policy relied on a theme ("all children must read well and independently by the end of the third grade") as well as specific uses of language, including metaphors such as "an army of volunteers" (see Edmondson, 1998). Reading researchers have often examined the themes and language of policy, although arguably more work can be done in this area (see Woodside-Jiron, 2004). Yet, there are aspects of policy study that extend beyond language that need to be taken into consideration as well. Two areas in particular seem to be worth mentioning here as possible ways to extend our work in relation to literacy policy study: (1) the use and impact of images and (2) the creation and maintenance of organic laws that govern our behavior.

Images

Political scientist Murry Edelman noted the importance of studying images in relation to policy. He explained, "Images are a major influence on social change and almost always act as a conservative force.... Images then, rather than meticulous descriptions, become the currency in which we think about and mutually negotiate changes in the world we inhabit" (2001, pp. 11–12). By "images," Edelman is referring to icons, or pictures that reflect ideas; indices, or terms that lead the mind in a particular direction; and symbols, which help us to realize the potentialities in a particular situation. Along with the image, study of the particular purposes and uses of the image also is needed. In other words, image can assume primacy in the promotion of policy, and when the image is tied up with messages about money, there can be particularly powerful influences. As one example, early reports of the No Child Left Behind (NCLB) policy demonstrated the combined influence of the image of money as people uncritically accepted the indices (or slogan) of the policy along with the accompanying reports of record spending on education from the federal government. Who could argue with a policy titled "No Child Left Behind," particularly when it came with promises of unprecedented federal spending in public education? Few people questioned what the image of "no child left behind" meant, and few among the media or the popular press seriously questioned how or where the supposed increases in money would be spent (for example, on testing and prepackaged reading curricula). For some people, the image is all that is known and all that matters.

Because of the important role that images play in brokering meanings, our policy work in reading education can be extended through consideration and analysis of images that dominate reading policies. Official policies are typically accompanied by a variety of images: two children reading *The Little Engine That Could* on the steps of the Bacon Memorial Library in Wyandotte, Michigan, USA, as the Clinton administration announced the America Reads program (see Shannon, 1998); the U.S. flag with the child's silhouette that is emblazoned on NCLB information from the federal government; the African American child's face on the cover of *Put Reading First: The Research Building Blocks for Teaching Children to Read*, a publication funded by the National Institute for Literacy; the school house and ABCs on the cover of the National Reading Panel report (National Institute of Child Health and Human Development [NICHD], 2000); and the charts and graphs reporting National Assessment of Educational Progress scores or the achievement gap, to name a few. In considering these images, we also need to attend to those that have been displaced. For example, we could consider the changes in the images on webpages at the U.S. Department of Education as administrations change. Why are some images removed while others remain? Who decides this? What meanings are conveyed?

Images contribute in part to our policy interpretations, helping to fill gaps in the policy text. Studying the images that accompany policy helps us to analyze the values, meanings, and ideologies of policy authors. Without a consideration of the fullness of these expressions, our understandings and analyses of policies risk being incomplete.

Organic Laws

Policies and their interpretations educate individuals and groups into particular "sets of tastes" or "public sense" (Miller & Yúdice, 2002). Philosopher Immanuel Kant suggested that tastes are conformity to the law without the law, in part functioning to create "organic laws" (see Marx, 1852/1963) that mark what is acceptable and what is not in a given culture. To extend our understandings of policy in reading research and education, we can turn our attention to those aspects of our lives that are taken for granted yet work simultaneously to disseminate information and understandings that contribute to our collective public sense.

As one example, in contemporary U.S. society, such collective sensibility is found through the organization of professional conferences (see Johnston & Spiro, 1990, for an explanation of how some conferences have been created). Reading educators who seek out ways to improve their teaching and knowledge turn to professional conferences for information and networking with other educators. The 2004 International Reading Association (IRA) Annual Convention in Reno, Nevada, USA, for example, had more than 20,000 educators in attendance, and none were ordered by law to attend. Although some educators may have been required by their states to earn continuing professional development credits, they likely had a variety of ways to fulfill the requirement. It also seems safe to wager that all educators in attendance at the conference expected they were engaging in acceptable and expected professional behavior. By attending this conference and others like it, reading educators can gain access to current knowledge and information in the field of reading, contributing to the reading community's consciousness of itself.

Throughout convention programs there are examples of policy work that crosses the categories of this book, offering explanations of the current state of affairs and asking critical questions. This work provides opportunities for conference attendees to develop shared language and communication with others in the field. However, such conferences and our participation in them should not go without question:

Who attends? Who does not? Why?

Who speaks? Who does not? Why?

Who advertises? What is advertised? Why?

Who gets paid? Who does not? Why? (see Johnston & Spiro, 1990, for consideration of some of these questions)

The structures of professional organizations that shape this collective consciousness are similar to others we find in contemporary society. Sessions at conferences sometimes resemble lectures held in university classrooms, town hall meetings, or even sales meetings. The organization and hierarchy of professional organizations resemble government structures, with elected governing bodies and committees. Sociologist Max Weber warned of the ways in which institutions that are affiliated become aligned in organization and values as bureaucracy and rationalization combine to direct individuals' lives. Through our professional organizations, we see the influences of schools and universities, government, and business. Through these influences, there are ideological state apparatuses (see Althusser, 1971) whereby institutions, particularly as they become aligned, enforce ideologies and sets of beliefs that people internalize. What ideologies and beliefs are forwarded through our professional organizations? Which are omitted?

Of course, Weber, along with other sociologists, recognized that people resist and work to change these institutions and society. Yet there has been little reading policy research to examine the ways in which institutions, including government, business, schools, universities, and professional groups, are aligned in organization, thought, and deed, and how these organizations influence our understandings as well as policy. There has likewise been little reading policy research that focuses on the organic laws that govern our behavior as members of a professional community. These organic laws and the corresponding habitus (Bourdieu, 1991) they endorse can be studied with careful attention to and questioning of the practices, thoughts, tastes, choices, structures, and ideas we most often take for granted. Jo Michelle Beld Fraatz (1987) and others who study the anthropological aspects of literacy have considered organic aspects of literacy education (see Street, 1995), but few have studied these anthropological questions directly in relation to literacy policies. To do so would be to ask probing questions about the ways in which our lives and understandings are ordered and why. Certainly power relations and hegemony shape these determinations of collective acceptability. Consequently, policies and practices need to be questioned and critically engaged so that we can better understand the influences, both subtle and overt, on our lives.

Beyond aesthetic judgments concerning interpretation and agreeableness, creativity is an essential element of policy study. In other words, we need to engage policy in part like artists, to "turn our world on end so we can see what we sometimes take for granted from new angles" (Bean & Konopak, as cited in Edmondson, 2000, p. ix). In this way, policy study is not just a science, it is an aesthetic engagement that leads to understandings and questions about why things are the way they are. This seems to be an area that needs further exploration among reading researchers that will lead to different understandings of the ways in which we might live and work together, the focus of the next section.

Collective Ways of Life

Because policies are regulative statements that can shape the ways we live together, involving people and consequences that are far-reaching, we need to consider carefully the anthropological implications they hold for collective ways of life. In part, these considerations have implications for governance and require some articulation of the roles and responsibilities of researchers, educators, and governments in relation to literacy education and research.

Government deals with both people and things (Foucault, 2000). Because of this, our approach to the study of policy, which includes governance, needs to engage some degree of skepticism about the relationship between rhetoric and policy practice (Miller & Yúdice, 2002) as we explore how policy, in turn, relates to both people and things.

Researchers and Educators

As Shannon wrote in the introduction to this volume, diversity of values in policy research increases the likelihood that policies will be more comprehensive and representative. There is no phantom objectivity (Lukács, 1971) in policy research, no way to fully conceal the fundamental nature of the relationship between people and the ways in which policy serves to direct those relationships. Nor should there be. People ask particular questions, engage particular problems, and arrive at particular solutions, all of which are based on their ideological, ontological, and epistemological understandings, experiences, and judgments.

Because ultimately it is people who make decisions concerning policy, as an education community we can work together to secure a moral commitment that will ensure that reading policies will benefit the community rather than harm it. Such a commitment would allow us to weigh our actions in light of benefits that are not just for us and those like us, but for the sake of all and with the broader commitment of enlarging the possibilities of freedom for all. We can delineate our own rules, but we need to do so with more inclusive notions of communities in mind.

Local and State Governments

Questions concerning the roles of local and state governments could be addressed more fully in reading policy research. Certainly, local and state governments serve important functions as they interpret federal law in relation to the structures, values, and conditions at the state level. Because education has traditionally been viewed as a state and local responsibility, and because the federal government by law has no direct role in public education, state and local entities can serve an important role in mediating between local needs and state and federal policies directed toward those needs.

In Pennsylvania, we have witnessed the ways in which a change in state administration has effected changes in education policy. In one case, the administrative change opened possibilities for federal grant monies to be disseminated to a rural school district formerly denied Reading First funds. The district was originally deemed ineligible for the grant monies because the former administration did not recognize the Ohio State Literacy framework to be "scientifically based" in spite of gains the district observed structuring curriculum around this framework. Instead, the district was told to purchase a prepackaged curriculum, and recommendations about which packages to buy were offered. Then, a new administration assumed office a few months after the original denial, and the district, without changing a word of its original proposal, was awarded approximately $2.5 million over a six-year period (Edmondson & Shannon, 2003).

Throughout the United States, there are states and local groups organizing responses to inequities and shortcomings of the NCLB Act (see Goodman, Shannon, Goodman, & Rapoport, 2004). Orfield (2004) reports that 20 states have taken steps in opposition to the law. Utah's Republican-dominated house voted 64 to 8 in favor of a law forbidding the state to spend its own money on the NCLB requirements. In Virginia, the Republican-dominated legislature voted 98 to 1 in favor of a resolution that calls on Congress to exempt the state from the law. Vermont passed legislation similar to Utah. Ohio and Minnesota have offered estimates of the millions of dollars needed to implement the unfunded mandates of the law (see Hoff, 2004). States and local groups do have power, and, as reading educators, it is important for us to understand the ways in which these groups organize and work to influence policy and reading education.

Federal Governments

In the United States, research in relation to reading policies has primarily been reactive, as educators study already existing policies to endorse them or critique them. Professional organizations offer position statements to explain a particular stance in favor of or opposition to federal policy. Yet, little work has been done to propose roles for the federal government to play in reading education and research. To do so would shift our relationship from one of service to the federal government toward a position in which we expect the federal government to represent and serve educators, researchers, and children. In other words, rather than Congress forming reading panels and articulating the charge to the panel (see NICHD, 2000), we could engage research and advocacy that would shift this role to one in which the reading education community would propose what is needed to representatives and senators.

Another area that needs to be explored further is how various governments are aligned in their efforts to ensure literacy among their various citizenries. What influence do policies in different countries have on one another? The United Kingdom's National Literacy Strategy has been controversial because of the heightened and prescriptive role the government assumed in this policy (see Fisher, 2000; Kelly, 2002; and Thorton, 2002, to consider some of this debate). Basically, the National Literacy Strategy delineates standards and practices along with teacher training in order for children to "leave school equipped to enter a fulfilling adult life" (Blunkett, 1998, n.p.). The "literacy hour" is central to the policy, and the National Literacy Strategy suggests the hour be spent in the following way: 15 minutes whole class (shared text work); 15 minutes whole class (focused word work or sentence work); 20 minutes group and independent work (independent and guided reading); 10 minutes whole class (reviewing, reflecting, consolidating teaching points). The content and debate surrounding this policy have many similarities and parallels with trends in the United States, Australia, and elsewhere. Yet, as a field, we have done very little to study trends across governments and institutions internationally.

There are new opportunities in the field to develop discussions around these international policy trends, and it seems to be important to use these opportunities to discuss policy research and issues. *Reading Research Quarterly* added an International Reports on Literacy Research column to its journal beginning with the first issue in 2003. This column, in addition to international journals such as *Thinking Classroom/Peremena*, could serve important roles in opening possibilities for more comparative policy research. Engaging such research will give us a broader perspective and help us to recognize larger trends in the field as they relate to other policy areas (including economics), and potentially such study may offer ideas for different possibilities for policy research and education.

Transnational Organizations

Transnational cultural policies in relation to reading and literacy are another area that can be engaged as we conduct policy research in reading education. Transnational organizations, including the United Nations (UN), have policy statements concerning literacy, and such statements contribute to broader understandings of what literacy is, can be, and should do. For example, a resolution adopted by the UN General Assembly on December 19, 2001, declared the 10-year period beginning January 1, 2003, the United Nations Literacy Decade. As reading educators and researchers, what implications does such policy hold, if any? Are such policies rhetorical, or are there practical and real effects from them? Who authors these policies and why? Who benefits?

Literacy policies from transnational organizations are certainly not a new phenomenon. The Sixth Assembly of the League of Nations, later the UN, adopted a resolution in 1925 that "set out quite clearly the need for media policies that would deal with the propensity of citizens to act intemperately as a collectivity" (Miller & Yúdice, 2002, p. 165). Just 20 years later, the same organization passed a resolution urging freedom of information and the ability of citizens to gather news from a variety of sources. The implications of these resolutions within the context of world wars seem to be of considerable rhetorical import. Yet, little seems to be known about the consequences such resolutions hold in relation to federal and local governments and individuals' lives. Although we may have brief reports of United Nations Educational, Scientific, and Cultural Organization (UNESCO) policies in *Reading Today* (see "IRA and UNESCO Support," 2004, for one report on a literacy collaboration called "Reading for All" between UNESCO and IRA in African countries) and other publications, there currently is no critical cultural policy study of these efforts to understand the influences, values, and consequences such policies afford.

In addition to the UN, there are other transnational organizations that are concerned with literacy policies. The World Trade Organization (WTO) has been involved in telecommunications and cultural policies. The North American Free Trade Agreement (NAFTA) has sponsored museum exhibits such as *Splendors* and cultural programs such as MERCOSUR that some believe serve government interests and a broader trend toward cultural integration that is considered to be troubling (see Miller & Yúdice, 2002).

Similarly, discussions and debates about the European Union have implications for language and literacy educators.

The field of reading policy research would benefit from consideration of these transnational organizations and their policies. In part, such study would give different perspective to the work we are doing in local contexts and within the contexts of our respective cultures and countries. In addition, such policy study would allow us to seek out broader trends, contradictions, and more specific understandings of the ways in which power and hegemony influence policy. Further, these understandings might allow for the development of broader based coalitions focused on literacy that are informed by the research community. Some questions that might be asked include whether the U.S. has disproportionate influence on the content, form, and implementation of transnational literacy policies as some researchers contend (see Miller & Yúdice, 2002). If so, what should be done about this? As these policies become part of a transnational public discourse on literacy, what role should reading researchers in the U.S. and in other countries play in their formulation, implementation, and analysis? While such policies have existed for quite some time, this seems to be an area that needs considerably more attention if we are to fully grasp the implications of policy in today's society.

Conclusions

Although reading researchers have engaged in various forms of policy study, as evidenced in this volume, we believe that our research and work in policy have only skimmed the surface of what can and should be done in this field. We need to expand and extend the policy-driven, communication, and critical policy study described in this book to consider aesthetic and anthropological questions and concerns. Such critical cultural policy study can help us to understand how policies become internalized and direct the ways in which we live together (see Lewis & Miller, 2003, for an introduction to critical cultural policy studies). Through this policy study, we will likely find new meanings and roles as we work collectively with others around the world to ensure that literacy policies benefit and enrich people's lives. This work is most certainly political, disruptive, and contentious, and hardly for the faint of heart. Yet, if we are committed to helping people develop voices, interests, and expressions of preferences and tastes, and if we hope to facilitate the development of coalitions that span the globe in ways that will ultimately lead to a more equitable and just world, then engaging in literacy policy study through the examples in this book, the ideas in this conclusion, and the spaces and forums our professional publications, organizations, and institutions offer seems to be a necessary part of this process toward social change.

REFERENCES

Althusser, L. (1971). Ideology and the ideological state apparatuses. In B. Brewster (Trans.), *Lenin and philosophy*. New York: Monthly Press Review.

Blunkett, D. (1998). Foreword. In *The National Literacy Strategy: Framework for teaching*. London: Department for Education and Employment.

Bourdieu, P. (1991). *Language and symbolic power* (J.B. Thompson, Ed., & G. Raymond & M. Adamson, Trans.). Cambridge, MA: Harvard University Press.

Edelman, M.J. (2001). *The politics of misinformation*. Cambridge, UK: Cambridge University Press.

Edmondson, J. (1998). America Reads: Doing battle. *Language Arts, 76*, 154-162.

Edmondson, J. (2000). *America Reads: A critical policy analysis*. Newark, DE: International Reading Association; Chicago: National Reading Conference.

Edmondson, J., & Shannon, P. (2003). Reading First initiative in rural Pennsylvania schools. *Journal of Research in Rural Education, 18*(1), 31-34.

Fisher, R. (2000). Developmentally appropriate practice and a National Literacy Strategy. *British Journal of Educational Studies, 48*(1), 58-69.

Foucault, M. (2000). Governmentality. In P. Rabinow (Series Ed.), J.D. Faubion (Vol. Ed.), & R. Hurley (Trans.), *Power (Essential Works of Foucault 1954-1984*, Vol. 3, pp. 201-222). New York: New Press.

Fraatz, J.M.B. (1987). *The politics of reading: Power, opportunity, and prospects for change in America's public schools*. New York: Teachers College Press.

Goodman, K., Shannon, P., Goodman, Y., & Rapoport, R. (Eds.). (2004). *Saving our schools: The case for public education*. Oakland, CA: RDR Books.

Hoff, D.J. (2004, February 4). Debate grows on true costs of school law. *Education Week, 23*(21), pp. 1, 22.

IRA and UNESCO support Reading for All in Africa. (2004, June/July). *Reading Today*, p. 37.

Iser, W. (1978). *The act of reading: A theory of aesthetic response*. Baltimore: Johns Hopkins University Press.

Iser, W. (2000). *The range of interpretation*. New York: Columbia University Press.

Johnston, P., & Spiro, R. (1990, December). *Artificial dissemination: The politics of knowledge and literacy conferences*. Paper presented at the annual meeting of the National Reading Conference, Miami, FL.

Kelly, J. (2002, November 27). Primary school literacy strategy needs an overhaul, says watchdog. *The Financial Times Limited*, p. 6.

Lewis, J., & Miller, T. (Eds.) (2003). *Critical cultural policy studies: A reader*. London: Blackwell.

Lukács, G. (1971). History and class consciousness: Studies in Marxist dialectics (R. Livingstone, Trans.). Cambridge, MA: MIT Press.

Marx, K. (1963). *The 18th Brumaire of Louis Bonaparte*. New York: New World Paperbacks. (Original work published 1852)

Miller, T., & Yúdice, G. (2002). *Cultural policy*. London: Sage.